CHIEF MARKETING OFFICERS AT WORK

Josh Steimle

Chief Marketing Officers at Work

Josh Steimle
Lantau Island, Hong Kong

ISBN-13 (pbk): 978-1-4842-1930-0   ISBN-13 (electronic): 978-1-4842-1931-7
DOI 10.1007/978-1-4842-1931-7

Library of Congress Control Number: 2016944614

Managing Director: Welmoed Spahr
Acquisitions Editor: Robert Hutchinson
Developmental Editor: Matthew Moodie
Editorial Board: Steve Anglin, Pramila Balen, Louise Corrigan, Jonathan Gennick,
        Robert Hutchinson, Celestin Suresh John, Nikhil Karkal, James Markham,
        Susan McDermott, Matthew Moodie, Ben Renow-Clarke, Gwenan Spearing
Coordinating Editor: Rita Fernando
Copy Editor: Kim Burton-Weisman
Compositor: SPi Global
Indexer: SPi Global

Distributed to the book trade worldwide by Springer Science+Business Media New York, 233 Spring Street, 6th Floor, New York, NY 10013. Phone 1-800-SPRINGER, fax (201) 348-4505, e-mail orders-ny@springer-sbm.com, or visit www.springeronline.com. Apress Media, LLC is a California LLC and the sole member (owner) is Springer Science + Business Media Finance Inc (SSBM Finance Inc). SSBM Finance Inc is a Delaware corporation.

For information on translations, please e-mail rights@apress.com, or visit www.apress.com.

Apress and friends of ED books may be purchased in bulk for academic, corporate, or promotional use. eBook versions and licenses are also available for most titles. For more information, reference our Special Bulk Sales–eBook Licensing web page at www.apress.com/bulk-sales.

Any source code or other supplementary materials referenced by the author in this text is available to readers at www.apress.com. For detailed information about how to locate your book's source code, go to www.apress.com/source-code/.

Advance Praise for *Chief Marketing Officers at Work*

The role of marketing has shifted from art to science, and nowhere is that more visible than in these interviews with CMOs who are not just creative thinkers, but heavy technologists. If you want to be a marketer of the future, rather than the past, this book will show you where the top marketing minds see things going.

—Michael Brenner, CEO of Marketing Insider Group and
Author of *The Content Formula*

In marketing, it seems that everyone wants to talk to, sell to, or become a CMO. But, most don't understand what it takes to succeed at one of business's most challenging roles. Josh brings you inside the inner walls of the C-Suite, introducing you to some of the world's top marketing leaders to help you gain insights and secrets that will guide your future.

—Brian Solis, Leading Digital Analyst, Futurist, and
Author of *X: The Experience When Business Meets Design*

Josh Steimle is an outstanding entrepreneur in his own right, but an even greater contributor in his insatiable desire to learn and improve and his willingness to share the lessons he learns with all others. This book is a great example, as he shares marketing advice from some of the greatest CMOs of all time. A must read.

—Cheryl Snapp Conner, CEO and Founder, Snapp Conner PR

These authentic, in-depth interviews with leading CMOs will help new marketers know what they need to do to succeed and enable experienced marketers to confirm they're on the right path.

—Kent Huffman, CMO and Principal, DigiMark Partners, LLC

Most marketing books tell you what to do. This book shows you what CMOs are actually doing to make their organizations thrive.

—John Rampton, CEO, Due.com.

Chief Marketing Officers at Work is an easy-to-read, yet substantive book that explores the Who, What, Why, and How they got there of a number of leading CMOs. Anyone considering becoming a CMO, or those already in the role, will find great value in the feedback offered by these luminaries and should definitely read it.

—Jeff Sheehan, IBM Influencer, Futurist, and Author

To my mother, who taught me to love reading

and

to my wife, who supported me during the process
of putting this book together

Contents

About the Author

Josh Steimle is the founder and CEO of MWI (mwi.com), a digital marketing agency. He has written over 200 articles for publications like *Forbes*, *Entrepreneur*, *Inc.*, *Mashable*, *TechCrunch*, and *Time*. Steimle is a TEDx speaker and sought-after presenter at marketing industry events. In 2016, Steimle was recognized by *Entrepreneur* magazine as one of 50 Online Marketing Influencers to Watch and data from social media research firm Leadtail recently ranked Steimle #11 on their list of People Most Mentioned and Retweeted by CMOs. Steimle has been interviewed for TV and radio appearances on topics related to technology and government policy. He is the director of the Hong Kong chapter of Startup Grind and consults with leaders in government on policies and practices related to entrepreneurship and startups. Steimle has held board positions at or otherwise worked with various nonprofit entities related to adoption, education, entrepreneurship, economics, and government policy. Steimle holds a masters of information systems management from Brigham Young University (BYU).

Steimle started his agency while a student at BYU, where he and his business partners won the BYU Business Plan Competition in 2001. Steimle and his partner were also jointly awarded Young Entrepreneur of the Year in 2002 by the Utah chapter of the Small Business Administration.

Steimle lives in Hong Kong with his wife and two children. He is a voracious reader, ultra trail runner, triathlete, and skateboarder. He is an active member of The Church of Jesus Christ of Latter-day Saints and served for two years as a full-time missionary for his church in Manaus, Brazil. He is fluent in English and Portuguese.

Email: josh@mwi.com

Twitter: @joshsteimle

Instagram: @joshsteimle

Snapchat: joshsteimle

Blog: joshsteimle.com

Acknowledgments

The reason that this book exists can be tracked to a specific time and date, and a single person. At 3:00 p.m. on Tuesday, October 28, 2014, I entered a conference room at the Hong Kong offices of Nexusguard, an online security company. I'm a partner at MWI, a digital marketing agency, and we had negotiated a contract with Nexusguard for our services. I was there to get the contract signed and have a kickoff meeting to get things started.

I was introduced to various members of the marketing team, including Hope Frank, who informed me that as of the previous day, she was the company's new CMO. She said she was interested in talking to me about my agency's services, but no contracts would be signed that day. I walked out of that meeting wishing it had been scheduled a week before.

Several months later, my management team and I had a meeting to discuss creating client personas for our agency. I recalled the meeting with Hope and said, "CMOs can make or break deals with agencies like ours. We need to understand them better."

Soon thereafter, I decided to write a book on the topic "What CMOs need to know about digital marketing." As I started doing research, I realized that while I knew plenty about digital marketing, I didn't know enough about CMOs to write the book. But I thought I knew where to learn more. A few years previously, my friend Peter Harris suggested I read *Founders at Work* by Jessica Livingston of Y Combinator. That was the first book by Apress in the "At Work" series. I was also in the middle of succeeding volumes *Venture Capitalists at Work* and *CTOs at Work* and knew there were several other books.

I went to Amazon to buy "CMOs at Work," but I couldn't find it. I found it hard to believe the book didn't exist, so I kept searching, and that led me to the Apress website, where I verified that there was no such book. However, as I was looking over the Apress website, I stumbled onto a page inviting authors to propose and write additional titles for the "At Work" series. The thought struck me that I could write the "At Work" book on chief marketing officers and that this would be excellent preparation for writing the book on digital marketing. I sent a message to Apress, explained that I was a contributor to *Forbes* and other business publications and I felt I had the network and means to contact CMOs and other top marketers to be part of this book; and I secured a contract.

In hindsight, I'm thankful that the meeting with Nexusguard happened when it did. Were it not for the impression losing that deal made on me, I would not have had the opportunity to interview 30 of the top marketing minds of our day, and this book would not exist.

And so my first thanks goes to Hope, who I kept in contact with, even after she killed our deal, and whom today I count as a friend. She was the first person I reached out to for help when I began writing this book. She has been influential in making introductions and providing input. In more ways than one, this book would not exist without her.

This book would also not exist were it not for the support and encouragement of many others. My thanks goes to my wife, Brynn, who not only encouraged me in this endeavor but also assisted extensively with editing and proofreading. To my mother, who taught me how to read and more importantly taught me to love reading by reading to me by my bedside at night when I was a small child. To my father, who kept up that tradition as I grew a bit older, reading Shakespeare and *The Book of Mormon* to me before I fell asleep. To my children, who had to bear with busy evenings and weekends that were the only time I could find to finish this book. To my siblings, who have always been interested and supportive. To my fourth grade teacher, Ms. Kuchinksi at the Anoakia school in Arcadia, California, who is the first person I recall, other than my parents, who enjoyed my writing.

My gratitude to my friend Cheryl Snapp Conner, without whose introduction to *Forbes* I would not have embarked on the writing career that gave me the confidence to write a book. Thanks also to Tom Post, my former editor at *Forbes*, Stephen Bronner at *Entrepreneur*, Gayle Kesten at CMO.com, and the many other editors and writers I've had the pleasure of working with.

A sincere "thank you" to the MWI team for their cheerleading and support, especially my business partner, Corey Blake, for his leadership and management, which gave me peace of mind while working on this project.

I'd like to thank my transcriptionist Kristen Cassereau Ng, editor Megan Van Dyke, research assistant Cynthia de Jesus, and the entire Apress team, especially Robert Hutchinson and Rita Fernando.

Thanks also to those who provided endorsements for this work, and others who were an inspiration to start it and see it through including Michael Hyatt, Gary Vaynerchuk, Joe Pulizzi, Ann Handley, Ryan Holiday, Tim Ferriss, Stephen King, Jay Baer, Shane Snow, and many others. Thanks especially to all my friends who supported this and to all those I forgot to thank by name and whom I will be mortified to have left out after this has already gone to print.

Finally, thanks to those who provided the content for this book. I didn't write this book, I merely had the pleasure of handling logistics. The real authors are those whose interviews are contained in these pages, who took time from their busy schedules to speak with me. I am forever grateful for your generosity. And thank you to the assistants and PR reps I worked with, many of whom went to great lengths to arrange these interviews.

Introduction

This book contains interviews with 29 top marketers. Most interviews lasted 60 minutes and are presented here with minor editing to ensure clarity and readability.

As CMOs increasingly graduate to the CEO role, the stories told in this book by marketers like Brian Kenny of the Harvard Business School, Trish Mueller of The Home Depot, and Seth Farbman of Spotify, are a roadmap for driven marketing executives looking to maximize the potential of their organizations.

This book will help C-level executives and others who interface and collaborate with marketing departments to understand how marketing drives growth at both startup and enterprise levels, and how marketing has moved from art to science. Trends in digital marketing, analytics, and marketing automation have pushed marketing to adopt data-driven approaches that would make a CFO's head swim. Marketing increasingly overlaps with business functions that were previously viewed as separate and distinct like sales, HR and recruiting, customer service, operations, and technology. This change in the status quo requires individuals in these roles to better understand how marketing works and how it can help them achieve their objectives. The interviews in this book deliver those insights.

Who Should Read This Book?

- CMOs, other marketing executives, and aspiring marketing executives

- C-level executives

- Advertising execs, media planners, public relations professionals, digital marketers, and other marketing professionals

- Advertising agencies and marketing and PR firms

- Entrepreneurs

- All others who interface with marketing functions in their own roles

What the Reader Will Learn

- How CMOs from leading corporations, nonprofits, government entities, and startups got to where they are today, what their role entails, and the skills they use to thrive

- How top marketing executives adapt to changes impacting their jobs in the areas of technology, language, and culture

- How the CMO works in an environment of ever-increasing collaboration where the roles of CEO, CTO, COO, and CMO are blurring

- How the CMO role is now dominated by data rather than gut decisions

Sample Questions

The interviews in this book start with the same question, asking how the marketer being interviewed began his or her journey and the path that led to the role he or she now holds. Here is a sampling of other questions that formed the basis for these interviews: Give us an overview of your career. How did you get your start and what were the steps that led to where you are today?

- Who are your customers?

- How has social media, mobile, and digital marketing generally impacted your company?

- What does it mean to build customer loyalty with your target audience?

- What does the structure of your marketing team look like?

- What is your philosophy on building and managing a marketing team?

- How do you attract and retain top marketing talent?

- What do you look for in hires?

- How do you make sure your team can produce the best results?

- How do you manage relationships with other teams? What challenges have you faced? What are some wins you've seen?

- Do you have experience breaking down silos, and how can a CMO facilitate that?

- How do you make sure your goals are aligned with the overall organization?

- What kind of metrics do you focus on?

- I know there's no such thing as a typical day, but can you describe a recent work day from start to finish?

- How is globalization affecting marketing for you?

- What do you see as future growth markets?

- How do you communicate value through your marketing?

- How do you make sure you're in touch with your customers and understand their needs and wants?

- Do you have any favorite books that have helped you be a better CMO?

- What organizations are you a member of and what value do you receive from them?

- What advice would you give to yourself if you could go back in time to when you first accepted the CMO position?

- What trends in your industry or with your customers are affecting you?

- How has your role changed since you came into the position?

- How is mobile impacting your marketing?

- Is there anything in your background that is not directly tied to marketing, but which you feel has been beneficial to your role as a marketing professional?

- What does it take to run a successful marketing campaign?

- How is the digital world affecting your marketing initiatives?

- What kind of data do you have access to and how do you use data in your role?

- What tools, such as social networks or CRM systems, have been the most helpful to you?

- What channels are you using to connect with your customers?

- Are there new forms of marketing or trends in marketing you're excited to experiment with?

- How do you keep up with all the different marketing vendors, channels, and opportunities?

- How do you get through to consumers in a world of ad blockers where consumers have control?

- What do you see as the biggest challenges facing today's CMOs?

- What advice would you give to first-time CMOs?

- What are the biggest mistakes you see today's CMOs making?

- What current marketing trends do you find interesting?

- How has marketing changed over the past 20 years?

- How has marketing stayed the same over the past 20 years?

- What do you think the future of marketing will be and how will it be different from today?

- What are the skills that students should be acquiring today to prepare them to be future marketing leaders?

- What are some of the skills CMOs need that don't get enough attention?

- What are your thoughts on marketing to millennials?

- Why does being a data-driven or data-informed marketer matter?

If there was anything unexpected from these interviews, it was how tech-savvy these executives were. These individuals are hardly the types to engage in "Mad Men"–style marketing. They are driven by data, yet also aware of the risks posed by depending too much on that data. They are always learning and progressing. Now you have the opportunity to learn from them.

CHAPTER 1

Seth Farbman

Chief Marketing Officer
Spotify

Seth Farbman has served since April 2015 as Spotify's first chief marketing officer. Farbman was previously global CMO of the Gap brand at Gap Inc., having held that position since February 2011. Prior to Gap, Farbman served as worldwide managing director for the ad agency at Ogilvy & Mather, where he developed marketing campaigns for brands such as Coca-Cola, Time Warner Cable, UPS, and Unilever; he then founded OgilvyEarth, a sustainability marketing practice where he held the title President of Integrated Global Sustainability Practice.

In 2014, Forbes named Farbman one of the "10 Most Influential CMOs."

Farbman holds a communications and journalism degree from Syracuse University.

Josh Steimle: What has it been like transitioning from an established retailer to a tech startup?

Seth Farbman: First of all, I think we're less a tech startup than we were a few years ago. With a hundred million registered customers—I think we're up to fifty-nine countries—it's a giant in an industry, and it still feels obviously like a startup because the attitude is mission-based. But it is now a fully functioning organization that is going through the normal adjustments from young to established. My work at Gap was to go back and find that founder's story, the essence of the company, the energy and excitement of building something, the belief that we're not just a company—we're something more. I had to go find that and nurture it and bring that back at Gap, and it's all here (at Spotify).

© Josh Steimle 2016
J. Steimle, *Chief Marketing Officers at Work*, DOI 10.1007/978-1-4842-1931-7_1

It's been a transition but an almost entirely good one. I still scratch my head at times and ask, "How do I get my expense report paid?" There are systems that are still being built in real time, but the vision and the ambitions for the company are clear.

What has made this exciting for me and why I think it's been such a good fit from the beginning is that the things I do well—taking complex ideas and simplifying them to a point where they seem self-evident—are especially critical in a late-stage startup that has grown quickly, where people need to understand the essence of the product and the brand. And, in a highly complicated and heady environment, these are brilliant developers, the best in the world, with incredible IQs.

I think it requires someone to remind people that what we do is fun, and what we do is put joy into people's lives. Listening to music, especially the way Spotify provides it, is not an activity in and of itself—you don't sit around listening to music anymore, right? It's applied to all these areas of your life, and it's applied to these areas to make it better. Understanding people and understanding the joy we bring and finding more ways to do so becomes essential. And that, I think, gives everyone a better sense of what they're doing. I'm not just building this or working on some feature. I am enabling people. I'm giving people music in a way that is individualized. We all benefit from that.

Steimle: Once you accepted Spotify's offer, how did you plan your transition? What objectives did you set for yourself? How did the transition work for you personally?

Farbman: The first thing I did was sit down in a rare quiet moment and write out everything I liked and didn't like about the culture, the team, the processes, and the work I had created at Gap. I wanted to be honest and understand what it was I wanted to bring forward and what I had not done as well and wanted to do differently. When you get to a certain point in your career, you have a series of playbooks. You know what works and what doesn't in most situations. You adjust the playbook. But essentially, this is why it's so important to pick a job where what the company needs is what you're really good at, because you can't try to be something else. I somewhat codified that, and I started to think about what it would feel like to be high-functioning and successful and build a team where people felt empowered to do their work.

The second thing I did was I found there's a tremendous amount of value as a new person—not in what you know but in what you feel and think. I've been a Spotify user for a couple of years, so I knew the product quite well, and I had a relationship with it, but I really engaged in a personal way, as a consumer would, and I started to look at the competition, and I started to think, "What are they saying about themselves? What is it they want us to know?"

At the time, Tidal had just launched, and Tidal was clear about being for artists by artists. That was sharp positioning. It was also wrong. But it was sharp positioning. You have to value and appreciate that. Apple had yet to launch

Apple Music, but that was certainly just around the corner. I started to think about how Apple made me feel and what Apple was all about. And I'd been an Apple fan for years, as many of us have.

Apple always has been by Apple for Apple. In a sense, that was the center of Steve Jobs' culture, right? "We're going to develop the things that we want to develop in the way we want to develop them, and you're going to be amazed by them." And a lot of times, that happens, and sometimes, it doesn't. And then, I started to think, "Where does Spotify fit into that? In a perfect world, what is my association with it?"

I always go back to the founder's story to look at the why—why did Daniel start Spotify instead of something else? He could have done anything. He's a music fan. He plays the guitar. He wanted to use technology to open up music and try to restore growth to this industry that threatened to dramatically reduce the ability to discover more music. It was choking off creativity because the business model was broken. Downloads, CDs, etc, were falling.

What I came up with quickly is what makes us special is being *for* music fans *by* music fans. That's an authentic place. My onboarding was going as deep as I could inside myself and my thinking before I learned anything.

And then, I was meant to start a few weeks after I actually did because we have this thing called "strategy days." Twice a year, forty or more senior people within the company come together, and we establish where we're going in the next six months. What are the priorities? What are the steps the company's going to make? We get clear on those. Daniel asked me to come to Uppsala, Sweden, which is a university town, and spend a week being involved in the strategy days. That was an amazing onboarding. I came out of that reinforced in what I had already believed, and realized how much I had to learn. But that was a tremendous way of getting myself oriented to all of the cultural changes as well as the process and industry changes. There was so much to adjust to, and that helped speed it up.

Steimle: You have access to massive amounts of data. How do you use that data effectively without getting sidetracked?

Farbman: We do have an amazing amount of data. I think it's sort of the secret sauce. Because of how people engage with Spotify and use music—seventy-some percent on mobile, for instance—we know where you are, what you're doing, and how you're using it. And we're able to find new ways to deliver what you need, maybe before you have even identified it yourself. When I first got here, I was fascinated by the discovery that there was an incredible amount of usage of certain kinds of music late at night. We looked at it, and we saw the patterns, and we recognized that these long listening sessions late at night were people falling asleep and sleeping to music. That's an example of how looking at data gives you an insight that allows you to develop around it and create a connection you might not have already had.

But for me, what's so amazing is that our level of data gives us narratives. It gives us stories. As a marketer, you're constantly looking for real-life demonstrations of why your product matters. And we mine social media for that. Sometimes, people make up the stories. But here we have the incredible ability to identify the role that it has in people's lives and how it can improve. And so we have storytellers. We have people who look for those red threads that go through many, many customers and are able to aggregate what might seem like an individual behavior and recognize that it's part of a larger cultural change.

The sleep thing is so interesting. Is it just about sleep, or is there something more? Is there something about the changing world we live in where sleep is no longer the simple thing that it was years ago? What does it say about us? What does it say about the role of technology in people's lives? What are the good and the bad aspects of this rapidly changing, adapting world, and is there a role we can play to understand and help that? It's much richer than, "Now you can get your music through the phone."

Steimle: What are some of the other trends that are happening either in the industry or with customers that are affecting you?

Farbman: Mobile has been an enormous one. Everything is now completely accessible in your pocket. What that means is that people have access, the ability to listen in so many parts of their lives. We talk about the trends. What are the macro trends? Waiting in line is a macro trend. People wait in line much more. That is normally a negative thing in people's lives. If you are able to listen to fourteen tracks while waiting in line wherever you are, we've just turned a negative into a positive. Suddenly, something that was frustrating is a respite. It's your quiet time. It's your "you time," in a way.

Mobility is probably the most massive trend that's affecting so many people in so many countries. Within the industry, we're also seeing an obvious trend towards discovery. One of the things that has personally excited me about streaming and Spotify—and we're seeing it across almost all of our customers—is that the very nature of how you engage with music has shifted from one of buyer's remorse: "I don't know. Should I buy the album? Am I really going to listen to it? Is it worth $12.99? Is the track worth $1.29?" And while those seem like small decisions—what's $1.29, right?—and we're willing to spend that on ourselves, there is always this sense of "Is this the right purchase for me? Is this the right track for me? Is this the right opportunity for me?" By having all the world's music for the price of a single album taking away that buyer's remorse, you see a tremendous amount of discovery. People say, "I will sample. I will expand my interests. I will trial. I will take a risk. I will see why so many people are interested in this artist." There is no downside.

What we're seeing when you release people from even small bits of anxiety or potential for regret or remorse is this explosion of this sense of freedom, and that freedom leads to a sense of empowerment, joy, and curiosity. And it means more artists connect to more people. It means that creativity can expand because people are open to it. And that overall trend is tied to the belief, especially amongst the millennial generation, that doing things the way they were done in the past, following a traditional safe route, is not necessarily the best way for everyone. This generation is much more open to discovery, to what we think of at times as risk-taking, to recognition that you can create your own world. Instead of getting a job, think about what the world needs and be the one who goes and does it. Those are trends that I think will continue to build the music industry, and it's why we see so much content even outside of music being shared at a much greater rate and with much greater breadth.

Steimle: How do you take these trends and turn them into things like marketing campaigns, visual content, and messaging? What are the practical steps to applying knowledge of trends?

Farbman: We start with our greatest asset, our tremendously large and addressable audience of a hundred million people from around the world. We start with them, and one of the things I've said to the team here is, "When you're coming up with an idea, if it's not right for the existing audience, throw it away. Let's start from the inside out because we have this asset that can be shared and deployed and empowered." People on Spotify are the ones who from the beginning understood and valued music, were open to discovery, and liked to share music. A lot of marketers are looking outside their audience and outside their company for so-called influencers. We just call them customers. But how do we deploy them? Looking from the inside out is the start.

I'll give you a practical example—something we launched recently called "Found Them First." There's a recognition that there's a sense of pride, a sort of personal accomplishment if you've identified early on in your listening an artist who's going to be huge. We all love when we've found something first. It's a powerful tool in marketing. You can't shove things at people anymore. You have to let them discover things for themselves. You have to be in a place where they feel like they are in control. Nobody wants to be marketed to anymore.

Found Them First simply aggregates all of your data. We know what you listen to. And, we know what people like you listen to, so what we've done is create a campaign that essentially goes to all of our customers and allows them to interact. There's a simple interface, and it will deliver back to you in real time a list of the artists that you've helped break and others who have done the same. Instantly, you feel special. You feel like your sense of individuality has been recognized and appreciated, and you also feel part of a community.

One of the things I learned at Gap that I find completely applicable here is that these human truths, like a desire to fit in and stand apart, seem like conflicts. That's what humans are. If you are able to understand, nurture, and respect that, then you get a lot of appreciation as a brand. People say, "You get me." That's what something like Found Them First does. It taps into that human need and at the same time reinforces the value of Spotify. So, what happens next? You share it. If you've broken some great artists, you're going to share that. You're going to brag about that. And you're going to identify yourself as a real music fan, a member of the Spotify community, and someone who is interested in sharing your knowledge of music. It's a powerful thing. That's how you take data and insights and respect for an audience and put them at the center. That becomes the essence of repeatable marketing.

Steimle: How does globalization affect marketing for Spotify? You guys are in about sixty countries, and you have a lot more countries that you want to enter. How is that affecting your planning for marketing?

Farbman: I'm creating a bit more centralization as we put more talent into the New York office here with me. Centralization creates clarity. It creates effectiveness, efficiency. As a global brand, you must be highly consistent about what you stand for, what your product does and means in people's lives, etc. When I was at Gap, I thought it was probably about eighty/twenty. Eighty percent could be globally centralized, and then twenty percent were local nuances. The product reflected that. The marketing reflected that.

Music is incredibly local, right? It's connected to culture. As a real example, we won't launch in Brazil without Brazilian music, and it seems obvious, but it's hard. Thirty-some percent of the listeners in Brazil are of local music. You can go to just a few places and get a global catalog and launch overnight, but you're not really connected to the people or providing a full service.

When we move into a market—and this is, I think, one of our competitive advantages—we take the time, and it does take time, to work with every single one of the local labels to create relationships and legal licensing and all that so we can have local music. The localization is much more important within music and within Spotify than it would be within most global brands. That means we continue to maintain strong regional and local marketing teams, but it also gives us the opportunity to cut across all of it. No matter where you are in the world, there are shared experiences, and they are of interest to everyone.

As a specific example, when the Supreme Court of the United States upheld marriage equality, that was a celebration around the world, and Spotify obviously responded like many brands did with appreciation, recognition, joy, and a few playlists as well. That's a global event, and that reinforces the point of view of the brand and also the quality of such a large, addressable community. But it becomes increasingly more difficult as you move into markets like India, China, or even Japan, where the rules are different, and the cultural nuances both in how you do business and how people engage with music just become greater. That's where you have to rely on partners. That's where you have to rely on people who understand music. That's why you have to have respect for local culture and the role that music plays in it.

Steimle: What's your philosophy on building a marketing team? How do you put your team together? How do you support or manage the formation of the local and regional marketing teams?

Farbman: My philosophy is to create a flat organization with a group of subject-matter experts who work as much as possible as a single team. My philosophy is to look at—in this order—first, structure. Do the right functions report in the right way so that there is both clarity and collaboration? That's the easy part. Secondly, I look at process. It's hard to evaluate the quality of ideas, the quality of creative, the quality of messaging, the quality of the people until you've got the proper process, so we're building that now. We have amazing ingredients and people, but we were a little light on process. The structure was not clear at times.

The third thing I look at is the people and which skills I have that meet their needs based on the vision that we have. I find it very systematic. And then, honestly, it becomes almost solely about the people, the culture. Did I feel better or worse after I talked to that person? Did I feel more stress or less stress? Did I walk out of the room with the thought of, "I have a lot to do"? Or, "I hadn't even thought about that"? At first, it feels like you've gotten quite a bit of information, and you walk out of the room thinking, "This is a person that I want to spend time with. This is a person who thinks like I do at the macro level but has an interesting and clear point of view," and then, you create as much diversity as possible.

One of the things I did at Gap that I will just sort of naturally repeat for the rest of my career is when I wanted to build a global marketing organization. Even though it was based in New York, I built an organization that was based on people who were from and had lived and worked around the world. It sounds so obvious, but if you want the right balance, if you want respect for local markets, and if you want a diversity of ideas, you have to have a diversity of people. That becomes a core tenet of building a team: diversity of ideas, diversity of points of view, and a diversity of people. And then, I think you avoid a lot of the pitfalls that especially some American companies have when they're expanding into markets that they're less familiar with.

Steimle: What are some of the specific tools and technologies that have been the most helpful for you in getting your job done?

Farbman: I'm building most of those now. For instance, we are building a CRM system pretty much from the ground up. One of the great things about being a tech company is it will be completely integrated into the customer experience, inside the client, inside the app, so we don't just have a hodge-podge of systems to spam people with. It is personalized.

I'm building tools that evaluate the effectiveness of marketing and create a deep understanding of the sentiment of the brand in real time—everything from social listening to political-style polling. We've actually purchased a couple of analytical companies that allow us to look at our user data in real time and then extract meaning from it, so I have this wonderful sense of what's happening inside the client. This allows me to do a couple of things. One is to provide more meaningful, contextual, personalized messaging to people to find the dark corners where we're not doing so well.

I don't think we're doing as well as we need to be in simple product education. How do I make it easier for you to learn the product more quickly, to find all the hacks, the special little features that only you know—you and another few hundred million? To get at the essence of what has made Spotify a brand people are passionate about, a product people are passionate about. That inside data has been useful.

As I mentioned earlier, I use it to find stories and narratives that I can then model. And I can identify where those same types of people live outside of Spotify so that I cannot just say, "Please buy Spotify." I actually know user interests—musical interests and others, so that even in our advertising, we're providing a value. Whether it's to sleep better, or run faster, or whatever, it is what you want in your life. That's the kind of way I can approach customers, rather than simply "Get your music here."

Steimle: What advice would you give to a first-time CMO? Somebody who has never been in the role before.

Farbman: Understand your company's culture. Successful marketing requires a level of truth and authenticity that cannot be faked. For a first-time marketer, a first-time CMO, there would probably be a great desire to show external value almost immediately. How do I increase sales? How do I increase engagement? What are the messages I'm going to send to my customers or prospects? But until you know what the truth of the company is, you're just going to guess, and you're going to miss the long-term opportunity to create an organization, a discipline that provides meaning even beyond the marketing. And that requires discovery. That requires a bit of digging in anthropology.

But take the time. Take the time to understand the why. Why does the company exist? Why does it deserve to exist? Why do people care? Why do people work here? And start to build off of that, because that's a solid foundation, and the rest will become easier to evaluate.

Now, we'll have a set of filters. Is this a good idea or a bad idea? Is this a feature that deserves marketing or not? Your message may resonate, and it may create a behavioral change with your customer, but then what? Once you've experienced the product or the service, are you just setting them up for disappointment? Stick to the truth as much as you can.

Steimle: What are some of the mistakes you see CMOs making today?

Farbman: There's what I call "shiny object syndrome." There's so much change. I mean, one of the great challenges for a CMO is that as soon as you learn something, it doesn't matter. You have to learn something else. It's difficult because the media world is in complete change and flux, and CMOs sort of run after that. You can try something new, and I think that's part of your plan, but I don't think it should be a complete distraction. Technology is not valuable if you don't know what you want to say.

I see a lot of marketers jumping into things without a proper evaluation in an attempt to stay current and relevant, add value, and show real knowledge of the industry.

The other thing is this proliferation of big data, which pales in comparison with the proliferation of talk about big data. We need to understand that data is a tool. It is something that is unbelievably helpful in validating your thoughts, desires, and narratives that you want to share. You look at it for insights, but that doesn't replace the spark of inspiration, the desire to create something never seen before, and the willingness to give people a reason to dream.

If you don't use it right, data's just going to tell you what people did yesterday, and it will help you find more people who want to do that same thing, but it actually can take away the power of marketing, which is all about meaningful emotional connection that makes people feel more in control of their lives and more connected to the people around them.

Steimle: There's some research that shows that a lot of CEOs, around eighty percent, are disappointed with their CMOs. Do you have any ideas about why that is?

Farbman: Not empirically. I've been sort of fortunate in having surprisingly long tenures at places. But at Gap, for instance, I think no head of marketing lasted even two years. But honestly, I think a lot of it is kind of a lack of clear expectations on what marketing is and can do. I think that the CEOs are as much to blame for that poor relationship—if it exists—as the CMO. And I think the CMOs largely don't have clarity around what it is that they're meant to accomplish. There needs to be that level of clarity.

Daniel and I have had these conversations ongoing for the last few months. What is the role of marketing? How do I hold you responsible and what for? You need to get aligned on that.

And marketing has always been and will always be a bit of a crapshoot, so if you're not trying and failing, then you're really not trying. I think it was John Wanamaker that famously said, "Half of my marketing budget is a complete waste. I just don't know which half." That remains true today. There's subjectivity in creative. Human beings are highly irrational. You need to have sort of an understanding that marketing is going to drive things forward but not every time and with complete success. But, there is an opportunity to learn from what doesn't work as much as from what does. I think it's about whether you are on the same page. And, are you willing to do that work ahead of time instead of just evaluating a TV commercial or something that's far downstream?

Steimle: For people who are maybe midway through their careers and looking at the CMO role as their goal, what are the key skills they should be developing?

Farbman: It's everything but marketing. If you want to be a good CMO, you should be a good scientist, a good social scientist, a good student of history, of literature. I often look outside of marketing for ideas, inspiration, and understanding. You need to be the best storyteller and the best at removing complication within an organization. And then, you need to simply define what you care about, what kind of CMO you want to be—there are different ones—and only take jobs that want what you have. Be deliberate and specific about where you go and why, and the why has to be because you believe in the brand, you believe in the product, you believe in your ideas, and you have a personal desire to share that. You're not marketing. You're sharing your own personal passion and the passion of others. And then, you're more right than wrong.

Heather Zynczak

Chief Marketing Officer
Domo

Heather Zynczak became the chief marketing officer of Domo, a SaaS company providing business management tools, in March 2012. She was previously global vice president of marketing at SAP and prior to that spent five years at Oracle as senior director of product strategy. She has led teams at multiple Silicon Valley startups and served as a business consultant for various firms, including Accenture, Booz Allen Hamilton, and the Boston Consulting Group.

Zynczak has authored several articles about women's leadership in publications such as ForbesWoman, Women 2.0, and The Huffington Post. She is a co-founder of Women at Domo, a professional networking group.

Josh Steimle: How did you get to be where you are today as the CMO at Domo?

Heather Zynczak: I grew up kind of a numbers geek. I loved math and science as a kid. It's where I excelled. From there, I went on to get a degree in finance and accounting and an MBA from Wharton. I went into technology right out of undergrad, and coded, and then went on to startups and then some of the world's largest software companies, such as Oracle and SAP, and kind of switched back and forth.

Mainly I was in marketing but also did some time in product strategy and outbound-focused product management, because I do have that technical kind of product background as well. I ended up at Domo about four years ago

J. Steimle, *Chief Marketing Officers at Work*, DOI 10.1007/978-1-4842-1931-7_2

because of the amazing opportunity. I had been in tech my whole career and had spent twenty-plus years helping companies automate their processes, and a side effect—what I call "scrap metal"—was all this data. Now, this amazing scrap metal is mounds of gold that people can go in and mine, and I think it's the next frontier.

Then, enter Josh James, and how innovative and revolutionary he's been in his career and other environments. With the product he was building, it just made perfect sense. At the time, a lot of people thought it was crazy to jump to a startup in the super-early stages with no revenue, but I wholeheartedly knew this was an amazing space, and I believed in the founder's vision. That's how I ended up in Domo.

Steimle: What does it mean to you to be the CMO at Domo? What does your role look like? Tell us a little bit about your day-to-day.

Zynczak: For CMOs of startups or hyper-growth companies, the role of the CMO is elevating. I first and foremost think of myself as a key member of the executive team. I stick my nose in and get involved, whether I'm wanted or not, in many if not all aspects of the business—everything from giving feedback on the product and strategy, helping with the rollout of the product, how we're taking it to market, working with sales on how we increase different things throughout the sales funnel, and conversions, all the way through the pipeline to close and enablement, which are not necessarily part of traditional "marketing."

To be a C-suite executive, you really have to wear the hat where you think about the entire business. If you really want to be more than just a marketer, you are there as someone who gives guidance to the entire business. That's the first thing. The second is I am responsible for the building of this brand and taking our CEO's vision of what Domo is and making sure we get that out into the marketplace. That's no small task when you're starting with a blank canvas as we did four years ago.

What I think is most important for a startup company or for Domo is that I am a contributor of revenue—and marketing at Domo contributes. Our leads contribute the vast majority of our revenue and ACV (annual contract value). If an early-stage or growth company CMO doesn't view that as the most vital thing in their role, they're massively missing the boat.

Steimle: How was it working at a startup as secretive as Domo, where you weren't allowed to share everything you perhaps wanted to share?

Zynczak: It was like pulling my hair out. I'm a product marketer by nature, which means I came into this job saying, "I'm really good at marketing because I'm good at marketing a product." And then, I couldn't talk about the product. It created some interesting challenges. It created challenges in getting our brand out there for people to understand what we did because we couldn't just show them. It created challenges in terms of our sales process. We would prospect into accounts and then ask them to sign a nondisclosure agreement, and they'd be like, "Hey, I didn't call you. You called me. Why are you asking me to sign something before you'll tell me what you do?"

It created a lot of challenges, but it also gave me some awesome opportunities. We were able to create some secrecy and intrigue around the product, which was Josh's vision. We would go to trade shows and have lines around the corner for people to see our demos and videos because it was secret, and you couldn't see it anywhere else. There were some real benefits from that, and it gave us a huge leap ahead of our competition.

When we did finally come out of stealth mode in April 2015, we were so far ahead of anybody else in this space. It's been really fun to now stand on the mountain and beat our chests with our competitive differentiators. It was a challenge, I won't lie, but there were some great things that came out of it as well.

Steimle: You mentioned working with other teams within Domo, like sales. Traditionally, marketing and sales work hand in hand. What are some of the challenges and opportunities you face there? How do you manage the relationship with sales?

Zynczak: I think it's something I've become pretty good at here at Domo. I've had to work with sales throughout my career, but most of our spending money—when we measured it—our ACV, and our revenue has come from marketing leads.

I view myself as part of the team that fuels the engine. I'm not successful if that team doesn't take the fuel and make something out of it. I'm held accountable to ROI at the end of the day. I have had to partner with them so much so that even a couple of years ago, for example, Josh called me and said, "Hey, you're delivering a lot of leads at the top of the funnel. The next team down, our inside sales team, isn't hitting their goals. I need you to be accountable for the number of opportunities they're delivering for outside sales reps."

I got really involved—everything from reviewing and changing comp plans to evaluating management and making management decisions on leadership in that team, to how and what we train.

As a marketer, you have to wear a sales hat, and you have to view yourself as part of the sales engine. If you don't, you're failing. If that means you've got to get in there and understand details on sales compensation plans, modeling, quotas, targets, or any other nuances that a marketer typically doesn't get involved in—roll up your sleeves and do it. You're not successful as a marketer if sales isn't successful.

Steimle: It sounds like Josh James has thrown you some interesting curve balls. Are there other ways your role has changed since you came into the position?

Zynczak: When I started, we weren't selling yet, and since then, we've had one hundred percent year-over-year growth, flying off the charts in terms of revenue growth and customers. I used to be one hundred percent laser-focused on prospects and generating demand. I still have those goals, but now I'm also really focused on our existing customers. How do I get our customers to engage and use the product? How do we upsell, renew, and make it stick?

It's the maturity life cycle of a company. I don't know if it's necessarily curve balls that have been thrown at me, but I think my job has changed over the last four years from "How do I market to and engage with a customer base?" They're just as important as our prospect base, if not more so.

Steimle: Let's back up a little bit and talk about your customers. What are some of the different types of customers you have, and how do you approach them?

Zynczak: Domo is a platform to manage your business, and it brings the information you care about as a businessperson into one place to help you make better decisions. The good and bad news for me as a marketer is that anybody in the organization who uses information could use Domo. That means anyone—marketing departments, the C-suite, financial, FP&A (financial planning and analysis) organizations, sales and sales operations, and HR departments. They all can use Domo, and they do.

Our customers are across every industry. If you look at an industry break-down of who uses Domo, it's like a pie that's been split into so many teeny, tiny pieces, because there's not one dominant industry. While that's really exciting from a marketing opportunity perspective, because everybody in every industry in every role that uses information can use Domo, it's also challenging as a marketer.

How do you target your message? I believe strongly in persona-based messaging, targeted messaging, and personalization. That has been a challenge. A challenge I think that we've navigated well is how to speak to everyone and find those unique conversations with individuals that resonate with them.

Steimle: How do you build customer loyalty with your target audience?

Zynczak: We spend a lot of time thinking about the customer journey. We use data and map the customer journey to see everything—from a welcome kit and an onboarding campaign via email and in the product, to regular communications through the product, through email, to physical in-person events that we host to identify different users of our product.

We have this role called the MajorDomo that's really the person who gets stuff done in Domo. We figure out how to cater content, materials, and training through Domo University. We've really tried to map out the customer journey for the different types of users of the product and make sure we're fulfilling their needs. We're still in the early stages of that. I don't want to claim victory, but we're working hard to understand.

We look at data. We look at who's using the product. How often are they in it? What are they consuming? We also look at where we're having upsells. Where are they referring it to other people? Where are they encouraging other people to use the product? Where do we have retention? How are our retention numbers, and how can we impact them? We try to customize content and outreach and communication programs based on that data.

Steimle: Tell me about the structure of your marketing department. How many people do you have? How do people work with each other and report?

Zynczak: When we started, we had a really small organization, and now we have somewhere around forty folks in the marketing organization, maybe thirty. I want to say thirty, so in case anybody reads it, I can make the case to get more head count. Because you know us marketers—we're always trying to hire.

But my strategy to building and growing the team first started with working with the data and the analytics. What markets are we going after? How do we go after them? Where do we go after them? We looked to the data for the right answers about who we should market to and the content on that. We've really spent time focusing on the content teams. I have a content marketing team and a product marketing team that build out the underlying infrastructure for everything we do and how we push it out. That message and content make it out to a communications team.

We have a digital team through the web, social, and advertising. We have a field team through associations and events that we do, like trade shows, etc. It's about starting with the data and the analytics around who we should market to, and building the content around that. Everything starts with this personalized content and the channels we push that through.

Then, we measure the whole way through that process to understand how we are doing. What content is resonating with whom? How is that working in the channel? How is it working with our customers? How does that impact everything?

Right now, for example, I'm looking at what the conversions are of the later stage in the funnel. Far down the funnel in our sales process, how can we help our sales team through the content and marketing teams to convert that customer in the final stages? It might be closing events. It might be certain types of technical documentation. What is it that's working best? We look at data for every aspect of the business that marketing is touching.

Steimle: Are there any trends in your industry or with your customers that are affecting you in your marketing role?

Zynczak: One of the groups we sell to is marketers, and I think the trends in marketing are moving away from the 1960s world of *Mad Men*—the Don Drapers saying, "Trust us, we'll create a great marketing campaign," where you spend a ton of money on it and win an award nine months later without having any idea if it succeeded.

Today, everything can and should be measured. Everything can show results. You can evaluate whether everything was successful or not. As a marketer, you have to do that, and I think all areas of the business are now being held accountable for showing results quantitatively, even HR.

I went to an event the other day, and our head of HR did a demo. I had three women sitting near me who said, "Wow, we should be showing how many open reqs we have, how far along we are on hiring, how many hires we've made, the retention rate of our employees."

Every department is being asked to be more data-driven and held accountable to quantitative statistics. Marketing is at the forefront of that because there's so much data in marketing, and there's so much money spent in marketing. You want to see the results of those efforts. I think the rise of Domo is because there's been such a need to have a tool to make this transition in business.

Steimle: There's a famous saying that goes something like, "Twenty percent of my marketing produces eighty percent of the results. I just don't know which twenty percent." Domo's helping answer that question.

Zynczak: It is. You should know, and to any marketer that uses that line, I would say, "Maybe you should be fired because you can measure it, and you should know."

Steimle: Now that you've been with Domo a few years and the company and landscape have changed a little bit, if you could go back and give yourself advice coming into the role, what would you change?

Zynczak: I think I would have pushed our product quicker. Now that I have the full functionality of our product, it's made my job so much easier. I probably would have gotten in our product team's face on day one and said, "This is what I need."

From a pure Domo perspective, three years ago, I would have loved to have seen my team's product adoption where it is today because we're all so data-driven now. For example, we decided to do our launch event at a conference in April, 2015. Josh made a decision at the end of December that we were going to do this, and we had four months to plan a gigantic event. We ran the whole thing in Domo, and it made meetings and planning so much easier.

We could quickly pull up Domo and see how many people had registered, the places and industries they were from, and their titles. We could see how many customer speakers had confirmed. We could see how much sponsorship money we had generated. We could see how many partners we had in the pavilion all the way down to how many people were staying for the ski day and what size shirts they wore so we could order the right size for them as swag giveaways.

And it made the conversations about the conference more meaningful because that data was just up there, and we could talk about all of the other things instead of the quick status updates of data, because we all knew. It was on the screen. We ran our business in Domo. So, I think that's one thing I would have done.

There are two other things I would say if I could go back and give advice to people coming into a startup in the role that I did. One, learn sales. Learn sales early. Be a part of the sales team early. Be accountable to the sales numbers early. View yourself as a part of the sales engine. Any CMO in an early-stage company who doesn't do that is failing.

The second thing I would say is quickly figure out how you show results. How do you prove your worth? How do you show how you're contributing to the bottom line? Make sure you track and measure that and shout it from the mountaintops. I think those two things, whether I strategically did them well or fell into them, were successes for me as a first-time CMO at a growth company.

Steimle: You mentioned some tools that you use for marketing. Are there other channels, other social networks that have been successful for you in your role to get the word out?

Zynczak: Oh yeah, we love social here at Domo. We're big fans of social, and it's one of the things I'm most proud of. Around 2007, I was at SAP, and I remember one of the teams I managed created a Facebook page for their product line, and it was so revolutionary. It won best Facebook page for the CRM products. It might have been because I didn't know if there were any other Facebook pages, but they came in first, middle, and last. I felt so cutting-edge and innovative.

The truth is, I look back on that and laugh. When I came to Domo, I had a meeting with Josh that resonated with me because he's so innovative, and he really wanted a CMO who was going to be cutting-edge. I knew he was going to push me and challenge me, and I was excited about that. I've tried from day one to be on the forefront, and one of those ways is social. A large percentage of our revenue comes from leads that are generated off social channels. I think every CMO can tell you social channels are significantly contributing to their revenue. We don't do anything on social that doesn't give us results, that doesn't give us revenue, that doesn't make us the ROI we need. I think that's rare and awesome all at the same time.

LinkedIn has been a great resource for us, mainly because of buyer personas and personalization. You can run very targeted campaigns on LinkedIn. I know if you're a VP, I know what industry you work in, I know what your title is—whether you have digital marketing, for example, or financial planning in your title. We've had times when we were running over a thousand different specific campaigns with unique landing pages off of LinkedIn.

At the same time, Twitter has been a real gem for us, and we've really worked with the Twitter team. They've been awesome to work with. I think we're in every beta program they offer, and we're always trying to do cutting-edge, and we're trying to get as personalized as we can. It's been a great tool for us.

We're cracking into other areas as well. We've seen some good results from Facebook lately, which is surprising because we didn't have great results with Facebook early on. I think it's historically been more of a consumer advertising place, but we've figured out some interesting things on how to have Facebook make us money as well.

I've been really proud. Social media's been a big deal for us.

Steimle: What are you doing internationally?

Zynczak: We've always had a global presence. We have decent-sized offices in Asia and now in Australia as well. We have a smaller presence in Europe, and we're expanding. I think that's one of the reasons Josh hired me, because if you look at my background when I left SAP, the majority of the revenue that I marketed was outside of the U.S. I'm very excited as we expand our global presence, and I've had some successes in using those skills to date in other regions. Even just thinking about how we build our website with localization in mind, so we don't end up in a situation that, for example, we were in at SAP.

We had many different websites with many different messages in many different languages that did not all have one brand umbrella. They were in the process of trying to fix that when I left. I've set up things here at Domo so that we don't end up facing those challenges as we scale and as we become this large global entity, because I've been there. I've seen those problems on the other side. I'm also excited to leverage some of my skills as we expand into new markets, which has been a lot of fun.

Steimle: How have you made sure you don't end up in the same situation as at SAP?

Zynczak: At a higher level, you need all the marketing resources around the globe to report into marketing, and you need to run from one budget, and you need to run one messaging platform and one content strategy. You have to make localizations from all of that, and then you need your process in place for how you localize, what the localization looks like. It's not just translation. It's localization. Those are two different things.

We're setting up the teams and how we allocate budget, how we do our content platform, and how we roll out our content with a global approach in mind. I have a strong lead in Asia who runs marketing for me there. He's been a great partner. I actually flew over to Japan to interview the first couple of marketing people we hired because our culture is so important, and I view those local offices as part of my team.

That's kind of the bigger picture. I sat down with our engineers when we relaunched our website a couple of years ago. We didn't have a ton of countries that we were needing to build it for, but I sat down with our web team, and we went through requirements. I had them build an entire document and strategy around the requirements needed for our website so we could easily localize for many different countries.

It took us longer to relaunch the website than if we had done it thinking, "Ah, we'll figure out the other countries later," but it was an exercise well worthwhile because as we brought on new countries and new languages at Domo. com, it's been a relatively seamless process.

Steimle: How do you localize your unique brand? You had a billboard in Utah saying, "Domo, the honey badger of companies." How do you take that kind of culture to Tokyo and stay true to it, but still communicate something people there will understand?

Zynczak: It all comes down to what I said earlier about personalized content. For example, the billboard you saw only ran in Utah. It was very much a Utah thing for recruiting for a certain type of profile we were looking to hire in the office there. We were focused either on engineering or sales when some of those billboards came out, and we did some billboards specific to hiring sales reps. So, I think it comes down to a couple of things.

One, you have to have a consistent voice and tone. As the CMO, I'm the builder of the brand, and that includes our tone and voice in the marketplace and any location. That has to be strong.

Then, you have to hire people who get that, who understand what you're trying to accomplish as a brand and who can help you navigate the nuances you need for their marketplace. Those are two big things you have to do.

And, you have to set up processes for localization. You can't just be using one-off companies to translate, because that's when you end up with screw-ups. I gotta be honest with you. We've made mistakes. We did a Christmas card one year with some pop culture in the U.S., and in our marketing automation, we inadvertently included some of our Japanese customers. It didn't resonate with them. We got it right away. The next year when we were doing holiday mailings, we made sure we were very thorough in what boxes we checked in the tool, but also in thinking about what would resonate in each and every geography.

Steimle: How do you manage relationships with outside agencies?

Zynczak: Do everything that you possibly can in-house. You keep control, you have people committed, and it creates cohesion. But, that's just not feasible when you're trying to scale the way we are. So when I have to work with vendors, we expect results. So, I share with them: "Here's what I'm held accountable to. I don't care how many impressions and how many likes we got, because I don't care about that. That's not on my radar of what's important. What I care about is how many qualified leads go down the funnel to our sales teams and at what cost." And you know what? It's been great.

If you expect results from your vendors and clearly communicate what those result targets are and give them a way to measure those targets, you'll be surprised how vendors will step up. For example, we've shifted money to Twitter recently because they hit goals on qualified sales opportunities at the cost that we needed them to. They got it. They came in and said, "Okay, this isn't normally how companies measure, but you guys are very results-oriented, and we can tell you're all about ROI. We're going to help you create a strategy, craft campaigns, and use the right tools at Twitter to hit your sales-qualified opportunities and goals in terms of number and cost."

I think when you're managing outside vendors, you have to let them understand they're held accountable to the same goals and targets that you as a company are held accountable to.

Steimle: What do you see as some of the largest challenges facing CMOs today?

Zynczak: I think it comes back to what we talked about earlier with how marketing is going through a transition and we're no longer in the Don Draper days of "trust us" and winning an award when you have no idea if your marketing really made you money.

Especially at big companies, a lot of the CMOs grew up on the creative side, and they weren't held accountable for hard numbers because you couldn't track that in television, for example, twenty years ago.

The industry is going through a transition, and CMOs are realizing they need new skill sets to survive in a predominantly digital world that requires showing results. You have to be extremely data-savvy and use that data to guide your strategy and show your worth to the company. I think this transition is where most of the gray-haired CMOs are struggling. I think that's the biggest challenge occurring right now in the industry.

Steimle: What advice would you give to somebody who's just coming into the role? They're brand new at this. They're not gray-haired. They're inexperienced. What advice would you give to them to prepare for what's coming?

Zynczak: Rely on data and get your data systems in place. You need the numbers and the reporting so you can take risks and be bold and do big things, because you need the numbers behind you so you don't make huge mistakes. Also, you need the numbers so you can show results.

That's my second thing: CMOs need to be able to walk into the boardroom and talk about how they're contributing to the bottom line, how much the money they're spending is making for the company, how much the efforts they're putting in are increasing sales, conversions, or customer retention. CMOs need to show results.

The other thing I would tell CMOs is, "Put on your sales hat early. You're part of the sales process. Their problems are your problems. If sales doesn't succeed, you don't succeed." That would be the third piece of advice I would give them.

Steimle: Let's say there's somebody in college right now interested in becoming a marketing executive. What skills could they be developing today that are still going to be valuable ten or twenty years from now, when it's more likely they could be in line to be a CMO or VP of marketing?

Zynczak: I think number one is to be analytical. CMOs in the future will have strong analytical, data-driven skills and be able to take numbers and make sense of them, both to craft strategy and show results.

The second thing I would say is digital. We are in a digital world that is becoming even more so. Even watching TV is digital. Digital, in every sense of the word, from marketing is important. It might be that you get more technical skills, that you understand how technology works, you take a computer class, but I think digital is extremely important. It also goes back to the skills that have made marketers strong, like being a good writer and being able to convey your thoughts and ideas to put them into words, campaigns, web copy, papers, and other things. I think writing and presentation skills can never be downplayed.

Finally, I don't know if you can be taught this in college, but creativity is really important. I joke that I'm a left-brain CMO who grew up loving math, and that's true, but I also think of myself as very in tune with creative. I know good creative when I see it. And I think I have a very good eye for it.

Brian Kenny

Chief Marketing & Communications Officer
Harvard Business School

Brian Kenny is the chief marketing and communications officer at Harvard Business School, where he brings over 20 years of experience in planning, program management, brand development, and corporate communications to his position. Kenny oversees branding, marketing, and media relations across HBS, including the MBA program, executive education, HBX, and HBS Publishing. He previously served as vice president of marketing and communications at Northeastern University. Prior to entering higher education, he oversaw global marketing for The Monitor Group and led marketing programs for Genuity.

Josh Steimle: What is your mission as the first CMO at HBS? What responsibilities have they given you? What does it mean to be the CMO at HBS?

Brian Kenny: The responsibilities were pretty standard of what you'd expect to see from any CMO role, and actually, there's an extra C in my title. It's "chief marketing and communications officer," and that's important because those functions had been separate before I got here. More and more, organizations are starting to bring the communications and marketing functions together because all communications have to be embedded in a marketing strategy, and they have to be consistent with the brand and the voice of the brand. When the person who was in my role left, it was much more of a traditional PR role, and I think Harvard Business School recognized that. They took a step back

© Josh Steimle 2016
J. Steimle, *Chief Marketing Officers at Work*, DOI 10.1007/978-1-4842-1931-7_3

and said, "We're a decentralized school. We have several major business units if you count our publishing, which does *Harvard Business Review,* our exec ed program, our alumni relations group, and our MBA admissions teams."

There are six or seven large organizations here that are out there talking about Harvard Business School and representing the brand, and there was nobody who was looking across all of those groups to make sure the message was aligned and the strategy was integrated. That was the big challenge on my plate when I got here—to find a way to get my arms around all those things that were happening and stitch them together, even though I had no direct authority over most of those groups, and I still don't to this day. I often describe my role as trying to find a way to have influence without having authority.

Steimle: What are some specific steps you've taken with marketing and communications to get the word out more accurately about what you do?

Kenny: I had the great benefit of being here during the dawn of the social media age. When I came here, Facebook was brand new. Twitter didn't exist. LinkedIn was in its infancy. All of these social platforms that are so common today—it's amazing the way those have taken off is. Aside from being impressive, it's also a boon for marketers like me who are trying to give accessibility to a brand.

Harvard Business School had always been this kind of mystical place. We were—by design, frankly—closed off, and there were deans here long before I got here who basically had a no-media policy. We didn't want people to necessarily know what was happening here, because it felt more special if you kept the brand under wraps. Times have changed, and that's no longer a viable strategy for most brands. We use social media as a way to bring life to the mission of the school, to give a voice to the people here so you can experience them and what they're really like and develop your own perceptions. I would say social and interactive marketing have been the greatest tools we've been able to use to change misperceptions.

Steimle: Are there other tools, such as CRM systems or other data-dependent systems, that have been useful for you in your role?

Kenny: Yes, but those are much more tactical. We've just gone through an implementation here of a big CRM called Salesforce. CRM systems are helpful for fine-tuning your message and giving you a deeper understanding of your customers.

When I got here, we weren't in a position to do anything with that information if we had it. We had to start with the fundamentals of making sure we were all talking about the school in the same way, so we did a lot of explorations as a group, trying to look at the information I heard on my listening tour, conducting more focus groups, and doing more work. We brought in outside research firms to help us do a global study of the brand and understand what brand perceptions were about HBS among business leaders.

All of those things helped us to form at least a baseline understanding of the current state of the brand in the world, and those are things you can build communications programs off of. Tools like Salesforce are now much more helpful to us because we at least think we are saying the right things, generally speaking, and those tools help us to fine-tune in a more specific way to individuals.

Steimle: Who are your customers as CMO? Are they business leaders, students, parents of students? What are all the different groups you have to help understand the message of HBS?

Kenny: It's a pretty broad group. If I had to rank-order those groups, I would say prospective students and alumni are certainly important to us. Those are the two groups I think about most, and that would be alumni of our MBA program as well as alumni of our executive education programs. Executive education is a huge part of our operation. We have 10,000 executives come here from around the world to do both short- and long-term courses each year. We only have 1,800 MBA students at a time, so exec ed kind of dwarfs the MBA program, but we're best known for the MBA and for good reason.

The case method and the innovations we've made there have changed management education around the world. So, those two groups are really important to us, and then there's a lot of overlap with the others: business practitioners, general managers, people who are out there and either building their careers or have advanced in their careers.

Everything we do, from research to things like *Harvard Business Review* and executive education, is designed to help people advance in their careers. We're a professional school, and that's how we got our start.

I also consider faculty to be an important set of customers because we're a service organization to the rest of the school. We're here to help faculty bring visibility to their work, and that helps me to continue to change perceptions of the school in positive ways.

Other important customers are people who are interested in business more broadly, which cuts a broad swath. We're not trying to help shape the perceptions of medical school students, but certainly, anybody who's got an interest in business as a practitioner or a customer should be interested in some of the things we have to offer.

Steimle: What is the structure of your marketing team? How many people are on your team? Who are they?

Kenny: I have a small team. There are about fifteen of us. It's an integrated group with a flat organization. My group is called central marketing and communications. If you were to look more broadly across the school, there are actually ninety-two people who do marketing and communications-type functions at the school, but they're marketing a specific offering or a specific program.

On my team, I have my right-hand person, who is the head of marketing programs. She oversees the interactive team, which includes social media, website design and development, and production of digital content. We've got a content producer on the staff who's doing videos and podcasts and things like that. She also has a creative team under her, which includes our creative director. He's got a couple of designers that work with him because we do provide design services both for interactive and print.

We also develop the look and feel and the brand standards for the entire school, so that's centralized under me. My right-hand person also has two program managers. These are people who are marketing generalists, and they meet with clients around campus to help them develop marketing plans. They bring in resources as needed to help them execute those plans.

I've got a communications team including a writer to help us to develop content and shape content for all the various channels. I've got a more traditional media and public relations director, who is out there pitching stories or providing subject-matter experts for inbound inquiries. A third person helps me manage internal communications, which we have ownership of. It's actually a huge amount of work, and she's also helping to manage the PR in India and Asia.

Everybody kind of crosses over into everybody else's area. We have two meetings a week. One is an editorial meeting that we have on Monday mornings, where we sit down as a team and talk about what's happening in the world. Pick your topic—let's say, Donald Trump. Do we have anybody on the faculty who's done any research on politicians and how they manage their brands, and can we find a way to peg that work to what's happening right now with Donald Trump? We try to take the work of faculty or existing content and peg it to something relevant and compelling that's happening in the world today.

This is a shift in strategy from where we were a couple of years ago, when we weren't creating our own content as much as relying on other people to write about us. That's kind of the old approach to managing your image through the media. Frankly, what's happened is the media has changed in such a way that it's much more beneficial for us to write our own content and create the context for our stories rather than relying on somebody else to do it.

Steimle: Have any other changes come up for you as the CMO or in marketing, generally, at HBS since you took this position?

Kenny: We're going through a period of growth. We were even growing during the recession, which was interesting. We had already put some pieces into place to do things in other parts of the world. Finding ways to manage our image in other countries has been a fun and interesting challenge and something we've become a lot better at over the last few years. But, every regional market is different.

The media operates differently in all these spaces. You have t₍ and customer service in different ways in all of these places. leading the charge to develop strategies in how we build our image ... of these markets around the world. The places we're going are much more emerging market-type economies. We've got a ton of activity in India. We've got a lot of activity in China. We've got a lot of activity in South America; Brazil specifically. These are all areas where faculty are interested in writing cases and doing research, so that's what drives our strategy to choose different parts of the world.

If you had been here fifteen years ago, Japan or Mexico would have been the hot places. This will continue to change over time, but I hope we're building the fundamental bedrock we need to understand how to go into new markets and create an image for ourselves in a way that's appropriate for wherever we are in the world. That's been a big change.

Technology has clearly driven a lot of change in the marketing field. We talked about social media and the emergence of that. CRM platforms are obviously important and huge investments. Technology is a double-edged sword. It's been an asset in terms of allowing us to better understand what our customers are thinking and experiencing and relate to them. But, it's also been a huge challenge to figure out how to manage the costs of technology investments and how to change behaviors in a way that allows you to get the most out of those technology investments.

Steimle: What are other trends in higher education that are affecting you right now?

Kenny: Online education is starting to come into its own. We launched an online program here last year called HBX. If you had asked the dean three years ago whether or not we were going to have an online program, he would have said no. It was pretty amazing. It was like he went home on a Friday and had an epiphany over the weekend and came back on Monday and said, "Not only are we going to do this, but we're going to do it fast, and we're going to do it better than anybody else does it."

For the following eight months, we built an online experience that captures the brand experience of being in a Harvard MBA classroom. I won't go into any deep detail about what we're offering, but what's important about it is that the program we have was developed entirely by faculty. There are four faculty members in particular who created a whole new set of cases that were going to be taught through the online medium because they didn't think they could teach a case the traditional way online. They re-created the development of a case so it would work online. And, they built a platform that relies heavily on social media tools for the learning experience.

In an HBS classroom, we teach by the case method. The students are essentially teaching each other. That's how it works. The social networking tools that were built into the online platform allow students to do the same thing in a virtual way. If you're taking the certificate course, when you log on to the program, you immediately see how many other people around the world are logged in. They show up like little circles on a map. You can click on a circle and the person's profile will pop up, and you can message them or the whole group.

We've even built a cold-call feature into this offering. You can be going through the lesson and a little message will pop up on your screen that says, "You've been cold called." You then have two minutes to answer whatever question it is they've put in front of you.

If you are familiar with HBS, you'll know the cold call is one of those things that is both terrifying but also unique to the HBS learning experience. When they start the class, the professor will just point to one person in the class and say, "Set up the case for us." They're referring to the case assigned for that day in the class. If you haven't read the case and you're the person that gets called, you're in a bad spot. We try to capture some of that same tension and drama in the online learning experience.

Every institution is trying to figure out what its presence is going to be like online. From a branding experience, we knew we had to create something true to the HBS brand that was excellent in terms of its caliber. We took a little longer to get there, but it was worthwhile. If you look at a lot of other schools, what they're offering are essentially videotaped versions of their courses. We tried to create something much different, and as a result, we've got something people are learning a lot more from.

Steimle: Speaking of other schools, what have you learned from how they market themselves that you've been able to incorporate into HBS?

Kenny: I'm learning all the time. I have regular meetings, a couple of times a year, with the people that are in my role at fourteen or fifteen other business schools, just to stay in touch with what other people are doing. We all share the same challenges and the same problems. There's always benefit in hearing how other people are thinking about social media platforms, CRM, or things like that. We don't share strategic things, but we share a lot of information with each other in the interest of common learning.

I can't think of any specifics offhand where we've actually adopted something somebody else has done. But, suffice it to say that in addition to getting out and meeting with people in higher ed, I also belong to two other CMO round-table groups, and these firms are all brand names that you would recognize, but they're all on the services side of the business, so there's a lot of commonalities between what I do and what these CMOs do. I learn a lot from listening to what people from outside of higher education are doing.

Steimle: Is there anything specific that you've been able to take from outside higher ed and apply at HBS that might be counterintuitive?

Kenny: I don't know that there'd be anything counterintuitive, and the reason I say that is because, having had the benefit of doing marketing in both private sector and higher ed, it's the same job in so many ways. Higher ed has changed and come closer to what firms have been doing for a long time in thinking about customers. We call our participants and our students "customers" a lot because that's how we have to think about them. If anything, the lessons I'm learning from the CMOs in these for-profit organizations are much more akin to the ways marketers in higher ed are thinking broadly these days.

Steimle: What lessons have you learned that other schools, corporations, or industries might be able to learn from you and your experiences at HBS?

Kenny: I think it's presumptuous to say I can teach somebody else in another place what to do or what to learn from me. If I think about what's worked well for us, it would be true in other places. I know it sounds trite, but it's hard to be transparent to the extent that people expect it these days. We've had to get comfortable being uncomfortable, and for this place, that was a big leap.

One of the first big decisions I had to make when I got here was during a centennial year. We got a call from CNBC. One of the producers there said he wanted to produce a documentary about Harvard Business School for the centennial. They wanted to do an hour-long program, so I engaged in conversations with them about it and assured myself through those conversations that they were going to treat the brand with respect, and it was going to be dignified. It wasn't going to be a whitewash of any kind.

They said, "Look, if we find things that are important to tell, we're going to tell them whether or not they reflect poorly on the school." So, we had to be accepting of that. I also thought about what a great opportunity it was to bring some awareness of the school, to usher in the new century in a way that could get lots of viewers, so I took it to the dean with my recommendation that we do it. I had to sell that to him and the school leadership. Again, this was coming right on the heels of the time when the school had basically closed its doors and said, "We've been burned a lot. Our reputation has suffered because we've trusted journalists to do a responsible job, and they haven't." I had to help people understand we needed to change the way we were thinking about that.

They filmed for three months, and I was never as nervous as I was the night that show was being screened for the first time, because I was not allowed to see it. I wasn't allowed to look at any of the transcripts. It was a restless night for me. But, they did a great job. They showed some of our warts, which was fine because otherwise, it wouldn't have felt credible at all since most of it was very praiseworthy. That was the beginning of being able to start building some trust internally. Transparency can be hard, and that's one thing we continue to try and get people comfortable with: the notion that we have to be willing to be honest with ourselves about our weaknesses and share those with the world as a way of humanizing the brand. That's worked well for us.

Steimle: It has been predicted that higher-education institutions will become increasingly divergent and differentiated. Have you seen that happening?

Kenny: No, I have not seen it happening. There have always been professional schools of one kind or another who are differentiated by the fact that they specialize in one area. But in my experience, if you look across the broad array of institutions, they still all seem similar to me. You could take almost any school's brochure and swap the names at the top of the brochure and it would still be pretty appropriate. That's a challenge every higher-ed marketer faces. Even if you just took business schools as a class unto themselves, it's hard to differentiate between them. We're all saying the same things. We're all using words like "innovation," "entrepreneurship," "leadership," and "global." It is hard to differentiate yourself in a space where we all look so similar.

Steimle: What can other marketing departments at higher-education institutions do to differentiate?

Kenny: I mentioned my prior institution was Northeastern University. They are fortunate to have made a decision over a hundred years ago that allows them to differentiate themselves today when they adopted a method of education called "co-op." Co-op is shorthand for "cooperative learning."

They were the second institution in the U.S.—the first was the University of Cincinnati—to build their year around trimesters rather than semesters. For two of the three trimesters, students are in class, and the third trimester, they are working in an organization. They are basically doing internships the whole time they're in school. The shorthand these days for that is called "experiential learning," but Northeastern University, having adopted that so early on, has built a huge network and a great reputation for creating amazing work experiences for students while they're in school.

Most other schools have some variation on that, but they can't differentiate on it the way Northeastern can now. Harvard has a little bit of that. Aside from just being part of Harvard, which is a little differentiator itself, the business school adopted the case method. We were the first business school to use it. We are the school that has basically shared that methodology with every other business school in the world by selling our cases, and now, eighty percent of the cases used by other business schools are written by HBS faculty, so that's a huge differentiator for us and one we use all the time. It's a great asset we have to talk about. Unless you have something like that in your history or you can zero in on something that pointed, it's hard to differentiate.

Steimle: How seriously are universities taking marketing these days? Have you seen marketing investments at universities increasing?

Kenny: Yes. If you were to look at the overall operating budget of most colleges and universities, going back maybe ten or twelve years, you wouldn't have found any cabinet-level positions reporting to the president that were responsible for marketing. There was much more of a government relations—type role, but it wasn't a marketing role. If you fast-forward to today, you would find the government relations person reporting to the chief marketing officer in most organizations, and you would find there's a line item in the budget specifically designated for marketing, branding, and image building for the institution.

I don't think we are anywhere near on par with what a private firm would spend for marketing. The benchmark for most firms is four percent of revenue goes into marketing. My guess is most universities are at a half of one percent, maybe one percent of revenue. But absolutely, the marketing investment has changed, and the way the marketing sits within the organization has changed.

Steimle: There's a lot of hype about big data these days and data in general. Can you speak to the use of data in your role?

Kenny: We're not doing anything with big data yet. We're not there. And I, frankly, am still trying to figure out what big data is. This is one of those things you'll hear marketing people talk about, but I don't know that anybody's put a fine point on big data and how we're using it. If you had to look at an evolutionary scale of where we are in terms of how we're using the data, we're in the beginning stages of figuring out exactly what to gather and how to mine it in a way that gives us insights that can affect our behavior and the way we go to market. I don't think we are sophisticated about it yet, but we understand we need to get there, so that's a work in progress.

Steimle: What are some of the biggest challenges facing today's CMOs?

Kenny: I would say change, the rapid pace of change. If you look at the pace of change back when I first got into the marketing field, fifteen years ago or so, even though it felt fast then, you had a lot more time to settle in on a strategy and execute it than you do today. If we look at technology and how quickly it's changing, we're kind of on a hamster wheel of sorts. We just keep running around and around. We're moving, and we're working hard, but we never quite catch up to what the next thing is. We never really have time to settle on one particular approach, because things are changing so quickly.

Another big challenge is that the millennials, people that are coming of age now and are becoming our customers, are much more savvy about how they make decisions. They're much savvier about when they're being marketed to, and it's a real challenge not to underestimate the intelligence of the people buying our educational products and services, because they're getting their information in ways that suit them, and they want to be able to engage in ways that feel genuine with the institution. If we lose sight of that, the exposure is much greater than it ever was before.

Steimle: Given these and other challenges you face, what advice would you give to first-time CMOs who are coming into the role?

Kenny: I would advise anybody to do what I did when I started in this role, and I did the same thing when I started at Northeastern University and every place I've been. Fight the urge to feel like you need to be the problem-solver at the outset. Fight the urge to feel like you need to demonstrate how smart you are. I go into every meeting assuming I know the least of anyone in the room, and at a place like Harvard, that's entirely possible.

It's important for people to realize they need to take a step back and listen and learn before they try to propose solutions to things. Although, when I first arrived at Harvard I can't tell you how many times people said, "We've been waiting to make this decision until you were here." You have to fight the urge to buy into that and feel like, "If I don't make a decision, I'm going to look bad," because it's not about you at the end of the day. I always try to remember that if it starts to become about me, I'm thinking about it the wrong way.

Steimle: What advice would you have for those who are aiming for top marketing positions?

Kenny: Fundamentally, if you look at what I do today versus what I did when I first started, the core of it hasn't changed. It's about being a good communicator with whatever tools are available to you at a given time. In fact, when I hire—unless it's for a specialized position, like a designer or something—I'm looking for people that are smart, creative, levelheaded, and good storytellers, people who are able to communicate and tell a story in a convincing way, because that's what marketing and communications are all about.

We're trying to sell something, trying to convince somebody to do something, and if you can't communicate convincingly, then you're not going to be able to do that. If I hire a person with the softer skills—creativity and being able to communicate well, being articulate, being enthusiastic—I can usually figure out how to teach them to do anything else that's needed.

Steimle: If the core of marketing hasn't changed over the past twenty years, do you think that will hold for the future? Will only the tactics change?

Kenny: The platforms we use will change. The way people access information and find out about our brands, products, and services is going to change just as it has. The way people are able to engage with us is going to continue to change.

Consumers have a broad platform when they want to talk about your brand or product. They don't need to check with you first. They can say what they want. That's only going to increase: the whole idea of a consumer as a marketer. I do think marketers will still need to truly understand what their brands are about, speak about their brands in honest and authentic ways, and tell the brand story in a way that is authentic but also clear and concise and helps people to appreciate what the brand is all about.

Louis Gagnon

Chief Product & Marketing Officer
Audible

Louis Gagnon served as chief product and marketing officer (CPMO) at Audible, an Amazon company, from January 2014 to January 2016. He oversaw branding, product development, marketing, and customer service activities within the business. Gagnon previously held the CPMO position at Yodle, after serving as senior vice president of global products for Monster.

Josh Steimle: Give us an overview of your marketing career. How did you get your start? What are the steps that led to where you are today?

Louis Gagnon: I had an atypical career path in the sense that I skipped a lot of steps and went in many directions, and, first and foremost, I am fascinated by the idea of change, social change in particular. All of my career, I've followed ideas that represented opportunities for me to change the world and have an impact.

That's what drives me. I started my career as an entrepreneur for a big international NGO[1] that was very small at the time. I went to Rwanda to do social marketing of reproductive health products, mainly condoms, to try and stop or slow down the AIDS epidemic. The idea was simple. We would go to

---

[1] non-governmental organization

© Josh Steimle 2016
J. Steimle, *Chief Marketing Officers at Work*, DOI 10.1007/978-1-4842-1931-7_4

the World Bank or a big international donor and say, "The cost of someone dying from AIDS is going to be fifteen thousand U.S. dollars to the economy. We'll pick up that tab if you give us one dollar per capita. We can mass-market condoms and build the brand, value, and distribution and do what mass marketers do, and in so doing, we'll create demand and save lives, and you will save a lot of money."

I think we were the eighth country to open up for this NGO called Population Services International. I did that in Rwanda for two years. It was a huge success, and after that, the genocide happened. I got out when the genocide happened and moved to London and tried to replicate my Rwandan experience with the European donor community targeting African and Southeast Asian countries.

In the following four years, I did that in seven or eight countries, and this time I was not the guy doing it in the country. I would hire people like me, and it was all about how you create demand for a product that is extremely hard to sell. Condoms are not easy to sell. There was the AIDS factor, which was a real knee-deep marketing problem. We saved thousands of lives, but in so doing, we also realized that mass marketing has its limits for health products, especially reproductive health as a category.

The real issue we had is we did not have the word-of-mouth effect. The innovators were not seen wearing the product, and the innovators would not necessarily brag about the product they were using because it had a social stigma attached to it. Therefore, using high investment in mass-media marketing and branding, we were able to raise awareness high, but adoption was limited to the innovators, and the innovators did not do the job of convincing the rest of the market, so we saturated sales quickly. So, after three or four years, sales would be saturated. We would still be saving tons of lives, but compared to the magnitude of the problem, it was not enough.

So, I went to India, and I founded a warehouse that would pay people for the economic effect of the word of mouth, the logic being that people don't want to talk about it. If I pay for it, maybe they will, so let's go test that. I got some funds from the U.S. government to go do that. I went to Chennai for three years and proved that the model worked, but it was heavily constrained in the brick-and-mortar environment. It was hard to manage exponential growth when you had the constraints of the physical world, especially in India at that time. We're talking mid- to late nineties.

It was at that time that I had this idea to take my technology and pay people for the economic effects of word of mouth and bring that to the Internet, specifically targeting telcos and the credit card companies. We had a few successes, but it never became what I wanted it to become, so I decided to take a job in the corporate world.

I worked as a vice president for marketing at Monster. When I started, the company was making ten million dollars a year. It was a small subsidiary. It was a distant number three in the market, and in two years, I made it a sixty-five-million-dollar company and in the number-one position, a super brand. It won all sorts of prizes, which got the attention of the headquarters. It got me into Boston to be head of consumer products, so I headed the job-seeker side of the house for a year, and then I headed the whole thing for another couple of years.

Then I left Monster. That was at the time when social was taking off, and I was not able to implement the changes we had built fast enough. I decided to move on, and I went to Yodle, which was trying to help small businesses leverage the Internet and technology in order to be successful and acquire more customers. It was an automated fast play. I did that for three years.

At that time, there was a turnaround, as I decided I would go with the title of chief product and marketing officer, which was based on my experience that you will lose a lot of opportunities to optimize the institution of marketing programs if you don't know how you're going to go to market. And if you don't understand the messaging of a product deeply at the cellular level, you don't build the same product. I brought those two things together with U.S.-Analytics and sort of pioneered the title. I don't know many people who had it, CPMO. I did that successfully.

We grew the company sixty percent–plus per year for the three years I was there, and it was a good gig. That's when Audible showed up, and I decided I would do the same thing at Audible—bring the integration skills I developed to bring data science, users, user experience, products, product marketing, marketing channels, marketing, and brand all together.

There's more to my job here. I also have customer service and strategic planning. The idea was, "Let's bring it all together in order to optimize customer simplicity." Customer simplicity is something we all claim we do and think about, and we all do to a certain degree, but unless you do it in a cross-disciplinary way, unless it's embedded in your processes and in the value that you deliver to the customer at each touchpoint, you're just talking about it. You're not really doing it. That is the journey I embarked on at Audible.

I am a marketer by heart. I think as a marketer. I have the marketing process deeply ingrained in me, and I believe in its values and virtues, but I also believe that a good marketer is more than just that. You have to be fluent with numbers and financial constructs, and in the end, when you get to be an executive in marketing, you realize that you're first and foremost an executive and then a marketer. But as an executive, the marketing *flavor* is the incentive and super important.

At Audible, we've had huge success. I've been here for about a year and a half. We've doubled the growth of the company. We're launching five new revenue streams starting this year and next year. We are expanding globally fast. This is the best time ever to be here, and I'm glad I was able to get the opportunity.

Steimle: How has your background as an entrepreneur helped you in the CMO role?

Gagnon: I said to a friend recently, "When you're an entrepreneur, especially in the early stage, every time you open your mouth, you play your life." You develop a reflex of thinking quickly about the scenarios in front of you and to think fast on your feet so you can communicate effectively and get where you want to be in an adaptive, dynamic manner. That is the skill that I've developed that is most precious.

I will always remember one of my first pitches to venture capitalists. The guy told me, "Hey, your presentation is great. You had lots of interesting details. Fantastic. The only problem is I had to sit through it for three hours. Unless you can summarize it in thirty seconds, three minutes, thirty minutes, and three hours, I won't do it next time." That was an interesting tip about how to think and how to think in hyperlink mode, where you can summarize or synthesize at a high level and then explode ideas as the audience requires. That is the skill. Of course, building things and motivating people is the other piece.

Steimle: What does your marketing team look like at Audible?

Gagnon: Marketing is together with all of the other functions I mentioned before, so I've got some product in two business lines. I've got data science. I've got customer service, strategic planning, and so on. And in marketing, I have two senior vice presidents. One is controlling all acquisition and product marketing, so we call it "product and channel marketing." The other is controlling the brand definition and the execution of that brand by creating an internal agency that actually feeds the channel group with their assets, and that also controls everything on the media side of things—social, content, marketing, PR, events, and so on.

So, splitting it that way, I have someone who's focused on the revenue and the conversion rate and call it "the science of marketing" and another one that's focusing on the messaging, the brand, the application of that brand, those guidelines globally, and how we execute those messages in the channel world. That's how I split it, and it's working well.

Steimle: What is your philosophy in building a marketing team? What do you look for in team members? How do you build that team up?

Gagnon: First and foremost, I look for complementarity. We should not all be clones of one another. That's a bad idea. I'm looking to surround myself with people who are not myself. Generally speaking, I'm looking for culture and values. The things I believe in for the team are we need to be open, intellectually honest, and transparent. We need to debate, and we need to be comfortable with debate and with trying to find the truth because nobody has it, so we need to trust there's going to be a rational process that's going to lead us there.

It takes a certain kind of person to want to go through those discussions and live those values on a daily basis. And then, you're looking for work ethic and attitude, people who want to win, people who work hard, people who are creative, strategic. You get into the technical skills depending on the job you want to hire.

Steimle: How do you manage relationships with other teams and executives? Are there any challenges you've faced, and how have you managed those?

Gagnon: There are always challenges, but that is inherent in being part of an organization. I manage them the same way I manage my team and the same way I manage myself. You want to be honest, you want to be open, you want to be transparent, and this is the best way to achieve collective goals. When I don't get that from certain stakeholders, I spend a lot of time trying to show by example and demonstrate with concrete examples how being that way is the best way for us all to be. I have not met a lot of resistance, and the relationships are pretty good.

Steimle: Are there outside teams that you work with? Do you work with any outside agencies?

Gagnon: We work with a lot of agencies on the media side. We just changed our agency in terms of locating everything under Assembly. On the brand side, we're dealing with R/GA. And of course, I'm dealing with a slew of technology and platform vendors. I don't directly deal with the agencies other than being there for the strategic discussions and hiring decisions. My SVPs are driving this.

My SVP of brand who works with R/GA, for example, was the number two at Razorfish in another life, so she understands that world a lot more than I do. She understands their inner working processes, their constraints, and all of that. I've outsourced the day-to-day management of the output of the agencies to that person. Same thing on the acquisition side. So, I'm there for the strategic discussions and signing the big checks, but otherwise, my team is doing it.

Steimle: You've been in this position for over a year now, right?

Gagnon: Yeah, two years in January.

Steimle: Has your role changed since you came into the position? Has it evolved in any way?

Gagnon: I would say my role is being established more than it has changed. Before, there was no such thing as a department that took all of those functions and brought them together, so I've spent a lot of time building the teams, establishing the processes, and getting us to work together well.

It's taken a year and a half, but I've demonstrated huge results. We have been successful in establishing results and in showing others that there is a lot of value in having your marketers sit together with the product persons, the UX persons, and the developers to find a solution and evolving power to create mini-startups in the company.

That is really the goal here. We want to be an incubator of smaller, what we call "streams," where we have multidisciplinary teams sitting around a table, never more than six or seven, and have them develop great products in an Amazonian way and give them the chance to take risks.

Because this approach was new at Audible, I've changed a lot, and I'm still changing a lot. I think I've tweaked my organization two times in a year. I will continue to do that until we find the perfect recipe, and in the meantime, it's a lot of value, and I think a lot of credibility has been gained in the process.

Steimle: If you could go back in time to when you first came on, is there anything you would do differently? Is there any advice you would give yourself of two years ago if you were going back to rework these last two years?

Gagnon: I would make a more aggressive move in building my data science department. It took me seven or eight months to get into that gear, and I think I should have done it earlier. I am convinced that data science is what powers the marketer of tomorrow, and if you don't get your act together on that front, you are losing a tremendous opportunity to streamline costs, to understand customers, and to do the right thing—so I would have accelerated that a little better.

I would have taken more time to explain the meaning of the changes I was proposing. You know, you come in, you know what it is, and you assume everybody knows, but it's not the case. Change is painful for most people. You need to invest the time to train and to program-manage such big changes. I would have spent more time communicating. There's never enough time for this, sitting down with the hundreds of people who are working for me and connecting more regularly than once a quarter and trying to keep them apprised of where we are, what we're doing, and why. That's something I could have improved. You never communicate enough, and if you're going to have a bias, having the bias to over-communicate is always better. Building a constituency early on with your peers and with people in the global corporation is also extremely important.

Steimle: What's some of the data you have access to, and how are you using data in your role?

Gagnon: Let me preface by talking about trends that are now dating three or four years, which are social, mobile, and local. These trends are now fully developed. They're not complete yet, but they're definitely deployed, and what these things are doing is generating data we didn't have before. You have the link between so many more things, which gives you points of understanding, provided you have the right system in a way that was unimaginable before.

We have access to all of the Amazon-related data sets. We have access to our own behavioral data sets. We have access to our own profile data sets, and we have access to third-party vendor data sets. We at Amazon spend *a lot* of time and energy protecting those assets. There is not one company in the world I've seen or worked with that spends more time and takes more precautions than us to anonymize data and to make sure our customers are protected.

We have an enormous amount to harvest. We have tools, technologies, and expertise to do that in a way I have never seen before. It's not like we just have a statistician crunching numbers. We now have statisticians, mathematicians, machine learning practitioners, computer scientists, economists. We have people from all disciplines trying to model out different pieces of the business using their own paradigms. Some paradigms are better for solving certain problems than others, so it's extremely interesting. It feels like it's day one at ground zero. Few companies do it well. We were able to recruit ten PhDs in three months to build a solid team.

On each piece of our business, from the customer to the acquisition side to the content side, I'm already seeing lots of interesting models emerging, which will change the way we interact with our customers. We're always trying to create more value and be more personal and try to get people more engaged with our services. At a high level, it's a huge amount of work and a huge amount of assets we put together.

Steimle: You mentioned engaging the customer, getting closer to the customer. Do you use buyer personas and, if so, how do you go about building and maintaining those?

Gagnon: Yes, we certainly use buyer personas. We have user research labs, and we constantly try and validate the data on who these personas are and how they react to different changes in our stack.

But we also use customer profiling to enrich the personas. It's not just a qualitative exercise. It's something we try and validate with data at the market level to try to understand the size of the personas and markets and to try to deepen our understanding of their ways and means and how they behave in the world other than with our products. What are the adjacencies around our products that affect them? How do they engage with them? It's a broad concept.

You know, the concept of personas is not very different from the concept of segmentation. It is just the application of the segment in the context of usage, so we try and marry both and get one to feed the other.

Steimle: How is globalization affecting your marketing and the customers you're going after?

Gagnon: We now have offices in six countries. We're going to go into many more in the years to come. We are spending a lot of time trying to go global intelligently. It is all too easy to look at the big market and say, "Hey, there are so many people." If you try to penetrate the market by this top-to-bottom approach to internationalization, you invest tons of money and it takes a long time to get a return on your investment.

We're trying to raise the bar on ourselves and be much more strategic in our approach. Looking at not only what the market is instead of trying to find the market for the product that we have, we try to find the right product for the market. For example, we're building new revenue streams. We're getting into the education field, teaching people how to speak English, and other things. If we were to look at a market like China, for example, we would not only look at what we should do for audiobooks in China but for the ESL market in China. What is this other market in China, and what could be the best way for us to enter with which product, and how would we move from there? We try to be more systematic in getting to the biggest value bucket. We're investing a lot of time doing this.

There is definitely such a thing as a global consumer of our products in the sense that we have customers in 220 countries using our dot-com app, which shows that you can live in Zimbabwe and read an American or English author in our app, and hundreds of thousands of people do that. There is definitely a group of people who identify with our English content in a global way, and we try to make their lives easier as we grow our products and try to understand them as much as we understand the others.

We just did our brand guidelines recently, and we had a major focus group with people in six countries, forty people in each country, telling us about ourselves and trying to participate in the process of building what our new brand will be. So, we invested in understanding that piece of it as well. But there is such a thing as customization and local content, so if you're going to be in Spain, you have to have the Spanish content from the local publishing houses. And we also invest a lot of time trying to understand what that is, what the critical mass is, and how to make it happen.

One big constraint in our business model is the publishing world. We don't control the economics of those firms or how they do business. It's definitely a factor to take into consideration as we try to grow our business. It's easier in some countries; it's harder in others, so that's part of a complex problem to solve.

Steimle: You're competing against a lot of options for consumers' time. How do you make sure Audible stays at the top of the list?

Gagnon: The first thing I said when I came to Audible was that we're not an audiobook company, we're a media company, and we're competing for people's time. How do you do this? There is no way to do this other than to deliver value, which means that whoever you are when you come to interact with our service, we need to put in your brain, your heart, or your soul the best content that is available for you.

That requires a lot of work for us to understand who you are and what content you actually use, and we need to make that social, relevant, and affordable, and we need to make sure we suggest the next thing, and that will get better each time. That is the priority—to build a service that no matter what you do, you're happy with your experience. That experience is going to feed the other one, and the idea is to create virtual circles in the experience as much as possible.

When you have a good experience with something, you remember to use it because it's nice. Having the best authors in the world narrated by the best voices in the world is something we stand behind and would put against anything. We're big believers in the deep psychological and human value of that, and our customers are people who love that. And, we need to invest in brand and marketing for people to discover that.

Onebook is a great way for us to do it. You use your social intelligence to decide who in your network could benefit from that book, which tells us that this person is going to have the best experience possible. We're not going to choose that book for him or her. You will. And since it's free, it's a great experience for everybody. This is building brand awareness through experience as opposed to brand awareness through recognition and frequency. Make the product great, and make sure it diffuses in smart ways, such as Onebook, social, viral, etc.

But, let me say this: you're never done with those things, right? We're only at the beginning. I'm not satisfied at all with where we are in terms of the number of members we have. I believe this company is going to go mainstream in a much bigger way. Right now, we are premium. We have *extremely* desirable demographics. We're over-indexing with the top of the pyramid, and we need to take that down in a significant way in the years to come.

Steimle: As far as that goes, are there any strategies you're working on that you can share?

Gagnon: Onebook would be a big one. We're also leveraging the intelligence we have around channel attribution to try and optimize our channel mix in a big way.

We're going to invest a lot in our relationship with Assembly, and we're doing so this year. We're going to go much deeper in rolling out our data science models, and that in turn will cede the intelligence we need to use to better target and be more precise and relevant.

And, we're just rolling out a new brand. We redid our logo. We have some new colors. We're working on all of our apps and all of our surfaces, trying to refresh the brand and make it a little broader. We are rolling out a brand idea that is about inspiring voices, and inspiring voices is much more than audiobooks. It encompasses education, information, all sorts of good things people want to put in their ears every morning. At that level, that's about all I can say.

Steimle: You have the benefit of being able to connect directly to your customers through the app and through the website. Are there other channels, social media networks and such, that you're experiencing success with in terms of connecting to customers and new customers?

Gagnon: We're investing a lot of resources in our social channels. Facebook, Instagram, Twitter, and now Pinterest have promising responses in reaching certain communities. It is not yet a mass phenomenon for us. We don't have fifty million Facebook followers. But we have super-engaged users that are totally dedicated to literature and audiobooks, and we try to have a special bond with them and have relevant conversations with all of them with the benefit of earned media.

Last year, with everything that we were doing on the earned side and on the paid side, we doubled brand awareness for the company. It took us one year to double that number for a company that had been in existence for seventeen years, and I think it speaks volumes in terms of the effectiveness of using the channels to not necessarily drive the transactions and direct the response but certainly to drive the awareness of the brand and the recognition and the preference for that brand.

Steimle: What advice would you give a first-time CMO, somebody who just entered the role?

Gagnon: Take your brand spiel and put that in the drawer. Today, no one is interested in adding a CMO who talks the brand lingo around the fact that brand is at the center of everything and wants to define what everything is and roll it out across all touch points.

It's a mechanistic model that does not correspond to today's reality in which everything is organic and dynamic. The new CMO needs to be a data-driven executive. That means you don't come in with brand theory. You come in with customer intelligence—customer understanding beyond, "Here's what the customers do, and here's who they are." You need to be able to speak to the why, because it's only that why that's going to give us strategic insights to move the whole business, not just marketing.

At the end of the day, the business is about the customer. You as the CMO are their constituent on the C-suite that is heavily invested in understanding the customer and making sure we're going to deliver the optimal value for that customer. So, you need to be fluent in finance, you need to understand human economics, you need to understand product, you need to understand test and automation. Coming in with humility as a data-driven executive that will be able to attract the data scientists to want to work for you is priority number one. Priority number two, like any good executive, is to be humble, open, and honest. That goes a long way. And then you take it from there.

Steimle: Are there any other marketing trends you find interesting today that you haven't already covered?

Gagnon: Besides the race to the data science Klondike, I would say two other things for me are really important and striking. One of them has to do with the fact that you have more information around consumer intent with the integration of all of those data points than Google can provide you with. As marketers, we used to have the marketing intent coming from search and SEO, and then you would make a wild guess and optimize as much as you could to get to the right economics.

But right now, you know customer intent or purchasing intent signals outside of search. Integrating that into your analysis is a huge trend. In the same way, search engines are becoming potentially intelligent enough to be powerful personal assistants. That's what's happening with Alexa at Amazon, and Siri, and Cortana, and all of those engines that are trying to be proactive, answer customers' wishes, suggest things, and have a relevant conversation. It's a major trend in terms of purchasing intent signals, interesting signals for us to understand as marketers.

The other thing related to that would be the fact that in the mobile world, there was a long debate around HTML5 and the browser versus the app. I think that debate has closed. The app has won. Eighty-eight percent of people's time is on apps, and that has strategic implications for marketers who are heavily invested in Google and in search engine marketing, because a lot of people go straight to the app store now. And when they go to the iOS app store, there is no Google search engine. How you get your piece of that organic and paid traffic is a new frontier everybody is trying to scramble to understand. And it's obviously true across marketplaces.

Steimle: Is there anything we haven't covered that you feel is important to communicate about the role of being a CMO?

Gagnon: I truly believe it is a privilege to be given the time and resources to be the one in the C-suite that understands the customer. If you understand the customer, you understand the business. Being able to leverage that knowledge, to talk to the CFO, to talk to the CTO, to talk about how we do business, understanding the interdependencies, and working together with others are the reasons CMOs are becoming more and more relevant in the C-suite.

I remember the time when the CFOs were it. The C-suite revolved around the CFO, and the CFO was the guy that would become the CEO. Around 2000 to 2005, that trend was starting to change. I think it's changing because of the fact that the CMO has access to that intelligence, and some of them can use it properly.

If you want to be that guy tomorrow, it's extremely important to understand that it's not a marketing degree that's going to do it. You need to have a deep, quantitative, financial skillset in order to be that CMO tomorrow. Those who will succeed are those who can do both the analytical thing and the creative strategic thing, trying to motivate hundreds of people who actually talk about your brand and present it in a good way. Marrying those two skills is the recipe for success. I think it's a unique opportunity. No one has been given the keys to the kingdom before our generation. Let's not ruin it.

Kevin Marasco

Chief Marketing Officer
HireVue

*Since 2011, **Kevin Marasco** has been the CMO at HireVue, named by Forbes as one of America's Most Promising Companies of 2014. At HireVue, Marasco leads product, outreach, and brand, promoting a combination of digital video and predictive analytics to build and coach employee teams. Prior to HireVue, Marasco served as Taleo's VP of brand and digital marketing for three years. Before working at Taleo, Marasco drove global marketing and sales support at Vurv (previously known as Recruitmax). Marasco has also spent time as an entrepreneur and investor with various startups. Marasco has a bachelor's degree in business from the University of North Florida and an executive education certificate in marketing for senior executives from Harvard Business School.*

Josh Steimle: What does the marketing department look like at HireVue? How many people are on your team, and how is it structured?

Kevin Marasco: Today, we have about fifteen people. It's in a continuous state of flux. When I started, we had twenty people in the whole company and only one person in marketing. It's continuously evolving as we start to build out.

Our core functions are demand marketing, solid content, digital, and web. We have a field and corporate marketing team that does events, promotions, and creative services. The product marketing team does all the product marketing and a bit of intelligence. Then, we have a go-to-market team, which takes everything and is responsible for the field enablement of our sales team, services team, and so on and so forth.

J. Steimle, *Chief Marketing Officers at Work*, DOI 10.1007/978-1-4842-1931-7_5

We have PR and communications as well as an important team within that that does customer advocacy. That's a huge, newer area of marketing that we're focused on—once we land an account, continuing to drive advocacy, expansion, renewals, referrals, and things like that.

We also have a social marketing function, which is another newer area, relatively speaking, for marketers. You used to see social placed in corporate comms, digital, demand, or even HR. We have a broader focus on social. We're trying to integrate it into all aspects of the business—social selling, social marketing, and services and support. Those are the core areas of how we're structured.

Steimle: What's your philosophy on building a marketing team?

Marasco: In general, I find it varies depending on the stage the company's at and what the biggest growth weavers are for the company. I don't find it all equal. For one business, one thing might add the most value the quickest, so there's a sequencing that needs to take place depending on the stage of the company, the market they're in, etc.

In general, marketing is evolving fast. I'm a fan of finding athletes that can hustle, that are quick learners, that can think outside the box and be innovative, and that are data-driven. I'm more a fan of those folks than of your traditional someone with x years' experience.

That said, for certain areas, experience can be really valuable. For example, it might be product marketing. Having someone who understands inside the mind of a buyer, positioning strategy, competitive intelligence—there are certain roles that really require that experience, but there are other areas where the experience can actually be damaging.

I work with marketers who get stuck in their ways, and the way we did something ten years ago is probably not the best way to do it today. I'd rather have someone who's intuitive, innovative, quick to learn new things, try new things, and hustle.

Steimle: Is there anything else you look for in new hires?

Marasco: It definitely depends on the role, but in general, I'm looking for people who are data-driven—in most areas, anyways—and people who are good at collaboration. In marketing, it's imperative that we work tightly with so many parts of the organization—sales, services, operations, HR, market. It's important that folks are good at teamwork and communication. I look for the ability to learn quickly and adapt. I think that's the other thing.

Other functions—for example, finance and engineering—are much more operational: "Here's your recipe. Just follow it and punch through this list." There are some exceptions, but for most roles in marketing, I find that doesn't really work. Things are so fluid and changing that you need people who quickly adapt to change and can work in a fluid environment. I find that works better than folks who are more rigid.

Steimle: Tell us more about who your customers are. What kinds of companies are using HireVue, and how are they using it?

Marasco: Companies are using HireVue to modernize the way they build and coach their teams, specifically using digital video and predictive analytics to get to know people at a deeper level and make smarter and faster decisions. We're disrupting things that have been in place for hundreds of years.

When building a team, traditionally, you look at résumés, which don't tell you a lot about a person. Then, you do a phone screen. We're basically going in and disrupting that process. Looking at résumés gives you access to very little information—where someone worked and maybe where they went to school. The deeper-level information, the things that really matter—soft skills, communication, people's potential, passion, capabilities, personality, communication skills—are things that we can pull out using video.

We can also apply that to allow people to actually demonstrate their true ability to work. For example, we're hiring a comptroller right now, and we just gave this person an exercise: "Look at this spreadsheet. Analyze this P&L. Tell us what's wrong with it." They have ten minutes to look at it, and then we capture video of their response. Those are things that you can't get off a résumé or even a quick phone screen. That deeper visibility allows people to make smarter, faster decisions. It can be applied to both building and coaching a team.

Let's take, for example, sales. Apple just rolled out the new iPad Pro. They need to make sure that all of their team members in every team around the world are able to articulate an understanding of the product, deliver the value prop, and explain how it differentiates from previous iPads, as well as competitive tablets. They need to understand the pricing, the objection handling, and so on and so forth. Right now, that's tough, because a lot of that is traditionally done through manual processes—old-school training, classroom learning, ride-alongs—so, we're disrupting that process using video.

An individual and a centralized team can demonstrate their abilities using mobile video. We're also layering that with predictive analytics. For example, if you're training your top sales reps on a new product, we capture those interactions. Using their audio, video, choice of words, etc, we compare them to the newer reps or whoever you're rolling this out to so you can understand where the gaps are, who needs more work, and what excellence looks like. Then, you can share that information.

It's really a way of improving the way companies build and coach their teams. Historically, we've focused on people who have big teams—the Fortune 1000. We have about twenty-eight percent of the Fortune 100 as customers—big companies like Nike, JPMorgan Chase, Accenture, Starbucks, Apple, and Amazon.

More recently, we started expanding and offering the same solutions to smaller companies, typically anyone with over one hundred employees. We're also expanding internationally into Europe and Asia. We're doing a ton of hiring and growth in those regions. It's broad compared to other industries in which you're focused solely on CIOs or something like that.

One thing I was surprised at: it applies to all verticals. I thought it made total sense for certain industries, like health care, financial services, and technology—and it does—but it also makes sense for organizations in the public sector, energy, construction, and manufacturing. They're competing for talent against a lot of these other industries.

Our technology can even connect miners and mining companies in the northern part of Canada that's difficult to access. HireVue uniquely applies to organizations of all types of industries, sizes, and locations.

Traditionally, it's been business leaders who run good-sized teams—your heads of sales, heads of engineering, and HR, which usually owns the process and spends a lot of time implementing any technology responsible for that. What we're finding is interesting because historically, we've focused more on the HR buyer. They're still highly involved, but we're finding more business leaders getting involved because they're the ones whose bottom line it impacts.

At HireVue, every day that we don't have a rep, we're missing just over three thousand dollars in revenue from the open quota. That's per rep. So for ten reps, that's thirty thousand dollars a day in missed revenue. We can cut the hiring time in half. So, for bigger organizations, it's millions and millions of dollars in additional revenue from the reduction in vacancy, not to mention better decision-making.

Steimle: Are there use cases for HireVue that have surprised you?

Marasco: Absolutely. Some of the industries and things like that have been surprising. Teaching has been one, and not just in higher ed. We happen to see school districts that require a whole process of decision-by-committee that used to take months and was done with surface-level information, like résumés and job applications. It not only took a long time, but led to poor decisions. Now, these folks are digitizing the process and getting it done in days instead of weeks or months, and making more informed, data-driven decisions. It's pretty cool to see such diversity in the industries.

The onboarding has also been interesting. We've had situations where you go up to a person in the office thinking they're a customer or partner and introduce yourself and realize it's actually a new employee that just started. Now, anytime someone has been hired, we do what we call an "introview," which is basically a digital introduction.

We have a few questions like, "Tell us a little bit about yourself. What are you going to be doing in your new role? How can the team support you? Tell us an interesting fact about yourself." I watch those. I'll go for a run on the treadmill and watch them on my iPad. I get to meet these people before they start. And then, the first time I see them, it's like, "Hey, you're a Broncos fan, right? Good game last week." It's pretty cool. And likewise, before they start, they watch all the introductions of the existing team members, so they feel like they know people before they start.

Another really cool use that one of our clients emailed us a couple of weeks ago and that a lot of companies are doing is using HireVue to reach underserved demographics of the workforce: military, working moms, the long-term unemployed, and underprivileged youth who are in some of these really poor school districts. It's very difficult for them to tell their story and be heard. With a focus on résumés or job performance, these stories are going to get skipped over.

One of our clients is a children's hospital, and they found this school district that no one was going into. No one was hiring anyone out of this area, and they used HireVue to meet and connect with people from there. They said, "We just found this person that's amazing. We never would have looked at this person based off an application, but she's incredible. If it weren't for HireVue, we would never have found her, and she never would have had this opportunity."

We've also been hearing a lot of that for the military. A lot of the vets coming back from Afghanistan fill out job applications that just get skipped over because they don't have the profile. If you looked at them on LinkedIn, you wouldn't even consider them. But their stories and their potential leadership capabilities—these guys have run teams of hundreds of soldiers and multimillion dollars' worth of equipment, but they get skipped over because they don't have ten years' experience at IBM or something like that.

That's been one of the most rewarding things: seeing the difference it can make in people's personal lives and giving these people, who are highly capable and have so much potential, the ability to connect with the incredible opportunities that they deserve, because, unfortunately, they are often overlooked.

Steimle: Do you have a process for discovering these additional use cases, or do they just pop up?

Marasco: One of the things we're trying to drive from marketing is to capture these stories. We've built a customer community as well as an advocacy program. It's basically a platform for customers to share stories like this, and we spotlight some of the customers in the community.

We also have point-based rewards programs. It could be anything from HireVue services to a pass to a conference for sharing their story. It can come in a variety of ways. We have people that will publish their story on LinkedIn in our community. Sometimes, we do a more traditional video or something like that. We'll capture that application, tell that story, and feed that to our product team as well because sometimes, they say, "Hey, this worked great, and if we added this one thing, we could do it at a greater scale across the rest of the business."

We also have an idea submission area for customers within this community. People are like, "Oh, wow, this is so cool. I could use it for hiring a nanny," or whatever. There's all kinds of stuff on this idea portal. You can go in and submit an idea, and then the rest of the customers can vote on it. You can vote up or down, or submit your own idea. We've built a few mechanisms like that to try to capture these ideas at scale and share them with our team.

Steimle: Have there been any unexpected challenges that HireVue has faced going into other countries and cultures?

Marasco: Absolutely. It's something I think a lot of companies struggle with, their international marketing entrance strategy and sequencing. Goodness, we could probably talk hours on that alone. The short answer is there are always challenges with that. A lot of it is the strategy, sequencing, brand preference, the overall go-to-market model.

Are we leading with marketing to create awareness? A lot of it depends on what the competitive landscape looks like. Are we taking a grassroots, hands-on approach to establish a beachhead? I've been surprised at how receptive, in general, the international market has been to what we do. There have been more headwinds domestically than internationally, which was kind of a surprise.

It seems mobile took off faster in Europe and even Asia to a degree. The workforce of some of our clients in these remote places can't afford a computer, but they can afford a smartphone. They can't apply online, but they can do it through an interview. The overall mobile and text messaging blew up in Europe before it did in the U.S. People were like, "Oh yes, this makes total sense on mobile. Of course, I can do this."

I was talking with one of our heads of recruiting who is based in London and recruits throughout Europe. She said, "When I bring hires in, it takes them two hours just to get on the Tube and get to our office in London. And they're local. Now, I just use HireVue before they do that, and it saves us all a ton of time. I love it." It's solving a lot of travel challenges. There are so many countries in Europe and parts of Asia where they've been super-receptive to it, which I thought was kind of surprising.

For us, the biggest challenge is breaking into these markets that have local competitors that built their entire business to serve a certain country, and HireVue is still a relatively small company. We're trying to punch way above our weight and enter a variety of countries with finite resources, relatively speaking. We really can't go put five people in each country, so we're trying to have this balance between a centralized and decentralized model. We're doing some aspects of sales and marketing in-region and then some centralized from here. It's trying to find that right balance and do it lean and effectively.

Steimle: How has your role at HireVue changed in the five years you've been there?

Marasco: When we started, we were so small that there was really no marketing. The company had over-hired in sales at the beginning, so we had like five or six sales reps and no marketing. The first challenge was giving them the basic tools they needed. At the time, they were having a lot of the challenges in positioning and sales enablement, and these six starving reps had some level of demand for pipeline leads to work. They were doing that kind of scrappy. They needed tools for better conversion. That was the first focus, getting the story together.

That was the early days, right? You're small, so you can roll up your sleeves and do that. Now, we're trying to build a marketing machine at scale. It's really all about scale and hiring. Instead of the five reps we had then, we can bring on five new reps a quarter and have everything they need to be successful—the demand, the pipeline, the tools for consideration of conversion and systemically helping to grow the company.

To summarize how things have changed, a lot of it has been about scale. It's been about putting the building blocks in place—getting corporate marketing, product marketing, demand marketing. We added social more recently, which is pretty cool because the first work is just basic blocking and tackling. That was honestly one of the biggest challenges at my last company. We had tons of demand nurturing, automation workflows, lead scoring, routing to twenty different countries, etc. And now, all of a sudden, it's like hitting a reset button. We have nothing. It's back to crawl, walk, run. It was a lot of crawling and walking.

Now, we're able to do some pretty cool stuff. It's an evolution from starting with a blank sheet of paper—there's so much to do—and getting the right team and processes in place and the right programs running. It was build-out mode, and now it's doing it at scale right across the different geographies and product market segments.

Steimle: What are some ways you've had success with social media?

Marasco: We're trying to empower our team, our entire business, even starting with recruiting people. We've developed dedicated social channels. We have a channel called VueNation. We have a website and social channels for it on Twitter, Facebook, and everything. We know that in order for HireVue to be successful, we've got to be able to attract the best talent, the best sales rep, the best marketers, the best engineers, and so on and so forth.

I'm a firm believer in marketing helping to drive all of that by partnering with the appropriate functions within the business. Other people have different philosophies and think it's strictly an HR thing. But in every company I've been in, the philosophy was that you're only as good as your people. In order for us to grow at scale, at the pace we're trying to grow, we've got to be able to attract great talent.

Look at how competitive it is in Utah right now with all these great startups. We're competing for the best engineers, the best marketers and sales reps against all these unicorns. It's like sales—building an employment brand and closing candidates. That's one area, and so is using social as a tool to let people know, "Here's a great company to work for. Here's how we differentiate. Here's an inside view to our culture. Connect with people who can tell you what a day in the life is like."

Being transparent about the culture and what success looks like in the company is one example. Then, we're taking that kind of approach across the other functions—sales, services, even engineering. We're trying to educate an entire VueNation in how to use social as a tool, so we have our engineers—like data scientists, for example—who are writing and contributing on LinkedIn. It's helping to elevate the HireVue brand and making us look like experts in a variety of fields, not just hiring or HR stuff, but things like data science. That's attractive, getting on the radar of some of the top data scientists in Silicon Valley.

Sales is probably one of the biggest areas, so we're really trying to train and educate. We've built a social selling process where what used to be "Call people five times and email them five times" is now "Engage with them." First, listen on social. Use social to understand what they care about, what they like, what they are commenting on, what they are contributing to. Understand their pain points, their value drivers, what keeps them up. Then, start to engage on social. Connect with them and share valuable content that's educational. Don't sell. Don't cold call them. Don't InMail them. Just engage with them. Then, continue the buying journey.

We've actually laid out the step-by-step process. Those are the things we're doing: trying to embed social into our DNA and infuse it with things we're doing in marketing—the content and things like that.

Steimle: Tell me more about the data you have access to and how you're incorporating it into HireVue's marketing.

Marasco: We're trying to track as much as possible, hence much more focus on digital channels, even for field marketing. Basically, all of our field marketing programs now have a digital overlay to them, so we have five events in the next four weeks, and they all have big digital components before, during, and after the event. A lot of that comes back to getting data and tracking everything. Part of it's operational, so we can ensure optimized conversion rates, responsiveness, and so on by best prioritizing demand.

But, it goes beyond that. We're trying to use it to cross all the areas—sales, customer marketing—to understand usage patterns for users. Who are our top users? I'll give you an example. We're launching some new advocacy programs. Instead of just rolling them out to all users first, we want to get some feedback so we can iterate and make them as effective as possible, so we're getting feedback from our most passionate customers based on their NPS (Net Promoter Score). We're basically mashing up data from our HireVue system, our CRM, and our customer service software that monitors usage and things like that and then pulling it into a couple of our marketing systems and advocacy and community programs. That helps us segment and prioritize: "Hey, launch this to these three hundred twenty-two customers that have an NPS of sixty-five or more first." Then, we'll iterate and roll it out to the next segment. It's cool. That stuff wasn't even possible five or ten years ago.

I boil it down to capturing data on usage, engagement, satisfaction, and buying patterns throughout the entire life cycle of the customer from first touchpoint. That includes capturing where they come from through the sales and marketing funnel, touch points, and dispositions. When an inside rep talks to them, for example, all that information is captured. Then, they go to the next step in the process, which we're tracking. We try to continue to funnel them to the appropriate place. At the end of the day, we're trying to capture data across all of those areas of an entire customer life cycle, use that data to optimize our programs and processes, and then prioritize and make decisions based on that.

Steimle: What have been some of the successful marketing campaigns for HireVue? What does it take to run a successful marketing campaign?

Marasco: One highly targeted segment of our market is the Fortune 100. There's a lot of regional and field marketing to go find those people versus a more broad-based digital approach that you'd normally do for small businesses or consumer marketing. We're trying to find out how we can take some of the principles of digital and apply them to what's historically worked for this high end of the market. There are more field events, and it's more network-based.

We've created this series of virtual events. It varies across market segments, but we try to maximize reach while keeping our costs per marketing-qualified lead under fifty bucks. We blended some traditional webinar concepts with content marketing and built virtual events where we'll get a group of subject-matter experts together—authors, bloggers, customers, a lot of whom are great brands—and have them talk on a topic.

From that, we'll build content like an ebook or a webinar that they recorded at their convenience, so they're not having to schedule anything and do it live. They do it on demand on their own time. We package it all together and then make it available. Then, we market it through every channel: social, email, etc. And then, we bring on partners to help fund it.

Actually, what was pretty cool is we were able to do this by allowing them to participate, giving them some access to some of the leads and things like that. We were able to do it at a net positive. We were actually able to generate revenue through sponsorships and things like that while basically getting our cost per lead net positive instead of paying fifty bucks or more. That's been pretty cool, and it's generated a ton of great content that's marketing on a shelf.

We continue to market. It's been great from a cost, economic, and reach standpoint and still drives some quality leads. Social campaigns would be a second example. Some have been more hands-on, like working with our outbound ADM team and empowering them with social tools where they're not just doing blind emails and cold calls and things like that.

Steimle: What are some of your favorite books that have been helpful in terms of marketing? Are books helpful in your role?

Marasco: Absolutely. I kind of geek out on that. I think I learned it from one of my earliest CEOs. You can learn from everybody, right? This early CEO of mine was a book nut. He'd fly to Europe and visit clients and come back with three books and say, "Hey, check this out! I have this idea." I inherited that, and I do it to my team. I think it's very important, but you don't need to take each book as gospel. If you're continuously pivoting directions, that's a mistake. Your team can get whiplash if you're always saying, "Hey, let's do this! No, let's do this because it's a hot new trend I just read about."

But that said, it's very important because you can always learn cool principles, concepts, and stuff that doesn't work—potential potholes. I think a lot of Daniel Pink's *To Sell Is Human*.[1] I thought *The Challenger Sale*[2] was good. I thought that was one of the better sales books I've read, not that it was that groundbreaking. There are other books that kind of introduce those concepts. Right now, I'm reading *The Challenger Customer*,[3] by Brent Adamson, Matthew Dixon, Pat Spenner, and Nick Toman.

The Challenger Sale and *The Challenger Customer* have been interesting to me because they've reframed my thinking about what we need to be doing as marketers as far as helping educate customers in a consulting role. The bottom line is that by the time an average buyer engages, he's over fifty percent of

---

[1] Riverhead Books, 2013.
[2] Brent Adamson and Matthew Dixon (Portfolio, 2011).
[3] Portfolio, 2015.

the way through his buying journey, and there are five other people involved too. How do we re-architect our marketing for that? That's been at the top of my mind lately.

Steimle: What advice would you give yourself if you could go back in time? What might you have done differently?

Marasco: I would tell myself to always be learning. I love marketing because it's so fluid and changing. The stuff I learned in college, like the five Ps, included principles I can still apply today, but there's a lot of stuff that has radically changed. We're not going to spend three million dollars on a Super Bowl ad and brainwash people because of some cool positioning. We can create a YouTube video for free, and if we know how to get it out there, it can be more effective at zero cost.

It's so cool how much has changed and that it requires us to be open-minded and always learning. I'd say, "Always be learning from what other people are doing." It's not always just other marketers. Something I try to ingrain in my team is to look for inspiration everywhere. Especially, don't look for it just from others in software marketing, because there's so much bad software marketing.

Look at what consumer companies are doing. There's a new trend of building a successful business that scales without traditional marketing—advertising, PR, and blah, blah, blah. I call it "unmarketing." If we can build that into the DNA of what we do, anything we do on top of it will just be icing on the cake. Depending on what your industry is, it could be building the marketing into the product social platform or, if it's in health care, providing such good services that people are talking about them, and it's easy for them to spread the word and recommend them to whoever would make a purchase. That's neat and easy.

We have to look for inspiration outside of our industries in what other organizations are doing. Our team will take a long time with this. What is Uber doing? What is Nest doing? What would Apple do here? There's something we can learn from that. Always be learning. You can learn from anyone anywhere.

I'd also tell myself to learn more in other areas even outside of marketing, services, and finance. I feel fortunate to have partnered with a lot of folks in other areas, sales especially. I'd love to spend more time learning in those areas at a deeper level because it continues to help us marketers arm and fuel the rest of the team.

Kraig Swensrud

Chief Marketing Officer
Campaign Monitor

*In 2014, **Kraig Swensrud** became CMO at Campaign Monitor, which provides email marketing solutions to top-tier customers like Disney, Coca-Cola, and Apple. Previously, Swensrud was the founder of the online survey tool GetFeedback, where he worked for three years before it was acquired by Campaign Monitor. Previous to founding GetFeedback, Swensrud was the CMO and head of product marketing at Salesforce. The first company that Swensrud founded, Kieden, an online advertising company, was acquired by Salesforce in 2006. Swensrud graduated from the University of California, Berkeley with a degree in engineering.*

Josh Steimle: Tell me more about who Campaign Monitor's customers are. What types of companies do you work with? What types of people are using the product?

Kraig Swensrud: One of the things I love about Campaign Monitor and the product we deliver is that we help companies of every size succeed and grow with simple, powerful email marketing tools. There are a lot of technology companies—including my very first employer out of college, Oracle—who are mainly focused on selling to companies in the Fortune 500. There are only five hundred companies in the Fortune 500, but there are millions of businesses around the world with the same hopes and dreams that want to grow and be successful. Small and mid-market growing businesses don't have million-dollar budgets and armies of people to bankroll a large complicated technology implementation. These are the companies that use Campaign Monitor.

J. Steimle, *Chief Marketing Officers at Work*, DOI 10.1007/978-1-4842-1931-7_6

Instead of servicing the Fortune 500, I like to say that Campaign Monitor is serving the Fortune 5,000,000—the millions of businesses around the world that want to use online marketing technology to help grow their businesses. Email marketing is the number one way that these businesses can grow their customer base, because it's easy-to-understand, cost effective, and has quantifiable ROI.

Campaign Monitor has three different types of customers. One type of customer is a growing small or medium-sized business. For example, there is a really cool company called Rip Curl, a global clothing brand, retail company, and surf apparel manufacturer. They are significantly smaller than their largest competitor, which is a company called Quicksilver. But Rip Curl has a mission to become what they call the "ultimate surfing company." In order to accomplish these goals with a smaller team and budget, they need to constantly educate their customers and launch new products with innovative technology.

The reason Rip Curl is top of mind for me right now is they just launched a new campaign with us called the Bombshell wetsuit. The Bombshell is the first-ever wetsuit made for women. Until now, for the decades the surf industry has been in existence, women have been forced to buy and wear men's wetsuits. We're coming on wintertime in the Northern Hemisphere, which is the right time to buy a wetsuit, and Rip Curl wants to launch the Bombshell to customers that live where it's Winter now. They want to be able to use their customer database and say, "I want a segment on people that live in the Northern Hemisphere" or "beach cities in California," and "I want to target this campaign toward female customers." Rip Curl has a relatively small team of brilliant marketers. They have innovative technology and want to launch targeted, personalized, global campaigns to millions of customers. They use Campaign Monitor to do that.

We also have a lot of customers that are agencies doing work on behalf of their clients. You're obviously familiar with Disney, but there is something that Disney does called Disney On Ice, a regional ice skating show that travels around the world, typically in wintertime. They've got all the princesses from Disney, and they skate around the ice and they put on a whole show. You probably have a child, a relative or somebody you know who's been to a Disney On Ice show. They do all of their demand generation and customer appreciation using email marketing. But, they don't do it themselves. They have an agency in whatever geography they're in at the moment handle their email marketing.

The third kind of customer that uses Campaign Monitor is a department within a big company. Selling to Fortune 500 companies isn't our model, but there are departments within big brands, like Coca-Cola, British Airways, and Toyota, that want to run a great email marketing campaign without a herculean effort. They want to get a beautiful, on-brand email out by themselves, that they can pay for with a corporate credit card, so we find ourselves serving that kind of customer too.

Steimle: What does it mean to you to build customer loyalty with your customers and target audience?

Swensrud: CMOs might answer differently depending on the industry that they're in, but one of the things I feel passionate about specifically as a product-based technology company is that customer loyalty comes from the entire experience they have using a service. In today's world of subscription services—like Spotify for listening to music or Campaign Monitor for email marketing—it's up to the company to keep their customers every month. Our customers aren't locked into a multi-year-long contract the way they would be with a cell phone or cable TV provider. Our customers are paying us every month, and they get to decide every month if they're going to renew, downgrade, or upgrade their subscription with us.

I think the experience of a customer engaging with Campaign Monitor to do their email marketing has to be the best builder of loyalty. From the very first moment they come in contact with our brand, all the way through to when somebody has a problem and how they engage with our support department, that experience is building loyalty. Or, when the technology has an issue, glitch, or bug, how our engineering team resolves that and communicates with the customer builds loyalty.

I think the role of the CMO spans that entire spectrum at a company like ours, and the sum total of those experiences is how we keep customers loyal, keep them renewing their subscription, and keep them buying more products and services from our company.

Steimle: While there's no such thing as a typical day, can you describe a recent workday from start to finish? What does your job look like on a daily basis?

Swensrud: My current role as CMO of Campaign Monitor is very different from my previous job as CMO at Salesforce. A typical day at Campaign Monitor is unique because our two largest offices are on opposite sides of the world—Sydney and San Francisco. Since we sell to businesses globally, we also have 24/7 technical support employees all around the world. Dealing with that time zone difference every single day can be a challenge.

Australia is 19 hours ahead of San Francisco. That means I have to plan my day according to when all of the people I need to interact with are online. Typically, that means checking email in the mornings before I even get into the office. The majority of our management team is in San Francisco, so when I get into the office, we'll talk about strategic initiatives that are important to the business.

A lot of the individuals I talk to after that are customer-facing folks. Most of our operations, sales, customer success, and marketing are also in San Francisco, including our CEO. We typically spend the morning focused on sales, marketing, customer operations, success, the numbers, and management team meetings and alignment. The product and engineering are in Australia, so at about 3 p.m., the product side of our business comes online. I spend typically from 3 p.m. to 8 or 9 p.m. engaging in aspects of our product.

Steimle: What gets you excited about the work you're doing? When you go into work in the morning, what makes you say, "Man, I'm excited to start the day. I'm excited to get to my job"?

Swensrud: I get excited by the size and scale of our customer base. When I say we've got two million people at 150,000 businesses around the world who are our paying customers, that's our company, our products, our team every single day making two million people more successful at their jobs. That's our company helping 150,000 businesses around the world grow. It's incredibly exciting helping these folks succeed with email marketing technology that is simple, powerful, and drop dead simple to understand and use. I think that's awesome.

I'm also excited about all of the changes in marketing that have happened over the course of the last fifteen years: the clear and obvious trend toward digital marketing, and all of the technology advancements happening in the world of marketing, and being a CMO.

There are a few people and vendors that produce charts about the marketing technology landscape. If you Google image search "marketing technology landscape," you'll see what I'm talking about. You will find an image on the Google search results that looks like an eye chart. The chart is meant to convey the companies you need to be familiar with if you're going to be a great technology-driven CMO in 2016.

There are close to two thousand marketing tech companies on that chart, which is representative of what's changing in marketing. I've been in the technology business for twenty years, CMO of two large scale tech companies, and I look at that chart and it makes me want to gasp. Think of all the CMOs of non-technology companies looking at that and saying, "What do I do?"

The state of how the Internet and tech is changing the marketing landscape is unparalleled. The pace of innovation in marketing technology is at an all-time high. Gone are the days of the mad men. Enter the new tech-savvy CMO. The awesome thing about digital marketing that appeared in the first decade of the 2000s was everything became trackable. I had a website. I could track what was happening on my website. I had an e-commerce store. I could track everything that happened on my e-commerce store. I could place ads on the Internet. I could track exactly what was happening with those ads, who clicked through those ads, and who purchased. That was never possible before.

I'm really excited about the technology landscape in marketing. I'm excited about how technology is producing innovation at a pace we've never seen before in marketing. Because it's my craft, I get excited about all of this innovation and the impact we're having on the economy and businesses around the world.

Steimle: As an email marketing company, I'm sure you use email marketing to grow your business, but what other marketing tools have you found successful for growing Campaign Monitor?

Swensrud: Of course, email marketing as part of our marketing strategy goes without saying. We use it every day to engage every one of our stakeholders—including employees, customers, partners, industry influencers and our investors—every day, and every employee has an account that they use as well. As I mentioned, there are millions of people that pay us to use our service, and every day we're working to make them successful and grow and attract new customers. On the demand-generation side, we tend to lean toward trackable media. It's where we spend our marketing dollars and includes email marketing, search marketing, display advertising, video advertising, and retargeting. We tend to use those digital channels to get the word out about Campaign Monitor.

We rely on companies like AdRoll for retargeting; Google AdWords for search engine marketing; Google's Display Network for display marketing; and YouTube, Vimeo, and other channels for video. That is all trackable, so I'm able to tell through any channel—whether it's a pay-per-click Google ad, a display ad, or a retargeted ad to bring somebody back to my website—how many customers I was able to impact and acquire for my business for every dollar I spent. That level of marketing is what my company calls "demand generation." That brings people to our website.

On our website, we have an objective, which is to explain to people what we do, tell them why it's valuable, articulate why it's different and unique, and get them to take the next action, which is to sign up for a free trial of our product. If you go anywhere on our website, you'll see big green buttons that say, "Get started for free." That's what we want you to do. We need to give you some information for you to feel comfortable doing that. We need to explain what we do. We need to explain why it's incredible. We need to show you why it's different. We need to entice you to take that next action.

Our website is the face of our company and our most important marketing vehicle—and I think that's true for almost any company. Whether you're a technology company or not, your website is the thing that articulates to people who you are. It shows people your identity, your brand, and what you're all about. It is the salesperson that is selling 24/7. I think of our website as our most important marketing asset. That means I need to know every single thing that's happening on our website. I need to be able to change it rapidly.

We use Google Analytics as a way to see every click and every path that someone takes. We use a technology called Crazy Egg, which shows us a heat map of everywhere people click on the website—what they're clicking on, what percentage of people are clicking on it, where they came from, if they're scrolling down the page or not.

We use an exciting technology called Optimizely, which is a company here in San Francisco that offers do-it-yourself website A/B testing. I can set up a page on my website, like my home page, for example, and it will look a certain way to you and different to someone else. Optimizely will then tell me how many of the people who saw version A and version B achieved our goal, which is to get people to sign up for our product and become a customer. They do the statistical analysis to tell me which variation is a winner. That technology came out of Google. Some engineers at Google developed it, and it is phenomenal for companies who care about tracking and achieving good things with their websites.

We also have some very important customers who want to do a lot of business with Campaign Monitor. They send not just ten thousand, or a hundred thousand emails with us, but millions and tens of millions, because they're very large companies with far-reaching customer bases. For those customers, we actually have a dedicated sales organization that uses Salesforce, so we plug our website right into Salesforce. That's kind of a wide array of technologies we use and why those are important to us.

Steimle: Tell me about your marketing department. What's the structure of the marketing department? What does it look like?

Swensrud: The structure of my current marketing department is based on the type of company we are, and also the type of CEO we have. For example, Campaign Monitor is a self-service application, so we are a very product-driven company. You can go to our website and sign up for free. You can poke around the application and determine whether it's valuable to you. That product experience and the way we showcase what the product does, and how it does it are really important to our company.

When I came onboard at Campaign Monitor, I was the first marketer at the company. The company had been around for a decade with an amazing self-service product. Beginning about a year ago, we decided to build out a whole go-to-market function. We were going to build out a whole marketing department, a whole sales department, and a whole customer success department. As the first marketer, I had the opportunity to start with a clean slate and draw an org chart from scratch, which articulated the future state of what I thought would be most impactful for a company of our size. I started with product marketing because we're a product company. I thought, "As a product-based company that's all about the product experience, we need to be the best at showcasing, articulating, and positioning that product in our market." My first thought was building out a product marketing function inside of the new marketing department.

The second thing I thought about was creative. That's typically not the first thing a CMO thinks about in a B2B business, but it's critical to a self-service technology company. Campaign Monitor has always been a design-driven company and one of the things we do in email marketing is help non-tech-savvy people at companies all around the world represent their brands through email campaigns in a gorgeous, phenomenal way. We've always been a design-led company and it was important to stay true to that. It's one of the reasons we're different. If you look at our website and click on "Customers" or "Gallery," which is the gallery of our top email campaigns of the year, you'll see examples of customer success from the world's leading brands. Those are marketers at companies large and small who want to showcase their brands in an amazing, modern way. Our own marketing had to pay that promise off. It was important to hire a creative team—designers and writers—so they could articulate that through our marketing vehicles, our advertising, our website.

Then, beyond product marketing and creative and design was demand generation, which I mentioned in relation to our marketing and advertising strategy. Where do you invest? Everything we've done to date has been on trackable media. We've been able to tell that for every dollar we've put into our marketing programs, exactly what value is delivered to the business. We're able to profitably acquire customers and we can quantify that. So, demand generation and content marketing as a core part of that strategy was the third thing to think about.

Customer marketing was fourth. A lot of companies don't do customer marketing. They don't dive deep enough into who their target customer is to fully understand that. They don't showcase their customers, but luckily, I stepped into the role at a time when we had 120,000 companies using our product. Now, we have 150,000. I was like, "Whoa, some of the most amazing brands in the world are using our products, and they love them. Let's showcase that success across everything that we do."

One of the most amazing assets you can have as a CMO is to have customers who love you and who want to tell your story, especially for B2B companies that sell to other businesses. Our potential customers do want to hear from us, but more than that, they want to hear from other companies and people like them. For example, if you go to our website you'll see customer stories everywhere. We also showcase customers, such as Rip Curl, Jaybird, South by Southwest, and others in customer films. You can watch those films right on our website. We want to tell their stories, how they use email marketing, and why they chose us. That's really impactful.

Since the core of our business is being able to quantify everything, marketing operations, infrastructure, and data analysis were the next major areas to hire in. Last came PR and awareness. I think a lot of technology companies, such as the company where I was formerly CMO, invest really heavily in PR because they've got a CEO who is invested in being very media savvy. We're a different type of company being a product company, so that was last on my agenda, but it was still clearly important.

Steimle: What are some of the core metrics you focus on to help you make sure your goals are aligned with the overall organization? What are you held responsible for?

Swensrud: I'm held responsible for the entire sales and marketing funnel. At the highest level, we have awareness metrics, which are best measured by the number of people who come to our website. They're measured at an even higher level with brand-awareness studies and advertising impressions and things we can definitely track and know. If I'm impacting those high-level awareness metrics, people will find my website. They will find my blog. They will find my content. They will find me somehow. At the highest level, I measure all of those things, which are brand awareness, advertising impressions, where we rank on Google, and how much traffic we get from different channels. Ultimately, I can measure that in terms of the number of human beings who are visiting my website, which converts into people signing up for our product or wanting to ask our sales team for help.

At the end of the day, we measure, and heavily scrutinize every aspect of the customer acquisition funnel. We look at the acquisition funnel every day, but we review it in detail at the end of every month, as well as the number of advertising and marketing dollars we invested relative to the customers we acquired and what those customers are paying us.

We also look at what those customers will pay us over time because, as a subscription business, the job of marketing doesn't stop when we first acquire a customer. The job of marketing never stops, because if a customer is unhappy, they can vote by clicking a button that says, "I want to discontinue your service," and they can do that at any time. As I mentioned before, they're not locked into a multi-year subscription, so we need to keep them happy. We need to keep educating them on how to get value from our service, so we also measure customer and revenue retention. All of those things are my job.

I roll these metrics out to everyone in the marketing organization using a management framework called the V2MOM, or VVMOM. The first V stands for vision, which defines where we want to go as a company. The second V stands for values, which is what's important to us as we charge forward. The first M stands for methods, which are the exact tactics that we plan to execute this year, this quarter, this month. The O stands for obstacles, where we think through what might keep us from achieving our goals. Finally, the last M stands for measures, which is how we know if we've achieved success or not.

That's the framework we've used to manage the company from the CEO all the way down to every individual contributor. Those are the metrics we use to measure the success of the marketing department—from brand awareness to advertising impressions, to website traffic, to signups, to sales leads qualified by our sales team, to customers, to the amount of money we generate from those customers, to customer retention over time. Those are our objectives and our measures, and that's how we determine if we're successful at the company and in the marketing organization.

Steimle: What do you think are some of the biggest challenges facing today's CMOs?

Swensrud: That Google search I referenced earlier for "marketing technology landscape" comes to mind. It shows the biggest challenge for today's CMO in that the world of marketing technology is exploding. The megatrend is that marketing budgets are shifting to digital marketing from traditional marketing. As a percentage of spend, we're seeing less investment in TV commercials, less in radio ads, less in television, and more online. As soon as you go online, you've got this explosion of innovation in the marketing technology landscape. How does any CMO make sense of it all?

The fact that marketing is becoming more explosive, targeted, and trackable is why marketing budgets are increasing and not decreasing. In 2013, I read a study from Gartner that said by 2018, CMOs are going to have bigger budgets than CIOs. I think that's what we're seeing happening, and that's because marketing is becoming more trackable than ever before. That means marketers are becoming more accountable than ever before.

I think the reason a lot of CEOs have traditionally had challenging relationships with CMOs is because there was a lot of hand waving and opinions about a specific ad campaign, piece of creative, or marketing brochure or material. Now that everything is trackable, the CMO is held accountable more than ever before to demonstrate and produce results for the business. The more tech-savvy CMOs, the more digitally focused CMOs, the more data-driven CMOs, are able to show that. Those are the modern-day CMOs that have great relationships with their CEOs and whose budgets are increasing.

But, it's not that simple and it's really hard to do. I'm sitting here at a tech company in the heart of Silicon Valley, and looking at that marketing technology landscape chart even makes *me* scared. How are the marketing leaders at millions of companies around the world supposed to understand what's going on? The biggest challenge facing today's CMOs is that marketing is going to continue to shift over the next decade and become more technology-focused than ever before. It's incumbent upon today's marketing leaders—whether they're CMOs, VPs of marketing, studying in school, or entry-level marketing managers—to learn. They need to learn technology. I think technology-savvy CMOs are the CMOs of the future.

Steimle: What are some of the biggest mistakes you see CMOs today making?

Swensrud: They're making decisions in the old way that marketing decisions were made—by a gut feeling, like in the TV show *Mad Men,* which is about an executive who gets in a room with an advertising agency and pitches them on some ideas, and they say, "I like that one." The CEO of Optimizely, Dan Siroker, wrote a book[1] where he talks about an age of marketing where decisions were made by the "HIPPO". "HIPPO" stands for "highest-paid person's opinion." In the past, the HIPPO was the one who got to make the marketing decisions. The assumption was that if you're the highest-paid person, it's your opinion about this campaign, creative, or program that is going to deliver results for the company.

For decades, it was untrackable. If you ran a global mass media campaign or a Super Bowl commercial and sales went up, you didn't know exactly how to attribute that spend to customer acquisition metrics. In today's world, everything is trackable. The CMOs who are not data-driven and who don't think about being able to measure every aspect of a campaign or every investment dollar, are the ones who are going to have challenges in the future. The biggest mistake a lot of CMOs and VPs of marketing all around the world are making is still thinking of marketing in a more traditional sense when the world around us is changing so fast.

---

[1]*A / B Testing: The Most Powerful Way to Turn Clicks Into Customers* (Wiley, 2015).

Patrick Adams

Head of Consumer Marketing
PayPal

Patrick Adams is currently the head of consumer marketing at PayPal. He is an accomplished strategic marketing professional known for creating and implementing high-impact, consumer-driven, omnichannel (brand, digital, direct mail, PR, in-store, e-comm/mobile, CRM) marketing initiatives. Under his leadership, these initiatives have driven both the top and bottom line for some of the world's most prestigious brands: Chase, Citibank, Bertelsmann Media Worldwide, and Victoria's Secret.

Adams has written for various publications, including Forbes *and* Business Insider. *He is also a member of several advisory boards, such as DMA's Social Media Council, The CMO Council, and AOL's Retail Advisory Board.*

In 2011, Adams was recognized as one of the Top CMOs to Follow on Twitter. In 2015, Adams was also named one of the 100 most innovative CMOs in the world.

Josh Steimle: Give us an overview of your career. How did you get your start and what are the steps that led to where you are today?

Patrick Adams: My career has been driven by looking for interesting opportunities and less of a planned sequence of events. I went to school for communications and journalism with a goal towards becoming a filmmaker. While I was in school, I was recruited to go into a management training program at one of the major banks in New York City. I thought it would be an interesting

© Josh Steimle 2016
J. Steimle, *Chief Marketing Officers at Work*, DOI 10.1007/978-1-4842-1931-7_7

experience for me, especially since I tended to operate on the more creative side of my mind. I thought it would be a good discipline to have because part of the program required credit training. Also, you were required to do rotations in the various sectors of a bank—marketing, customer service, back office processing, credit and lending, cash management, private bank, retail bank, middle market, small business, etc. It felt like it would be a great investment in my career and might help me better understand what I wanted to do and what else I might be good at. Until then, I had not thought much about marketing because I was so immersed in filmmaking.

When I got into the two-year MBA management training program, I quickly became enamored with anything that was marketing related. Marketing came naturally to me, and I felt invigorated by it. From that point on, I just let my gut drive my every move. If there was an opportunity that could get me closer to interacting with consumers or driving consumer engagement, I took it. I didn't pay a lot of attention to the level of the role or how much I was compensated. It was more about the experience and scope of responsibility. To this day, I've driven my career that way.

I graduated from the program at a time when the major banks were consolidating. This was during the massive mergers and acquisitions of the late eighties and nineties. Actually, my first day on the job, my employer announced a significant merger (Manufacturers Hanover Trust and Goldome). I was put on the integration team to do much of the grunt work. That's where it all began. I lived through the Manufacturers Hanover to Chemical Bank and Chemical Bank to Chase, Citi to Travelers mergers. And as each bank was being acquired, I just looked for opportunity. I always did well with the acquiring bank and subsequently the acquiring bank chose me for a larger role in the new organization. It really wasn't my goal or objective. I was just going where my instinct and curiosity told me to go or where I thought I would be challenged.

I had been in banking for about eight years when a recruiter contacted me and said, "You're a financial services marketer. Do you know any packaged goods marketers?" For whatever reason, that stuck in my craw. I didn't think of myself as a financial services marketer. I thought of myself as a *marketer*. At that moment, I knew I had to prove that I was much more than just a financial services marketer or I would be pigeonholed in financial services my entire career. That was not my intention. I had a passion for marketing and envisioned being able to market in many different industries. I began an eight-month effort to see if someone outside of financial services would hire me. I was shocked by the mindset of many industry experts who often said you are a great financial services marketing talent but we need a non-financial services marketer. I thought: "Shouldn't a great marketer be able to be effective in any industry, any field?"

I was lucky enough to be hired into BMG (Bertelsmann Music Group)—the direct to consumer American arm of German multimedia conglomerate Bertelsmann Media Worldwide. I was hired to do exactly what I was doing in banking, which was customer segmentation and customer management. Also at that time, there was this new thing called the Internet, and BMG was interested in having someone explore how they could leverage the Internet (and email) as it related to the negative-option music club, which at the time was catalog only.

Within six months of getting into BMG, I launched a customer segmentation focus and discipline—something I was very familiar with. Then I was given the gift to figure out how to launch both a website and supporting email program. This was circa 1999 and game changing for BMG Music Service and career defining for me. No one else was really doing anything like that. Unbeknownst to me, it was setting a foundation for my professional future.

I spent ten years at Bertelsmann and when I left the business I was SVP, head of consumer marketing, responsible for multichannel marketing (catalog, email, Internet, phone), merchandising and customer service for BMG Music Service, Columbia House DVD, YourMusic.com, Book of the Month Club, Doubleday Book Club, and approximately twenty other book clubs. It was a substantial job. I loved every aspect of it because it was multichannel, dealing with so many different types of consumers and interests. Personally it was gratifying because I was able to market movies, music, and books—all of which I had a passion for.

In many ways, BMG is where I grew up, from a direct-to-consumer and digital marketing perspective. In 2008, Bertelsmann announced that it was interested in selling their direct business. I spent my last six months with Bertelsmann selling the business, meeting with many VCs and large media companies across the country. This was a very new experience for me, a great learning opportunity. I helped Bertelsmann sell the business to a private equity firm in July 2008.

While we were on the circuit selling BMG, Victoria's Secret contacted me. They asked if I was interested in doing for Victoria's Secret what I had done for BMG, which was to take an old-school cataloguer and figure out how to drive the business digitally. I thought, "Well, that's something I know how to do. It's in yet another industry I've never been in before: retail. So, why not?" In 2008, I joined Victoria's Secret as SVP, head of direct marketing (digital, mobile, e-comm, catalog). When I joined the company, much of the direct business was catalog-based. By the time I left Victoria's Secret, about ninety percent of the direct business was driven via mobile and the dot-com. During my time there, I got a great flavor for retail, merchandising, planning, and how to optimize in-store consumer marketing opportunities. We launched social, mobile commerce, and redesigned and reengineered the dot-com. During my tenure, Victoria's Secret consistently ranked high on *Internet Retailer*'s annual list.

My last year there, we were listed as the number-eight mobile commerce site, up eighteen positions from the prior year.

After five years at Victoria's Secret, I was ready for something new. I often wondered what it would be like to work with a startup. I had spent my career with fairly significant brands: Citibank, Chase, Bertelsmann, and Victoria's Secret. I began to seriously consider the startup world. How would it feel to be part of a scrappy, lean and mean, no-red-tape business? I started connecting with a couple of small startups. In particular, I became passionate about two e-comm startups—Adore Me and swimsuitsforall— and spent about two years working closely with them to elevate their brand, digital business, and direct to consumer muscle. It was awesome. I loved the small team passion, smart people, energy, and the ability to think of something in the morning and execute it in the afternoon. So refreshing! It was at about that time that the PayPal opportunity came my way.

PayPal contacted me with what seemed like a dream job crafted specifically for me. They were looking for someone who could help them shift their business from primarily a merchant facing business to a consumer facing business as well. They needed someone who could build out a consumer marketing muscle in North America and transform the way in which they connected with, acquired, engaged and serviced their consumer base.

I met several times with the head of the Americas. I liked him immediately and thought I could learn a lot about the payments business from him. Also, he had a great appreciation for marketing and I loved his interpersonal style. He also convinced me that in a lot of ways, PayPal is the best of both worlds. It is a scrappy organization with very little red tape and politics like a startup but also extremely financially sound and stable. I thought, "That's kind of cool. I could have my cake and eat it too!"

I also loved where PayPal was going. They were intent on reinventing themselves. They wanted to transform and enhance their consumer based offering from simply being a secure, safe way to transact online to serving the underserved and changing the way people manage their money. That was something I could get behind and something I'd be good at. I said yes, and I joined PayPal in 2014 as head of consumer marketing for North America.

Steimle: What does a typical day, if there is such a thing, look like for you?

Adams: PayPal is a highly matrixed organization and involves a tremendous amount of cross-functional teamwork, so my team works closely with the product teams, the brand team, the analytics teams, and the merchant teams. A typical day is filled with cross-functional work sessions and meetings. We're either strategically planning for a product introduction or a feature enhancement, or looking at analysis on how a plan or effort is working out. We also drive an ongoing dialogue with our customers. Ultimately, we're trying to create great consumer interaction that will drive greater productivity for the business and that will be an unforgettable and unbeatable end-to-end customer experience.

Steimle: How is globalization impacting your marketing as you're dealing with a global audience, different cultures, different countries, and different regulations?

Adams: Our marketing teams sit within the regions, so they are very familiar with the consumer—what they want and what they need. They are immersed in the culture. In general, marketing within financial services is a bit more complicated due to the many compliance requirements we must adhere to. In the end, we endeavor to serve up great product, with a stellar digital experience—from in-store, to the dot-com, mobile, or app. Something truly integrated.

Steimle: In a large company like PayPal that has so many customers around the world and so many different types of customers, how do you make sure you're in touch with them and understand their challenges and their needs? Do you have any specific tools or methods?

Adams: We do everything from your standard consumer research (quantitative to qualitative at the global, regional, and segment levels), and all the satisfaction studies that you would imagine we engage in. We have an outstanding customer services team that we're tapped into, so we understand exactly what the customer's going through, what their pain points are, and what their feedback is. It's a constant dialog and loop of information coming back to us so that we can leverage it and use it to make what we do better.

Steimle: You're on a few advisory boards, like the CMO Council and the Retail Advisory Board at AOL. What value have you received from being involved in industry or peer groups?

Adams: It depends on the council or group. It's super valuable when you can talk with your peers, compare notes, share best practices, and leverage varying points of view. That's what I like most about the councils I engage with. Sometimes it provides an opportunity to mentor and help those who are younger in their career or have less experience. I really enjoy that. Great way to give back.

Steimle: How has marketing changed since you began your career? What are some of the trends you've seen? Which trends are you excited about?

Adams: The biggest trend I've seen is that when I first started marketing, it seemed to be a sort of back-office function. Marketing didn't hold center stage and was more of a support group and less of a driver of the business. Today, some of the best CEOs and GMs are coming out of the direct-response marketing discipline because they drive P&Ls, they drive productivity, and they have a tremendous amount of financial weight on their shoulders.

Back in the day, the most recognized type of marketer was a brand (above the line) marketer who focused on brand advertising and brand awareness. There wasn't a tremendous amount of attribution associated with it. Over the years, direct-response marketing and focus on ROI came into its own. As e-commerce started to develop as a discipline and a driver of retail business, typically, a direct-response marketer would drive the e-commerce channel.

More recently, the melding of the marketing, technology, and product teams is a trend that I am noticing. The disciplines are morphing and melding, and the teams are becoming a lot more seamless. They plan together. They drive insights together. They create programs and initiatives together. It's a more immersive operation.

Steimle: What does the structure of your marketing department look like?

Adams: It's a functional organization. There's a team that focuses on consumer strategy around the seasonal, quarterly, and annual consumer marketing planning. There's a focus on consumer segments, one of which is new customer journey. Another, for example, would be around the youth market or highly engaged customers.

The next team is a pure digital team that focuses on a best-in-class digital acquisition discipline (display, affiliates, SEO, SEM), and digital experience optimization. There is a priority to optimize all of our digital properties, whether it be the dot-com, the mobile site, or the app. True end-to-end optimization.

The last team is a traditional marketing services team that is responsible for marketing ops, project management, database management, creative, and QA that services all of North America.

Steimle: What's your philosophy on building a marketing team? What do you look for in hires?

Adams: First and foremost, I look for someone who is passionate about marketing and consumer interaction, has a tremendous amount of curiosity, is bright, and understands how to work within a team. He or she must have the potential to make the team better.

I run into a ton of really smart people who are not effective in a team environment. They are individual contributors. That person typically will not do well on my marketing team.

As for other qualifications, the standard qualifications need to be met. Great discipline around strategy, digital, execution, insights and research, analytics, profitability, and incrementality. On a personal level, I look for someone who really wants to win, who likes being challenged, and who has an innate drive to do more. Sometimes, you can detect those things when you're meeting people or having several rounds of meetings, and sometimes, you can't. You try to take a balanced view and look for all the bits and pieces that you think will fall into place.

Steimle: You mentioned that a lot of your day-to-day job is managing relationships between teams. What are some of the challenges of managing multiple teams and getting them to work together? How have you overcome those challenges? Do you have any tips for getting different teams on the same page?

Adams: The majority of my job is helping to set up and drive marketing strategy that will ultimately help us achieve our overarching business needs. In the process of doing that, I'm required to lead and manage many cross-functional teams. Managing them starts with having a common goal and objective.

Most of the time, people or teams fail because goals are misaligned. Focusing on a common goal and objective with a lot of clarity and simplicity ensures greater success. It always loops back to "Does this get us here? Does this make sense for the customer? Does this make sense for the business?" It's a constant evaluation of "Is that where we need to be? Is this getting us to *x*?" You have to be very thoughtful and mindful of where you want to go.

Steimle: Is it a matter of remembering to step back and look at the big picture?

Adams: Definitely, but it's easier if you start everything with a complete level set. We're all trying to accomplish the same exact thing.

Steimle: What are some of the metrics you focus on to bring everybody together and align goals?

Adams: Customer experience is very important to us, so we usually align out the gate on a seamless and delightful consumer experience—the typical KPIs I'm sure you've heard time and again around usage, interaction, and satisfaction scores. We look at several profitability measures as well. But I think what makes PayPal super interesting is how maniacally focused we are on consumer satisfaction, surprise, delight, and engagement with our products and services.

Steimle: How do you attract and retain top marketing talent at PayPal?

Adams: Attracting talent is fairly easy for me because I've been at this for thirty-plus years. I've met and worked with a tremendous number of talented people over the course of my career and have been very lucky that my network is extensive, robust, and connected. Word of mouth has been fantastic. That helps build my personal network, so I have great access as it relates to attracting people who have awesome skills.

In terms of growing folks, there's really only one way to do it, which is to become completely invested in every single individual on your team, know what their goals and objectives are, and where they want to go to next, and figure out how you can help them on their path to that. Your leaders must be committed to doing the same.

I just spoke to a woman who's coming onto my team next week, and she told me she talked to someone who worked with me years ago. The reason she was so excited about coming onto my team is because the woman who she spoke to said I was so committed to development and growing my team. That was meaningful to her because she hasn't had a leader who was committed to that. That word of mouth builds trust, credibility, and reputation.

Steimle: Based on some things you've said, I assume you've read Joseph Michelli's book *The Starbucks Experience*[1] where the phrase "surprise and delight" is used extensively. What are some of your favorite sources to go to, be it books or other sources, to learn more about the marketing craft?

Adams: I read a ton every day. What inspires me most about becoming better at my job is my relationship with the customer. Nothing inspires me more than having a conversation with a customer and watching how they are engaging with our product. Listening to what's working and what's not is the ultimate way to jumpstart ideas, ideation, excitement around getting better, and figuring out what's next. I love to read success stories on impactful initiatives that others are doing. I think the earth-shattering, innovative stuff happens when you have an intimate understanding and knowledge of your customer and focus deeply on what they want and need.

Steimle: You have a lot of data at PayPal. Can you talk a bit about how you use data in your position, how you analyze it, and how you don't get lost in what you have access to?

Adams: We do have access to a decent amount of data. All of it is highly guarded. We try to use what we know to improve the product experience and drive a much more relevant conversation. It's our mission to surprise and delight as much as possible. That said, we do not just collect data for the sake of collecting data. I think many organizations spend so much time collecting data with no real strategic use or intent. That is a waste of time and an ineffective use of resources.

Steimle: Security is huge for PayPal. How does security factor into your marketing?

Adams: Security is a cost of entry. It's expected to play in the space. PayPal has built its business on security and convenience. I believe the brand resonates that feature and sentiment quickly and easily, so we benefit from that. In financial services, you have to exude that. You have to stand for it, or you can't establish a basic relationship with a customer. It's an expectation we don't take lightly. We work very hard at it, but it's an absolute expectation. Although you do want to remind customers how safe and secure you are, it's not enough, because you have to be so much more.

---

[1] McGraw-Hill Education, 2006.

We plan on being so much more. In 2016, we are branching out and serving the underserved, helping consumers manage their money in ways they never thought possible.

Steimle: Another facet of marketing that's becoming an expectation these days is having mobile-friendly applications, websites, and such. Can you talk about how the shift to mobile has impacted your business and the way you approach marketing?

Adams: Mobile is extremely important. A significant number of our consumers engage via the app and their mobile device. We are a mobile first organization and design first for that experience. We are committed to creating optimal and impactful mobile experiences because our customer requires it.

Steimle: Are there any particular initiatives you've had success with in terms of driving more mobile adoption or taking advantage of the shift to mobile?

Adams: A few years ago, several retailers made the major misstep of mirroring their dot-com usability and experience on their mobile site or app. It was a disaster. The device, the size of the screen, how people use it, what the keypad looks like, and a natural flow or sequence of events, all of those things are meaningful and have to be taken into account when you're creating an app or mobile-led experience. Since then, most have gotten much better. A majority of organizations today tout a "mobile first" methodology and leverage responsive design.

Steimle: It seems like common sense, but somehow, it's easy for people to skip over the basics.

Adams: Probably not by design. Usually, unclear objectives, time constraints, or talent challenges drive less than stellar productivity. You don't get many chances to win or retain someone's business. You almost have to act as if you get one shot. You'd better do it right.

Steimle: What are some of the channels you're using to connect with your customers as far as social media? What are some of the most successful ways you've found to reach out and engage?

Adams: A multichannel approach seems to be the best for customers. We have a pretty robust email marketing program. Additionally, we leverage messaging and experiential opportunities via the dot-com, mobile site, and our app. We're always looking for new opportunities that will be relevant and resonate with the customer. Consumers are interacting less and less with email, so as email winds down, we look for other touch points. We are also active in all social channels. The best programs I've led and have been engaged with leverage brand, PR, social, and performance/digital. Connect with customers where they are.

Steimle: What advice would you give to somebody who's new to the CMO or top marketing role in their organization?

Adams: I would say find a mentor, someone who's been in the business, who is seasoned, possibly been in the role you aspire to get to. Or someone who you respect for their experience, skill set, and how they get things done.

You also must be very self-aware of your strengths and weaknesses. Surround yourself with the best talent you can find, people who can fill in the gaps where you might be light or less deep. Don't be afraid to ask for help. Contrary to what most people think, asking for help is a sign of strength, *not* weakness.

Steimle: What do you see as the biggest challenge facing today's CMOs?

Adams: There are a tremendous number of CMOs in roles today who came from a brand/classic marketing background. They tend to struggle with driving a P&L because ATL (above the line marketing) typically didn't require them to prove out a return on investment. The very best marketers and those who I believe will make the most effective CMOs are marketers who cut their teeth in direct response (performance) marketing but transitioned to a more digital/tech focus early on in their careers. The role of CMO today is very challenging. You need to have a great understanding of technology, data, analytics, usability, profitability, product, and digital. And you need to understand brand management, development, and evolution.

Steimle: What are some of the mistakes you believe CMOs are making today?

Adams: It cracks me up how loosely we use the term "CRM" (customer relationship management). Everything is "CRM this" or "CRM that," but very few get exactly what CRM is. "CMO" is also a term loosely used to mean everything and anything. I'm not even sure whether the term "CMO" is an effective title for how leading marketers need to drive a business today.

I think the biggest mistake people make around a top marketing job is thinking they know all the answers, not making a point of creating an intimate relationship with their consumer, not developing their in-house talent, and maintaining too much distance between their product, technology, and financial peers.

There are creative marketers, strategic marketers, financial marketers, and operational marketers. The best marketer is somebody who's balanced, who can sit and play on the creative side, the strategic side, someone who understands ROI, someone who can jump in on analysis, set up testing, interpret test results, and leverage data. You need to have a great understanding of all of those things in order to drive a productive business. It's rare today to find someone who can do all that.

Steimle: How has marketing changed over the course of your career?

Adams: I think the basic tenets of marketing have not changed—consumer marketing, that is. The vehicle might have changed, and with digital, different ways to do the same things have certainly surfaced, but the basics haven't changed.

Over the years, marketing has come to the forefront and is much more of a lead position or a lead function than it ever was. A lot of e-commerce marketers function more like GMs than traditional marketers. We not only need to have the creative, strategic side but also have to be super astute when it comes to ROI and financials. You need to be able to deep dive into technology as it relates to e-comm and digital. You also have to be a strong and committed leader. You have to be someone who can attract great talent, maintain it, and grow it. You must be multifaceted.

Steimle: What do you see in the future of marketing, and how will it be different from today?

Adams: I see the current trend continuing. It's going to be less of what you want to tell the consumer and more of what they want to hear from you, what you have permission to tell them and sell them. It's going to be less about you wanting to send an email to them and more about "I know this person is in this location at this time, so I'm going to communicate with them on a topic they find relevant via their preferred channel to engage." How they like to receive content, and what type of content they want. That will continue to evolve. We are highly reliant upon great cutting-edge technology and a deep understanding of what the consumer wants and needs to deliver a stellar experience.

Steimle: It's interesting how two hundred years ago, marketing was one-to-one out of necessity. You couldn't do it any other way. Then, we went to mass marketing, and now, we're going back to one-to-one with the aid of technology and data. Do you have any comments or other insights on this trend?

Adams: One-to-one marketing back in the day was cumbersome and restrictive—so time-consuming and not very accurate—more mass customization. Today, thanks to technology, you get a more impactful result and at significant scale. I think that great marketers will continue to search for something that feels as close to the corner shopkeeper who knows you and knows your family, your likes, dislikes, how best to meet your needs. I think that the ultimate goal is replicating that relationship. Much of today's methodologies and technology will get us very close to that.

Steimle: Is there anything we haven't covered that you're itching to talk about in terms of the CMO role and marketing?

Adams: When someone is considering a head of marketing role—beyond the skill-set requirements we just discussed—there must be a passion for leadership. A large aspect of your role and responsibility has to be focused on leadership. How you show up to lead a marketing team and what the interaction model looks like when you're growing your team, developing, and retaining marketing talent is paramount to success. It's an important topic. I don't think a lot of thought is given to it and it is a place where many fail. You have to be focused on talent development, leadership style, and leadership shadow. Some people are naturally good at it and some are not. Your ability to master it effectively can make or break you.

Edith Wong

Chief Marketing Officer
InvestHK

Edith Wong is CMO at InvestHK, a department of the government of Hong Kong that manages 29 offices worldwide, each focused on attracting entrepreneurs, startups, and foreign investment to Hong Kong. Wong entered the CMO role in 2015 with the aim of using advertising, events, PR, social media, websites, publications, and other channels to promote Hong Kong as a leading international business center, as well as to offer the help and services of InvestHK both locally and globally. Before stepping up to become CMO, Wong was head of Advertising and Communications at InvestHK. Wong has both a bachelor of laws and an MBA in international business from the University of London. She has a BA and a MPhil in English from the Chinese University of Hong Kong.

Josh Steimle: Give us an overview of your career. How did you get your start? What are the steps that led you to where you are today?

Edith Wong: I have been working for InvestHK for ten years. InvestHK is the government department established in the year 2000 to attract foreign direct investment to Hong Kong. InvestHK is the marketing and PR arm of Hong Kong as a place to do business, and that's why marketing plays a very important role within the department. I joined the department in 2005 and since then I have worked on various teams.

I started off on the China business team, and then I moved to overseas promotion, where I managed and attended overseas events organized by InvestHK, giving me a good opportunity to understand what really matters to our overseas audience and get a good grasp of the issues and concerns of the international business community. A couple of years ago, I moved on to head our advertising and communications team.

Looking back, these ten years have been very helpful in building up my career and moving towards the CMO role. When I first started with InvestHK, I didn't have this role in mind saying, "I want to be the CMO." But, taking into account the depth and breadth of experiences I gained with this organization, I am aware of the different facets of marketing within the department. And, I'm very happy that I am able to play a part in this role and contribute to this area.

Steimle: Is there anything in your personal background that's not directly tied to marketing, but that you feel is beneficial to your role as a marketing professional?

Wong: In terms of academic background, my bachelor's and master's degrees are in English. I have an interest in language, communication especially. My first language is Chinese. English is my second language. In a sense, I'm more aware of the nuances of words. I sometimes ask a native speaker, "What's the difference between these two words?" and he or she will say, "Oh, I haven't thought about that," because if it's your first language, you might not think too much about it. I'm sensitive to language, and I love language and communications.

I have an MBA in international management, which is logical. The odd thing, though, is my law degree. I find it useful because even in the marketing world, you need to review contracts. A law degree is useful to people who want to move to more senior executive positions because it trains you in logical thinking. Marketing today is more data-driven, technology-driven. It's not based on intuition anymore. Logical thinking and using precise language are the things I got from that law degree that have been quite helpful in my career.

Steimle: Who are your customers and what are your responsibilities within InvestHK?

Wong: InvestHK's mission is to attract foreign investors to set up or expand in Hong Kong. We have about one hundred staff members within our headquarters in Hong Kong, and we have a presence in twenty-nine cities around the world. We have five offices in the mainland. While it's a government department, the setup is very much focused on the private sector.

We have a matrix type of organization. In the headquarters, we are structured by the sector teams. We have eight priority sectors, like creative industries, innovation and technology, ICT (information and communications technology), and tourism and hospitality sectors. Of course the overseas teams are responsible for specific geographic areas. We also have some cross-sector function teams in the head office such as research and knowledge management, global events management, and so on.

My team, which is Division 4 within the department, oversees a bunch of areas, including advertising, branding, events sponsorship, publications, gifts and souvenirs, PR, videos, websites, IT, and social media. Our remit is pretty broad, and we make use of all these channels and strategies to reach our potential targets. By "potential targets," we mean companies or entrepreneurs that have an interest or plans to set up or expand their business in Hong Kong, to use Hong Kong to grow their business either regionally or globally.

Despite the uncertain global economic environment, Hong Kong manages to attract overseas companies, mainland companies, and entrepreneurs to set up businesses. InvestHK's role is to constantly put Hong Kong on the global scene and make sure people get the latest update of the business environment in Hong Kong and how we compare with other competitive cities in the region, like Singapore and Shanghai. That's our role and our mission.

Steimle: How does marketing for a government entity differ from marketing for a private company?

Wong: InvestHK is quite business-oriented because we have to get in touch with business people and other stakeholders in the business world. The comment from people who are familiar with InvestHK is we are not like other government departments. Based on our client feedback, InvestHK is perceived to be a friendly, non-bureaucratic, and responsive government department.

In terms of marketing, we try to stay as close to the latest marketing trends as possible. Take, for example, social media. Understand that it's not easy. There may be certain issues or concerns for government departments to take up social media. At the moment, we have a Facebook page at InvestHK for our StartmeupHK campaign. Social media is really 24/7 and therefore resource intensive. We do not currently have an external agency to help us manage social media. We manage that in-house.

While InvestHK is a government department, we are quite open to new ideas in marketing. At the same time, we also have a limited budget because what we are spending is taxpayers' money. Luxury consumer brands in the commercial sector can put quite a lot of resources in advertising or other marketing channels, whereas we face the issue of a limited budget. The challenge is in spending our resources wisely and cost effectively, and promoting Hong Kong both locally, so that people are aware of InvestHK's role and mission, and globally, where our potential clients are based.

Steimle: You mentioned you have twenty-nine offices around the world. Talk a bit about globalization and the importance of thinking globally for InvestHK.

Wong: Every year, we work out a business plan for the year ahead and define our priority markets and sectors. Some of the emerging sectors are fintech, maritime, and IoT, which we are paying a lot of attention to. In terms of priority markets, we have to look at the global trends and analyze in terms of our top sources of completed projects.

According to the latest survey on overseas and mainland parent companies running regional and local operations in Hong Kong, the top five sources are the U.S., Japan, mainland China, the UK, and Taiwan. These are the markets that have traditionally been reliable, strong, and promising sources of completed projects for InvestHK.

We also look at emerging markets, such as South America. We have recently set up a new office in Mexico. We also put in resources in the ASEAN[1] region because of the "One Belt, One Road" initiative. Recently, we signed an MOI (memorandum of intent) with the Board of Investments, Department of Trade and Industry of the Republic of the Philippines to exchange information on the investment environment and opportunities, and share experiences in attracting foreign investment and best practices regarding investment promotion. We've also signed an MOU (memorandum of understanding) with the Office of the Board of Investment of the Kingdom of Thailand to achieve similar objectives. There are two key things in terms of globalization: one is to identify our key source of completed projects—and we will continue to put resources into these territories—and another is to keep an eye on emerging opportunities and, if necessary, strengthen our resources in those areas.

Steimle: Because Hong Kong is such a small territory, it is forced to think globally in terms of economic development, whereas a large territory like the U.S., for example, can perhaps afford not to be so globally focused. Do you think the need to go outside and think more globally works to Hong Kong's advantage?

Wong: I do think it's an advantage, because if you look at the history of Hong Kong, it has been a free trade port all along, and we value free trade, the free flow of information, the free flow of capital. These are Hong Kong's fundamental and enduring advantages.

In terms of playing a bridging role between mainland China and the rest of the world, Hong Kong is getting even more important. The central government has announced the "One Belt, One Road" initiative, and Hong Kong's role as a super-connector between mainland China and global companies has become all the more important. Hong Kong is often perceived as the first step for mainland companies to go global. They go global via Hong Kong. They set up in Hong Kong and build their brands, and that makes it easier to expand globally. It also helps to build their brands' credibility.

For overseas companies wanting to have a share of the mainland market, Hong Kong is again the first port of call because of its regulatory and institutional frameworks, which meet even the toughest of international standards. The taxation and accounting standards are different from mainland China, so

---

[1]Association of Southeast Asian Nations

overseas companies find it easier to set up in Hong Kong before they venture into the mainland market. It really plays to Hong Kong's advantages, and InvestHK's role is figuring out how to promote these advantages.

Living in Hong Kong, we assume people will know Hong Kong, but many people in other places may not be fully aware of Hong Kong's role and how it has been changing. One useful source of information is the *World Investment Report 2015* released by the United Nations Conference of Trade and Development (UNCTAD). For the first time ever, Hong Kong is ahead of the U.S. and just behind the mainland in terms of global FDI (foreign direct investment) inflow. For the first time, Hong Kong ranks second in terms of both FDI inflow and outflow. This shows how Hong Kong is really a prime conduit of investment in the global scene.

Steimle: What does it mean to you to build customer loyalty with InvestHK's customers?

Wong: One of the things we keep targeting are the potential customers—companies that have not yet established in Hong Kong. But, it's also very important to keep close touch with our current clients, and we have different ways to do that. We organize networking receptions from time to time, like sector-specific or more general receptions. Every year, we have an annual reception hosted by the chief executive of Hong Kong to thank overseas investors for their vote of confidence in the city. Part of my job is speechwriting for events, for officials. That's part of why I need to have an overview of what's happening in Hong Kong and not just narrowly focus on InvestHK.

For building customer loyalty through networking events, we do email our clients on our CRM on a regular basis to keep them posted so that they are aware of what we are doing. We treasure our existing clients, companies that have set up in Hong Kong. Our sector colleagues continue to engage with them and if they need any further support, they can always approach us. That's the message we want to send out to the investors, to the companies that have cast their vote of confidence in Hong Kong.

It's very much one-on-one account management. For example, from the marketing perspective, if a company needs marketing and PR support, if they want a success story to be featured in the newsletter, my team is happy to help out. Or, if they want a press release to be issued, we will work closely with our sector teams to provide the best marketing and PR service we can to our clients.

Steimle: What kinds of metrics do you focus on?

Wong: We measure the number of enquiries because it reflects how effective our marketing effort is. In the last few years, we have re-deployed resources to digital marketing, where you can measure the results, the click-through rate, the number of impressions, and the number of enquiries generated from the website. Another KPI is the overall website traffic and which pages are most visited. On the PR side, there is the number of press releases we have issued and the resulting media coverage. In a nutshell, we have lots of measures to monitor our results and identify ways we can do better.

Steimle: What have been some of the most successful campaigns or marketing initiatives for finding customers or reaching out to them?

Wong: In 2003, we first started the StartmeupHK venture program, which is an integrated marketing campaign combining advertising, events, PR, website, social media, and so on. We saw how Hong Kong's startup ecosystem was booming. In fact, Hong Kong is traditionally perceived as an ideal city for multinationals, big companies, and SMEs. But there is a growing awareness of the worldwide startup trend. In 2013, we started this integrated startup campaign. We created a venture forum and organized a competition. The result was quite good. We had hundreds of entries in the first year.

In 2014, we organized that venture forum again, and the number of entries increased, arousing even more interest in the local and global communities. In January 2016, we organized the StartmeupHK festival, which is a weeklong festival featuring four key industry verticals, including data analytics, financial technology, health tech, and consumer IoT. It's been very fulfilling to see how marketing has played a key role in pushing this startup initiative in Hong Kong and overseas, and how we can contribute to promoting Hong Kong's startup ecosystem around the world.

Steimle: Are there ways you've engaged your customers to become part of your marketing strategy and act as evangelists for InvestHK?

Wong: We have what we call IPAs—investment promotion ambassadors— and of course, some of them are very well-known names in Hong Kong and in their home countries, and they all love to promote Hong Kong. Some clients may actually become our ambassadors. We have a nomination and vetting mechanism because they then become like ambassadors for Hong Kong. This points to the fact that relying on testimonials or third parties to say how good we are is always better marketing than saying how good we are ourselves. Some of our clients do become our ambassadors and share with the audience their firsthand experience with Hong Kong, how easy it is to set up in Hong Kong, and so forth. It's better that these messages come from their mouths rather than through propaganda from us.

Steimle: What does a typical day, if there is such a thing, look like for you? What do you do on a daily basis?

Wong: In theory, I'm on the job 24/7, especially considering I have to look after PR and social media, and all the more so because we are global. We have offices around the world. That means there is something going on around the world every minute that is related to InvestHK.

In terms of branding, the CMO role is a kind of brand guardian, even down to small things like whether our logo has been used properly. That is the kind of thing you have to pay attention to. We review our brand every few years to see if it's time to refresh it. I also look after event sponsorship. On a frequent basis, we receive event sponsorship proposals, so we have to exercise judgment as to whether something is an event worth sponsoring or supporting. Another key area is publications, which involve quite a lot of writing, proofreading, and editing, which also take up part of the day.

PR is one of the services that our clients really value. We provide PR support like issuing press releases and attending opening ceremonies, to help boost their PR and brand awareness in Hong Kong and globally. I review the press releases and give advice if necessary. We have a very robust social media calendar. We look ahead every month so we know on a daily basis what we are going to post and how to align our events with other marketing initiatives. We keep an eye on what's happening in Hong Kong day to day that may have an impact on the work of InvestHK, and this is a broad and fascinating area. There is positive and negative news about Hong Kong every day. We figure out how to distill this information and what kinds of posts to share on social media. That is a daily job.

I rely on the IT team to make sure the infrastructure and network are functioning properly and leave it in their good hands, but the website has to be reviewed and updated on a regular basis. The team is not very big. We have a dozen people in this division, but there's quite a lot of work going on, on a routine basis. And on top of that, there may be crises to handle from time to time, and crisis management cannot be predicted, so you need to stay alert and be resourceful.

Steimle: What gets you excited about coming into work?

Wong: That's actually my job as well—not only getting myself excited but getting my team, my colleagues, excited. I do want them to have that passion to come to work every day, and I want to bring out the best in them. Different people will have different strengths, and my role as the CMO is bringing out the strengths and encouraging them to learn more, to always keep up with the latest marketing trends and techniques.

One of the reasons I like going to work is actually the unpredictability. You can never know everything that the day will bring. You have an overview of what you need to resolve and get done during that day, but every day, there will be some unexpected issues you need to handle. Some may be positive, some may be negative in a sense, but this is indeed the challenge.

Another thing I really enjoy is that in my current role, I have the privilege to meet with many industry players and experts in this field. The conversations always give me insights and new things to think about.

Steimle: How do you manage relationships with other teams within InvestHK? How do you make sure your goals are aligned with their goals?

Wong: One key is constant communication. We have regular meetings, and as the CMO, I attend other division meetings to tell them what our division has been doing and to get the latest updates from their teams.

The key points are communication and aligning the objectives of our overseas teams and the local sector teams based in Hong Kong. It's quite an open environment where people can share their ideas frankly.

Steimle: What's your philosophy on building a marketing team?

Wong: When my colleagues come to work every day, I want to give them a sense of looking forward to accomplishing something. That's the spirit I want to develop and build to bring out the best in people, to encourage learning and to develop skill sets that can complement the whole team. As you know, different colleagues will have different strengths. Some may actually be quite resistant to certain tasks, and my role is really to encourage them to step out of their comfort zones.

Steimle: What does the structure of the marketing department look like? How many people work in marketing? What are some of the different roles? How do people report?

Wong: Within my team, I have twelve colleagues, including myself. There are essentially three teams under my purview, including IT, PR, and marketing communications. Everyone is fully engaged and occupied every day.

Steimle: Being in government, recruiting top marketing talent can be a challenge because a lot of people are looking to work for private industry. How do you attract and retain top marketing talent as a government entity?

Wong: Unlike a private organization or company, we don't have the flexibility in terms of the salary and fringe benefits. It's all pretty much fixed by the government. When we publish a job ad, the salary is open, and the benefits are all transparent. But, more than the salary and the package, some people are attracted to the job. They have a passion to promote Hong Kong, and they want to do what InvestHK is doing. I've been working here for ten years, but I still feel very passionate about what I'm doing. In terms of attracting top talent, it's never just the salary, especially when they move into the more senior positions. It's about whether they love the job they're going to do. That's the most fundamental thing.

Steimle: Which talents and skills do you look for in new hires?

Wong: The most important quality I look for is passion for Hong Kong. As regards specific talents, at the moment, I want people who can bridge digital and marketing. I am nurturing my existing team to bridge the divide between digital and marketing because that is where we are going forward.

Steimle: What trends in marketing are affecting your role as CMO in terms of technology, globalization, or transparency?

Wong: We cannot avoid data and technology in marketing these days. The key point is how we can make use of the data we have to make better marketing plans and decisions, especially in terms of media buying and so on.

Another thing, of course, is social media, which has revolutionized the way we do marketing. We don't have to spend a lot of money on advertising, but can rely on social media to spread the word. This is especially phenomenal in the startup scene. When we were building the startup website, one of the comments I heard is that no one looks at websites anymore. They just use social media, Facebook, and Twitter. One of the challenges is to listen to the ideas of the people in that community. You listen and decide whether to take that step forward, and you have to balance the interests of different people and stakeholders.

Steimle: How important are traditional marketing practices in the face of this trend towards digital?

Wong: Events and networking are important. Face-to-face contact is still important, and that's why we didn't stop doing events just because there is social media. Events and some traditional marketing, such as press releases or newsletters, are still important because if we look at our target companies, some of the decision makers still rely on traditional marketing tools. With startups, entrepreneurs, or millennials, we can use social media tools, which may be more appropriate to reach out to these groups of people.

InvestHK's target audience is diverse. They come from different backgrounds and industries. For example, the financial services industries are very regulated and may not rely on Facebook or Twitter to get in touch. Taking into account our very diverse audience and their backgrounds, we still have to rely on a multichannel approach in our marketing strategy. I wouldn't rule out the traditional media as such.

Steimle: How has marketing at InvestHK changed since you've taken on the CMO role?

Wong: One thing is this position was held by expatriates before. The CMO is the marketing leader in the organization, and I think being able to read and write Chinese is advantageous in promoting this leadership role within the organization. It improves the role of the CMO in terms of being an integrator and a leader in marketing within the organization. As a Chinese taking up this CMO role, another change is that I look after advertising and social media in the mainland. This is one of the key changes, because in the past, the CMO looked after English-speaking and other overseas markets, but not the mainland.

Steimle: What are some aspects of marketing to mainland China that people without experience in the region might not understand? Where do organizations outside Asia make mistakes when marketing to the mainland?

Wong: First of all, when it comes to marketing to the mainland, we have to use their language. While Hong Kong people also use Chinese, we have traditional Chinese characters. In the mainland, they have simplified Chinese, but it's not just the difference between traditional Chinese characters and simplified Chinese characters. The tone and the copywriting are totally different. If we want to speak to them and appeal to this audience, we have to use their language.

The second point is that the social media channels and behaviors in the mainland are also different. Mainland China itself is changing rapidly, so how we are going to target this market is an important question. We are using an offline/online approach. For instance, when it comes to events in the mainland, they still do very traditional trade fairs with a mass audience. Of course, we distribute our traditional publications. And actually, they are advanced in the sense that most people have all their QR codes to Weibo and WeChat on their business cards. How are we going to capture this and make use of this? This is something we need to think about more.

Digital marketing and e-commerce are also going strong in mainland China. How are we going to capture this, not only for InvestHK but for other consumer brands, commercial organizations, or companies? The challenge is that things are changing so rapidly.

Steimle: What are some of the skills that students today should be acquiring to prepare themselves to be C-level marketing experts?

Wong: It's important to have not only communication skills but a very broad education, including humanities and social sciences, because in my experience, you come across people from all walks of life and very different backgrounds. Having a broad education in the humanities and social sciences is important because a business degree is just an entry ticket, but then, you need to be very broad-minded and aware of world affairs—what's going on in society. It helps shape your perspective.

Michael Mendenhall

Chief Marketing Officer &
Chief Communications Officer
Flex

Michael Mendenhall is CMO and CCO at Flex, formerly known as Flextronics. Mendenhall first gained experience in the CMO role at HP, where he worked for three years. Before working at HP, Mendenhall held various positions at The Walt Disney Company, including executive vice president of global marketing. Mendenhall is a board member of the Advertising Council. He is a member of the Emerson College Board of Overseers and the Academy of Television Arts & Sciences. Mendenhall holds a bachelor of science from Emerson College in business communications and speech.

Josh Steimle: Give us an overview of your career. How did you get your start?

Michael Mendenhall: I graduated from college in business communications, which was where marketing and advertising existed when I was in school. It was a school that specialized in the business communications of media and entertainment. When I came out, I joined YBI, which was a unique firm in that it worked on product development and product branding. It was one of the foremost firms that looked at how to take a product from an idea into

© Josh Steimle 2016
J. Steimle, *Chief Marketing Officers at Work*, DOI 10.1007/978-1-4842-1931-7_9

manufacturing and make it a reality. We did a lot of work early on and were one of the first firms to work on consumer shopping behaviors. We researched how people shopped and what motivated them, everything from product design, packaging, placement in the store, store layouts, and retail layouts, to positioning. We worked with Black & Decker on the first cordless screwdriver, the first cordless product to come out. Then, it morphed into the industrial DEWALT pieces.

We worked on the product design and packaging. We were doing a lot of research in the psychology around the good, better, best, and the fact that lighter-colored products tend to be the least expensive, while a darker color indicates more value, the more expensive and richer product. We did a lot of work on strikeLINE. We learned that 5.3 feet up on a shelf was the placement that drove the most product. We did all kinds of work where we mocked up stores and watched people's behavior in terms of shopping and price points. Early on, we did a lot of consumer research and behavioral research in terms of motivations and behaviors around buying. We did that for a lot of major brands, and then we partnered with the ad agencies.

It was through that—right out of school—that I got great experience managing and developing these accounts. I was business development and the senior account representative for the firm. I got great exposure to a lot of the major advertising and marketing personnel in each of these companies. I was young at the time, just out of school, and I was learning a great deal because we were so advanced relative to where a lot of firms were. Most were just working with ad agencies. They weren't working with product specialty firms that did what we did.

Through that, I got exposed to Disney and decided that it was a terrific brand. It was a company that really didn't have marketing at that point. It was a company that had the idea, as Walt would say, "You build it and they will come." They started to feel the competitive pressures in the marketplace. They were no longer the only game in town, so they decided to invest in marketing and advertising. I was then hired to move to Orlando and become the senior representative within the advertising department, and begin to help them build out what would be their first advertising programs for Walt Disney World. I literally was there a week when I heard about Euro Disney, which was going to be under construction in Paris. After about six months of working in advertising at Walt Disney World, I was asked to go over to Paris on a business trip to help them set up advertising.

We also did cooperative advertising. We did advertising with our partners at the time, whether that was General Motors, Hewlett-Packard, Delta Airlines, or American Express. The idea was to go over and set up advertising, begin to build the entire process from creative all the way to market through the channels, and then build out cooperative advertising, which was new for Europe.

In fact, Europe never did it, and the publishers wouldn't allow it. It was introducing this whole new concept to Europe.

I went over, was there for about two weeks, and then came home. I was called in and they said, "We're going to move people over to Paris as expats, and we'd like you to go over there." I was there for about three and a half years, opened the park, and was with the turnaround of the park after we opened it. It is now one of the most successful tourist attractions in all of Europe with around eighteen million people visiting a year.

I then came back to Orlando and was moved into marketing. I moved from advertising into a more marketing role. I began to build out big, cross-asset management plans for the park, and that was Michael's synergy. He called it "synergy," but it was really cross-asset management and figuring out how else we could build franchises and leverage the parks to make the whole greater. How could we leverage all of the parks? We knew that once you built a park in a given region in the world, the entire company's performance went up, from consumer products to film. It became a brand anchor. When it came to thinking about the brand, how to position it, leverage off it, and leverage its parts again to make the whole better—we knew that incredibly well.

I worked on a lot of the franchise plans for Walt Disney World. I was then asked to move out to California and become the vice president of marketing for all of our feature films, both animated and live action. We had four labels at the time.

Disney was good at moving people around divisions and around the company. Michael Eisner believed executives should be moved around and have great overall experience within the company, instead of staying in one sector or industry within the company, because you thus became a more well-rounded executive. I also had to fill in at Disneyland when we didn't have a president. There were a lot of little things I did here and there within the company. Through that, I was not only responsible for the marketing and the positioning of the films but also how we built the franchise. What was the vertical and the horizontal franchise of the company? When did we go with the feature film? When did we go with the sequel if there was one? When did we go online? When did publishing release the books? When did the soundtrack come out? What was the soundtrack? It included the entire franchise plan for the films, including *The Lion King, The Little Mermaid, Beauty and the Beast,* and the Pixar films, from *Toy Story* to *Finding Nemo* to *A Bug's Life*. I did that for well over a decade.

After doing the marketing and franchise planning, I wound up being president at the studio through that period. At the same time, I was not just doing the marketing promotions, advertising, media, strategic allegiances, and these franchise plans, but was also then asked to do some production. I was producing some TV at that point for the studio as well. And I was then asked, after a decade, to come back to the park division to be the global head of all of marketing, sales, and entertainment. That was all of the shows, the parades, and the fireworks spectaculars at all of our parks around the world. I did the marketing, sales, and entertainment globally and opened Hong Kong while I was doing it.

I moved back into the park division and then took on the fiftieth anniversary of Disneyland, which we celebrated at all the parks around the world, including our cruise lines. We launched a tour business and continued to grow. In the five years I did that, when I came back to the park division, we had record attendance, record per-caps. In fact, you could not have gotten a hotel room. We were completely sold out and were at capacity. At that point, we recognized we would have to build more hotels if we were going to continue the growth trend that we were on.

That's when I was recruited by Mark Hurd and Shane Robinson, who came after me to be the global CMO and head of corporate communications and some of corporate affairs for HP. I certainly questioned it. I said, "I'm in a consumer brand. I'm not in a tech industry." I understood technology through Walt Disney Imagineering, but I did not understand the enterprise technical field. Their comment was, "Listen. We have over one hundred thousand engineers in this company. We don't need another engineer. We need somebody who is an expert at communicating what we have so people understand it and it's comprehensible."

I said, "Well, that's interesting because technology has really disrupted our industry. We've seen that in music. We're seeing it in television. We're seeing it in film." Steve Jobs had been on the board at Disney, and I had worked with him for six years marketing his Pixar films. I understood the role technology was going to play in the future. I thought, "If I were ever to make a leap after seventeen years at one company and industry to move to another, this would be the moment." I took advantage of that and moved to Palo Alto, and didn't look back. I was there with Mark Hurd for about three and a half years up until he left. I stayed there shortly after, until we transitioned into a new CEO, and then I left.

At that point, I had taken on an even broader role because that's when I expanded beyond marketing comms and the traditional CMO role and took on the corporate communications role—the executive communications, corporate communications, analyst relations, financial communications, earnings, and crisis comms. As a part of that, I took on all internal communications at the company, including employee engagement. Then I took on global citizenship, CSER, the foundation work, and that whole piece. I took on all of HP.com, which had its own P&L line.

It was a much broader role when I made the move from Disney to this corporate role because I had, up until then, been in business groups. That was another great experience. After Mark left, I stayed through Cathie Lesjak's time as the interim CEO. When they hired a new CEO, I stepped out. I invested in several startups. One of them was created by a friend of mine. I went in and ran it as the CEO. I did that with an agreement that I would only do it for a year. I stepped out. That project is still going today. Some of my investments have done quite well in that space.

I was then recruited by Fusion-io to consult with them. I said fine, I would consult. I didn't want to go into a full-time job at that point. They convinced me to do that after a couple of months. I went in, and we turned that company around. We launched the third-generation product. In that role, I had all of the corporate and financial communications—the same that I had at HP, I had at Fusion-io. Then, we sold to SanDisk. I exited. One of our board members at Fusion-io, who was the chairman of the board here at Flex, said, "What you have done in your career and what you've touched, the transformations and new business startups you've done, would be incredibly valuable to this new company called Flextronics." I knew them on the periphery because they had worked with HP—HP was a customer—but I didn't know the company well.

I spent time with Mike McNamara, the CEO, as well as all the senior executives there. As I got in underneath it, I began to understand that this company touched and impacted so much new technology and innovation. It was enabling all of these enormous brands that were getting incredible credit from businesses and consumers alike in terms of the equity they were creating and the brand they were developing based on the products they were taking to market. Flextronics was the brand behind the brand that impacted that.

The other thing I recognized was that over the last five years, the company had developed capabilities and solution sets that weren't a part of what it was known for as a contract manufacturer or manufacturing firm. The company forty years ago was one thing. It had pivoted and iterated and was agile in how it adapted to the marketplace needs, and built this capability of what we now call "sketch to scale" through rebranding. I knew it had extraordinary potential and world-class people. I decided it was at the forefront of what IoT is today. This will be one of the companies at the center of the IoT—the Internet of Things—that will play a pivotal role in the success of many products in multiple industries.

In fact, we do business in twelve industries, and we do over a billion in each of those and probably touch over three billion-plus in commercial merchandise a year. I thought it would be a great move in my career and journey because it would give me a set of experiences across both the CMO role and the CCO role, as well as a strategy role. And, it gave me the tools to transform the company into what it was becoming.

My biggest thing in terms of career trajectory was that I always took advantage of the opportunities as they were presented to me. I was never one to question the company when they wanted to make a move and wanted me to go do something else. It always turned out that when I took advantage of the opportunities they presented to me, I learned something that would become incredibly useful to me in my career path and the experiences I've had that I could apply to each job. I wouldn't have had those experiences had I not taken advantage of the opportunities as they presented themselves.

A lot of people ask, "How did you get into the movie business?" That was never in my career trajectory. I never said, "I want to be in that business doing that." What I knew was that Disney was a great brand and a company that was known for leadership. I knew I wanted to be mentored by the best in leadership. I wanted to go work for a great brand because usually, great brands have great mentorship. I've always, in every piece of my career, looked for good leadership. I also wanted to go to a company that would give me extraordinary opportunities and a path to grow. For me, it was one of the best moves.

Hewlett-Packard was also a company that had extraordinary equity. It was the heart of Silicon Valley, but it had become the silver-haired lady of Silicon Valley. It started to feel old, stodgy, not as cutting-edge, yet it fostered most of the entrepreneurs. The founders of these new companies came out of HP and out of its system. It was known for the HP way. It was known for how it managed people. It was known for how it innovated and for how it thought about innovation, but it had let itself stagnate. For me, it was another great opportunity to get in, make a difference, and leave an imprint.

I have always believed that when you take a brand on, you should leave it in a better place than when you found it. Those were the questions that I asked myself. Could I do that? Could I take my skills and use them to leave the brand in a better place? Does the company have good leadership? Is it known for leadership? Is it known for mentoring? Those are just some of the guiding principles.

Steimle: Tell us a little bit more about Flex's customers.

Mendenhall: Flex's customers range from startups all the way to the Fortune 100. They come for design, engineering, rapid prototyping, small batch manufacturing, scalable manufacturing globally, global distribution, logistics, tax and trade solutions, and forward and reverse logistics. For some companies, we do everything. For some companies, we do pieces and parts. For some, it's a little bit à la carte. But most understand that if they want to take full advantage in this rapidly changing marketplace, they need the sketch-to-scale. They want the velocity, they want the help, they want the experience.

We do everything from medical, automotive, aerospace defense, industrial, agriculture, consumer electronics, energy, and renewable energy to retail and fashion. Recently at their analyst and investor day up in Beaverton, Oregon, Nike announced that we were their innovative partner for product design and advanced manufacturing solutions moving forward. We've been working with them for over two years, and they made the announcement. You're going to see some interesting developments come from Nike with our ability to help and enable them. We are broad. It's well over twelve industries, and we do over a billion dollars in each of those industries.

We have a program called Lab IX where we incubate startups. We have over twenty companies in that right now. Some of those we just bring on and help incubate and get them started. We do small batch manufacturing as well as some prototyping for them and hopefully allow them to grow into what is a scalable idea globally. With some of those companies, we act as a venture, and we actually invest in them as well as incubate them. We go the full gamut. Some are later stage that have already done series C-level fundraising, and they're coming to test out the working prototypes and do small batch manufacturing that will eventually lead to a more scalable, global solution.

We're everything in between and that's what makes it unique, because we can be competitive with the small startup and the guy who has an idea that's a sketch on a pad, which we have done, all the way to a major brand.

Steimle: Tell me what the structure of your marketing department looks like.

Mendenhall: I've gone from having several hundred people to several thousand people to a handful of people in marketing, to now what is probably around thirty people. I started with a core of seven people—seven people globally, not seven people with teams under them. It was seven people that transformed this company. It's always about world-class people who are engaged both emotionally and intellectually. We tend to think of B2B people as having no emotion or EQ (emotional quotient). Marketers tend to forget that we're all people, we all have emotions, and we're all intellectuals to different degrees. You have to respond to both as you think about marketing. As you think about your team, you have to make both an intellectual and an emotional commitment to the brand and believe in where you're going and what you're doing. I built a team of seven core people who worked incredibly hard to transform a thirty-billion-dollar company.

There's the traditional corporate marketing arm, which has event sponsorships, promotions, brand, the creative directors, the media directors, and the graphic designers, and manages that corporately. They also have the whole global citizenship piece, which comes in under corporate marketing. We have corporate communications, which is everything from content creation, employee engagement, social media, financial communications, crisis communications, some product communications, and executive communications.

We then have another team, which consists of my VP of marketing strategy and operations and research. That's a strategic arm of the company. This is where the senior data scientist sits, where the analytics team sits, the director of research, the business intelligence group, the director of corporate strategy, the strategy team, and our operations for marketing. Then, we have the digital marketing team. That's everything from our web, our email strategy, our SEM, our SEO, and our technical leads. Then, I have a bucket marketing innovation team, which is thinking even further ahead than the team reporting to it.

Steimle: How do you attract and retain top marketing talent for your team?

Mendenhall: It's a combination. Here at Flex, we have internal recruiters. LinkedIn is an unbelievable resource for recruiting. Certainly, there are some key recruiters that have given specialties around marketing in some of those larger firms, some of them more boutique. Using LinkedIn has also become incredibly important relative to recruitment. As you think about us as a brand building reputation, reputation becomes incredibly important.

To participate in the marketing community becomes important, and you have to be selective because there are hundreds of marketing events around the world, and it's important that you participate and share in some of those and build a marketing and communication brand around your company within those specialties and functions. You have to participate in those communities. Through thirty years of working, I have met and worked with a lot of great people in the companies, as well as through marketing specialty firms, marketing service firms, and communication firms. That becomes a great resource.

In keeping the talent, it's about the culture of the company. A lot of people always go to compensation, but it's not necessarily about that. I think it's about the mission, the vision of your company. What are you doing? More and more, it's "Why?" Why are you doing this, and what are you doing as a global citizen? Can I feel good about working there? An important piece is leadership. Am I going to learn? Am I going to mentor? Am I going to feel a part of a community at work? All of those cultural and leadership things become important. Certainly, somewhere in there, compensation's important, but it's not the first thing. You better know why you're doing what you're doing. You better understand socially what you're doing as a company, the impact you're having on the world, certainly in today's climate. How people are going to learn and be mentored and led becomes important.

Steimle: What are you looking for in the people you hire?

Mendenhall: Many brands come to us at Flex, and we have to suspend disbelief and industry conventions and think differently about the product. If you're going to disrupt something or be disrupted, it's going to come from an unconventional place where somebody has seen a friction point or opportunity and seizes that moment. Today, a lot of these companies can do that with very little capital, so a competitor can come from anywhere. For me, part of it is finding someone who can appreciate that. The people I look for when I hire are world-class and experienced but agile and adaptive because that's what each day requires.

Steimle: I know there's no such thing as a typical day, but what's typical for you in terms of your work? What are you doing on a daily basis?

Mendenhall: A lot of the formality of how we built organizational structure in the past was based on a decades-old sort of military approach to operations and organization. In fact, General Stanley McChrystal ordered an entire reconstruct of the military based on where the world is today. I think that has to happen in organizations. I don't have a formal schedule. I have certain meetings where I touch base with the people that work for me, and then from there, it becomes agile.

As you can imagine, when you have the footprint we have with two hundred thousand employees on the comm side alone, it's highly real time and dynamic. You're hearing things, you're responding to the market, you're engaging, you're announcing things. The CEO's office, the CFO, and the general counsel are all in an open environment, which is typical of Silicon Valley, and we are in and out of each other's offices all day long. We text each other, we call each other, we use every means of communication.

I was asked just last week, "How do you engage your CEO? Do you have a formal meeting with him once a week to catch up?" And I said, "In today's world with how fast things move, I am engaged with him every day, multiple times a day, through multiple communication devices." There is never a day that I have not communicated with him in multiple forms. The same is true of our CFO and our general counsel.

The things that I deal with during the day are highly unpredictable. There are things that change rapidly because of priority, and there are things that remain pretty stable. It's hard to give you a normal day because it depends on the market and the world and what unfolds. One day, there's an enormous explosion in Shenzhen, China, and we're dealing with that because there's an enormous operation from our company there. We have to figure out how to mitigate any event or impact to the supply chain or our customers.

Any given day, there's a typhoon that comes through, or there's a Nepalese earthquake. Because we're in a global economy, those all impact a company of our size and scale. We operate a large, multibillion-dollar supply chain. We are spread geographically around the world. What most people don't realize is a power outage in North Carolina in the United States is going to affect the plants in China. We're all interconnected, and it's that mapping and sophistication of real-time data that will allow us to help our customers. Every day is new and every day brings something unexpected. The more we globalize, the more impact it has on all of us. What happens around the world, whether it's a labor strike or social unrest somewhere, that will impact product and brands. And generally, that means it will impact our company.

Steimle: How do internationalization and globalization affect Flex and marketing in particular?

Mendenhall: We are a global company. We are in thirty countries with one hundred locations. We are clearly a global company based on our senior leadership team. Many of them don't even reside at corporate headquarters. They reside around the world. They commute in. In the world today, agility, flexibility, and speed are important, so we don't spend a lot of time in formalized meeting structures. We are an informal company. We move and pivot fast. We are agile in how we manage the teams and the company. I like to say we are the biggest startup you will ever meet, but we move fast, which gives us a competitive advantage.

We are a global footprint. With the trends happening today, we have a growing middle class—sixty percent growth in Asia alone. With consumption on the rise and consumers having more buying power than they've ever had, the demands for hyper personalization, product, and services are becoming incredibly important. As that happens, you can no longer import and force—if you're a Western company—other markets to take Western product. You're going to have to customize or mass-customize. Then, it will move to hyper personalization, which means you're going to have to start thinking about regionalization and manufacturing. You're going to want to have distribution and manufacturing as close to your end retail point as possible. You're going to start to see more regionalization take place across the globe, not less, and I think we're going to become more global in the future as a brand.

Steimle: What are some of the key metrics you focus on that you're held responsible for?

Mendenhall: Some of the key metrics have to do with communications, share of voice, and sentiment about that, as well as the reputational research we do around the brand. We are interested in what our stakeholders think of us and what attributes they assign, how well they think we're doing against those attributes, and how we build programs around that.

To build the shareholder value becomes incredibly important. Our share price becomes incredibly important. Our top-line revenue, what our OP is, what our margins look like—I'm held to all of that too, just as a corporate official would be. I'm held to the brand reputation. I'm held to an enormous amount of metrics around global citizenship and CSER. We're held to metrics around a number of leads and the cultivation of those leads. I won't get too specific, but we're held to all of the metrics around engagement in social and our digital efforts, whether that be the web or otherwise. There's probably over one hundred metrics that my team and I pay attention to. Most of those are auditable and quantifiable.

Steimle: How has marketing changed during your career? What future trends are you excited about?

Mendenhall: One thing that has never changed in marketing is the art of telling a brand's story in multiple ways through multiple channels. That is still incredibly important today. What has changed is the means, delivery, channels, the gross in those channels, and the ability to use analytics and data to better understand the customers and their needs and wants. It's given us the ability to listen better. If people use the data well, they'll listen more to the customer. That's where you'll see extraordinary change. Technology has changed, particularly in terms of the idea of mobility, always being on and connected. It is pervasive. It has changed how people engage, how people communicate, how people purchase, and how people react to information.

It's also changed the transparency. A brand can't hide. Customers can't hide. It's put more accountability and transparency into the system, which I think is a very good thing. Those brands, products, and services that provide real solution sets to the customer with authenticity and transparency tend to move to the top, and people appreciate that. These changes have thus affected the skill set of what marketers need to understand, the knowledge base they need to have. Agility, speed, and the ability to react with precision have become incredibly important.

Virginie Glaenzer

Executive Vice President of Marketing &
Customer Experience

Great Eastern Energy

*Since 2014, **Virginie Glaenzer** has been the executive vice president of marketing and customer experience at Great Eastern Energy, where she is responsible for
digital and social media brand marketing as well as lead generation. Before coming
to Great Eastern Energy, she was vice president of marketing at LiveWorld, a social
content technology marketing company. Glaenzer's move to LiveWorld was awarded
fifth place in Social Fresh's Top 21 Social Media Career Moves of 2012. In 2015,
Glaenzer received the SmartCEO's Executive Management Award. Glaenzer has
been published in* Social Media Today, iMedia, *and* Entrepreneur.

Josh Steimle: Give us some background on Great Eastern Energy. What is
the company? Who are its customers? Which regions does it cover?

Virginie Glaenzer: Great Eastern Energy was founded seventeen years ago
in Brooklyn, New York to provide gas, electricity, and renewable energy to
businesses. Today, about fifty percent of the U.S. states are deregulated—and

© Josh Steimle 2016
J. Steimle, *Chief Marketing Officers at Work*, DOI 10.1007/978-1-4842-1931-7_10

New York, New Jersey, and Massachusetts are some of those states—in which you can choose an energy provider to buy energy commodities. We offer energy services to real estate management companies, restaurant owners, and small businesses who want to reduce their energy cost by better understanding how to lower their energy consumption. Our company has about sixty employees and we did $400 million in revenue in 2015 and we've been growing tremendously over the last four years.

Most of the time, businesses will only have one energy bill from their utility company, which displays the name of their alternative energy supplier.

I started as EVP of marketing and was later asked to manage our customer experience department, which is composed of customer service agents.

Steimle: Can you talk more about customer service being part of marketing and how you see the relationship there?

Glaenzer: We look at the customer experience with a holistic approach, so it starts with marketing, whose function is to do brand messaging and lead generation. Once the leads are in the pipeline, there's a prospect journey. At some point, those leads are being converted by our sales team or through our online portal. From the first time a customer interacts with our online properties or through word of mouth, he or she is having a customer experience.

The customer service team starts with greeting customers online and on the phone through the reception desk. Creating touch points to build a real relationship is a big challenge for us because in the past we didn't capture that relationship. Most of our customers come through brokers and they will only see our name on the bill of their utility company. So we are trying to innovate and create new ways to capture customers' data and engage with customers.

Steimle: How do you develop customer loyalty when the customers don't know who you are?

Glaenzer: In this industry, people have the assumption that the reason they are with your company is for price and nothing else. We need to change that perception. The deregulation market doesn't really provide financial savings as much as price protection with a fixed-rate plan. As a business, you can do budget forecasting easily as you'll know that the cost of the commodity will not fluctuate.

Steimle: What initiatives are you taking to change that and build customer loyalty by reaching out and developing relationships with customers?

Glaenzer: Our mission is to help our customers reduce their energy consumption, so with that in mind, we're trying to teach them that turning out lights matters. Exchanging the incandescent light bulbs for LED light bulbs matters. There are many things we can do on a daily basis to lower the amount of energy we're consuming. It's a different approach from the one most energy vendors take.

We use social media to engage with customers who are online and interested in understanding what energy is, customers who buy into the whole sustainability effort. They're comforted by the sense that they're making the right choice.

We create loyalty by being true to customers. We want to help them thrive in their business. If we want them to focus on growing their businesses, we have to remove their worry about energy commodity fluctuation. We want to help them change their behavior so they can reduce the energy they're consuming.

Steimle: You've been an entrepreneur, so you understand saving money for businesses. What other ways has your entrepreneurial background led you to be successful in marketing and the CMO role?

Glaenzer: I don't know if it's the entrepreneur side as much as the technology side that helped me. Today, we're seeing a new type of marketers with a strong background in technology. I've spent more than 15 years in sales and technology and that gives me a completely different view on the objective of marketing.

I try to inspire my team to go beyond their limit and become technology savvy. Marketing SCO, CRM, email marketing, A/B testing, and all the tools and technology we're using can be very technical and complex, and you have to know all that. It has nothing to do with content. It's driven by technology. One of the things I'm trying to teach my team is to be what I call "growth hackers," which is a term that comes from Silicon Valley. It's being at the crossroad between product, data, and marketing by creating a different mindset.

Another growing trend is "agile," which also comes from the software world. Agile goes hand in hand with a growth hacking mindset. Going agile allowed Spotify to be faster, better, and cheaper than the industry Goliaths like Google, Amazon, and Apple. Our team needs to be agile, which is that ability to shift, to change, to adjust and adapt quickly.

Steimle: How do you make your team aware of that mindset, and how do you train them to adopt it?

Glaenzer: It's an everyday practice, and it's a combination of multiple things. First of all, we provide them with opportunities to learn new technologies as well as prioritizing ongoing training and resources. Second, every time I stumble upon a new tech company that provides a new cutting edge tool, I will send it to them and say, "Please evaluate and take a look. Engage with this startup and try to understand what they are offering." Keeping up with the latest tech start-up is an investment but it doesn't mean you're going to use it because every new tool has a cost.

Finally, I think creating a culture of risk and understanding the meaning of failure is another way to keep an open mind. After all, how do you try new tools and processes, which are risks, if you're afraid of failing? I've recently been thinking about how you change the perception of failure, because society doesn't help you. It tells you, "Yes, you should fail," but no one wants to fail. Why? Because it feels bad. We haven't been taught the right way of looking at failures.

I've been telling my team that we're going to change. Every time we fail, we're going to raise our hands and say, "How fascinating," because if you think about it, failing is the opposite of what you've worked for. It's fascinating—not getting what you want and having a scientific approach, looking at the failure, trying to see why you failed. What other thing can you learn and connect together so that failure becomes an insightful experience? Then, you're not focusing on the failing. You're focusing on the insightful experience that comes from failing.

Steimle: And the next time, you can get it right.

Glaenzer: Exactly!

Steimle: How do you make sure this interest in failure doesn't become a crutch or an excuse for more failures in the future?

Glaenzer: I was brainstorming with my CEO on how to create a company culture that enables people to take risks, and reward people who take risks. We talked about failing and how if people cannot fail, they're not going to take any risks, but ensuring that we are not creating a culture of failing. Ultimately, no one wants to fail. Does it feel good to fail? No. So from a human stand-point, even if you're opening the door to the possibility of failures, no one wants to go there. We're just creating a soft cushion so people are able to push themselves back up if they fail. It's putting a perspective on something that no one wants to go through and focusing on the insights. If we're failing but we are able to find something insightful, something we can learn, then we haven't really failed.

Steimle: Tell me more about the structure of your team.

Glaenzer: We have a director of digital communications. Her role is to overlook the content strategy from a holistic point of view to ensure that our brand story is consistent across platform, across our customer journey phases, and across departments. We have a marketer in charge of advertising, SEO, and web management, which includes our newly launched e-commerce portal. Our social media manager is focused on social media outreach, engagement, and blogger outreach. Our graphic designer oversees our brand image throughout our online and offline presence and he works closely with our webmaster. Finally, our copy editor reviews every single piece of content and creates engaging content.

Steimle: What does a typical day—insofar as there is such a thing—look like for you and your team?

Glaenzer: I usually have two to three meetings per day, during which we review, we create, and we plan. We use Smartsheet, an online collaborative tool that allows us to do project management, as well as Skype. We also use Google Docs which allows us to co-create projects in real time. I believe that two people can produce more and better results than one individual alone. It's also a good exercise to put your ego on the side.

Steimle: What's your philosophy on building a team and recruiting top talent?

Glaenzer: I think it starts with finding people who desire something you can give them. Sharing similar values is also a key element in building a great team.

When I hire someone, I try to assess their story and identity and then their skill set. The skill set is something you can acquire, but you're not going to change the individual's personality. Hiring people who fit within our brand culture and company culture is really important. Yet at the same time finding different styles or personalities that can also complement the existing team can make a big difference. It's a delicate balance.

Part of my job is to help our CEO build an employee culture, which transfers into our customer experience. We've recently been nominated as finalists in the Best Employee Engagement Award from the 360 Loyalty Marketing Association. It was a good achievement for our last year's effort.

Steimle: How do you manage relationships between your team and the other teams they have to work with within the organization?

Glaenzer: Marketing has become the center of most organizations, yet from my discussions with other CMOs, efficient collaboration between departments remains a challenge. I work hard to create a true collaboration between sales and marketing departments. And it is known that when you have people with opposite personalities, it can be quite a clash. However, I see technologies like Salesforce as a new way to create a common language and increase collaboration.

Steimle: What are some of the metrics you focus on that you use internally with your team?

Glaenzer: Every month we look at our number of leads, the number of converted leads, the number of customers, and the amount of website traffic. How many people are we reaching on our online platform? How many people are we getting on the phone? Our pipeline goes from the website traffic to marketing leads, marketing-qualified leads, sales-qualified leads and converted leads.

Steimle: What are your customers looking for when they find your company and how are they finding your company?

Glaenzer: The energy industry is being disrupted for a number of reasons: customers are being more educated, we are seeing a sustainability movement, and most recently the NY State energy commission is working on new regulations. All this creates an environment where the traditional marketing strategies do not work any longer. In the past, marketers believed that if you create a good story that people could relate to and share it on enough platforms enough times, at some point, customers would start believing and start buying into the company and the product. That doesn't work anymore.

Today, customers are overwhelmed with data and are very distrustful towards most brands and active discerners. They have changed from being passive to active customers. If something goes wrong, they're going to complain on Twitter. It's out there in the open. You can't hide it as a brand. The risks for brands have increased tremendously.

All of this has created an environment for marketing that requires you to understand your customers' beliefs. In other words, we need to know what people believe, and until we find out what they believe, the brand story we're going to tell has no meaning. That's what we've recently worked on. We're trying to understand what people believe on the topic of energy.

I sent my marketing team out on the street, knocking on small business doors and asking people, "Can I ask you questions? Do you know about energy deregulation? What do you think?" You've got to remember that for marketers, this is *unusual*. Most marketing people are rarely in the field so it can be an uncomfortable experience. We went out there and talked to about twenty small businesses.

We're now at the phase of trying to look at what people think. I hired a consultant—business speaker and brand author, Tom Asacker, who wrote a book called *The Business of Belief*.[1]

Steimle: Do you build buyer personas? Do you use buyer personas in the work you're doing?

Glaenzer: We have identified several buyer personas, but we need to be careful as they can oversimplify the customer's needs and desires. Building personas creates an easier way to target an audience, but the challenge is that you're putting people in a box and today's customers are evolving quickly. Their needs are changing so you take the risk of misunderstanding who they are.

---

[1] Tom Asacker (CreateSpace, 2013).

Steimle: What do you see as some of the biggest challenges facing today's CMOs?

Glaenzer: They're twofold. The first one is technology. Technology is disrupting organizations. If you're not technology savvy as a CMO, if you don't understand the impact, you're going to be left on the side.

The second challenge is customer experience. Customer experience is an effort that needs to come from the entire organization, from the cashier to the person on the phone to the delivery partner. Who owns the customer experience? Who should be responsible? Is it marketing? It touches every single department, even finance—the way we bill, and the story we tell in our invoices.

Steimle: That's so far away from the traditional idea of marketing—which has been grounded in advertising—to go from "I'm going to meet with an ad agency and talk about an advertising campaign" to "I'm going to scrutinize our receipts and see how they're formatted to see if they're confusing or if they're user-friendly." It's such a different mindset.

Glaenzer: Exactly. It's almost like CMOs are becoming COOs. The COO used to be the person who managed the inside of the organization with a flow process. The CMO is doing the same thing from a customer standpoint, not from an employee standpoint.

Steimle: You hear a lot of this talk about how the CMO role is merging with the CIO, COO, or sales. It's not hard to see why a lot of CMOs get targeted to eventually succeed to the CEO role.

Glaenzer: Absolutely.

Steimle: Let's say somebody had been working in marketing and just got promoted to be CMO. What kind of advice would you give to a first-time CMO who's just getting started?

Glaenzer: I would say looking at technologies, as an enabler of customer experience, should be the first priority.

Steimle: What do you wish you would have known when you came into the role for the first time and took over at Great Eastern?

Glaenzer: I would have liked to better understand the financial backbone of an energy supplier. There are a lot of new business models, such as software as a service and recurring revenue, and new ways of selling, and these can help transform an organization. Every industry is being disrupted by startups because of technology. Uber is disrupting a 200-year-old industry. The finance industry is also being disrupted, and even though they might be trying to hide the fight or pretend that it's not happening, it is happening.

Steimle: What do you think CEOs need to understand more about marketing and about the CMO role?

Glaenzer: It is known that many CEOs have lost touch with customers. However, there are a few CEOs out there, like Richard Branson and John Legere, who seem to have that desire to be close to the customer and understand how the desire of the customer changes and how they can best serve.

Ada Chen Rekhi

Vice President of Marketing
SurveyMonkey

Ada Chen Rekhi has been VP of marketing at SurveyMonkey since 2014. She co-founded Connected HQ, which provided a professional contact management system, in 2011. Less than a year later, Connected HQ was acquired by LinkedIn, where Chen Rekhi became a product marketer. Previous to founding Connected HQ, Chen Rekhi served as both director of product management and director of product marketing at Mochi Media in the online games industry. Chen Rekhi began her media career at Microsoft.

Chen Rekhi has a bachelor of science from The Wharton School of the University of Pennsylvania in economics, operations and information management, and marketing.

Josh Steimle: Tell me about SurveyMonkey's customers. Who are the people using your products?

Ada Chen Rekhi: SurveyMonkey is the world's leading online survey platform. The vision is about much more than being a survey tool, though. It's about being a decision platform and democratizing access to data. Our customer base is just about everyone. We see folks using SurveyMonkey from the education space—students, K12, teachers collecting feedback—all the way to health care—How satisfied are you with your care today? How clean were the facilities?—to training to events to feedback around the customers to more professional use cases like HR and employee engagement.

© Josh Steimle 2016
J. Steimle, *Chief Marketing Officers at Work*, DOI 10.1007/978-1-4842-1931-7_11

We see people through the whole spread. We're seeing more and more excitement around how you take these initial surveys, create surveys, send out and collect feedback, and transform that story into how you democratize access to data. The act of collecting feedback or having context on how to interpret that feedback is often inaccessible unless you have professional services or other things. We've done a lot with products like Benchmarks, which is a way to see how you're doing on your survey results relative to others. It's a powerful way for us to take certain segments of our customer population and give them a way to see those answers in context. If you have an NPS—which is a Net Promoter Score of customer satisfaction—of forty-four, that might be a great or terrible score, but it all depends on how that score of forty-four compares relative, in this case, to technology companies in the Bay Area and in this particular industry.

Steimle: How do you manage relationships with other departments and give and receive feedback?

Chen Rekhi: Part of the SurveyMonkey story is growth. I've been here almost two years. We've more than doubled the employee count of the business. We're pushing seven hundred. When I joined, it was three hundred. We were in a much smaller office. Communication and collaboration between teams is always an evolving process because what works with three hundred is not the same thing as what works with seven hundred.

One of the major changes we've made which is continuing to evolve is a more robust quarterly planning process. We start every quarter with a running list of what we gathered from all the product counterparts, the other teams within the organization that we work with, and the international teams to get an overall understanding of everything we could potentially do, and then we overlay it against the broader context of our business strategy to determine the most important things. The ability to collect all the initiatives, size them, and communicate what's above and below the line has been one of the biggest aids in terms of us working closely with teams. It gives us a sense of what everyone wants from us and what to try to do by the end of the quarter.

As always happens in any rapidly growing and changing environment, when new information emerges, it's easy at that point to look at the list and say, "Here is a set of tradeoffs that we need to make. Either we need to get more resources for this or something needs to come off the list, and here's the proposal if we want to fit it in." It creates a much more transparent conversation given all of the moving pieces within an organization of what's going to get done, what isn't, and what else is getting worked on.

In many cases, teams interact with marketing on a specific area of projects they're trying to finish. They may not be aware of the broader activities, because marketing is one of those central resources that everyone ends up needing to leverage in some way or another. We want to be an enabler of that, not necessarily a gatekeeper. There's a huge difference between the semantics of those two terms.

Steimle: Can you tell me more about how you manage the relationship between sales and marketing at SurveyMonkey?

Chen Rekhi: We have an international sales team. They're primarily based in Palo Alto, Sydney, London, Dublin, and Ottawa. To support them, we have a demand generation and field marketing team. The charter for the marketing team relative to sales is figuring out how we help them fill their funnel and enable them to win deals. How do we partner with sales and make sure they're successful? There's always a special relationship between sales and marketing. We think about it in two different ways. The first one is making sure there's clear alignment and accountability across roles and responsibilities. We're transparent about what we're doing: "Here's what we expect to get out of it, here's what we're planning, and if x comes through the door, here are the tradeoffs—should we really be doing A instead of B?" That's been a huge part of building the relationship with the sales team.

The second part is that aspect of data. Because we are a business that gets a lot of traffic from online sources and thus has a high level of measurability and accountability, a lot of what we do with the sales team is to help them understand the actual leads we're tracking, the metrics we're holding ourselves to on a weekly and quarterly basis, and the initiatives and targets, what we're actually trying to get to. That clarity of communication and metrics has helped the relationship a lot. Building a business together and being one team has been helpful because on a lot of levels, we're marketing new products all the time.

We're launching new solutions all the time, which means being incredibly agile in taking feedback from the sales team and saying, "You guys are the experts. You're the ones who talk to the customers. How do we bring that feedback into the marketing materials and messages? How can we help bridge the gap between sales and product to make sure the next version addresses what we're hearing from the field sales team?" That's an incredibly important area where marketing can add value.

Steimle: What are the key metrics that you focus on?

Chen Rekhi: We think about our business in two major buckets: the self-serve surveys product and the SurveyMonkey for Business sales channel. The self-serve business product is the SurveyMonkey you are probably most familiar with—coming to the website, evaluating different plans in terms of how you would like to be able to create surveys, collecting feedback, analyzing the results and what type of functionality you need for that, and then transacting with a credit card. For the self-serve business, we care most about our metric called "new paid," which is the number of paid subscribers we're bringing in. We look at the trim rate of the new paid and we look at the lifetime value of the new paid, which is dependent on the mix of what level of plan they signed up for on a given channel. It's quantitative and performance-driven. It's understanding the initiatives that we can take to drive the most revenue relative to new paid and the lifetime value of the customer over time. We drive that across a variety of different channels and initiatives.

The other metric we look closely at is certain measures of customer satisfaction, which we proxy through their engagement. When someone signs up for an account, what percentage of them made it through initiating a survey, deploying a survey, and collecting responses from a survey lets you know if you're introducing friction in that process. If they get confused and throw up their hands, you can see it through that product process and the metrics you have.

The other half of the business, which is SurveyMonkey for Business, offers the more high-end products and solutions that we sell to businesses and organizations. The marketing organization looks a lot like a B2B marketing organization. It's much more focused on how we drive demand through marketing-qualified leads into the funnel from the sales team. Then, we look further down that funnel and we understand from the marketing-qualified lead how many opportunities are being created at what value and how much revenue is closed from the sales team side. Working with that broader sales team, we also look at opportunities to grease the wheels in that funnel.

Steimle: How much is the growth you're experiencing driven by internationalization and globalization? How is that impacting your role?

Chen Rekhi: There are many different types of growth. From the business standpoint, internationalization is the focus for us. We've seen a pretty major shift in terms of the mix of our business that comes from the U.S. moving to more and more international markets. We've localized our site, and we've expanded the currencies we support. We expect there to be more and more growth in the international frontier in addition to what we're seeing already in all parts of the business, whether it's the self-serve surveys product or SurveyMonkey for Business.

The way we approach international growth is leveraged. We have central teams here in Palo Alto and a couple of marketers in different places. We do have offices in Sydney and London, but a lot of it is thinking about the things we can do at scale that can impact the entire rest of the world—the way we think about it versus going in on a country-by-country focus. The other part of growth is adding more and more employees. We're also diversifying our product portfolio and the set of solutions we offer when we're thinking about expanding beyond that surveys product, so we've had more and more growth in terms of employee count to go with that as well.

Steimle: What does your team look like? What is the structure like?

Chen Rekhi: There's been a ton of growth in the marketing department. More than half of my team has started this year. When I started, my team was six people. We're now thirty. It's grown five times the size over two years and it's been a remarkable transition. As the business grows, we have more leverage and more resources to take on broader opportunities. When I first came on, we were focused on the initial frontier of making sure our scalable, paid marketing channels were performing well. It's a huge avenue of growth, but once you get that humming, there's a lot of additional low-hanging fruit to take. We've seen growth from the team not only on the online marketing side and the product marketing side but have started to think about selling through more of a sales channel. We've also built out a demand-generation and field marketing team in the last year.

Steimle: What's your philosophy on building a new marketing team? What do you look for in new hires? What do you do to train and retain?

Chen Rekhi: One thing that drew me to SurveyMonkey was this growth story of starting with a small team and then building it out. Build the organization in a way that optimizes what marketing should be—a source of insights and data that helps inform the product roadmap. It should be a facilitator and enabler of how products get to market, reach the customers, and communicate value to the customers.

Knowing that we're on this growth trajectory, I've focused on finding high-quality people that over-index on curiosity as an element, people who ask questions and wonder why. The analogy I always give folks when I'm interviewing is there are people who know how to operate a car. They can drive it, they can shift, they can make turns, they can use signals. They understand the rules of how you operate the car. Then, there's a set of people—and this is leaning back a bit on my entrepreneurial background—that understand fundamentally how the car works, and they're curious about going under the hood, understanding the engine, understanding how the parts interconnect, and tinkering with it. Since so much of our business and where we're going is fundamentally around building new processes and solving problems related to issues other people have seen in the past, we need people who are excited about rolling up their sleeves and building the car. We're focused on curious people that are builders.

I think of this initial team I've been building in the last year as the DNA of the future of the marketing team as we get larger and larger. The first set of people you hire become the groundwork and set the DNA for what the organization looks like at scale. If you think about the marketing department as a microcosm of the startup, it's important that the kind of people you hire are right in terms of talent, curiosity, and sense of ownership rather than saying, "This is what's in the job description." You're getting that right balance, and you're also actively encouraging and reinforcing that value system as you grow the team. It's an area I'm curious about.

In a technology-rich product-centric environment like SurveyMonkey, marketing must have a deep understanding of the product. They have to be incredibly curious and understand how it works, who would want it, and how to get that relatability to the end customer. The idea of black box marketing—where you can give a marketer anything and they can go sling it—doesn't really exist because so much of what we do is intertwined with the product experience and what we offer.

Steimle: How do you stay in touch with your customers and make sure that you understand their needs and wants?

Chen Rekhi: In many different ways. There's always the high-level view of the quantitative data. We're very data-driven here at SurveyMonkey. We run daily reports of dashboards against our key performance indicators. At that point, we look at specific markets, channels, and customer sets and quickly identify any leading indicators that might be something bigger to dig into. That's the overall health metric. We have a set of different ongoing initiatives to make sure that we as a marketing department—and also the entire company—are staying close to the customers. Once a year, we run a voice-of-customer summit. We bring folks from our support teams down to the main Palo Alto office and actively encourage a lot of the employees and marketers to look at real-life customer feedback, field their concerns and questions, and think, "We're seeing this question all the time. What are the ways we can fix it or help educate customers better about these pieces?"

We also have a market research team that sits down with different product groups. They do two different sets of activities. The first one is they track the more longitudinal metrics of customer satisfaction and feedback. When customers come in, we naturally run surveys against them and try to understand trend lines in their satisfaction and needs as well as certain demographics that are fluctuating over time. We want to understand the makeup and composition of our customer base from a needs, profile, and demographics basis. The other portion of what the market research team does is help get answers to key and burning questions from the product organization or other areas within the company to drive specific decisions.

For example, if the product team is trying to understand how to implement a certain survey feature, they may have identified there's a need for it, but they also want to make sure that from a usability standpoint, it makes sense to the customer. When you think about the broader category of the feature, they deeply understand the use cases and the specific path the customer is trying to go down in order to leverage that feature. We'll do a set of customer interviews to facilitate those product managers getting a chance to talk to the customers. We'll take the designs that the design team creates, show them to the customer early on, and ask, "Does this make sense? Is it what you expected?"

Once the prototypes get built, we'll do usability studies with customers and help the product and design team tweak the experience before it gets launched. For the final phase—which is really neat for tech companies—we can do phased launches of product features when they come out. When something gets shipped initially, it's not like you turn it on and everyone gets it. You can turn it on to a percentage of your population and talk to them once they've been exposed to it to see their reaction and find out whether it's easier to use. You can go look at the quantitative metrics, whether or not they're using it and how they're leveraging it to introduce something positive rather than negative into the experience. You're able to essentially A/B test between those two experiences.

Steimle: What are some of the most successful marketing campaigns or initiatives you've taken that have grown the user base? What's worked for marketing?

Chen Rekhi: A lot of our success has been on the online marketing front, like our scalable online marketing campaigns that exposed customers to the idea of using SurveyMonkey or made them more aware of how SurveyMonkey can help answer those questions. A lot of the expansion we've seen has been in search and display channels, helping capture mid-funnel intent. You have this idea, and you think you want to create a survey, but how do we show up in the right place at the right time when you're looking for it—whether it's a search result or a display ad—and then also target you with the right messages? Based on the contents of what you searched for or what parts of the site you browsed, what are the different messages we can show you later on?

That and the expansion of our ability to hypertarget customers based off of the information we have about them have been huge areas of gain for us. In addition, we've started to look more and more at social channels. Facebook is a great way for us to reach those customers. That's been a huge win for us, and we've been learning quite a lot about how you engage with those channels, whether it's through our mobile applications or to drive a broader awareness of SurveyMonkey.

One of our products, Question Bank, is tied to some of the customer insights. When a customer is excited about creating a survey, we often hear them start not with, "I want to create a survey," but with, "I want to answer a question." They eventually get to the point where they say, "I'm trying to answer this question and I want to have a credible answer, but I don't have the ability, budget, or time to hire a firm. It sounds like I need to create a survey, but I don't know whether I'm doing it right. Walk me through the process of doing it right."

Many people are often left to a gut decision or a survey made without using the best methodology. We've done two things to decrease the friction in that decision-making process. One is a question bank. Our question bank offers a whole set of methodologically correct, correctly phrased, non-leading questions to help you get to the right answers because you don't necessarily want to ask yes-or-no questions like, "Do you agree with this statement?" There's a bias toward agreement. You may not want to ask questions in a way that skew people one way or the other in terms of your examples. A lot of people know there's a correct way but just don't know what it is.

The second thing we've done besides our question bank is our marketing campaigns introducing the concept of templates. If you're trying to measure customer satisfaction, or you're an HR leader of a small company and are trying to measure employee engagement, there are preexisting templates. For instance, we've partnered with the Society of Human Resource Management (SHRM) to get to an employee engagement survey, which is the official SHRM-stamped way of collecting information from your employees based on feedback. In addition to that, we can benchmark and tell you if forty-four percent of your employees said such and such, is that good or bad relative to others? That becomes powerful because you're not only measuring it but putting it into context.

Steimle: What are some trends in your industry or with your customers that are affecting you?

Chen Rekhi: Data is the massive trend—the massive prevalence of data, the fact that you don't ever have enough, and then once you do have it, getting it all to fit together.

Steimle: Once you have it, you have too much.

Chen Rekhi: Yes, exactly. You simultaneously have too little and too much, and then you don't necessarily have the tool sets to be able to go implement them. Embedded within the wins in marketing—whether it's online marketing, trigger marketing, hypertargeting all of those things in terms of how we can communicate with customers, all of that—is the need for data.

We want to target customers based off of who they are, what they want, when they want it, all of that classic stuff. It turns out that getting to effective marketing campaigns is dependent on tying into, for instance, the product database and understanding that if a customer comes in and they haven't initiated a survey, the message we want to send them is encouragement to initiate a survey. If they've already created a survey and filled in the questions, the message we might talk to them about would be a little bit different to ease them along that path. You see this all the time in terms of email communications. The more targeted you are and the more specific you can be in terms of providing value to that customer, the less likely they are to delete your email and keep moving on in the world.

It's getting noisier and noisier. Underpinning a lot of it is this need for data to be the groundwork for marketing campaigns to be successful. But that data is all over the place, whether it's billing data, site behavior data, pixelating to understand a customer's journey from the ad, all the way to your end conversion point. Even marrying a lot of the more implicit or explicit data of survey responses back into how you message and market to them. That's a major trend I've seen throughout my entire career, both here at SurveyMonkey and previously at LinkedIn.

A lot of the gains marketers make in their campaigns are based off of finding ways to execute and implement that data. A lot of what my team spends time on is aggregating more data feeds, making sure tracking is working well, and making decisions based off of the data for whether to turn something on or off. We're far away from the days where you throw a billboard up on 101 and hope it works. We're being held to pretty strong metrics. You spent *x* amount of dollars on this event. How did it go? Did we see a lift? It turns out a lot of that stuff is measurable now, but the demands in the marketing organization to have the infrastructure and the ability to market and act against it are increasing over time.

Steimle: What do you see as some of the big challenges facing today's CMOs?

Chen Rekhi: We can't be everything to everyone. The CMO or head of marketing role is expected to be simultaneously left brain and right brain. You're supposed to be incredibly quantitative and understand down to a T the performance, and impact, and the ROI of the specific quantitative marketing campaigns. It's a huge part, leveraging that data and reaching the customers.

At the same time, marketers are also stewards of the brand and they're stewards of the voice, the tone, and the overall experience of the customer. There are cases where in order to be effective at that, you have to be incredibly creative in terms of thinking outside of the box and breaking through the noise of the customers. It's hard to create an environment that is balanced across both the left brain and the right brain, because you need both in order to have an effective marketing organization.

As there's been more and more of a pull towards this trend of data and analytics, finding a way to simultaneously assert the fact that we do need to be customer-centric, think about the story, think about the narratives, and craft great experiences while being married to the data is a unique challenge that faces all marketers today. You can't be too much one or the other.

Steimle: Where do you see marketing going in the future?

Chen Rekhi: Specific to the industry and the sector, marketing will probably look more and more different over time. Moving between industries and companies and having your job be transferrable will get tougher because so much of the marketing role is now tied to having a deep understanding of your product, your customer, and the specific space or set of problems you're trying to focus your product and company vision against.

I also think the marketing world is going to become increasingly technical and merge with product. The traditional marketer may think of the channels in their toolbox—online media spend, offline spend, or other traditional marketing channels—but the new marketer also has to think about the context of all the channels to communicate with the customer inside of the product, through push notifications and mobile, through triggered email, through the receipts. Having a deep understanding of the product flow and being able to help shape that with the product and engineering organization is going to lead to a fundamental shift, where in order to be successful, you also have to be technical. What does that look like? Does that look like marketing departments with engineering teams?

You already see it with web development teams sitting within marketing or analytical teams sitting within marketing, but I think that trend will continue. It's a bit mind-blowing, having marketing sit with engineers, but a lot of our initiatives use search engine optimization. It's impossible to be effective at search engine optimization given how many of those changes are on the site level without the support of an engineering team.

Steimle: What are some of the skills new marketers or college students interested in marketing should be developing today?

Chen Rekhi: The environment is changing so fast that I fall back on this concept of trying to be an endless learner, being curious throughout your life. For the candidates I see as well as the people I talk to about broadening their careers at any point, wherever you're working, spend time understanding the whole system. Spend time understanding how the system interacts. If you're a marketer sitting in an entry-level job and performing a specific set of duties, look at all the people in the departments around you, below you, above you, and try to understand how all of it fits together. How does your role fit within that role?

When you've then been taken on to a smaller company or a startup or have become a leader, you may be in a position where you need to rebuild it from scratch. You saw the engine. You sat in the engine and you operated it, but if you didn't look under the hood and understand all the pieces, then when you get into the role where you're actually running the engine, you have no idea how all those pieces fit together.

A lot of what we do as marketers is not just the activities within the scope of our job description and our responsibilities. It's broader. How does marketing work with sales? How does marketing work with product? What does the product team do? What does the finance team do? How does finance enable marketing to be successful? What do all these different tools and vendors do? Endless curiosity is important.

In terms of hard skills, have a deep understanding of market research. There's a science to it, but have the underpinnings of understanding customer insights and the right ways and methods to measure them. When I think back on what I leveraged from undergrad and business school, statistical understanding, modeling, and a lot of things that may not be typical to a marketing background involving familiarity and comfort with data—even on a high level in terms of understanding how to evaluate it—are very useful.

Get a good understanding of the diversity of available marketing channels, even if it's just playing around with the tools or finding opportunities to be exposed to them. Not having a good sense of how paid marketing can drive ROI and whether it's search, display, retargeting, global display networks, or the different providers and how all those pieces stitch together is a steep learning curve to take on. In many ways, marketing organizations are becoming increasingly responsible for driving growth and the new acquisition of customers. Having a deep understanding of that and staying on top of it is really useful.

Steimle: Is there anything we didn't cover that you want to say about what it's like to be a CMO or about the CMO role?

Chen Rekhi: The one thing I would highlight is there's an incredible amount of change. There's an incredible amount of change taking place because of data in terms of the marketing function being much more proactive, leveraged, and impactful on the broader business organization and goals. A lot of it is creating the culture and having a good understanding of how data, marketing, and customer insights all come together and help the product and the organization reach the customer base. Because of that, there's no longer a playbook for being an effective marketer.

With someone who has lots of experience, there's a ton of value in terms of their ability to take apart a problem. There's a ton of value in terms of their ability to lead, manage, and run teams. There's a ton of value from the perspective of their being a great general manager of a business and understanding the fundamentals of how you guide a team, how you drive them, how you state clear objectives, and how you work well within organizations. That's absolutely key and critical to the job, but the nuts and bolts of making any one business successful are specific to that industry, that particular business problem, and those customers.

Part of being a marketer is being agile and adaptable rather than saying, "At my previous company, we did this channel, that channel, and this channel, and this was the playbook. I'm just going to carbon-copy it and move it here." It's about coming into an organization and saying, "Let me learn. Let me understand how customers experience a product. Let me understand the value, and let's take what I did at my previous roles and match them up. How is this different or the same, and what can be leveraged from my past experiences in a different way rather than simply copied and applied?"

That makes for a very interesting and fun challenge as a marketer in this present day. I also think there's a huge opportunity for marketing to be much more impactful and work more closely in the development and sale of the product.

Kieran Hannon

Chief Marketing Officer
Belkin International

Kieran Hannon has been CMO at Belkin International since May 2013. Prior to coming to Belkin, Hannon spent two decades focused on the mobile experience. During that time, he held various marketing roles at UBM Canon, Sidebar Inc., Cooking.com, and RadioShack Corporation, as well as a few startups. Hannon also served in executive and advisory roles at several advertising agencies, including Grey Group, Saatchi & Saatchi, and J. Walter Thompson.

Hannon attended St. Paul's College and has a degree in civil engineering from the Dublin Institute of Technology. In 2015, PR Week named him one of the Top 40 Marketing Innovators to Watch. Onalytica counted Hannon within the top ten of the Top 100 Influencers at CES 2016.

Josh Steimle: How did you get your start in marketing? What were the steps that led to where you are today as CMO of Belkin?

Kieran Hannon: I'm originally from Dublin. Growing up in Ireland, I had the opportunity to do a couple of different things. My father had a vertically integrated company which was ahead of its time, particularly in Ireland, where they designed, built, and developed commercial projects like shopping malls, government buildings, and large housing estates. He wanted me to take over the family business, so he encouraged me to study civil engineering, which I did, in college.

J. Steimle, *Chief Marketing Officers at Work*, DOI 10.1007/978-1-4842-1931-7_12

While I was in college, I was elected to be college sports president. I was also president of the Irish Intervarsity Swimming Association. Between those things, I was very involved in organizing swimming events in Ireland. While I was organizing and packaging the swimming events, I came to the attention of the brand manager for the European equivalent of Philip Morris, a company called Rothmans International. The brand manager and I met when I was working as a lifeguard during the summer. We got to talking, and he said, "Hey, I could really use someone with your skill set to work part-time during the winter on weekends and then go full-time in the summer with my promotions team."

Back then, the promotions team was the consumer demand, the sampling teams that go out with the product. What was attractive to me was not that it was a cigarette company, but that they were heavily involved in motor racing. They were the works Porsche racing team, rally endurance group racing teams and stuff. I was attracted to being involved in car rallying in Ireland and England. And Europe was huge. It was a dream part-time job. I learned marketing under the shadow of the brand manager who hired me, and I got much more interested in marketing. Our agency at the time was based out of London, and I enjoyed working with them as well.

When I finished college, I came to the U.S. on June 1, 1985. I came over on a work visa. I decided I wanted to go and work with an ad agency in San Francisco. From there, I spent about twenty years in the ad business in San Francisco, moving over to the client side in the early 2000s, where I was VP of marketing at RadioShack. I'm at the intersection of mobile, digital, retail, and tech, which is kind of my sweet spot when it comes to marketing.

I was CMO of Helio, which was one of the first mobile virtual networks. The very first smartphone in the U.S. That was sold to Virgin Mobile. I've done a couple of other startups. That brings me here to Belkin International, where I'm the first CMO the company has ever had. When I joined, they had one brand—Belkin—and as I was joining the company, they bought another brand—Linksys—in the networking Wi-Fi space. A year and a half ago, we launched another brand, which was a product under Belkin, but we pulled it as a stand-alone brand in the net home automation, smart home, connected home Iota space called WeMo. So now we've got three brands: Belkin, Linksys, and WeMo. We're a house of brands.

Steimle: How did your agency experience prepare you to be a CMO?

Hannon: The agency experience is extremely helpful for a number of reasons. Firstly, you have a service mindset because you understand. One of the goals of being a great account person and agency president is to understand the client's needs and to help them achieve their goals, so it made me able to ask those questions.

Secondly and most importantly is creativity. I love the creative output. I'm very involved in the creative output, so for me, the ability to understand, nurture, and champion great work that's meaningful with the end user, i.e., the consumer, has been a hugely invaluable part of my agency experience. Thirdly, most of the jobs I've been in on the client side have also involved in-house agencies, where we've done the best of both worlds—in-house agencies alongside external agencies helping us craft, build, and magnify our brands. Having had the agency experience and background working on the client side is immensely helpful with that as well.

Steimle: What does the marketing team you manage at Belkin look like?

Hannon: We're a privately owned company. It's a thirty-three-year-old brand. We're a billion-dollar-plus corporation. The founder and CEO, Chet Pipkin, who started the company in his parents' garage many moons ago, is the visionary, authentic leader you would want to work for. Chet and I were chatting, and he said, "You know, we've got a great brand," but he recognized the need to help harness the brand globally. That's why I joined the organization—to help bring a professional marketing structure to bear with strategy and so forth.

When I joined, we were a regional-led organization, meaning those three brands were managed at the regional level. Our European headquarters were in Amsterdam. That was the sales office that led all three brands across third channels. I managed global marketing and global customer care as well, but I was initially brought on board to help manifest global e-commerce and put the voice of the customer front and center in that conversation. We've evolved from being a regionally led organization to being a globally led organization with global strategies and priorities that are then executed regionally and locally in-market. We've undergone a major shift in how marketing has deployed globally. We're in the middle of finishing an implementation of the Adobe Experience Manager, which is a set of key tools that allow you to develop, create, and deploy marketing assets globally. That has two modules: the Digital Asset Manager and the Marketing Resource Management tool set, the MRM. That's one example of how we are being effective as a global organization in delivering, developing, and deploying comprehensive programs around the world.

Steimle: How can a CMO come into an organization that needs a lot of changes and get that job done without ruffling too many feathers?

Hannon: That's the toughest challenge because the body can reject the organ. If you're too aggressive, too harsh, too disruptive, the rest of the organization structure can shut down. As an organization, we've got a phenomenal culture, and that's been a real blessing in helping achieve our goals.

It's a three-year process. It's a crawl, walk, run. You have many success stories along the way that continually reinforce what you're doing. For example, one of the big projects I had on my plate when I joined was at CES of 2014. That was the most successful CES we had had as a company in terms of the recognition for our brands and products. Every year since then, CES has become a better and better show for us. We've won numerous awards for our three brands, not only from a products standpoint but also from a presentation standpoint—Best in Show for products and also one of the Top 10 Booth Experiences at CES. Those are the type of success stories we've had on the way, tangible results that point to a grounded brand and meaningful engagement.

In each of the brands, when we set up and manage the campaigns throughout the year, we determine what success looks like at each stage and how we achieve it. Being realistic, we're driving towards monumental successes that continually build towards the broader brand plan. That's a key goal.

Steimle: What are some of the KPIs you're measured on or are tracking for marketing at Belkin?

Hannon: There's a wide range of KPIs depending on the objective, but the one overarching KPI that we look at as a company universally is the Net Promoter Score. That's the most foundational KPI we look at. You achieve a result by the actions that you and your team take. Net Promoter Score is the one we track carefully across the board.

Then, there are the obvious campaign results: tracking to sales, campaign KPIs, conversion, engagement. Depending on the campaign goals, it could be—if it's a direct response—cost per order level-type goals all the way up to awareness, where we have ongoing tracking studies to understand not only brand awareness but brand comprehension. We use a wide variety of tools to track our KPIs.

We're a big believer in understanding user behavior. For the Belkin brand, we talk about people-inspired products. That's one of our visions for the brand. One of the ways we achieve that is we constantly do research. As an example, on-site, we have our own qualitative facility with a conference room for focus groups with our users, looking at and evaluating products, packaging, in-store presentations, and larger campaign and program elements as well. Consumer feedback is a big part of our core DNA, whether it's qualitative or quantitative.

We are always looking at that, shopper marketing, and in-store research. We're constantly looking at not only our brands but also our competitors, how they are engaging, and the consumer response. But, at the end of the day, it's a thirty-three-year-old brand for Belkin, a thirty-year brand for Linksys, and a three-year brand now for WeMo. Storytelling is hugely important for all three, helping people to understand and connect the dots between the devices and the experiences that they want to have and enjoy. That's what we're all about.

Steimle: What are the challenges a CMO faces in managing a global marketing organization? How do you handle the growth in emerging markets versus established markets? How do you modify your marketing to cater to different groups?

Hannon: It's interesting because markets can be evaluated in different ways. Obviously, e-tail in emerging markets has a bigger percent of people focused on it than there might be in other markets, where it's more established with the brick and mortar. E-tail is also a key part. You modify your distribution and your channel strategies based on those market needs, but at the end of the day, the ways people consume and enjoy our categories are similar worldwide. There's a commonality in how we talk about the end-user benefits to our products, and the storytelling is part of that richness in delivering those stories. The challenge in strategy is really the way it is tailored to those markets. It's the best of both worlds.

I have a marketing lead for each brand. They manage all the consumer touch points for that brand. We call it 360-degree communications. Those are mapped out for each brand, so we're ensuring a cohesive, consistent, yet flexible approach to marketing in each of our respective markets. It's a flexible yet preordained approach so that we're focused and effective at using the resources we have in deploying those programs.

Steimle: What's your philosophy on building and managing marketing teams?

Hannon: As a marketer, you have to have that innate curiosity. If you don't have it as a person, how can you be a great marketer? Understanding people, their needs, wants, and psyches, and how you connect is so critical. That's the number one rule. Have the curiosity. If you don't, then don't be a marketer. It's about the person. If they have the aptitude and attitude, most people can learn or be put in a position where they can be most effective.

With a team, you understand the strengths and weaknesses of each player, and you create a team that harnesses stuff in a complementary manner with everybody else. When I build out teams and I'm hiring people, I look to complement the organization, not duplicate it. It's a merry band of warriors. Each has their own distinct traits and skills that we harness, deploy, build, and grow. For me, that's the most exciting part: seeing people thrive, giving them the tools and resources necessary, but letting them win and make mistakes or try things out that might fail. That's fine once you learn from it and continue to grow.

We're big believers in helping people achieve their goals in an experienced manner. Each of the team members is active in that. The nice thing about our category is it's fast-paced, so there's no downtime. You don't have time to screw up. If you're not in the vein of what's happening, you're missing it. That's what we do. It's having the ability to be strategic and understand what's happening and constantly revisiting the objectives.

Are the campaign objectives aligned with the marketing and business objectives? Most people lose sight of the business objectives, sometimes even the marketing objectives, and you can have campaign objectives that are not aligned with those. You constantly have to be evaluating those and getting execution. The forest and the trees are both important when you evaluate things.

Steimle: There's a lot of competition for marketing talent these days. How do you attract and retain top marketing talent?

Hannon: By letting them be the best they can be; giving them the support, mentoring, and coaching that they need; and giving them the freedom to develop and grow themselves. We're big believers in everyone being an adult. We let people achieve their goals and their dreams in what they want to do. We never hold somebody back, so if you can achieve it, you will do it here. That's what we're here to support. It is important to have grounded people with self-awareness about what they can achieve, who are willing to help out.

I have one great example from when I was in the agency world. There was an account team on one particular piece of business that had multiple account teams. One of those account teams was staying late, working hard to get a deliverable out. One of the other groups was ready to go out—it was a Friday—and start enjoying the weekend, but what did they do? They put down their bags, came over, and stayed with the other team to help get the work done and be there with them. No one even had to ask them. That is a true testament to a great team and a great way of viewing their teammates and colleagues. They were there to help them out. That's when you know you've got a winning formula.

Steimle: What experiences have you had breaking down silos and ensuring communication across the organization?

Hannon: We've got a good planning process in bringing products to market. We call it E-squared. For each milestone in E-squared, marketing is very actively involved from their initial product concept development all the way to execution. That's a huge part of having everyone on the same page, setting expectations as we bring a product to market, and figuring out how that product fits into our overall priorities and focus.

Then, we clearly outline what we will be doing for that product as part of a certain launch. Categorizing products, creating stories around those products, and delivering those solutions is a huge part of it. Our team is actively engaged in understanding consumer behavior, so they're always out in-store, doing research and learning how users interact with products, whether it's the physical product itself or the content that people use to learn and understand the products.

A big part of our focus as we move forward is where the business is going, particularly for us in the consumer electronics space. The new form of content marketing is actually user reviews that are posted not only on our own sites but also sites like Amazon, Best Buy, and all the other global e-tail sites. Those are the new form of brand currency. People look to those reviews to understand the star rating for the product and then the actual quality of the review itself to learn more about the product.

We spend a lot of time helping our customers not only get access to those reviews in a timely, sensible way but in encouraging users to share the great news about products we enjoy. That's a great example of how content marketing is shifting. For example, sixty percent of all searches in the U.S. in the consumer electronics space now start on Amazon, not Google. Amazon is a media platform, not just a selling e-tail platform. The reviews and star ratings are a new form of media content. We have to think about that at every touchpoint as well.

Steimle: What are some other ways that digital marketing, mobile, data, and so on have affected marketing at Belkin?

Hannon: It's pretty phenomenal. I love it because of the instantaneous nature of the feedback and the ability to have a conversation with people without it being filtered, influenced, or tarnished. You get all the raw feedback in a very nice way. For instance, I'm very active on Twitter personally, outside of our brands. I have engaging conversations with people. We get great suggestions and feedback on products and channels in areas that we can improve. That's important. I love that.

If you look across our channels with our brands around the world, as a global organization, we probably have the most square feet of any brand in stores around the world. If you look at the square feet between our Belkin, Linksys, and WeMo brands, we probably touch more consumers than any other brand in our space globally. Just understanding that is an advantage for us. Those insights are huge.

If you look at programs of our key customers, for example, Target with their Target Cartwheel app, that's a huge monthly and weekly user engagement. Over ten million active users each week engage with the Cartwheel mobile app, learn about products, look at offers, and engage in that way, so there's no loss of opportunities for brands like us. Can you imagine ten million unique users every week, looking for your brand, wanting to understand the products you have available, and then engaging with it? It's a meaningful way to have that high-quality customer engagement. It's understanding the ones that have the most impact, the ones that our users want to engage with, and then fueling those fires. That's my job.

Steimle: Do you have any favorite books that have helped you to be a better CMO?

Hannon: One book that had a huge impact on me was *The Paradox of Choice* by Barry Schwartz.[1] The premise of the book is incredible. It debunks the myth that consumers want a wide range of choices. Actually, the more choices consumers have, the less they make a decision, and the less they buy. Having a

---

[1] Harper Perennial, 2005.

curated choice is important for them to be able to make a decision. That, for me, was quite foundational, quite eye-opening. It has great insight into human behavior, albeit it started in a time when there was less e-tail happening, but nowadays, it applies more and more to e-tail. That's why the recommendation engines are so important to brands like Amazon and how they can have related products to the purchase that you're making. It helps serve that up. That's why it's such a compelling proposition. Curated choice and helping people understand good, better, and best and what that means for them is so important.

Steimle: What are some events that you attend or organizations you belong to that have been helpful for you in your role?

Hannon: You have events that I would call vendor-sponsored, where essentially you are "brand-napped," for want of a better word—a new way of being kidnapped—where you're isolated and at their behest. They're pitching you, which I'm not a huge fan of unless you have a distinct need and have some vendors you want to spend time with.

Other than that, I always evaluate events based on the ability for me to promote my brands, to be able to talk about my brands one to one to many. With media in attendance, I can talk about the Belkin brand, about connecting people's experiences with the devices that they have. With Linksys, it's talking about the importance of Wi-Fi and how Wi-Fi is the center of your smart home. With WeMo, it's bringing your home to life in connection with all the wonderful devices that we have to create those experiences.

If I can promote the brand, it's not about promoting me whatsoever. It's about promoting my brand. That's my key litmus test. When I go to conferences, it's whether I can connect with those audiences and the media that will promote my brands. Beyond that, it's the quality of attendees and my peers that are there and where I'll have a chance to share and possibly do business. Business development is a big part of it. Some of the best conferences I've gone to are where we've come out of it and created great programs with someone we've connected with there.

Also, we're helping to position the brand from a thought leadership standpoint. As a marketer, I find the CMO Club invaluable. I'm on the advisory board of VentureBeat. VentureBeat has the Marketing.FWD Summit, which is equally good. That's primarily targeting growth brands and growth hacking, so it's a strong environment for growth brands.

There are a number of other conferences that target the data side of things that are good to go to. For the tech space, CES is a large presence for us. As an organization, it's quite a sizable focus for us, and it's a great way to engage with our customers and our brand, so we love CES.

For me, there are a couple of new conferences that have emerged over the last few years in the U.S. One in particular is called the Collision Conference. It started two years ago in Las Vegas from the people that brought you the Web Summit in Dublin, which is rapidly becoming the largest tech-startup conference in Europe. (In 2015), they had over 35,000 people out in Dublin. This year, Collision is happening in April in New Orleans. They'll have fifteen thousand–plus attendees. That's a great place to see startups, new products, new industries, and their collision, for want of a better word—it's aptly named. There's a collision involving all these things. MarTech, ad:tech, Fintech—all the various tech seats that you could be part of, you can see them at Collision. I find that highly stimulating. There's a wide range of other conferences all the way from social media and the various sub-functional areas of marketing as well as the e-tail conferences, iMedia. I look at the quality of attendees and what makes the most sense based on the business that I have, and decide from there.

Steimle: What do you see as some of the biggest challenges facing today's CMOs?

Hannon: One is the ability to find people who have that rare talent of being highly strategic and highly executional at the same time because of the speed of how business transacts, the demands on the business from our consumers, and the quality and content of information that they want us to be able to share about our brands. Being able to map to both of those is probably the most important trait a global marketer needs to have.

The second thing would be the ability to attract, retain, and motivate talent. That's hugely important because you're only as good as the quality of the people you have to bring it to life. Thirdly, it is being the full stack marketer. People should have the ability to work at all levels of the stack—all the way from classic direct-response techniques up to global brand-building capabilities, and mapping all that with great creative sensibilities. Those people are few and far between. Those are the people that are hugely successful marketers.

Steimle: What is one of the biggest mistakes you see CMOs today making?

Hannon: They let data drive all the decisions. Data is a great indicator, but at the end of the day, you have to wrap it around with broader human insights. This is oversimplified, but at the raw level, let's say I have a product that's currently being sold for twenty dollars. The data shows if I reduce the price to fifteen dollars, I would sell an immense amount more—increased volume, right? One would believe I should reduce the price to fifteen dollars, but guess what? What does that do to my gross margins? That's one great example. There's a lack of understanding it in the totality of what you're trying to achieve, and more importantly, what it says about the brand. How do users evaluate and see the brand when it's a fifteen-dollar price point versus a twenty-dollar price point?

Price is one of those key indicators that helps users evaluate where a brand fits into a category vis-à-vis its competition, because, as you know, if all things are equal, price is one way for people to understand if there's a higher value versus a lower value with that brand. There's a lot of science that goes into it, both hard and soft, and then the blending of the science with the art, both hard and soft. The combination of all that together is really critical to achieving, sustaining, maintaining, and growing the brand.

Steimle: What do you see as the future of marketing?

Hannon: I think it will be different in a hugely transformational way, which is the fourth industrial revolution that we're seeing right now with the Internet of Things. For brands today that have a one-to-one relationship with consumers, that's going to change because they will now have to understand how their brand relates to other brands as part of the experience a user is creating.

As an example, you could be a brand that has an appliance that's used for cooking. That cooking appliance can now be smart-home-enabled, where it can turn on and off, change temperature, and do different things based on a set of circumstances that are derived from the owner's behavior. What's the product? What are the ingredients? What's the end output of that appliance that people are cooking with? How your brand interacts with all of these other brands is going to be important, so I encourage people to revisit the brand architecture, putting the consumer front and center in that brand architecture and making it three-dimensional in terms of how their brand interacts with other brands that are related to that consumer's behavior. Having the pliability and flexibility with the brand DNA to engage, nurture, and be complementary to that user experience is going to be critical. People have no idea how this is going to change consumer behavior.

I'll give you an example. With the Amazon Dash button, you don't even have to go online to buy a product. You don't even choose it now. You know when you're ready, and you know you're about to run out. You just hit the button, and it automatically reorders. In a year's time, you're not even going to have to worry about that. It will understand that you're already low.

The beauty of it is it allows people to spend time doing the things that matter the most. You shouldn't have to worry about all those other things that are happening within your home when you're at lunch with friends or at sports practice with your kids. Did I remember to do this? Did I remember to do that? Did I turn off *x*? Did I leave on *y*? Are my kids home safe and sound? All of those things will now take care of themselves for you so you can enjoy living in the moment and have the peace of mind and reassurance that comes with that. That's going to be a wonderful thing.

Phil Bienert

Executive Vice President of Digital Commerce
and Chief Marketing Officer
GoDaddy

Phil Bienert began his corporate career at Ford Motor Company, where he served in various roles, including brand strategy manager. Afterward, he became senior manager of CRM, e-Business, and e-Retail at Volvo of North America, which was his first role in the digital world. He was then approached by Citigroup and AT&T, respectively, to digitally drive customer experience. Bienert started at GoDaddy in 2013 as executive vice president of Digital Commerce. He now serves as both EVP of Digital Commerce and CMO at GoDaddy until mid-2016.

Bienert has a bachelor of arts in history and Asian Studies from Georgetown University and an MBA from The University of Texas.

Josh Steimle: Give us an overview of your career. How did you get your start? What were the steps that led to you becoming the CMO at GoDaddy?

Phil Bienert: My career has been a heck of a lot of fun. My path was somewhat atypical for most CMOs. For a large part of my career, I tried to stay away from CMO roles, and I'll explain why. I started my career nowhere near the corporate world. After college, I lived in China for a while to teach English. I had been lucky enough to have a great college experience and I wanted to give something back to the world. I had studied a lot about Asia at Georgetown. I came back from China and started my "real working career," much like a lot

© Josh Steimle 2016
J. Steimle, *Chief Marketing Officers at Work*, DOI 10.1007/978-1-4842-1931-7_13

of GoDaddy customers. I was a small businessperson. I worked at a small company of about three people. We were helping other small companies to be successful.

At the same time, I started up a couple of little companies along the way—private equity, venture capital businesses—just little ventures here or there that I would run into in that consulting job. A lot of my career has been informed by thinking of business decisions like a small business owner, meaning these are decisions that have a financial impact—and if they don't, then we need to do something different. It also has to do with never thinking about a business decision as spending someone else's money, never thinking about personnel decisions of hiring and firing in terms of anything other than a personal thing, working with real people, impacting real people's lives.

I did that for a couple of years and then decided to get an MBA. I decided to get it based on advice I had gotten from a lot of folks that happened to be early mentors in my career. I'm a big believer in finding somebody who's had a career path that you admire and asking them questions, even if it's not as a formal mentoring relationship, and always trying to learn from somebody who's gone ahead of you. Based on that advice, I got an MBA, and from there, I really started my corporate career.

I started it in the automotive business at Ford Motor Company with an advanced fast-track marketing executive program meant to bring folks with significant non-automotive experience into the marketing organization. It was one of the first programs of its kind. Now, many corporations have it.

What was great about that experience is I was able to get a wide variety of both marketing and general management roles in my career across pretty much all of Ford's brands. I started in the corporate strategy in the customer service organization and went from there into product development, co-located with engineers working on a car, a product that would be sold in every market around the world. I was in the role that Ford called the "Jaguar liaison," meaning I was the Ford person at Jaguar representing Ford's interests there and representing Jaguar's interests back in Detroit. I learned a lot about brand and everything from market representation to brand management to M&A.

From that role, I went and helped start Ford's first advanced design studio in Southern California. I was the businessperson co-located with a bunch of engineers and branding people doing concept cars, retail redesign, and auto shows. I spent about a year and a half back and forth in Japan helping to rebrand the whole company there. I worked on a lot of unique and cutting-edge future projects and products in that role. After that, I was transferred. I was the second employee to go to Volvo after Ford purchased Volvo. At Volvo, I got my first real digital role. I had worked on the Volvo purchase. I put together all the sales, marketing, and distribution components of the pitch to the Volvo board, so I knew a lot about the brand, and that's why I was sent over early.

The job that happened to be open at the time that was senior enough for me was head of CRM and ebusiness. This was 2000, the early days of the notion of ebusiness and digital. We were right in the middle of the dot-com bust, and it was sort of counter-trend to say, "I'm going to go into digital," when at that time, people were declaring that the Internet was dead.

It's funny. I talk with folks that I've known over the years, and for those of us who stuck it out through today and always saw the potential of the Internet, even when people were talking about its demise, it was an exciting time to be there. This will give you some context for how I think and how I've managed my career. The power of digital, the power of the Internet, was never about the craziness of the late nineties, what I called the "dancing bologna days of the Internet." All you needed was to set up a website with a name that made no sense and put a picture of a dancing bologna on your home page, and you could get venture capital money. None of that ever made sense.

What always did make sense to me was that the Internet offered a direct way for the brand to communicate and have a relationship with customers. There's no in-between, no intermediary, no media company in the middle. Yes, there's advertising, but that ability to contact, remember, and respond to a customer directly lets you take advantage of the fact that it is, at its heart, a data-driven medium.

In the early days of the stuff we did at Volvo, it was taking that approach when everybody was, particularly in automotive, pulling out of their investments in online and digital. We were going all in, including doing the world's first online car lot, Ship Volvo, where we actually launched a car just with online advertising—no TV, no print.

This was all based on the fact that the data said it made sense. Our customers for Volvo tend to be highly educated with a high utilization of the Internet. It made sense for us to launch a car online. We were one of the first companies to do advertising in a video game. We did mobile advertising in 2002. According to *The Wall Street Journal*, we did the world's first integrated ad campaign in 2001, where we built a campaign to connect creative and tracking between TV, digital, email, print, and direct mail in 2001 during the NCAA basketball tournament. We did a lot of cutting-edge things to move the business forward in a way that nobody else in the industry was doing using the power of the technology, data, and platform.

There were a lot of things we were doing then that the automotive business uses today: the idea of pre sales, the idea of trying to sell a vehicle and get orders before it actually goes on sale. When we brought an SUV to market, everybody said we were late to the market, but by cultivating our CRM database, by using direct marketing, by using digital, we were able to sell out almost a year of inventory before the first TV ad ran. Now, most of the automotive companies go to market with digital first before running their TV campaign.

By the time I left Volvo, I was managing all the direct-to-customer marketing outside of mass TV and print.

From there, I had been bitten by the digital bug. I could have gone on to bigger marketing jobs and maybe even head of marketing or CMO types of roles in automotive or other places, but I wanted to stay in the digital world. A lot of things about marketing earlier in my career were not necessarily based on the types of business results that I like to track and measure—like the customer impact and the impact to the P&L, which did not appeal to me. There was a disproportionate amount of time spent on TV ads, awards, and other nice things, but I saw so much potential in where the Internet was going that I wanted to stay in.

I ended up being approached by Citigroup to come run the online function for their credit card business, which was the biggest part of their business. That was exciting for me because I tend to be wired to look for the "alignment of the planets" opportunities. The alignment of the planets opportunity there was that financial services was going through a massive transformation, digitally driving it, getting away from the branch, moving to online services because that's where customers wanted to go.

With the industry going through this transition and the opportunity to be at what was the largest financial services company in the world, the largest division in that company, and the person brought in to drive that change, I had to go for it. I needed to prove to myself that I could do what we had done in the automotive industry, that I could do it somewhere else. I always need to challenge myself to try something new and harder to see if I can do it, and that was one of those opportunities. We had a great run. We were able to make some huge strides growing the business through improving the customer experience and the digital platform.

When people ask me, "What is it you do?" I can give the title, but what I've done through most of my career is use the power of customer experience, personalize the customer experience—which you can do in digital platforms better than in most touch points—and grow businesses by improving the experience. We radically redesigned the whole digital experience at Citi. While we were there, we were able to shift volumes. Digital quickly became the number one volume platform in the company through those improved experiences. There was great P&L impact.

While I was there, I then started applying that to other retail businesses outside of cards. While I was in that business, I got contacted for another of these "alignment of the planets" opportunities from AT&T. The combination of things that got me hooked was wireless telecommunications going through a significant transformation, wireless growing, and digital growing.

AT&T had just merged with BellSouth to become the new AT&T, so it was pulling together BellSouth, SBC, AT&T, and Cingular. The role was to take all of these separate digital businesses and pull them together into one that made sense for customers anywhere in AT&T's business, whether there's a wire line or a wireless customer. It made sense to the business for the customers to take the experience to the next level. To go to what was the largest telecommunications company in the world and drive this for them was a pretty unique opportunity.

I was the first senior hire of the new AT&T at the time. The ability to use data to influence the experience has improved, and by focusing on personalizing the experience and being smart with how we advertised—with the largest digital ad budget in the country, maybe one of the biggest in the world, plus a pretty large online business—we were able to grow it from the hundreds of millions to the multiple billions in a short amount of time.

People ask, "What was behind it all? What was the secret sauce?" The secret sauce was using the experience. I remember the first time we turned on personalization in our logged-in experience and the instantaneous uptick in the business results, both on Net Promoter Score and on revenue. That was just the tip of the iceberg of where we were able to take that business. I had a great run there. They were all great companies and great experiences.

I joined GoDaddy a little over two and a half years ago. On the surface, it might seem counterintuitive to go to GoDaddy from running digital at AT&T, a multibillion-dollar business. What appealed to me about GoDaddy was what's under the surface. A lot of people have seen the Super Bowl ads, NASCAR, and things like that over the years, but this company is surely special. It's one of the only companies in the world that is singularly focused on helping very small businesses, these mom-and-pop businesses, the type of place where I started my career. We're helping them succeed and grow their businesses with our digital products and services.

To me, it's an incredibly personal and important mission because these businesses are the lifeblood of the global economy. They're small, but they're incredibly important, and helping them be successful is incredibly important. That's our mission. That's what hooked me. What also hooked me was there were a lot of things in this organization that reminded me of my time at Volvo. You walked the halls and could talk to anybody from a customer all the way up to the CEO. There's a sense of purpose. There's a sense of knowing why you come into work. At Volvo, it was because cars are driven by people, and they have to be safe. At GoDaddy, it's because these small businesses need help. They need someone looking out for them. That's what we do.

I came in as head of digital commerce for the company, which means running most of the channels, driving revenue, driving business results, and driving customer experience through those touch points, which we did early on. We redesigned and improved the digital experience. We improved a lot of things across a number of touch points. The addition of CMO to my role was a natural progression. I finally agreed to take the CMO role mainly because marketing has become a broader discipline. It has finally moved to where I always was interested because today, a CMO is a digital person. That's why it was such a natural thing to me—my interest in the ability to take data and operationalize it for the sake of customers, to give them the right message at the right time at the right place.

It's real and seamless now. I won't say addressable and programmatic TV is as seamless as, say, display advertising, but it's way closer than it was five years ago when I was telling companies or recruiters, "I don't want a CMO role. I want to stay in digital." Now, it's all the same thing.

GoDaddy is going through a number of changes and is transitioning to be a truly global company. We're in thirty-seven markets and seventeen languages, fully localized around the world—that's a new thing for GoDaddy in the last two years—while still making sure our marketing messaging reflects that feeling you have when you walk through the halls here.

Some of the messaging we've had in the past was, frankly, out there. It was certainly controversial. To be honest, if I'm looking at the data for the right reasons, it certainly got the company noticed, but it's not necessary now. We have eighty percent plus brand recognition, and that allows us to talk more about the mission and what we do every single day for our customers.

Our customers know us for being helpful. We'll sit on the phone with you for an hour until what you have is right. The chance to message that and to back up that messaging platform with a digital, data-driven approach is certainly an exciting part of our transition. We're a public company now. There're a lot of things that have been changing, and where we're going with marketing now is the natural next chapter for GoDaddy and for me in my career because it's the type of marketing I always wanted to do.

Steimle: What does the structure of your marketing department look like? How many people do you have? What do they do? How do the roles work?

Bienert: Every department, every team I've run has been structured a bit differently, but the way I tend to approach it is by cleanly compartmentalizing areas of accountability. I have a head of brand marketing responsible for the brand message, the brand voice, and campaign directions. I have a head of digital sales and marketing. We are an e-commerce company, so I have a person who is running that major portion of our business. I've got a head of online advertising. We're a digital company, so that digital advertising component and percentage of our marketing mix is much larger than if we were in, say, CPG (consumer packaged goods) or automotive.

We have somebody running our logged-in experience, our existing customer experience, and how we continue to take that experience to the next level for everything from account management to personalized messaging. We have a head of mobile. We have a head of pricing, which includes all the pricing in offer management around the world.

I have somebody running my technology and business operations, the actual text stack for the digital experience, as well as our business operations, keeping email running. The head of user experience, the head of design for the company, reports to me as well.

Steimle: What's your philosophy on building a marketing team?

Bienert: I always try to hire people who are not like me because I already know what I think. I try to get folks who have different and complementary skills. If I look at my direct report team, I have some folks who range from highly analytical to super creative to massively passionate about NPS and customer experience to folks who are just really sharp salespeople. It spans the full range of backgrounds, talents, and mindsets. Having that set of complementary perspectives is interesting.

My team right now is a mix of folks who have been at GoDaddy for a while, folks who are new to GoDaddy, folks who are new at GoDaddy but that I've worked with before, and many I haven't worked with before, which also is on purpose. I look for a diverse set of opinions at the table. I try to build a team dynamic where we can have heated discussions, where people are fine trusting and handing off things to other people on the team, but where we ultimately make decisions and move forward. I've worked on teams in my career where there was a lot of debating after the election. We like to have the election and then move forward.

Steimle: How do you attract and retain the top marketing talent? How do you get the people you want and keep them?

Bienert: It's about getting folks who believe in the vision we have. My vision for marketing here is to use the investments we've made in the people, tools, and technology behind data. Our CTO, Alyssa Murphy, is one of the best technical minds in the world. She's built all of our data platforms. We've hired some of the best data scientists in the world to take strategic advantage.

Our vision in marketing is to take advantage of this capability, these platforms, this ability to know our customers better than anyone in the world and bring them to life as they touch customers in the marketing mix. It's personalizing messaging, what I call transitioning to micro-funnels, meaning tens of thousands of message combinations to prospect and existing customers at any touchpoint.

That's our vision. That's where we want to take the company. We want to take the marketing discipline combined with a brand message that talks about what we do every day for small businesses. That's the vision of where we're going, and I use that vision as a recruiting tool.

There are a lot of talented people. I want talented people who come here, hear this vision, and just have to be a part of it. I want people who can get excited about what we're doing, who can have that empathy with these very small businesses, who want them to be successful, who want to use marketing and what we can do with messaging and the right message at the right time—which, by the way, is not always about buying something. Sometimes, it's advice: "Other small businesses like you at this stage have more customers come to their website. Give us a call. We want to help you." That type of message—that's marketing.

We're using the power of our technology to be there for the customer at the right time, whether it's a prospect or an existing customer, and that's what attracts people here. I get pinged many times a week from folks who want to join, and that's different from what it was a couple of years ago when I joined. At that time, you had to do the preamble of, "Let me explain. Here's what you may think about GoDaddy. Here's what the company really does." I can't remember the last time I had to tell that story because people are feeling it in the marketplace, and folks see the vision and want to be a part of it.

Steimle: Tell us more about how internationalization and globalization affect your job and what that means for you.

Bienert: It's something that affects pretty much every decision we make. Every decision we make today has to take into account that we're global now. The growth in this company going forward is going to come from markets outside of the United States. The United States is a huge market for us. We're still growing like crazy, but in recognizing that—whether it's campaign development, media planning, technology decisions, all of those—we have to take into account that the decisions we're making have to work as well in India, Brazil, Turkey, the UK, or Australia as they do in the United States. That's something new for GoDaddy.

Most of my career has been at companies that are global. I've spent a heck of a lot of time doing marketing work in markets outside the U.S. As much experience as I had, you go into the market like I've been doing the last couple of months, and you remember how much you forget. That's what that means for us. There are few decisions that are domestic-only decisions, with the exception of a local sponsorship or something like that.

Steimle: How do you make sure you're in touch with the customers in all these different markets and that you understand their needs and wants?

Bienert: We make sure that our own business is highly instrumented, meaning we can see at a granular level what's going on with the customers we have. We always start with the customers we know. We ask what those dynamics are. What products are they using? How are they shopping on the site? How are they interacting with us in different media touch points? We start with that, and then we do a lot of research, like in any other marketing organization.

There's nothing like actually going into a market, visiting the market, seeing what's happening on the ground, seeing customers in-market. It provides context that a report is never going to give you. It's not that we're putting the entire marketing organization on a plane and sending them around the world, but we are looking more and more at those types of opportunities to get folks immersed in key market dynamics.

We do a lot of stuff with technology using videos. We've done a lot of videos from our markets around the world, whether it's a focus group or recording a one-on-one conversation with a customer. We're using all those types of input to help ground the marketing organization on how different it is in every market in the world.

Steimle: What are some of the successful marketing campaigns you've seen lately? What's working today?

Bienert: It's interesting. The answer I'm going to give you is probably the answer I'll be giving to that question for the rest of my career in marketing, which is there's no one thing, because there's not any one campaign. We will be rolling out our newly named global brand agency, but if you look at the way we're operationalizing marketing, at any one time, we're doing hundreds and hundreds of things around the world.

I can point to the growth of the impact of social media on our marketing in Brazil, or I can point to some of the things we've been doing specifically with localized language in marketing in India, where they have multiple languages. Although Hindi and English are common, those regional languages are important to take advantage of. We've done some things with social and PR in Turkey. There's not any one thing.

We've seen success in connecting more of the dots across more touch points. In the past, a lot of our campaigns focused on the traditional above the line versus below the line, meaning online versus offline. As we've been more explicitly connecting the dots between the addressable touch points and the math touch points with messaging and implicitly building campaigns to feed different parts, different stages in the funnel, we've seen those results.

I'm happy about where we're going with programmatic TV in those markets where we can do it, particularly in the U.S. It's probably dissatisfying to hear the answer, "It's a bunch of different things," but it really is a bunch of different things. In the old days, the CMOs I observed managed the cycles, the rhythms of business in these big campaign cycles. The way it's going is about orchestrating hundreds of things all at once and using the technology to make sure that they stay in sync and that the customer, the individual customer, doesn't get messaging that is inconsistent from the brand. Ultimately, we're trying to communicate a consistent promise of what we're going to do for the customers and when we're going to do it for them.

Steimle: You mentioned working with an outside agency. How do you manage relationships with outside teams like marketing, PR, or ad agencies? How do you make sure those relationships are successful?

Bienert: GoDaddy has not traditionally worked with a lot of outside companies. It's something that's part of the DNA of the company—this drive for self-sufficiency. Most of the Super Bowl ads you've seen were done entirely in-house. We started working with ad agencies for the first time about three years ago, and we just named our first-ever global marketing agency for the full marketing mix—traditional and digital. We have the opportunity to set it up the right way, which is great. We're in the middle of kicking off and onboarding with TBWA, who we just named as our agency.

To get that right, I created a position to make sure we work well with our agency partners around the world. It's a senior person on the team, and it's worth having that type of role because those partnerships are so important. Done right, it's truly a partnership. It's truly an extension of the team, not this agency-client-vendor kind of thing. The best agency relationships I've had have been those where you get to a level of working where, to put it bluntly, you can call bullshit on each other. I've had those relationships. They've been incredibly successful because folks aren't worried about who the boss is. It's more about letting the best idea win, and you can argue it out, decide, move on, and make great decisions. That's how we're approaching onboarding our first true global agency partner.

Steimle: What do you see as the future of marketing? What are the trends? What skills do people need to focus on to be relevant in the marketing world of tomorrow?

Bienert: If marketers are not comfortable with technology and data, they'll have a hard time being successful. It really is the future. More and more, customers expect an experience from a brand that makes it feel like the brand is talking to them. The only way you pull that off is with creativity tied to technology. It's that blend. I don't think it's feasible to be creative *or* to understand the technology. It's about marrying the two to be successful.

When I'm interviewing folks, I always look to see how they can articulate what they've done for the customer, how they've taken data and insights to drive their decisions, and how the decisions ultimately made a business impact. That all gets to an understanding of using data to understand the problem you're trying to solve.

Steimle: What do you think are some of the biggest challenges facing today's CMOs?

Bienert: Depending on which survey you look at, the average lifespan of a CMO is eighteen months or twenty-four months. A lot of money flows through the budgets of a CMO. To me, the biggest challenge is being able to articulate to the company, to your board of directors, "Here's why we made the decisions we did. Here's what we did with the company's money to drive the business results."

The CMOs I see out there are either not comfortable or not empowered because of the org, politics, or whatever to truly be able to pull enough customer-touching levers to make that impact. It's hard to do it with just TV spots because a TV spot is not a direct response medium, even if it's DRTV. It's being able to show the impact by pulling the levers that touch the customer. More and more often, those levers are digital.

Defining the job that recognizes where customer experience is, where the marketing world is, is challenge number one. When I see friends or colleagues who have not made it to the twenty-four-month mark, it's generally been because they didn't understand the data or weren't in a position to respond to the business data in their span of control.

Steimle: What are some of the biggest mistakes CMOs today are making?

Bienert: I see CMOs making the mistake of spending more time answering internal questions than answering external questions, responding to what their peers, colleagues, and the internal narrative say instead of what the customer data says. It's easy to please your own employees or investors and miss the mark in the marketplace.

Thankfully, we don't have this at GoDaddy because our investors are also very data-oriented, and that's what has been a pleasure in my role as CMO here. Colleagues at other companies have a hard time when the marketing work is a product of the internal dialogue because it can be an arm's length from what is happening in the marketplace.

Margaret Molloy

Global Chief Marketing Officer & Head of B2B Business Development
Siegel + Gale

Margaret Molloy is the global CMO and head of B2B Business Development at Siegel + Gale. Before coming to Siegel + Gale in 2013, she gained experience as the CMO at Velocidi after holding a variety of marketing and customer strategy positions at Siebel Systems. Molloy has received a number of awards and recognitions, including being named by Forbes as one of the Top 5 Most Influential CMOs on Social Media and a Must-Follow Marketing Mind on Twitter in 2014. Molloy was in the top one percent of most-viewed LinkedIn profiles in 2012. In 2015, Molloy received the Executive Management CXO Award from SmartCEO.

Josh Steimle: Talk to us a little bit about Siegel + Gale. Who are your customers? What exactly do you do for them?

Margaret Molloy: Siegel + Gale is a global strategy design and experience consultancy. We help our clients design and deliver brand experiences for their customers. Our point of view is rooted in simplicity. We believe that simplicity pays. The brands we create and build and the experiences we deliver to our clients are predicated on the notion that they are seeking simplicity. By "simplicity," we mean experiences that happen at that gorgeous intersection of clarity and surprise. To create a simple experience, you need to be both clear and surprising, and for us, that's where the magic happens. That's been our perspective on how to build brands.

© Josh Steimle 2016
J. Steimle, *Chief Marketing Officers at Work*, DOI 10.1007/978-1-4842-1931-7_14

We've just issued our Global Brand Simplicity Index. You can find it on my Twitter and on Siegel + Gale's Twitter as well. The top line on the study is that simplicity pays. Not only is it desirable, but it pays for brands to provide simpler experiences to their customers. Specifically, customers are willing to pay more for simpler experiences. They're willing to recommend brands who provide simpler experiences to their friends, family, and connections. Also, the stock market performance of the top ten brands in our index outpaced the market indices for the past six years for which we've conducted the study. We firmly believe in the importance of simplicity, and clients who choose to work with Siegel + Gale support that perspective.

Steimle: What does the structure of the marketing department at Siegel + Gale look like?

Molloy: At Siegel + Gale, we have a combined marketing and sales department, which I head. We have a core team at corporate and we have colleagues in our regional offices with a dotted line to me but who also report to the heads of those offices in London, LA, and China. Within our marketing team, we have someone who handles PR and community management. We have colleagues who handle field marketing and events, colleagues who handle sales operations and proposal generation, and a colleague and his team who head all our content marketing. Finally, we have a number of colleagues who are focused on business development, whose jobs it is to win the right business for Siegel + Gale.

Steimle: What's your philosophy on building a successful marketing team?

Molloy: There's a lot of merit to having marketing and sales integrated within one organization. It leads to clarity and focus, and it's one tenet of my philosophy, that where feasible, marketing and business development should report into the same leadership. There should be one head. That's one philosophy.

The second philosophy is that communication matters. It's vital that everything marketing is doing is in the service of business development. The nuance to that is the subtlety between the long term and the short term. BD colleagues are incentivized to close deals, but the marketing team's incentives have a dual focus: to support business development in winning deals and that long-term horizon of building the Siegel + Gale brand, building our reputation. Sometimes that means marketing may do things and create content that is more indirectly in support of the sales cycle—for example, putting our literature and events content that closes business in that quarter. That's the tension. And there's a healthy tension between BD and marketing because of the time horizons of the different groups.

Steimle: What are the key metrics that you focus on?

Molloy: The model we employ is the sales funnel. We have metrics for every stage in that customer journey. From the awareness stage, we look at metrics like media mention, social media engagement—pretty classic measurements in that stage. At the far end of the funnel, we look at deals closed. We look at the types of deals, meaning the size of business won. We also look at our search performance because search can play a role in the nature of our business. Search is one important metric. We look at the source for all of our deals. We look, for example, at whether a deal comes from reputation, marketing source deals, or outbound engagement on the part of our BD colleagues. Those are among the metrics.

At the farthest end of the funnel, the advocacy stage, we also look at awards. Our business is conducive to awards, so we look at the number of awards won. We also look at the number of case studies we published because our business is inherently all about showcasing the work we do for our clients.

One of the metrics we're working on is the long-term value of a client. Keeping in mind that I run business development and marketing, I not only look at the size of the first piece of business a client has hired Siegel + Gale to do, but at how the client relationship has monetarily grown for the firm over the course of years. We look at everything from media mentions to social media engagement to activity measures like events, case studies, LTV, and the long-term value of the client.

Steimle: What processes do you have in place to make sure these team goals are aligned with the overall organization and the goals of other departments and parts of Siegel + Gale?

Molloy: I sit on the management team at Siegel + Gale, so I participate in our off-site management and have a role in setting the goals. For example, I have a voice in the conversation about which industry verticals we go after. We have quarterly meetings with leadership where we report back on the performance, the publications, the PR, and the event performance of the preceding quarter. We also publish a weekly update in the marketing department where we showcase—it's all about transparency—what we're doing. My marketing team sends a weekly email to all of our colleagues across the firm. We also have a monthly dashboard meeting where marketing and every other business head participates. We look at the metrics. For example, in another department, the metric is utilization. We're a services business, so my colleagues in different departments report on their utilization, whereas I report on the deals closed, the pipeline, the close rate, all of that. The processes are predicated on frequent meetings, transparent communication, and quantifiable metrics.

Steimle: How do you make sure you're in touch with your clients? How do you know you understand their needs and wants and are able to deliver them the kind of marketing messages that will connect with them?

Molloy: We do that in a couple of ways. A key success factor is that the marketing team has access to clients. Members of my team interview clients for case studies all the time. Other colleagues and my team are the business development people, so they are in touch with prospective clients day-to-day.

We host events frequently. We are in the middle of hosting The Future of Branding roundtable, a lunch series around the country, where we convene existing and prospective clients. The purpose of that is for us to listen and understand the conversation that's going on in the market around branding. Those events are attended by marketing and business development people.

We also actively watch the conversations on LinkedIn and other social media channels to understand what is top of mind for our buyers. Finally, both the marketing department and our practice colleagues go to marketing events that we don't necessarily convene. We're involved in the CMO Club and other organizations to make sure we're part of the conversations that matter—and conversation is a two-way street, obviously. While we have a point of view, we also have wisdom, I hope. I aspire to having the wisdom to listen and understand how simplicity applies differently in different companies and what's top of mind for our prospective clients. Our group is also quite active on social media to be aware of who the tastemakers are and play our role in that.

Steimle: How is marketing changing for an agency like Siegel + Gale? What's different today about the way you're doing marketing than it was three, five, ten years ago?

Molloy: The core elements are not materially different. The channels are different, but the core aspect of any professional services firm is around having a point of view, being differentiated in that point of view, and delivering excellent work to clients upon which you build your reputation. Those core elements, for any professional services organization, are critical. Another factor that's the same is a lot of our business is word of mouth. Good work begets other good work. Those dimensions are constant.

What has changed is the marketing tools at our disposal and the pace at which we use them. Content marketing is a big topic. We exploit that aggressively in promoting our points of view through every social channel, through our PR efforts, and through our search marketing optimization. That's a new mechanism at our disposal on the supply side.

On the demand side, what has also changed is that the buyer is much more sophisticated and knowledgeable by the time they come to Siegel + Gale seeking a branding agency. Because consumers can search and seek peer input, and because we all—including my peer agencies—put out great content, the client is much more educated than ever before. When they come to us, whether it's in a pitch situation or similar, they have a lot more knowledge. We need to be more sophisticated and go deeper in the answers we provide them as we advance them through the relationship from prospective client to happy, engaged client. The tools have changed, and the frenzied pace of the pitch has changed. Often, clients need to make decisions faster or have more urgency, but at the end of the day, there are a number of facets that haven't changed.

Another obvious but perhaps neglected aspect that hasn't changed is the need for chemistry. In our business—professional services—clients are buying people. We need to offer them the smartest and most appropriate people to help drive them and their business forward. At Siegel + Gale, we are maniacally focused on being three things: smart, nice, and unstoppable. We endeavor—not just in the marketing department but across the firm—to live those values every day. We've learned that if we hire people who are smart, nice, and unstoppable and put those colleagues in front of clients, we do well. That hasn't changed since our firm was founded over forty years ago.

In fact, any professional services business is about getting to a scenario where a client finds someone with like values but different expertise. That's the success. In finding a firm to partner with, you're looking for people who have deeper expertise in something that you don't, but who share your values. That combination of different expertise and shared values is what makes magic happen for our clients at Siegel + Gale.

Steimle: Can you describe a somewhat typical day for you—what your day entails, the types of meetings you go to, what types of interactions you have with other teams?

Molloy: I typically start off the day looking at social media feeds to understand what is topical from a branding perspective and the CMO's perspective as well as general business news, whether it's looking at mergers and acquisitions news, splits, or what have you, because they are all drivers of our business. I often have team meetings with various colleagues, whether it's to discuss an event we're planning, PR coverage, or a piece of content we're working on for a report or study. Those are all meeting scenarios with the individual or colleague who's leading the effort.

Other key meetings would involve teams here at Siegel + Gale from the different practices. For example, if we're about to do an event focused on our naming business, I would be involved in a meeting with the head of the naming department—to understand how he wants to focus that content and who the right attendees are—as well as my own colleague in the marketing department who will execute the event.

Another typical meeting would be with a business development team member to understand his or her pipeline of deals and to talk about how we're going to advance a particular deal. Often, that means pitch preparation or pitch rehearsal. We're about to go into a pitch, rehearsing the roles in that pitch, talking together to come to consensus with all the participants about the content we would show in that pitch.

Depending on the day, we'll have conference calls with colleagues either in London, LA, or China to understand their business and marketing priorities and to help provide guidance to support their attainment of their regional business goals. More often than not, it could include speaking once a week.

That could mean putting in a speaking engagement, going to a conference for a couple of hours, talking to guests at conferences, moderating a panel. Participating in speaking is a frequent activity. Maybe three nights out of five, I go to some event in the city and meet other CMOs, business leaders, or clients in a networking situation.

Steimle: You mentioned the importance of having a point of view and getting it out there. Talk a little bit more about the importance of thought leadership in content marketing at Siegel + Gale.

Molloy: Content marketing is the cornerstone of our marketing plan. Within content marketing, we have point of view. Specifically, the thread that goes through everything we do is simplicity. We believe that great content for our clients happens at the intersection of three variables: the topics the client is interested in, the topics the PR world or press is curious to have insight around, and our business development goals. If it were a Venn diagram, it would be those three circles. We ask ourselves these questions about every piece of content: Does it support our business development goals? Is it something the news media or other PR outlets are interested in? Does it answer actual client questions? That's the framework that informs our content.

When it comes to form factor, we look at making sure we diversify across platforms. Within the past year, we started publishing a number of videos because we found the engagement with video content is much greater than with written content, and frankly, they're internally easier to produce because some colleagues love going on video. It's easier to get them on video than to get people to pen an article. We try to cover all our bases from a form factor perspective. We've got video, and we have byline articles, like how-to articles on third-party properties. We maintain our own blog property. We publish ebooks and studies like the Global Brand Simplicity Index.

What's important in all of this are three things. Number one is that the magic of simplicity must go through all of it. It must be on-brand for Siegel + Gale. Every piece we write, every video we publish, every graphic we create, every slide share deck we perpetuate must have that valid simplicity. We're strict about that.

The second thing is we try to achieve balance across the different practices. At Siegel + Gale, we have ten different practice areas ranging from naming to research, design, content, communications, etc. We have to try to attain balance to make sure every practice is represented proportionate to the business opportunity.

The third factor is that we optimize the different form factors—that balance of video, long-form articles versus short-form articles, ebook versus tweet, SlideShare versus LinkedIn post, blog versus quote—opportunistically with the press. Those are the three vectors we try to balance: simplicity branding, representation of each practice area, and optimization of the different form factors and platforms.

Steimle: You mentioned the international scope of Siegel + Gale. Talk a little bit about globalization, internationalization, and how you're approaching the world as your marketplace.

Molloy: Siegel + Gale is a global firm. We've offices in London, Shanghai, the Middle East, New York, and LA. A lot of our clients are global companies too. We may commence a relationship in New York, but we may do work in China for a division of that company there, or we may localize our work. I don't mean the marketing department. I mean the actual client delivery. For example, our China, New York, and London teams all worked on a project for a client of ours that went live last week. Clients increasingly have an expectation that you have a global footprint.

In terms of the marketing, my team, for example, has both field marketing and business development colleagues in London and China. Their job is to understand the nuances of their market, take content, tweak it for the region, and come up with themes that are still on-brand for Siegel + Gale but are relevant for their market. We have a video series called *Brand Matters*. That series shows my colleagues in the different departments talking about their specializations—for example, a researcher, a designer, a content creator. We create this one entity, this series called *Brand Matters*, but the protagonists are featured from different regions. Two weeks ago, we shot *Brand Matters* in China. My colleagues went to London and shot a whole series of videos for *Brand Matters*. We have representation to reach the nuances reflected in the content.

Steimle: What do you see as being some of the biggest challenges facing today's CMOs?

Molloy: Marketing is a people business, so the biggest challenge is around talent: finding it as you identify it, retaining it, motivating colleagues, all the while making sure they're people who know how to continually learn because marketing is changing so fast. Hiring colleagues, retaining them, exciting them, and making sure they learn because the skills are becoming so finite and specialized—that's the most critical challenge facing marketing today, and it's even more acute than in the past.

The second challenge is making sure the profession of marketing is perceived as strategic. That's been called "making sure marketing has a seat at the table" and "marketing within your organization." We've made a lot of progress in the profession in the last decade with marketers being strategic—senior marketers taking on roles at companies, marketers who have a strong strategic background being elevated—but that's still a challenge, making sure people understand marketing and its strategic intent and not merely the tactics and the platforms.

The third challenge for all marketers is to be simplifiers. Marketing is a complex science and art form. Will marketers know how to distill what matters, make prioritization choices, and communicate the merits of those choices and the action and exclusion platforms for their colleagues within the marketing department, the rest of the firm, and externally? The challenge is to be able to simplify. That's the biggest challenge facing marketers in a world with so many choices and so much data—not to lose sight of the strategic aspects of the profession married with the storytelling, all the while simplifying it. That's what will set great CMOs apart: their ability to simplify.

Steimle: What do you see as some of the biggest mistakes that CMOs today are making?

Molloy: I don't like the word "mistake," but learning opportunities, maybe. Generally, one of the biggest mistakes is not trying something new and piloting. I commend CMOs who pilot and try new programs. The biggest mistake is making things too complicated, hiding behind big data, or being paralyzed by the bountiful nature of the channels that are out there and not doing much creative on any one of them, or not really—and I see this from my conversations with CMOs in general—getting back to the basics around their brand and understanding their brand purpose. That is the biggest mistake—getting caught up so much in the tactics and the whirlwind and losing sight of the brand purpose of the organization and why their firm exists. It's important to be a real steward of your brand and hold your colleagues in delivery, customer service, and retail, accountable for creating a substantially fabulous brand experience for the customers.

Steimle: You mentioned the CMO Club. Are there other organizations, like peer organizations, that you're involved with? What's the value of being part of these organizations?

Molloy: The CMO Club is probably the most interesting. I'm also a member of the Harvard Business School Club of New York as a peer academic group. Marketing is a social experiment. You can enrich your understanding by talking to peers in a candid, honest, and open way. I get tremendous value from talking to my peers about what's working and what's not. Also, because we sell to marketers, I get tremendous value listening to what's keeping them awake at night and map that to how Siegel + Gale can help them. To me, the events and clubs I'm involved with are powerful—obviously, I've won a lot of clients through them and made a lot of friends, but it's really because marketing is a social activity.

Steimle: Other than the CMO Club, are there any CMO-specific organizations or events that you highly recommend?

Molloy: I get invited to a lot of digital events by being asked to them in the social media realm. As an agency, it's tricky because when we get invited to events, it usually requires sponsorship. Recommending people makes me a little uncomfortable because it's usually pay to play for marketers because we sell to marketers. Sometimes, it means I don't go to events that look great because I don't think it's worth a large check from Siegel + Gale. I love in-person events, and I do a lot of them, but there's a lot that can be appropriated from being active on Twitter virtually and watching what CMOs are sharing. In spending time engaging with other CMOs—even if it's not in person—I find that if you work hard to get to know someone on social media, when you meet them at an event, you know them so much better. It's a much more advanced conversation. When I think events, I also think of virtual platforms like Twitter.

Steimle: Is there anything in your background not directly tied to marketing that has been directly beneficial to your role as a marketing professional?

Molloy: I grew up on a farm in Ireland, which instilled in me a work ethic that certainly helped me as a marketer. It also instilled in me a curiosity about other countries and other people. Anyone who's an immigrant, who has come to another country and left their own, has a natural curiosity, and curiosity is such an important skill as a marketer.

The Irish thing is material, but perhaps the immigrant thing is more so. Coming into another environment makes you sensitive to that environment, and sensitivity and empathy are powerful skills for a marketer. To be concrete, it's almost like in biology. If you take an animal out of its habitat and put it in another habitat, it creates a certain awareness on the part of that animal that instigates a survival instinct. They're more aware of their environment, and they're more curious and more attuned to the various cues of that environment. In the same way, if you go from one country and choose to live in another that's so vastly different, it invokes your curiosity. It helps you develop empathy for others who may find themselves in disparate situations, and it makes you always challenge yourself and never be complacent. If you self-select to come to New York City, you're obviously motivated to be in a new environment, you're curious, and you're hardworking. I think those skills serve me well as a marketer.

Steimle: Where do you think marketing is going over the next ten to twenty years? What's the future of marketing?

Molloy: Well, I'll take out my crystal ball and polish it up. Brand is so important, and recently, it's become a new focus. The notion that a company needs to understand its purpose and what it stands for is an important back-to-basics thing. It's having a renaissance. I think that will continue into the next decade. Also, marketing is going to be much more about experiences. There was a time when marketing was about advertising and broadcast media, and even branding was about words and pictures. Now and into the future, marketing's job will be creating experiences that inspire buyers and inspire a community.

Also, marketing in the future will be much more strategic. You will see more heads of marketing running companies because of that ability to understand such a wide variety of data from the analytics to the ability to tell a story. Those skills will mean that you will see many more marketers in the CEO seat, which will bode well for customers because great marketers have an appreciation for the customer. The consumer will win if the CMO becomes the CEO.

Steimle: Is there anything we didn't cover that you think is important to communicate about the CMO role?

Molloy: There's never been a more exciting time to be a CMO or even to be in a marketing organization. There's a confluence of diversity of channels, an availability of technology that enables data-driven decisions, and the imperative to be an engaging storyteller. Those demands render the profession so exciting right now. I entered marketing twenty years ago. Twenty years ago, we didn't have the data we now have to know what's working and what's not in our campaigns or general efforts. Nonetheless, I am a huge proponent of data. I'm also a huge proponent of great storytelling, being from Ireland, where storytelling is important in our DNA. There's a marriage of availability of great data to make informed decisions plus the capacity to tell great stories. There is no other profession that gives you the ability to use both sides of your brain at the same time and use them together and not separately. It's a wonderful time to be in marketing.

If marketers apply themselves strategically and commit to continuing to learn, they should and will be the CEOs of the future because if you can understand great data, make informed business decisions from data, and at the same time tell an engaging story that inspires others to act, what better qualities do you need to have as the CEO? There is no better career path for people who want to make a difference. When I was in business school a decade ago, I don't know that people saw marketing as the path to the C-suite. Today, we can see it's a logical path if the CMO is desirous of that role. Great marketers play great roles at their companies. It's an inspiring time to be in the role.

Marketing is a very social activity, and there is nothing more social and more important than hiring the right team. Try to spend as much time thinking about your people and creating environments that are inspiring for them as you spend time talking about big data. At the end of the day, you need people to interpret the data and ask the great questions of the data while technology is advancing in leaps and bounds, and it will only get better.

The human factor is so important to delivering great business benefits to your firm. If you love people and data in equal parts, you're in a great place as a marketer. The other thing I would emphasize is this whole notion of being a simplifier. Here, we often joke that my job as chief marketing officer is also as chief simplicity officer. I think all great CMOs, whether they play with that or not, are also the chief simplicity officers of their organizations because they need to pick the voice of the customer information from the market, marry that with the creativity and the storytelling, couple that with the big data they're getting from their systems, and ultimately simplify it so people don't get paralyzed and can actually move to execution.

The final thing I would say in general principle is that execution is the ultimate differentiator. You can have as many fabulous ideas as there are raindrops falling, but unless you can pick an idea with confidence and execute, you won't see the benefits. I've talked about marketing being a place where there's a confluence of data and creativity, but it's also a process function. Having clarity of purpose is what dictates execution. If you have a pathway and can bring others along on that journey, then you're essentially executing. It's not enough to be a great data analyst, although that's essential. It's not enough to be a creative storyteller, although that's helpful. You must also be a process engineer because otherwise, great ideas and great analysis don't ever see the light of day. People often underestimate the role of execution.

Tom Buday

Global Head of Marketing and Consumer Communication
Nestlé

After over 25 years of experience at Nestlé in the pet care category, **Tom Buday** *became the company's Global Head of Marketing and Consumer Communication in 2008. In his current role, Buday is responsible for defining and embedding best practices in brand building and consumer communication as well as for setting strategic direction for the Nestlé corporate brand. Prior to that, Buday served as VP of marketing of Nestlé's Friskies Petcare Division for four years in the U.S. before becoming European Marketing Director of Nestlé Purina. Buday holds a BS in marketing from Penn State University and an MBA from the University of Cincinnati College of Business.*

Josh Steimle: How did you get your start? What were the steps that led to where you are today?

Tom Buday: I got my bachelor's degree in business with a marketing emphasis from Penn State in 1980. At that time, I was focused on consumer research. I ended up going straight to graduate school at the University of Cincinnati where I received my MBA with a marketing research and quantitative analysis focus.

© Josh Steimle 2016
J. Steimle, *Chief Marketing Officers at Work*, DOI 10.1007/978-1-4842-1931-7_15

After graduating from UC in 1981, I started my career with Procter & Gamble in Cincinnati where I stayed for two years working in consumer research. I then moved to Los Angeles for personal reasons, so I interviewed with a few companies there and ended up with Carnation Company. At the time, Carnation was a mid-sized food and beverage company, primarily U.S.-focused. About a year after I started there, Carnation was acquired by Nestlé.

At Carnation, I continued to work in consumer research, and more specifically in pet care, a business I fell in love with because my wife and I are passionate dog lovers and owners, and because it's just a fascinating category. I did consumer research in pet care for five years and then moved into marketing, as I wanted to get more involved in operational decision-making and running a brand. I did that still within pet care and gradually worked my way into the position of head of marketing for what was called the Friskies pet care division of Nestlé USA. That was in 1995.

Four years after that, I had my first opportunity for international experience, relocating to Nestlé's global head office in Vevey, Switzerland as marketing manager in what Nestlé calls a strategic business unit, or SBU. SBUs in Nestlé are charged with defining long-term strategy for a particular product category. I worked in the pet care SBU for three years and was actively involved in the project team that put together the business rationale, financial valuation, and the plan to acquire and integrate Ralston Purina's pet food business. Until then, Ralston Purina was a competitor of ours. After the acquisition in 2000 I worked on integration and then ended up moving to St. Louis with what became Nestlé Purina Pet Care, the combination of the two pet care businesses.

Less than a year later, I was asked to come back to Europe as marketing head for Nestlé Purina Europe, a position I held until 2008. I spent 25 years in pet care and enjoyed it immensely, not least because we were—and still are—singularly focused on creating richer lives for pets and the people who love them. And, because we did it well, our pet care business grew substantially and made important contributions to Nestlé's financial performance.

In 2008 I was offered the opportunity to take my current job, which is global head of marketing and consumer communication for Nestlé. Leaving pet care was not an easy decision but this was an opportunity I couldn't pass up.

We tend not to use the term "CMO" at Nestlé, at least not at a global level, partly because we're so decentralized—more so than perhaps any company even close to our size in food and beverages—which means a lot of the marketing decision-making authority is local.

Steimle: Is there anything in your background not directly tied to marketing that has been beneficial to your role as a marketing professional?

Buday: I was focused on consumer research early in my career. I've always had an affinity for data and analytics, and developed that affinity naturally at an early age, well before anybody was talking about big data. It turned out to be a useful area in which to develop competencies given the explosive growth in data-powered brand building.

Even more off the beaten path from marketing is my dog and animal-loving nature. When I was a kid, I wanted to be a veterinarian and was convinced that was my future. Lo and behold, many years later, I stumbled into the pet care business but from a completely different angle. I have an inherent love for everything about the pet-owning experience, so working in a category centered on enriching these experiences was fortunate. I understood and embraced the mission of my business unit every day, and was highly motivated by it. That was a stroke of good luck, and sometimes, I wonder what would have happened had I started my career working on brands that I had less innate passion for. Perhaps I would not have even stayed in marketing. Luckily, job opportunity, personal passion, and conviction overlapped, and I was more satisfied and more productive as a result.

Steimle: It sounds like you and your department act as marketing consultants to the rest of these individual units. Is that correct?

Buday: "Consultant" might be too soft a word because it implies a service that clients can use or not depending on their need. Our best practice implementation is a bit more institutionalized than that. We have an operating platform called "Brand Building the Nestlé Way," and it's exactly what it sounds like, similar to the platforms some companies in our peer group use. Unilever has one. P&G certainly does. Diageo has their approach to doing things.

We spend a lot of time thinking about the nitty-gritty but important details of successful brand building: selecting target consumers; deeply understanding them; identifying the problems or tensions in their lives that we can solve with our brands; developing brand communication; getting the best from our agency partners; winning in social media; and delivering content and communication that's attractive, rewarding, and business building. The approaches to doing those things should of course be simple and efficient, but equally, they must be managed professionally and rigorously.

We believe that, while there is no one best way to do things, there should not be wide divergence across Nestlé in how fundamental brand building tasks are carried out. And, while there are certainly no guarantees when it comes to marketing or brand building outcomes, there are ways of working that increase the odds of success, and it's on these "best practices" that we focus our energy. The way we interact with colleagues is consultative, but it's not a take it or leave it proposition. We have a Nestlé way, and we expect our people as well as agency partners to adopt it, or to propose a better way if they see such opportunity.

Steimle: How do you take the lessons you learned from all your years of experience in the pet food industry and apply them to the diverse mix of products at Nestlé?

Buday: Luckily, the "Brand Building the Nestlé Way" philosophy applies across product and service categories, even if small adaptations might be required. That includes categories as diverse as ice cream and confectionary on one extreme and Nestlé Health Science, which offers nutritional solutions for people with specific medical conditions or predispositions, on the other. We have found that the fundamentals of successful brand building are fairly universal.

Steimle: You mentioned that you took the opportunity to work overseas. How critical do you think that international experience was for rising to a top marketing role at Nestlé? And how important is international experience for today's CMO?

Buday: At Nestlé, it's very important. Because we're headquartered in a small country of eight million people, we tend not to have the domestic bias companies headquartered in big markets like the U.S. sometimes have. We are a truly international company. Taking international professional assignments is in fact very much part of the Swiss mentality and culture.

Moreover, food is a category where local insights, culture, and habits are a lot more important than, for example, with technology products or even personal care, which tend to be more similar in consumer motivations and usage patterns from country to country. When it comes to cooking aids, coffee, tea, or even ice cream, local preferences, culinary habits, cooking routines, and flavor affinities really matter. You have to get the local dimension right, and it's pretty hard to understand what that means unless you've been around a little bit. I can't speak for other companies but for us, this is critical.

Steimle: As far as decentralization goes, how do you make sure that lessons learned in one part of Nestlé don't have to be relearned from scratch by another part?

Buday: It's a continuous opportunity and challenge, and I think we get better by the day, but still, there's lots of opportunity to get better.

Steimle: Do you have any specific processes in place to manage that or to encourage sharing between groups?

Buday: One of the big advantages of "Brand Building the Nestlé Way" is that more than anything, it's a philosophy. It's a set of beliefs about how to put the odds in your favor. Behind it, of course, are tools and processes, but at its most fundamental level, it's a set of convictions that takes only about five minutes to read. It's not overly complex.

We also felt it was important to establish a consistent vocabulary across our company because we have a lot of marketing people, not to mention agency partners, involved with brand building across Nestlé. Consider that we have about 2,000 brands, most of which are local.

If we don't have a consistent vocabulary, we waste time trying to communicate with each other because we're using the same words to mean different things or different words to mean the same thing. When we say "big idea," that's our terminology for a high-level, creative idea. Everybody in Nestlé gets that. When we say "core insight," everyone in Nestlé knows what that means. Vocabulary consistency is a huge time-saver. That in itself doesn't empower sharing, but does make it a lot easier and more efficient.

Then, we have various sharing platforms, the most recent being an internal social media platform called Chatter, which is a Salesforce.com product that we've adapted to Nestlé's reality. We've been using Chatter for three or four years now and have learned a lot about the benefits of a less structured communications and sharing approach, as compared to traditional meetings, emails with restricted distribution lists, and more hierarchical communication.

There's still a role for those things, but the internal social media network has allowed people to share in more natural and human ways, similar to the way they share in their personal lives. We've seen that a social media approach to sharing tends to bring people together who share common interests, challenges, or problems. You see these natural communities forming that wouldn't otherwise have formed if we were to remain slaves to fixed distribution lists. That's been an insight and a breakthrough for us, but we keep trying to work that harder to make sure we get maximum sharing value out of it.

Steimle: How can CMOs work better with other executives, with the CEO and so on? What's the structure of communication between you and other executives, and how do you make sure your objectives and actions are aligned with those of the overall organization?

Buday: I report to an EVP, who reports to the CEO. I'm two levels below the CEO but have an open and productive relationship with him. My boss runs marketing, sales, and all the strategic business units that I mentioned earlier. He and our entire Executive Board do a good job in my view of articulating the company's priorities.

Steimle: How does a one hundred fifty-year-old company adjust to the new reality of social media and digital marketing? How do you keep the core fundamentals while adjusting to the new tools that are changing consumer behavior?

Buday: There're two relevant and timeless fundamentals here. One is to make sure our communication content is attractive, rewarding, and business building. The business-building part should be no surprise. The attractive and rewarding part is worth getting into more deeply.

We feel that that successful brand communication, regardless of channel, has to be attractive. The notion of chasing consumers across contact points, trying to surround them so they have no escape route from our communication, doesn't work today, if it ever did. Consumers are in absolute and total control of their content consumption experience and will avoid or reject messaging that's irrelevant, annoying, or uninteresting.

That wasn't radically different thirty years ago. While it's true that consumers back then consumed publisher or broadcaster and brand content a bit more passively, they always had the ability to tune us out, simply by closing their eyes or ears, stepping away from the TV and walking into the kitchen. There were lots of ways they could ignore us and this has not changed.

So the notion of attractive brand communication has always been relevant, but it's mission critical today. Consumers, particularly in younger generations, have no patience for communication content that doesn't warrant their attention, and they'll make this judgment in a fraction of a second.

Then if we succeed in getting them to invest three minutes, thirty seconds, or three seconds of their time with us, we need to reward them. They need to feel somehow that it was worth their time. That means we need to inform in a way that is useful to them. In some cases we need to entertain and provide content they feel good about sharing with others. Bottom line, we need to make it worth their while, otherwise, they won't come back.

We're in product categories where one-off communication, one-off engagement with consumers won't build our business. We need repeated opportunities for brand and consumer encounters, and therefore must reward them in each encounter so that they feel good about coming back.

Of course, we need to drive business impact. We are not purely in the content business. For us, content is an enabler to selling wonderful experiences with Nescafé coffee, Nespresso, KitKat chocolate, or Purina pet care. That's where we make our money. Our content has to be attractive and engaging, and that increasingly means it has to be entertaining or at least useful. It has to be worthy of consumers' attention and compete effectively against all the content out there. Then, unlike publishers, we have the additional commercial obligation of making sure that our content, directly or indirectly, sells more coffee, more cat food, more chocolate or ice cream. It's a huge creative and communication challenge.

We've always believed in communicating with consumers when and where they're receptive to our brand message. We've never subscribed to the notion of a 360 communications plan, this naïve notion of surrounding the consumer in every conceivable contact point, which never made sense because consumers don't live 360 lives. They live their lives. Even if you understand the contact points your consumers are engaging with, they are not necessarily receptive to a message from our brand on each of those contact points at any time of the day.

We encourage our people to work hard with their agency partners in understanding at what moment of the day and in what communication or social channel might they be most receptive to a message from our brand. We work hard to prioritize our media investments on those receptivity moments, which could be on Facebook, Twitter, at point of sale, or on traditional TV media.

Steimle: What is the structure of the marketing team you work with directly?

Buday: The team I'm directly responsible for is about thirty people, but to put that number in context, there are a lot of other global marketing people sitting in specific product categories—the coffee and beverage global marketing people, the confectionary global marketing people, the ice cream global marketing people. Then, we have marketing people at the local level.

Steimle: What are the typical daily activities or projects your team is working on to support these other organizations?

Buday: We do ongoing training of marketing people according to "Brand Building the Nestlé Way." We travel the world or train remotely. For new people, we do webcasts to teach, remind, and refresh the way we go about things. We bring that to life with examples to make it tangible. A lot of it is capability-building efforts.

At another level, we do operate as advisors, which means we get called in to help markets or business units solve particular business challenges. Maybe they've not been able to crack a particular communication brief. Or they're struggling to define the most appropriate target consumer. Maybe they have their target consumer defined but haven't been able to uncover a core relevant tension or a problem in the consumers' lives that the brand can resolve. Or they haven't figured out how to properly define their brand essence. My team gets involved in helping them work their way through those challenges.

Steimle: Is there any one story that stands out where you were able to get involved in assisting a brand or turning a brand around?

Buday: I'll talk about two examples. The first one, KitKat, was about contemporizing it for the new reality of digital and social media while staying absolutely glued to its historical fundamentals. The KitKat iconic product design, the four-finger bar of wafer and chocolate, has remained the same for I don't know how many years. The iconic packaging and logo have also remained essentially the same. The core fundamental selling proposition of KitKat, which is about bringing a smile to your break—the slogan is "Have a smile, have a KitKat"—has remained consistent as well for a long time. What has rapidly changed, thanks to the leadership of our global KitKat team, is the way the brand engages with consumers to bring that proposition to life when and where they're receptive based on a deep understanding of how the target consumers are living their lives.

To give you a couple of concrete examples, we partnered with Google a few years ago in allowing them to brand the Android operating system upgrade as KitKat. We developed a joint promotion with them that was highly successful worldwide. To be honest, we got a little bit lucky on that one because a gentleman at Google working on Android happened to be a big KitKat fan. Until then, Google was using generic dessert-type names for naming their operating system releases, and this guy had the idea, "Why not use KitKat?"

They contacted us through our advertising agency, JWT (J. Walter Thompson), and one thing led to another. No money changed hands between the partners, but we arrived at a promotion that was great for both of us. There was logic to it all even though the opportunity came to us with a little bit of luck. The team understood that, while people have been taking breaks from work or the daily grind forever, the way they're taking breaks today is very different. More often than not, when they take a break, they have a mobile phone with them. Why not exploit that breaking moment, exploit the branding partnership with Android, and see if we can bring a smile to people's breaks in a Web 2.0 way?

Steimle: Imagine traveling back in time thirty years and trying to explain to somebody that in the future you will co-brand KitKat with an Internet search engine's mobile operating system. That would be a tricky one.

Buday: It was very successful. Since that time, we've continued our partnership with Google. KitKat has among our best presences in social media across platforms and we continue to do well there. It's not really a turnaround. It's more a contemporization, staying true to fundamentals and adapting them to new realities.

Regarding turnaround, Lean Cuisine frozen food in the U.S. has been a challenge. Frozen food, in general, has been a difficult category in the U.S., not only for Nestlé but the whole industry. Moreover, consumers are far less interested in dieting than in years past, more likely to reject media and advertising stereotypes of physical attractiveness and health, and more focused on simple, positive nutrition. They're interested in eating natural, simple, and understandable food they consider to be healthy, but don't want to be reminded of what they're not getting. For a long time, Lean Cuisine was associated with dieting, so we needed to pivot pretty quickly. The team put a complete product and packaging redesign and a whole new communication approach that recognizes what we know to be truly important to women today, which is their own personal success and accomplishments. That meant pivoting one hundred eighty degrees away from dieting, which as you can imagine is not easy when the brand has been associated with it for so long. Indications from the relaunch are positive, so hopefully a year from now I can tell you with confidence that it's been successful.

Steimle: What's your philosophy on building a marketing team? How do you attract and retain top marketing talent?

Buday: It sounds stupidly obvious, but for me, it's critically important that they care about the product category and the brand they're working on. They need to believe in the brand's mission, what the brand is trying to do. For instance, the mission of Purina Pet Care—the corporate brand we use for our pet care products—is to enrich the lives of pets and the people who love them. We tell people all the time, "If that doesn't get you out of bed every morning, then you might be a great marketer, but you probably want to work in a different business." Purina consciously recruits people who actually care about enriching the lives of pets and the people who love them.

On top of that, we need functional, technical, interpersonal, and leadership skills. Not surprisingly, of increasing importance is digital marketing skills. We still use the term "digital marketing" inside the company, but I think that term is going to disappear soon because there's essentially no other type of marketing these days. Everything is connected to digital reality one way or the other. Even so-called offline or non-digital activations have a digital component, so we need people and agency partners who know how to build brands in today's reality, not the reality of ten years ago. That means digital competence is a key priority.

Steimle: What do you look for in hires when you're building your team?

Buday: We look for curiosity, the desire to understand things deeply. We look for collaboration skills, the ability to work in teams, to reach productive compromise where needed, to listen carefully to others, and strong, inspirational leadership skills. Leadership comes from all over the organization, but marketing is a key source of leadership when it comes to building our brands and delighting consumers. We need people who, in whatever style comes natural to them, can find a way to motivate others, because we're all busy with many things to do and we have a lot of brands as a company.

There is a bit of internal competition for resources, so you need to be strong and inspirational. You need to give people a reason—and not only internal people. We need to get the best of our agency partners and even our social media platform partners like Facebook, Twitter, Pinterest, whatever. Our marketing people need to be inspiring. They need to be energy givers, not energy takers.

Steimle: Are these the same skills you would recommend students today acquire if they want to be future marketing leaders?

Buday: In some sense, they're the same skills that were always required—some of the softer skills, the collaboration, inspirational leadership, listening, the ability to work with others, communication skills, the ability to get in front of people and express a compelling, energizing view and vision. Those have always been important and are still important. The technical side is changing pretty rapidly. I mentioned digital and social media, but even more than that, data and analytics are increasingly important skill sets.

Steimle: Based on your experience, what advice would you give to somebody who's entering the CMO or VP of marketing role, the top marketing role in the organization?

Buday: Decide concretely how you're going to add value. Where does the greatest opportunity lie to make brand building more successful and more productive in the company? Depending on the company, it's going to be in different ways. In some, it might be in understanding consumers more deeply. In others, it might be modernizing their go-to-market approach and getting a contemporary view to winning in digital social media. In some, it might be brand fundamentals—getting the brand essence, communication framework, and visual properties properly defined, protected, and leveraged if there's a lack of discipline. Scout out the terrain and look for where in the marketing brand-building value chain you can get the biggest wins.

Steimle: What are some of the markets that are exciting for a global organization like Nestlé?

Buday: They're all exciting for different reasons. Developing markets are exciting because of their inherent growth, even if that growth rate has tapered off in some markets like China. Many developing market families are entering middle class or reaching socioeconomic status where they can afford more when it comes to food and beverage products. As they enter that world, it creates tremendous and exciting opportunities for us.

Developed markets like Western Europe, U.S., Canada, Japan, and Australia, are exciting for a completely different reason—if you're going to grow, you're going to have to take it from others. You have to be better than your competition or create new categories, new market opportunities, consumption occasions, or need states and fill those well.

I can't think of a non-exciting marketing opportunity now. I think my colleagues also feel challenged and enthused by opportunity wherever they are.

Steimle: What do you see as one of the biggest challenges facing today's CMOs?

Buday: One of the bigger challenges is consumers having more control at their fingertips and proactively exercising control of their advertising consumption experience. The latest threat at some level to the industry is ad-blocking technology, technology in web browsers, applications, or wherever, that consumers can use to block out the majority of ads they see. A big challenge for us as an industry to discourage consumers from resorting to ad blocking is making sure that we deliver attractive and rewarding content experiences. We need our advertising to be as delightful as the content they normally wish to consume. It's a major challenge to do that and at the same time sell more cat food, coffee, or whatever.

Another big challenge and opportunity is to leverage data. Like in other industries, the amount of data available in all aspects of our business has never been seen before. And it's multiplying fast. The companies that win in the future are going to be the ones that get the fundamentals right but also understand how to leverage data. Leveraging data well requires us to establish a trusting relationship with consumers where they understand and agree to provide data to us in return for better value, better service, better and more relevant content. We need to demonstrate every day that we warrant their trust. Otherwise, the data will not come our way.

Once we have data on our individual consumers, we need not only to serve them better but to serve them more efficiently and effectively. We need to target better, deliver more relevant content, eliminate waste, and add service layers that expand the brand's value proposition. The mastery of consumer data is a big challenge because it requires new skill sets for a lot of marketers, but at another level, it's a huge opportunity for competitive advantage.

Steimle: Is there anything we didn't cover that you've been itching to talk about or need to get out before we wrap things up?

Buday: It's a recent trend or fad in the industry to talk about brands having a purpose. That's not a new concept to Nestlé. Our company was created by a German pharmacist named Henri Nestlé, who created an infant cereal product to save the life of a neighbor's baby nearly one hundred fifty years ago. And we remain committed to that purpose. When we hear people talking about the notion of brand purpose as if it's a new concept, it seems strange to us. We're a company that tends to be wired with that in mind. It doesn't mean we always are successful, but I think we always have the right ambition. That sense of purpose is a key part of our success.

John Costello

President of Global Marketing and Innovation Dunkin' Brands Group, Inc.

John Costello began his career in brand management and marketing at Procter & Gamble. Throughout his 30 years in retail, consumer products, technology, and digital, he has held traditional management positions as well as launched successful marketing campaigns for prestigious brands such as Crest, Dunkin' Donuts, Sears, and The Home Depot. Costello is currently the president of Global Marketing and Innovation at Dunkin' Brands Group, Inc., after serving as CMO for four years. Costello is also the current global chairman of the Mobile Marketing Association. Dunkin' Donuts currently has more than 11,700 locations worldwide serving 3 million customers per day.

In 1997, Costello was elected to the Retail Advertising Hall of Fame. Costello has been named one of the 30 Most Influential People in Marketing by Advertising Age and one of the Top 50 Marketers by Adweek. He was also voted one of the Top 10 Merchants by DSN Retailing Today.

Josh Steimle: What were the steps that led to where you are today?

John Costello: I've been fortunate in that I've got thirty years of experience in consumer products, technology, and retail. My career began at Procter & Gamble brand management. And I find that thirty years later, I still rely heavily on the principles I learned at P&G as a young marketing assistant up until when I ran marketing for the beauty care division. Prior to that, I was a brand manager on both Head & Shoulders shampoo and Crest toothpaste.

© Josh Steimle 2016
J. Steimle, *Chief Marketing Officers at Work*, DOI 10.1007/978-1-4842-1931-7_16

The first part of my career was spent in fairly traditional jobs like Procter & Gamble and PepsiCo, and the later part of my career has been helping companies navigate high change, from Nielsen Marketing Research U.S. to most recently at Dunkin' Brands, where I'm president of Global Marketing and Innovation for both Dunkin' Donuts and Baskin-Robbins. I've been fortunate to observe significant changes in marketing, but while the tactics of marketing and product development have certainly changed over the years, the fundamental principles have not.

Steimle: As you prepare for your retirement next year, what are some of the most valuable lessons you've learned with other companies that contributed to your success as a CMO?

Costello: I've been fortunate to have a broad range of experiences in consumer products, retail, and technology, including roles as CMO, president, and CEO. I've found that what I enjoy most is helping to grow businesses. At Dunkin' Brands, over my time here, I've had global responsibility for Dunkin' Donuts' and Baskin-Robbins' advertising, marketing, consumer engagement, digital, mobile, social marketing, consumer and business intelligence, and overseas research and product development, and also the culinary team and the retail consumer products business for both brands globally.

As I look back at my career, the two most important lessons I've learned are, number one, focus on the consumer. The key to success is understanding consumer needs and then meeting those needs better than the competition does. I call that "brand differentiation," which is how you answer the question, "Why should consumers choose your brand over all their other choices?" The second most important lesson is to surround yourself with the best people that you can and create an environment and culture that lets them achieve their best.

Steimle: What lessons did you learn as a CEO that have aided you as you've gone back into a marketing role?

Costello: The two underlying principles of focusing on the customer and surrounding yourself with great people can apply to whatever role you have, from an entry-level manager up through the CEO of a company. Rather than "CEO," why don't we go back and call it "general manager"? The key thing that distinguishes a general manager is the ability to lead across functions and to find a way for functions to work well together.

For example, Dunkin' Donuts has had a strong record of product innovation. Dunkin' Donuts introduced over forty new products in the last twelve months. That new product success was the result of a talented culinary team working closely with marketing, operations, our franchisee partners, and training. The key thing that distinguishes a general manager is his or her ability to lead across functions.

Steimle: What is it like to take an established company that's been around for sixty-five years or so and transition it into the digital world?

Costello: Dunkin' has strongly embraced the digital world and more recently the move into mobile. "America Runs on Dunkin'" is more than a tagline. It really is Dunkin' Donuts' brand purpose. Our goal is to help people get running in the morning and to keep them running all day long with great beverages and food at a great value in a fast, friendly, and convenient environment.

Given that, mobile was a logical next step for us. It's the perfect platform for a brand designed for people on the run. And I think a lot of our success in mobile has been listening to what our customers want and then developing solutions in a collaborative way. Our mobile app has over fifteen million downloads and was built with world-class technology and features that our customers wanted. For example, you could pay with the Dunkin' Donuts mobile app from day one. We have a store locator on there to help locate a Dunkin' Donuts when you're traveling, as well as personalized marketing when you sign up for our DD Perks® loyalty program.

I think a lot of the success of the mobile program was that it was our most collaborative project to date. As you would expect, marketing and IT were very involved in leading the effort, but it also involved strong collaboration with operations, our franchisee partners, HR, training, PR, and customer service. The collaborative nature of the mobile app combined with listening to our customers are key factors of its success. In exploring new technology, it's easy to get caught up in the latest gee-whiz technology, but we found there's no substitute for listening to your customers and providing what they want in an easy and seamless way.

Steimle: With that app, you get some great data. How are you able to use that data to help serve your customers better? Are there any standout examples?

Costello: Building that data has been a big part of the success, as we're able to better learn what our customers want and then tailor product news and offers to customers based not only on what they've purchased but also what they're interested in. For example, beyond providing incentives on their favorite beverages and food, we've also learned that our customers love new products, so we inform them of all of the new products we introduce. The data does provide an opportunity for more targeted marketing, but I would offer two caveats to that. First, data should supplement your judgment, not replace it. Secondly, with increased data comes the need for a careful respect for customers' privacy.

Steimle: Tell me about your team. What does your marketing department look like?

Costello: Our marketing departments continue to evolve as the business evolves, but it's a team-oriented organization focused on the key things that can drive our brands, that can build our brand, as well as drive profitable sales for Dunkin' Brands and our franchisees. We have teams overlooking brand marketing, consumer engagement, business and consumer insights, digital, social, and mobile efforts, as well as our culinary team, which leads product development. While people in the marketing and product development teams have functional responsibilities, they also work collaboratively together.

We also have a close working relationship with our franchisees. I believe our franchisees are Dunkin' Donuts' and Baskin-Robbins' secret weapon, as they know our local markets better than anyone and can provide us with real insight into what their customers are looking for. This has enabled us to launch regional products. For example, we launched a chicken biscuit at Dunkin' Donuts restaurants located in the southeastern markets of the United States, which has been very successful.

Steimle: Dunkin' Donuts is a global company now. You have locations in China and elsewhere around the world. How has globalization and going international affected marketing?

Costello: We're fortunate in that we have a strong international marketing team at Dunkin' Donuts and Baskin-Robbins who also work closely with our international partners to tailor marketing and our product for countries. While you'll be able to find global favorites like Dunkin' Donuts' Original Blend coffee and glazed donuts around the world, we'll also have local favorites as well. In Asia, you might find more savory products, like a donut with shredded chicken, in addition to favorites like chocolate and glazed donuts. Our global marketing and product development efforts blend both global needs as well as local needs.

Steimle: You talked about the franchisees being a secret weapon in the focus on region. What methods do you have for staying in touch with the customers through these franchisees? What other channels do you have for making sure that you understand your customers?

Costello: We do extensive consumer tracking to measure our brand attributes and customer satisfaction at both the national and market level. We also meet regularly with our franchisees to discuss the business and review out front business plans, marketing plans, and product development. We combine what Dunkin' Brands corporate is learning from our in-market research with what the franchisees are seeing in their markets on a day-by-day basis.

Steimle: What do you see as some future growth markets for Dunkin' as you're expanding worldwide?

Costello: We think there are significant growth opportunities for Dunkin' Donuts, both in the U.S. and globally. We plan to add between 430 to 460 net new restaurants in the U.S. in 2016 and internationally we plan to increase our presence in key regions such as China and India, as well as Europe.

Steimle: What's your philosophy on building a successful marketing team?

Costello: The most important criteria are an interest in understanding consumers and what they're looking for, a real agility to adapt to all of the rapid changes occurring in marketing, and being a team player, because marketing is more collaborative than ever before. I'm looking for people who are intelligent, curious, agile, and great team players.

Steimle: How do you attract and retain top marketing talent?

Costello: The most important factor is creating an environment where they can accomplish things, achieve their personal goals, and have fun. We work hard to create an environment where people can have an impact, are valued, and also enjoy coming to work every day. We work hard at Dunkin', but we also create an environment where people are valued.

Steimle: What are some of the metrics you're held responsible for? What metrics do you focus on?

Costello: Sales, profitability, and the strength of our brands are the key corporate metrics. We're focused on helping our franchisees grow profitable sales because we believe our success is tied closely to our franchisees' success.

Steimle: How do you measure the strength of the brand?

Costello: We do proprietary external tracking that measures Dunkin's brand strength on key attributes.

Steimle: In the digital world, all this marketing, and tracking, and everything is going onto social media and such. What's been successful for Dunkin' in terms of those forms of digital marketing?

Costello: Dunkin' Donuts is a very responsive brand, and as a result, digital, social, and mobile marketing have worked well for us. However, traditional marketing, like TV, out-of-home radio, and in-store point-of-sales materials also continue to work well. The new digital media is growing faster than traditional marketing, but it needs to earn its way. One of the key barriers to more rapid growth of digital is the lack of common ROI metrics across new and traditional marketing.

I expect digital and mobile marketing to continue to grow at a rapid rate, but the industry needs to make more progress against common ROI methodology. The Mobile Marketing Association has a new initiative called SMoX, which does provide cross-media ROI. That's a very good first step, but the industry needs to do more on cross-platform ROI.

Steimle: If you could go back in time to when you first came into the CMO role, what's some of the advice you would give to yourself as a new CMO?

Costello: I would give myself two pieces of advice. The first would be to focus. A CMO has a broad range of responsibilities and projects that he or she oversees. The most important advice is to make sure that you spend the bulk of your time focused on those initiatives that will provide the greatest return to your brand and company.

The second piece of advice would be to surround yourself with the best team and create an environment where they can do their best work. As a CMO, your success is determined more by your team than any individual activity you may personally do. The two most important pieces of advice are to make sure that you are focused and are building the best team aligned against your objectives.

Steimle: What do you see as the biggest challenges facing today's CMOs?

Costello: There are two big challenges facing CMOs today. The first is balancing short-term results against long-term brand building. The second is to remain agile to understand and adapt to the rapidly changing market environment.

Oftentimes, it's easy for marketers to look in the rearview mirror, analyze what's worked in the past, and do it a little better. Today, I think it's much more important to look out the windshield to see what's coming. Agility is far more important in a CMO than it's ever been because of the rapid change in the marketing world.

Steimle: What do you see as the future of marketing? What's changing and what doesn't change over time?

Costello: The tactics will continue to change, while the fundamental principles will remain the same. We'll continue to see rapid growth in mobile, social, and digital marketing. We'll also continue to see growth in one-to-one marketing and loyalty programs.

At P&G, I learned that the most effective marketing is to be recommended by a friend. Mobile, social, and digital offer the opportunity to take one-to-one marketing to scale, so I would expect to see continued evolution of new marketing techniques as the cost of new technology continues to climb.

On the flip side, I think the fundamental principles will remain the same. Do you understand what your target customers' unmet needs are? Are you focusing your brand and company against serving those needs better than any of your competitors? Customers today have a lot of choices. You need to answer the question, "Why should I choose your brand over all my other options?"

I see a world in which marketing tactics will continue to evolve at a rapid pace while the fundamental principles of building brands and driving profitable sales remain the same.

Steimle: How does a business thrive today when there are ad blockers, when people are increasingly able to tune out marketing messages? How do you get through to consumers in a marketing environment where the consumer has more control?

Costello: There are a couple of factors. Marketers need to make sure that their advertising is relevant, authentic, and contextual. Most of the consumer concerns about advertising are due to the bombardment of irrelevant ads. As marketers, we need to focus on making sure we're developing relevant ads and delivering them to the right consumer at the right time. As a result, you'll see more effective advertising, a greater use of native advertising, and greater contextual advertising. If you're looking to buy a new SUV, automotive advertising is relevant. If you're not in the market, it's much less relevant. Advertising needs to evolve to be more relevant and more targeted than ever before and we need to reduce the amount of less relevant advertising.

Second, the industry needs to do a better job of helping consumers understand that the people who create content need to be fairly compensated. Today, there really are only two ways to compensate the creators of content: either advertising or subscription. Consumers need to understand that if they want to watch their favorite programs, the people who are creating and offering those programs deserve to be fairly compensated, either via subscription or advertising.

To summarize, I think we need to see more relevant and contextual advertising along with helping consumers realize that the creators of content need to be fairly compensated.

Steimle: What are some of the skills that university students or young businesspeople just starting out should be focusing on if they want to prepare to be future marketing leaders?

Costello: I would advise students today to be inquisitive, to learn as much as they can about what motivates consumers and how to reach them. I would also suggest they focus early on building their skills and working hard, and worry less about their next promotion. The early part of your career is a great opportunity for you to learn about your chosen profession and begin to build your toolkit.

I was fortunate to spend the first twelve years of my career with Procter & Gamble, who placed a lot of emphasis on training, mentoring, and developing people. That gave me a great opportunity to understand consumer marketing as well as build my own skills in building brands and driving sales.

Steimle: Is there anything in your background or experience that is not directly tied to marketing but that you feel has been beneficial to your role as a marketing professional?

Costello: There are two things. The first is to be naturally inquisitive and learn as much as you can outside of marketing as well. That will make you a more effective marketer and businessperson. Secondly, it's important to have work/life balance and to develop interests outside of work. It's important to focus on your work, but it's also important to continue to develop as an individual and make sure you have time for family, friends, and your outside interests.

Steimle: What are some of your outside interests?

Costello: I've always had a strong commitment to volunteering. On the business side, I'm the past chairman and board member of both the Association of National Advertisers and the Advertising Council. I'm the current global chair of the Mobile Marketing Association. I've long been involved in the not-for-profit sector. I'm currently on the board of directors of the Yellowstone Park Foundation.

Steimle: What are some of the benefits marketers can receive from being a member of associations and industry groups?

Costello: It's an opportunity for you to broaden your exposure to different people in different industries. That exposure can make you more effective as a marketer. It's also important if you have the time to give back. For example, the Advertising Council coordinates the bulk of pro bono advertising in the United States. It relies on donations of media funds and people to achieve its mission. For marketers, it's the opportunity to contribute to the U.S. society, as well as an opportunity to meet new people in different industries. It's a good example of doing something that benefits the U.S., as well as helps broaden you as an individual.

Steimle: When you think about your time at Dunkin', what keeps you excited? What gets you coming into the office each day excited to go to work?

Costello: Dunkin' Donuts and Baskin-Robbins are unique brands in that both are over sixty years old but are as relevant today as any time in their history, so they are a fascinating combination of tradition and current relevancy. I think it's exciting to work on brands that have these deep traditions but are also relevant to consumers today.

The second part is the people that I get to work with every day. We have a great team across all functions at Dunkin', are able to work with some of the most talented franchisees in the world on both brands, and have great agency partners as well.

One thing that gets me excited is the ability to work on two very cool brands. The second is the ability to work with a great group of people at Dunkin', among our franchisees, and with our agency partners.

Luanne Calvert

Vice President and Chief Marketing Officer
Virgin America

Luanne Calvert is vice president and CMO at Virgin America, where she leads brand strategy, marketing, PR, advertising, and more. Prior to working at Virgin, Calvert consulted for LVMH's Fendi brand, as well as Moleskine. She served as Google's creative director for three years after founding Mixed Marketing, an agency specializing in buzz marketing, where she also served as CEO. Calvert has a bachelor of science in marketing from San Francisco State University.

Josh Steimle: Give us an overview of your career and history. How did you get your start?

Luanne Calvert: Some parts of it were traditional and others were nontraditional. I studied advertising and marketing in college. It's one of those unusual situations where you're actually using your degree. My first major was fashion illustration, but I wasn't able to draw and that was definitely holding me back. I came to realize that I wanted to do something that was commercially viable but also allowed and even encouraged creativity, so the two areas that made sense were architecture or advertising and marketing, which is where I ended up.

I'm happy I chose the field of marketing. It offers the chance to be creative in a business setting. It's also much more measurable than when I started off. I studied marketing. I studied advertising. The first job I had was all about finding good training and learning the basics, the foundation. I spent the next twenty or thirty years figuring out how to do things differently. In a discipline like marketing, it's almost like you have to learn the rules first, if there are rules, and then figure out how you can do things differently to encourage new ways of getting attention.

Steimle: Give us an overview of Virgin America. What's the history and place of the company in the Virgin family?

Calvert: Virgin America was launched over eight years ago. We are a licensor of the Virgin Group. There are about four hundred Virgin companies around the world, of which we are one. In the U.S., we're the most well-known. There's also Virgin Mobile and Virgin Hotels. Virgin Atlantic, of course, has a good presence here as well. Virgin Produced is a company out of Los Angeles that we also work with.

When the company was launched, the reputation of domestic air travel was below the customer satisfaction of the IRS, so there were very low expectations when we came in. I guess you could say that was a good thing. We came in and the company took a fresh look. What do people want in air travel? Granted, there are a lot of constraints, but if you could have anything, what would it be? A lot of it is about control. As soon as you get to an airport, you lose control. So, we offered control.

For example, we have food ordering available on your seatbacks. You can get food when you want it, not just when the cart goes by. People also want options. They also want to have the same things in the sky that they do on earth. People want Wi-Fi. We were the first airline that had full-fleet Wi-Fi, full outlet seats. Of course, after a couple of hours when your battery runs out, you need to recharge your phones, so we give people that option. People want fresh food. People want to look at things that are nice. We have a stylized, chic airline. Why not make things look beautiful? Our mood lighting, which is what we're known for, makes it a relaxing environment. Air travel can be stressful, so why not make it relaxing? Give people control. Make it as good of an experience as possible.

We're also proud of our service. We try to do our best to hire people that are optimistic, and proud to work for the company, and all that went into creating a unique experience. Because of that, we're able to differentiate amongst the other airlines by creating a good experience. It's not just the utility of getting from point A to point B. It's giving people a good experience that starts when you check in.

We were the first to do responsive design. You'll notice something different when you get on the plane. You'll see the safety video. It's the first airline safety video set entirely to music and dance, and it's now at 11 million views. We try to take things that are generally mundane, the details, and make them interesting, compelling, and fun for people. Our goal is to try to create an airline that people love. That message comes from the top. And we try to do things in a way that respects our guests, gives them a good experience, and encourages them to become loyal flyers with us.

Steimle: What happens when other airlines catch on and start offering similar amenities?

Calvert: Our goal is to keep ahead. Other airlines do catch up, so we have to keep pushing forward. A lot of times, they are not as consistent as we are. We're still the only airline that has one hundred percent Wi-Fi, one hundred percent outlets. Because we started as a new airline, everything was built in at the beginning. We incorporated all of these items into the aircraft. We just announced a few months ago that we're going to have satellite Wi-Fi that will be faster. We offer Netflix for *House of Cards* and other programming for free on our aircraft. Hopefully, for the good of consumers, other airlines will start to catch up and be more customer-centric, but our goal is to still maintain our competitive lead.

There are five areas where we focus on differentiation. One is the style and design of the aircraft. We're constantly looking at that, what we can do with our mood lighting and seating. We just upgraded our software for our in-flight entertainment system to have a lot more content and games. There's Wi-Fi and we're looking at how can we be faster and offer broadband. We're always looking at new ideas for ways we can offer fresh food on our aircraft. We just won an award for healthiest food from one of the gourmet people that evaluate airline food. Service, too—that's a hard one for people to catch up on. It's intangible.

We have a team-oriented culture here. Our culture is important to us. It's about how we can be excellent for our guests. And we believe that if we put our teammates first, they will put our guests first. That culture permeates the entire company. Everyone is a teammate. Our flight attendants, pilots, and guest services people—the people that check you in—have very similar uniforms. It's set up to be a team-oriented environment. We put a lot of effort into the culture, even though it's not tangible like the product that we fly.

Steimle: You said there are four hundred companies within Virgin. Do you have the opportunity to collaborate, work, and share services with the marketing people in these other groups? How do you share ideas?

Calvert: There's formal and informal collaboration. Formally, we do have opportunities where we meet once or twice a year with the larger brands globally. We all meet and share ideas and do our best to collaborate. The company is run very interestingly. There's not a lot of control on the day-to-day operations. We work pretty much as individual companies, but we also know that the brand is one and we can affect each other, so we do work together. For example, Virgin Atlantic, Virgin Australia, and Virgin America are the three airlines.

A couple of years ago, we integrated our frequent flyer programs so you can earn and burn points, or miles, on all three airlines, and we made a program to launch that called *Departure Date*. It was the first and only film ever made in an airplane. It was a twenty-minute program filmed on all three airlines. We worked with our friends at Virgin Produced to make it. It was produced by Kat Coiro, who is a pretty well-known director. We had Philip Baker Hall, Luis Guzmán, Janeane Garofalo, and a few other celebrities participating in it. It's a fun movie that we launched at the Los Angeles Film Festival. That's an example of the kind of marketing we do. It was unexpected and new, so we had a nice PR event to introduce it. Of course, the film was then put on our aircraft and became content for us.

We also have Virgin Hotels in Chicago, so that's a natural partner for us. We also work with them on points and loyalty. We want people to stay there when they're flying to Chicago. It's a great hotel. When they opened up, we did everything we could to help them promote it. And then they were nice enough to invite us to their amazing party, which was a lot of fun. It's a beautiful building. It's a beautiful hotel. It's a good property. They're going to roll out to other markets as well. We do work collaboratively.

Steimle: Tell me about your marketing department. What does it look like? How is it structured?

Calvert: Instead of the "marketing funnel," I call it the "marketing bow tie." We have everything across the funnel. We have our brand team, which is handling all of our social media, PR, brand advertising, our integrations with entertainment, our sponsorships. As you get a little bit further down in the funnel with our digital team, that's more about consideration of purchase. That's where we have social media. We have our online advertising, email, search engine marketing. We have the front end of our website. All across the funnel, we have our creative team. We have a small in-house creative team. For product preference, the team works on all of the in-flight entertainment: the Wi-Fi upgrades, the content that goes on the in-flight entertainment system, the design of how things are delivered in the catering, the uniforms our flight attendants and front-line folks wear.

We have an impact on the actual product. We're involved with the design of the cabin as well. We work closely with other departments on that. Finally, for loyalty and advocacy, we have our Elevate loyalty program, our credit card business, our social media guest care. That comes through social media. That's changed a lot over the years as people flock to social media, not just the call center, for guest care. We have that and our Gold and Silver tier programs. We have all of corporate communications as well. I think of them as part of the foundation to make sure our corporate reputation is as solid as it can be, especially now that we are a public company.

Steimle: What's your philosophy on building and managing a marketing team?

Calvert: There are a few things that are important to me. One is—and I work very hard on this—to create an environment where people feel like their ideas matter and that they can be creative and feel comfortable in taking risks. That's an easy thing to say, but it's a hard thing to do because it means that people are going to be doing things differently from the way you might do them. Sometimes, they'll be right. Sometimes, they might not be. You have to live with the fact that sometimes, things aren't going to go as expected. Creating an environment where people feel free to contribute their ideas and take chances is important to me.

The second part is that I try to make sure that people are pointed in the right direction, that there is a plan in place, and that everyone's clear on what the goals are for the company, what their role is within that, and how their job is measured. Everything within the marketing funnel has a KPI (key performance indicator) associated with it, but at the end of the day, we still want to be provocative and do things in ways that are going to differentiate us from the rest of world.

We also want to work collaboratively and try to be nice to each other and have a good time because it's a crazy business. Things are changing every day. When I look over the week, there are so many different things that pop up that I can't even plan for. We have to be able to work together, collaborate, and depend on each other in order to compete because we don't have the resources that the other airlines do. We have to make up for our fewer resources by being smart in how we integrate so that we can be more nimble. We're smaller, so we can be more nimble, but being collaborative and having a good team-oriented environment is crucial to that.

Steimle: How do you attract and retain top marketing talent? Why do people come to work for you?

Calvert: Well, the good and bad thing is that people love Virgin. We have a good reputation. I've been fortunate. In my first job, I worked at an agricultural chemical company, and now, after I've spent some time in the industry, I get the luxury of working for brands that people really love, like Google, Moleskine notebooks, and Virgin America. It's a great thing to get to work for a company that you believe in.

A lot of people come to us after they've flown with us, so they love the brand. We get a lot of people that love Virgin America, so that's fortunate. Hopefully, people see a lot of the creative work that we've done, and it gets their attention, but it's the good and bad. We're a big target. We're in Silicon Valley, where there's a lot of competition for top talent. We work hard to create a good culture, a good environment. We're flexible about working from home. And we try to create a culture where people like the people they work with and learn something.

Steimle: What do you look for in your new hires?

Calvert: We have a broad range of people. I want them to have really good analytical skills but also be flexible, creative problem-solvers, that idea of doing things differently and coming up with new ideas. I have other people that are leading with more of their creative thinking, but they also need to be able to measure the results. From the creative front, what's important is being able to think not just in terms of paid media, but in terms of getting the word out.

With a brand like Virgin America, a lot of the brand is built by our guests, so a lot of our job is about putting out what I think of as idea seeds, getting the conversation going, and getting people to talk about the brand. It's finding people that can be creative, but it's also about not being controlling. How do you encourage other people to do a lot of the brand building for you? That's an important skill. Digital is crucial. Most of our business is booked online, so people have to have a natural or good experience in digital marketing and digital creative work. That has to be the default mode.

Being nice to people is also key. We're a customer-oriented, guest-oriented business, so that has to be reflected in all the departments, including ours, where taking care of our guests is a front and center priority.

Steimle: Do you work with outside marketing agencies?

Calvert: We use a number of agencies for our promotions, for advertising, for media. We have quite a few external companies. And having had my own agency, I know that good communication and trust are important. As with any relationship, I try to set up what the objectives are, what we're trying to accomplish using the right audience and right strategy. It's important to give freedom to the agencies to come up with what they think is the best approach. I try to make sure that they're measuring and that they have a clear idea of the metrics.

Steimle: What are the metrics that you get judged on?

Calvert: There are two big ones. One is the unit revenue goals. As a public company, that's really important. We look at that. The other one that comes to mind is employee surveys. That's probably my favorite metric. So far, I've been pleased with the results we've gotten. That's an important one, making sure of the engagement of the team that I'm managing. Looking at our tracking study, seeing what the awareness is and what the positives and the challenges are within our brand and our sentiment are others. Our Net Promoter Score is an important metric that we have. It's an airline. We have no shortage of metrics. There's online, too. What are people talking about? Are we getting our story out there within social media? We can see how engaged people are with a lot of the stories we're telling.

Steimle: What is the value of having been an entrepreneur? How does that help you in the CMO role?

Calvert: What helps is it probably gives you empathy. You learn to empathize with what your agencies are going through. Empathy is a big part of what can make a good environment and the ability to collaborate. Empathy is definitely a big one and so is trying to pay the bills on time. People forget that the agencies need to get paid on time. I've been on the other side of that and we do a good job with that.

Steimle: When you were running your agency, you were directly in touch with the results of the company. How has that aided you in your work?

Calvert: Because of that experience—and even having been at a company with an entrepreneurial spirit and culture like Google—I probably expect things to be faster, which we're pretty good at. Being nimble and quick is an entrepreneurial trait. An entrepreneurial culture gives importance to experimenting, trying things. Planning is certainly important, but you have to put some bets out there and keep on trying, and then see what takes off. For example, we just used some new technology that allows us to refer a friend. It's something we tried quickly and it worked out well. We're going to continue to see how we can expand that technology.

Another example is a video we did called *Blah Airlines*. It was pretty funny. It was done with our agency, Eleven, Inc. One of our biggest challenges is that people are really addicted to their frequent flyer programs. I think of it like the Stockholm syndrome, where people start to relate to their captor. They might not like the airline, but they won't want to leave it because they have so much invested in it, so they start to relate and almost defend a company they don't like. Trying to examine that behavior in kind of a funny way is something I've been experimenting with a lot. I've been trying to figure out how to get people to have that aha! moment: "Yes, ten hours of my life is a lot. Why am I spending it with an airline I don't like so I can buy a 'free' ticket on an airline I don't like or get an upgrade that I'm probably never going to get?"

The agency came up with this idea to do a five-and-a-half-hour video, which is the exact time that it takes to get from Newark to San Francisco, and call it *Blah Airlines*. It makes the worst experience seem reminiscent of some of our competitors. The idea was that you probably wouldn't want to watch this or fly the experience, but at the same time, it's hilariously funny. It was a great job and another thing that took off well. We have this great content, so how can we now use it in other ways? To me, this is entrepreneurial. They try different bets and figure out new ways that you can actually use those ideas.

Steimle: Has being in Silicon Valley around all these startups and technology companies helped Virgin America succeed?

Calvert: Absolutely. It's a big part of who we are. We're the only airline based in Silicon Valley. What that means is, first of all, our guests expect more from us. We need to make sure we offer the technology and the flight that they want, that our website offers an easy way to book and check in, that it's mobile. We're one of the first to do something so that it's responsive, so that it configures to whatever device you're on. The expectations are higher.

At the same time, what I also love is that our guests bring us ideas, so we try things. One company, Here On Biz, was doing something where you could connect with people based on geography using your LinkedIn profile as a platform. We used them almost like an incubator. I want to be an incubator to our creative guests. In the sky, if you enabled it, you could actually make business connections. If you were on your way to South by Southwest, you could meet people even before you got to the event by using the Here On Biz app.

We've also met with different VCs. We hear out different pitches on new products that are coming up, different startups. We have technology and research tools that we use for our A/B testing that came out of some of these meetings. So it's a real differentiator for us from a guest standpoint and also brings us new ideas.

Steimle: What are all the ways you build customer loyalty with your audience?

Calvert: We look at our brand tracking survey. The biggest thing is that once people fly us, most of them prefer us after having had that experience. Even if they have to go a little bit out of their way for the time of the route, we get a lot of preference after people fly with us. The biggest thing we do is offer the experience. Our loyalty program, Elevate, offers a lot of perks. When you get to a certain level of points, you get a status. Probably one of the biggest things that is unique to Virgin America is that we don't have any blackout dates. Whatever the price is—$300 a flight, every flight converts into points. It's really simple. There's no small print. There are no blackout dates. If there's a flight available, a seat available, you can buy it with points.

The strength of our program is something that drives loyalty. A lot of it is just rewarding people for flying with us. We do encourage people to then share their experience, which is probably something a lot of other airlines couldn't do. We have different promotions in place where if people refer a friend, they will also get points back once that person actually flies on Virgin America. We've come up with ways to encourage that. It's something unique because of the experience we offer.

Steimle: What do you see as some of the biggest challenges facing today's CMOs?

Calvert: I've learned everything has a flip side—challenges and opportunities—but when I started off in advertising, there was not a lot of measurement. Models were built. There was some tracking study, so if you spent a lot, you could probably get an idea of what moved the needle. What's great now and what also makes it challenging is that everything is much more measurable. When we do have a need for, let's say, weekend sales, we're called to the table: "What can you guys do to help us sell some seats?" Having those tools in place, you have to think more. It's not just marketing. It's about the brand, but it's also about delivering on sales and being smart with the investment money. How do I invest to maximize the revenue but still keep the brand, the Virgin brand, as provocative as it is?

Steimle: What do you see as some of the big mistakes that CMOs today are making?

Calvert: A lot of it is staying relevant considering how it's so much more complex, making sure that you've finely honed your digital skills as more and more people make their shopping decisions that way. It's harder to build a brand, to get the emotional connection out. In an online way, you can do it with video. You can do that, but you have to make it compelling because people are going to choose whether or not they want to engage. You don't have the control that you used to when you were pushing your message out. Now, people have to really choose to want it, so with digital, it's making that emotional connection and differentiating your brand. Going further down the funnel and having a measurable impact on sales can be challenging, especially for companies that have been around for a long time.

Steimle: How do you keep up with all the different marketing channels and opportunities?

Calvert: I know what our goals and priorities are for the year, and then it's a matter of bringing in the people that are the experts because in a lot of ways, things don't change. People want to hear a good story. They want to have a good product. They want to have an authentic message, but they want to be entertained. A lot of the basics have not changed, but how you deliver the message and how you measure it have changed. I definitely have to keep up. And I have to read and make sure that my folks aren't overlooking anything. But a lot of it is that I expect everyone to be an expert in their field. And they are.

Steimle: Is there any trend in marketing that gets you excited about the future and where marketing is going?

Calvert: It's two things. One is there's so much discussion about content. When you have a brand with such passionate followers, a lot of the times, they're creating the brand for you. How do you continue to codify the marketing that your guests are almost doing for you? How do you incorporate that message? You have it on social media, but how is it getting into your website, into your content? How do you bring your guests even more and more into the fold, into the brand?

That's related to the second part, which is referrals. How do you encourage people to authentically share when they like a product or when they have feedback for you for improvement? A lot of it is about marketing being unleashed. It's about the community, the guests that are involved, and how those messages continue to be amplified. That's always changing on all the different social media tools, so you have to keep up on that, but how are your guests sharing your message and doing the brand for you? They're building it in a lot of ways. Your job is to encourage those loyal guests out there to spread the word.

Steimle: With marketing changing so much, what are some of the skills new marketers can acquire that will continue to be relevant as they rise through the ranks?

Calvert: The importance of social media—a lot of students understand it, but that's how they're spending a lot of their time communicating, texting as well as all the other ways of messaging. If you're working in marketing, balancing out that communication channel with the fact that it has to have a commercial message can be an adjustment. How do you build it? You still have to have the story about your brand. Word of mouth can be great, but if it doesn't have a relevant message about Virgin America, then it's not going to make a difference. How do you balance out creativity, the digital communication tools people are using, with how to make sure there's a commercial message that's integrated?

Steimle: What are the skills that people can develop to help them succeed at that kind of challenge?

Calvert: In some ways, it hasn't changed. You still want to have great communication skills, and you need people that have excellent quantitative skills as well. The basics haven't changed. It's how you then use them, how they're then translated into the tools we use to communicate and measure.

Steimle: Do you have any thoughts on marketing to millennials?

Calvert: They aren't the focus of our target. We don't have an age. Our target has been focusing on the business traveler and making sure we deliver on what the business traveler needs, which is Wi-Fi and a good loyalty program. That said, the millennials tend to prefer Virgin America because we offer the options, because we have the Wi-Fi, because we have extensive—and it's not censored or edited—in-flight entertainment, because it's well-designed, youthful, chic. We have music when you check in. We're pretty modern in how we do things. We do well with that group, although they're not really the focus of our target unless they're business travelers.

Steimle: Is there anything we haven't covered that you're itching to say about the CMO role?

Calvert: It's changed so much in the past few years, but there are a few things that will never change. You have to get along with people. You have to use your common sense. That's something that never goes out of style but can be in short supply. But those are the things that really come to mind: getting along, working well with people, trying to be nice, making smart decisions, having common sense. Everything has changed below that, but those main things haven't changed. As my father would say, nothing replaces a kind word and a smile, so even with all the great digital stuff, people are still flying to do business. There's still the in-person, the relationship that you have between people that will probably continue to be the most important.

Trish Mueller

Senior Vice President & Chief Marketing Officer
The Home Depot

Trish Mueller became senior vice president and CMO at The Home Depot in 2011 after over 20 years of experience in various sales, advertising, and marketing roles. Previously, Mueller served as VP of advertising at both The Home Depot and American Signature, Inc. Mueller was also senior vice president of broadcast sales at ShopNBC and senior vice president of marketing and advertising for The Sports Authority. Mueller has a business degree from the State University of New York at Plattsburgh.

Josh Steimle: Describe your roots in marketing. What steps led to where you are today as the CMO of the Home Depot?

Trish Mueller: I'm a third-generation retailer. I had a grandfather who worked for Sears for thirty-five years. I had an uncle who was with Montgomery Ward and I have another uncle who was with JCPenney. Growing up, I was always exposed to retail conversations about how to sell things and what was selling. You can imagine the family barbecue with those three guys sitting around the picnic table. From an early age, I was fascinated by the conversation. One of my earliest memories as a fairly young person, maybe six or seven years old, was sitting in my grandfather's chair in his office at Sears. He ran stores for Sears. I remember him having me come to see him at work and sitting in his chair behind his desk and thinking how cool that was.

© Josh Steimle 2016

J. Steimle, *Chief Marketing Officers at Work*, DOI 10.1007/978-1-4842-1931-7_18

As I grew up from that young age through high school, I was an overachiever. I graduated fifth in my high school class and went to school with scholarships because I come from a humble background. I went to college for business, earning an associate of arts from a two-year college. Then, I went to the State University of New York at Plattsburgh in their business program and I graduated magna cum laude with a business degree. Some of my studies there were specifically retail coursework. I remember coming out of school determined to work in retail, and I interviewed, not shockingly, with Sears, JCPenney, and Montgomery Ward. I looked at the groups of people working at all those companies and I had a distinct impression that Sears and JCPenney stores employed predominantly older white males. In my early twenties, my read on that was, "Wow! It's going to take me forever to climb that ladder."

At the time, Montgomery Ward made a pretty tough revolving-door impression. I chose that on purpose because my feeling was if they were constantly changing people out, I would have more of an opportunity there than I would at Sears or JCPenney. I remember being in the interview process and they asked me, "What do you want to be in five years?" and I said, "I want to be a district manager." They kind of chuckled and said, "Good luck with that." Clearly, it took a little bit longer than that, but I did climb the ladder fairly quickly. I started with them in 1984 as an assistant manager in training in Rutland, Vermont, and I worked for—I will never forget—Joyce Lanfear. She was the general manager for apparel and that was men's, women's, children's, lingerie, jewelry, and fragrance and cosmetics. As assistant, I had oversight for lingerie and women's.

I did that and then moved out of that business into homes, home furnishings, and became a general manager myself. I moved to Bedford, New Hampshire. I started running that business. It had a commission sales component, which goes back to my love of selling things. Early on, I learned how to understand what people wanted, what they were motivated by—whether that was a commission salesperson or the customer—and figuring out how to sell stuff, including my ideas, to management.

It's important to note what happened in Bedford, New Hampshire, because we had a store visit from the new CEO, Bernie Brennan. I knew he was coming, so I was reading a book called *It's Not My Department.*[1] The theory of it was you should never talk badly about any other part of the company in front of a customer. You should always take ownership. One of the things my grandfather, who was a great mentor to me, taught me was to take care of every single customer like you're going to see them every day and like they're family. Two percent of the time, they'll be taking advantage of you, but ninety-eight percent of the time, you'll build a customer for life. That book espoused that to me.

---

[1] Peter Glen (Morrow, 1990).

My grandfather also taught me to offer my card every time I helped someone. And you'd be amazed how many people would come back and ask for me when there were issues not in my department. I shared the book with Bernie Brennan. He took it with him on the plane. He was a voracious reader. He read it and sent me a thank-you note.

From then on, he followed my career and would show up at interesting times. And I would find myself moved to a new assignment, a new store, whatever. My philosophy of my career has been to take every opportunity that's put in front of you and pretty much never say no. No matter what the opportunity was, I never said no. I relocated.

I got married and moved from Bedford, New Hampshire, and took a job in Port Richey, Florida, which was a little bit of a hike, but it's where there was an opening. When I was in that store, I got asked to help a store opening, so I found myself running the home departments in Port Richey, Florida, and then being asked to go to Baltimore/Washington to open a store. I was making sure that I never dropped the ball on my responsibility to Port Richey and that when I was in Baltimore, I was building relationships with people. I struck up a conversation with our EVP at the time, Bill Dane. Obviously, I did a great job and went back to Port Richey and then went on to open a new store as the GM in Melbourne, Florida. Each of the times I moved, whether they were lateral or not wasn't the issue. The issue was more about whether I was getting exposure to leadership and growing my skill set. Learning to open a store was a huge up for me.

One topic I like to teach young people about, which is important for most people, is to prioritize their understanding of the personnel recordkeeping for the company. I had a situation in Melbourne where a peer I had met was in the same role as I was and she was promoted. I went to my then boss, which was the store manager, one of my favorite bosses in retail, and I said to him, "Roosevelt, why did Kelly get the job and I didn't?" He said to me, "Well, you only have a two-year degree and she has a four-year degree." I said, "Roosevelt, I have a four-year degree, magna cum laude." He was so embarrassed. He said, "Well, your profile just shows the two-year degree." I went home that night, pulled my degree out of the frame, and faxed it to the regional HR office and said, "Please update my file." Six months later, I was promoted.

Make sure you understand what people think or know and don't be afraid to ask. If I would have just let that happen and waited for the next thing to come, it wouldn't have come. They would have always assumed that I was not as educated as the rest of the group.

Then I was promoted and I went on to the next role and the next role. Another formative thing in how I think and act was when I was offered a role as a store manager. The district manager, who was a great guy, called me up and offered me the store manager role for Altamonte Springs, Florida. I had a general sense of the salary they were paying most of the other guys. And they were pretty much all guys at the time. It was quite a bit lower. I said to Rick, "Is the salary negotiable?"

He said, "No, it's not."

I said, "You do realize that it's a substantially lower salary than what the other guys are making?"

He said, "Yes, I understand that, but they have more experience than you do."

I said, "Yes, I understand that, but you're going to expect me to do the same job they do, correct?"

He said, "Yes, that's correct."

I said, "I'll take the job, but this is what I ask: I will run a fifteen percent comp ninety days into the job. If I do that, I'm going to call you and ask you for more money because, in fact, I'll be doing a better job than they're doing."

He laughed and said, "Absolutely."

To his credit, eighty-nine days later, when I was running a fifteen comp, he called me and gave me a raise. It's important to establish for yourself, fight for yourself, without being difficult or unprofessional, and set the groundwork: "I want the role, but I also want to be compensated fairly." This was in the eighties, maybe early nineties. My dad and grandfather taught me that you have to advocate for yourself.

Anyway, Bernie Brennan was in the background and popping up indiscriminately in different locations that I was in, visiting and sussing out. Throughout my store career, I was flown up to Chicago on three occasions because he wanted me to come and work in corporate. I turned them down for multiple reasons—mostly financial, in recognition of the fact that the cost of living was a lot higher in Chicago and there were taxes and so forth. On the third trip, I told the HR people, "Hey, I love you. You're great and it sounds like a great role, but unless you can meet my compensation expectations, please don't call me again because I don't want to waste your time and the company's money again coming up here." The fourth time that I got called up, they met my request for salary and so forth, and I was recruited into the marketing department.

I joke around with folks since then that I complained too much about how screwed up things were, so I got invited to help come fix them. You know the history of Montgomery Ward. I was only so successful at accomplishing that. I spent five years in the corporate office in different marketing roles. My first role was as marketing director for the home division, which was where most of my experience was. My last role was marketing director of planning and advertising operations. I ran all the marketing planning, the calendar, the events, who got space—because we were very print-driven at that time—who got TV spots, who got radio. I did all of that.

I hit a glass ceiling, if you will, where I was managing. I was reporting to a senior VP as a director and could not seem to get to the next level. I set a boundary with that boss and said, "Hey, how do I get to the next level? Tell me the things I need to do." We had a conversation. I said, "Okay, I'm going to go work on the things you've given me and I'd like you to work on the things I'm looking for in terms of my experience in the company, and let's touch base in six months." Six months went by and I did everything I said I was going to do, and he did nothing. In the meantime, one of the EVPs left the company and went to a shopping television network in Minneapolis that was pretty much a startup, and he called me and said, "I'm doing this. Are you interested?" I said, "No, I really want to play out this role here and see what happens." I gave the then boss six more months and nothing happened, and then I left.

I went to a company then called ValueVision, which later became ShopNBC because NBC's network took a stake in it. I worked for five years in different roles in that company in what I call "then-real-time retail," which is as close to the dot-com world today as it could get without it being as sophisticated. We did have a website. It was called ShopNBC.com. When I went there, the company was ninety million dollars total. When I left, it was six hundred million dollars, but by no means do I take credit for that leap. Some of it came from forming the distribution of the network through different channels. NBC obviously had networks and cable relationships, so that helped. The roles I had there were formative in who I am today.

My boss was the CEO, Gene McCaffrey. Gene basically believed in throwing everything at me that I could possibly handle—or maybe not—just to see if I could stretch, which was wonderful because I had more and more responsibility in different roles. I had a stint in strategic business development for a while. I ran marketing. I ran broadcast sales. And in my last role there, all the on-air talent reported to me. I was responsible for programming and what we were going to sell and when. It was a 24/7 job because television shopping doesn't end. The only day every year it was closed was on Christmas Day, when we ran tapes. I had twenty-one people reporting to me that, to be kind, were very focused on how they looked and what hours they worked. That was a whole new learning experience for me in terms of managing egos and not hurting people's feelings, figuring out win-win situations.

At that time, I did some professional training at a seminar for several days on negotiation skills. It turned out to be one of the best things I ever did. It has served me well even up until today in terms of how to work with people and negotiate whatever terms you need for what you're trying to accomplish.

I was then recruited away to go work for American Signature Furniture. And the home background served me well again. I did that for a couple years and absolutely loved the job but did not love the geography. I found Columbus, Ohio to be too gray. If you've spent any time there, you know what I'm talking about. I loved my job and it killed me, but I just couldn't live there anymore.

Sitting in the hot tub with my husband on a gray Sunday afternoon, I said, "I've got to get out of here. Are you in?" My husband is phenomenal—I could write a book about him and what a supportive person he is. He said, "Okay, no problem. Let's see what's next on the horizon."

I went in that day in February and fired off my résumé to a guy named Mike Powell, who was a recruiter down in Florida, and I said, "Do you know anyone in Denver?" because we had a second home in the mountains. He said, "As a matter of fact, I do, at Sports Authority." He fired my résumé off to this other person he knew at Sports Authority, and as luck would have it, they had a need. I found myself working there by Labor Day of that year, which was kind of crazy, pushing the envelope in terms of networking, being open to new experiences, and moving around.

I was at Sports Authority for three years and loved it. It was great experience in terms of working for a private versus a public company. Then, a recruiter called me and said, "Hey, I have this opportunity for this really huge company and you should call me back." At that time, we were pretty happy with the hiking, biking, skiing, and all that, and I looked at my husband and said, "What do you think?" He said, "I don't know. Why don't you call him and see?" It turned out to be Home Depot. That was in 2009. You know how bad the economy was. My husband and I looked at each other and said, "Are we crazy even contemplating this move?" I called my dad, who's not a retailer. He's an electrician. I said, "Hey, what do you think of Home Depot?" He said, "I think you have to do it." I give my dad huge credit for my confidence. My dad's always said, "Hey, everyone always puts their pants on one leg at a time. You should never be afraid to speak your mind. You should always go for it. You're smart. You're capable." He's always been very encouraging, as was my mom. He said, "I think you should go do it because probably one of the few things you haven't marketed yet is home improvement."

I came to Home Depot and interviewed three times. There are two specific people here that convinced me to make the leap in one of the worst economies of our lifetime. One was Carol Tomé and the other was Frank Blake. Carol Tomé indirectly convinced me because I read up and was so impressed with her CFO skills and her presence of mind. I had read a lot about how she managed cash flow for the company. I was inspired by the fact that the company is very focused on women and growing women in the workplace, so that was motivating for me. Frank Blake, when I interviewed with him, was probably the youngest person over sixty that I'll ever know. He was so passionate about what he was seeing his kids, his early-twenties kids, doing. He was like, "I need you to come here and help me help the company make a shift away from print to digital because I really believe that's where everything is going, but I need you to do it."

I packed up from Denver. My husband left his job and moved here with me. He has followed me through every career move I've made, making a leap without a job, and every single time has been hired without a contract or entitlement because the company hired me. Every single time I've introduced him to the company and the leadership, he's been hired. Yet again, he came to Atlanta with no job and later went on to work in HomeDepot.com.

When I think about books that have helped me in my role, *The CMO Manifesto* by John F. Ellett is such a great primer. I read it and had my team read it. I read it after I did what I've accomplished here, and it checked every box. It was just a happy accident that I went through the paces that I did, but one of the key things that I did when I got to Home Depot was I aligned on expectations: "Here's what you need me to do. This is what success looks like," which was helping lay the groundwork for that digital shift.

I was at Home Depot for about a year and a few months when the then-CMO, Frank Bifulco, retired. I was put in as CMO. The first thing Craig Menear, who is now CEO and was my boss at the time, said was, "You've done a phenomenal job building relationships because our company runs on relationships." I made the digital shift and had laid out the groundwork for that at the beginning of 2010. That playbook still exists today and it is what we use. We actually didn't deviate from it. I attribute that to one part luck and two parts skill. But I had a vision and laid it out on paper and got buy-in. We actually just got done talking about it to our investors in our call a few weeks ago. And we're going to talk about the shifts we've made again tomorrow in our investors' meeting, which is pretty exciting.

Steimle: What does the structure of your marketing team look like today?

Mueller: The consumer insights team reports to me. We also have the customer relations marketing team reporting in. I also oversee our gift card business. I oversee our marketing, both strategy planning and our private brand's marketing team. We also have the management of the Home Depot brand, all the creative and production teams, and the media team reporting to me as well.

Most recently, we blended the digital marketing practice with the rest of our marketing practice. It was housed in our online team, which has a separate leader, and that's because we have a high level of commitment to the online piece of our business. The digital practice for marketing is now rolled up under marketing, and the strategic reason for that is so we can do a better job of integrating our buys and how we spend and allocate our media but also importantly because much of what marketing is today is data-driven. We're using all of that insight and all the data we're acquiring to fuel more digital strategy. It just made sense. It was a great time to make that pivot.

I manage anything facing the customer for the Home Depot brand other than the Home Depot website. I do that for U.S. only. I partner with our Canada and our Mexico operations to guide and inform them, but they are run by separate marketing leaders.

Steimle: What is your philosophy on building and managing a marketing team?

Mueller: My philosophy is you have to invest in your people and empower them and enable them to do a great job. I attribute all the success we've had in marketing to my team. I'll quote Mark Holifield, who is the EVP in our supply chain distribution and fulfillment. He once said to me, "If you're working too hard, you need to look at your team." A light bulb went on. This was years ago when I basically first got here. I thought, "Wow, I have got to think differently about the people I surround myself with." I put a tremendous amount of effort into recruiting talent and taking the talent on the team already and enabling them and empowering them by training and development. Over the last couple of years, we've spent one entire day every single month with both internal speakers and external speakers in training and developing them because the world outside of Home Depot keeps changing. I felt—and I still feel this way—that I have to continually expose them to new ways of thinking and new tools, but I also have to step back once they have that mindset and let them do their jobs. It's important for our talent to know I'm invested in their success.

I also have a philosophy of test and learn. Go really fast. And it's okay to have things not pan out as long as you learn from it. We spend a great deal of time constructing tests, theories, and pilots. They don't all work, but that's okay. That's how we have been successful the last five years, specifically with digital, as we continue to push forward successful programs and then divest of tests that aren't deemed a success.

I've evolved a lot in the last couple years specifically. I know my team would agree because we just did a survey with them for me to get their feedback. I tell them all the time, "You guys are running the show. I'm here to help you. I'm here to support you, to give you information, to give you air cover, to help you make the case for your ideas, to make your job easier, and to take friction out by making introductions throughout the building."

In a lot of cases, I help them network, putting them in front of the right leaders in the company to get exposure to new opportunities. I'm also pretty passionate about kicking people out of marketing into other areas of the company. I could go through a whole bunch of individuals that have moved out of marketing, and I'm so proud of what they've accomplished. I have a couple folks who are now officers in the company who worked for me and then went onto other things. I'm excited and happy to see them go because that's what they wanted in their careers.

I'm also excited about recruiting from within the company. We have six thousand people, give or take, within our buildings. On any given day, I can bump into lots of strangers, but when I meet someone who seems to be excited about what we do, I make sure to sit down and talk with them. We're actively recruiting talent.

I believe in a concept called "raw talent," which my team would tell you is a little bit painful. About a year ago, I embraced that fully. I believe in bringing people that are genuinely curious and motivated, whether or not they have any experience at all. I had been chatting with a peer who is the CMO at Georgia-Pacific, Douwe Bergsma, who's a great guy. He was sharing with me an approach he was taking in media of hiring people who were not media buyers. So I asked him, "Douwe, how's that working out?" It turned out to work really well for him, so we've embraced that concept here.

We've been pulling people with similar skill sets and that curiosity, motivation, and passion and have seen great success with that. People are excited to try something new versus "This is how we've always done it." What I find today in marketing is that "This is how we've always done it" has no place in the business. It's much better to bring people in who have different lenses on the business. I'm really passionate about my team, building up my team and what we've accomplished as a result.

Steimle: How do you make sure you're in touch with your customers and understand their needs and wants?

Mueller: I'm sitting in a room right now with three life-sized fiberboard cutouts of our pro customer, our consumer, and one of our associates, who's wearing an apron, and they're all holding signs that say, "What's in it for me?" We try to always remember who we're here to serve. The insights team reports to me, and we spend a great deal of time talking with our customers, not just third-party research but first party. We also have two panels—one of our pro or contractor customer and one of our consumer—with thousands of people that we can ask questions to, and they'll tell us what they think. I also spend time with our customer relationship marketing analytics team. They're the folks that are driven off the specific transactional data and other data that we can use to know our customers at the household level. I spend a lot of time observing what people do.

One of the things that I do that helps me the most is I get out of the building. I try to live my life through the lens of the customer: What am I doing with my mobile phone? What's happening with my family? How are they consuming media? Then, I pressure-test. I try very hard not to be a focus group of one. It makes me crazy when people do that. It's seeing what's happening outside and trying to run that through our own data set to see if it holds true.

In terms of knowing the customer, the most important thing I do is pay attention to the outcome of things we're doing, because you can do research all day long and people will tell you what they'll do, but it doesn't necessarily mean that's actually what they do. I learned that early on, so we spend a great deal of time testing our theories and seeing if they actually play out. We come to know the customer much more by what they do than by what they say.

Steimle: What metrics are you measured on that you have to report on?

Mueller: I'm measured on the same metrics that all of our leadership team is measured on. We all have one complete set of goals. We're obviously here to drive shareholder value and to drive wealth for our associates. We all have sales goals. Carol talks publicly about how we drive return on invested capital, operating profit for our shareholders, and earnings. We all have the same goals and that's also helpful in terms of everyone being on the same page. I do have subgoals that I've created for myself that leadership holds me to and I've identified what those goals are. There was never a day when our CEO would have said, "Trish, I want you to answer for return on ad spend." But tomorrow, Craig, Carol, or Ted is going to talk about our ongoing improvement in return on ad spend. That's a metric I didn't create, but I told them I need to be accountable for it, so that's a key one that my team looks to when we think about what we're doing. Those are the key metrics.

We all hold ourselves accountable to customer satisfaction. I don't have a specific metric for that, but I'm always working towards making sure the marketing efforts we have don't dissatisfy the customer and that we stay relevant in the marketplace. Our insights team actually manages our social listening, so we help inform how satisfied our customers are by listening to that as well.

Steimle: What do you see as some of the biggest challenges facing today's CMOs?

Mueller: Pretty much the standard ones you read about: data and what to do with it. Talent. There's a war for talent. You think about boiling all that data down to something to act on and having great people that can find those kernels of knowledge for you. That's huge.

Motivating and continuing to inspire the team when there's a lot of pressure is another. None of these is specific to Home Depot, but when I think about our talent, there's a lot on their plate. It's a challenge making sure they know they're appreciated, and that they're compensated, and that their development's important so we retain talent. It's tough to hit the reset button with all we have going on. It's important that our folks stay here and feel like they can contribute and we see the impact of that over time. Those are really the big ones. It's the people, technology, time kind of components, having the right people and using the data and the technology right.

Data is a huge top of mind for us right now in terms of how we use it. How do we not just mire ourselves in it? Once we have those insights, how do we act on them quickly?

Peter Horst

Chief Marketing Officer
The Hershey Company

Peter Horst became CMO at The Hershey Company in 2015. He first gained experience in the CMO role at Ameritrade and TruSecure, which is now Verizon. Previous to working at The Hershey Company, Horst served as senior vice president of brand marketing at Capital One Financial. Horst has a bachelor of arts in history and literature from Harvard University and an MBA in marketing and general management from the Tuck School of Business at Dartmouth.

Josh Steimle: A lot of people may not be fully aware of all the products that Hershey makes. Can you give us a quick overview of the product line?

Peter Horst: Hershey has a wider array of products and plays in more categories than most people realize. We certainly have the core confection brands that everyone's familiar with: Hershey's Milk Chocolate Bar, Hershey's Kisses, Reese's Peanut Butter Cups, and a whole array of brands that are not quite on the same mega scale as those. We have Twizzlers, brands I certainly remember from my childhood, like Zagnut, and other big brands including KitKat *(Note: KitKat is manufactured and distributed by The Hershey Company inside the United States, and outside the United States by Nestlé).* We also play in the breath freshener space. We have Ice Breakers and Breath Savers.

© Josh Steimle 2016
J. Steimle, *Chief Marketing Officers at Work*, DOI 10.1007/978-1-4842-1931-7_19

In the last several years, the company has also been expanding more broadly into snacking, with the intention to play across the spectrum from the great-tasting, like the Reese's cup, to the quite good-for-you protein-based snacks and so forth, and everything in between. We acquired Brookside Brands several years ago, which is a dark chocolate and fruit and nut brand that plays both in confection and snack bars. We acquired the Krave brand, which plays in the culinary end of the meat jerky space. We are launching a soy-based protein snack with a wonderfully clean nutrition and ingredient label; a great-tasting snack that comes in a variety of forms. Through both acquisition and organic innovation, the company's spread across a pretty broad array of snacking categories.

Steimle: Now to you. How did you get started? What are the steps that got you where you are today?

Horst: The path that took me from college to where I am today was a bit of a magical mystery tour. I majored in history and literature, which was a wonderful thing to study, and I'm glad I did it, but it certainly didn't point me in any particular career direction. In the early days of my career, I ideated across broadcast journalism. I then explored working at a talent agency, then spent some time at a law firm as a paralegal, then in magazine publishing, and then finally realized what I needed was business school to get some marketable skills.

It was at business school that I discovered marketing, which to me was particularly exciting and satisfying because it was clearly a whole-brain profession, where you had to roll around with the numbers and wrestle with analytic, strategic issues but then turn around and go through a more purely creative process to develop big ideas, craft magic language, and make two plus two equal five. In my bouncing around in various roles before business school, I had found positions that were either creative roles lacking in any kind of intellectual vigor or cerebral roles that were not tapping any kind of creative instance. I found marketing at business school and from there went to General Mills where I spent a bunch of years and had a wonderful experience across a great variety of categories and business challenges—kids' products, adult, new products, established, price-driven, brand-driven, regional, national. A wonderful portfolio of experiences.

With the impatience of youth, after six years there, I was starting to feel the itch to explore new territories and went from there to U.S. West, which was one of the Baby Bell phone companies post-AT&T breakup. They were one of the more aggressive in getting into the new territories of the unregulated spaces around wireless and interactive television and entertainment. The world of telecom in the early days of conversions was everything the world of packaged goods was not at that point: lots of strategic upheaval, new technologies, converging of industries, new consumer opportunities that had never before been conceived or possible. It was a very exciting place. I wore a bunch of different hats there. I worked as an internal marketing strategy consultant on various new media opportunities. I held a couple of line roles and did a lot of internal entrepreneurial work building up some internet businesses.

From there, I had the opportunity to join Ameritrade, which was just at the dawn of that brand. It had been functioning as four separate brokerages with different uses of technology and different consumer value propositions up to that point but had the opportunity to build that brand and drive an integrated, aggressive marketing program in a hotly contested space. It was great learning, great experience, literally a "build the airplane and fly it at the same time" sort of thing.

From there, I took what may look in some respects like a career left turn and went into B2B technology and joined a small technology company that focused on information security. This was back when e-commerce was just starting to take off. And security, even then, was a primary consumer hang-up. I saw an opportunity to help build this company to be the Good Housekeeping seal of approval for an increasingly networked world.

Given the turn of the digital economy and the April 2000 stock meltdown in the tech space, the agenda shifted from building a B2B consumer brand into a pure thrifty B2B play. I suddenly had to go deep in learning how to get the most out of a modest budget in the context of driving leads to a high-end enterprise salesforce. It was a painful experience at times, but it was great learning. I had to go deep in technology product management, learning that always tricky balance with marketing, sales and the management of lead flow processes. I did lots of work with public relations using that as a primary brand-building tool.

While it was great learning, after a few years of that, I started to think I was not leveraging the experience in consumer marketing skills that I'd developed over the years, and the 80/20 of stretch versus comfort zone was off. I wanted to get back into something with more of a consumer bent and on a bigger stage as well.

That's when I joined Capital One, where I spent twelve great years in a founder-led company that was extraordinarily bold in its strategic objectives and continually moving from one improbably audacious objective to the next. That's what kept me—a guy who'd had some career ADD craving new chal-lenges and moving between industries—there for twelve years. I spent most of my time at the tip of the spear of the company's diversification as it moved from credit cards, to home loans, to auto loans, to branch banking and digital banking. I got to wrestle with a great array of fascinating challenges: How do we evolve a brand to increasingly embrace all those different categories and product segments? How could we drive innovation so that when we entered a category, we had a better mousetrap to sell? How do we evolve the market-ing model to embrace increasingly digital and social channels? It was a great experience, especially working in a company that was so steeped in data and analytics from its inception.

Then, I was presented the opportunity to come full circle back to CPG (consumer packaged goods) and join the Hershey Company. I found that too great an opportunity to resist. It's a company of tremendous iconic brands with great history, richness, and attachment. Yet, I had a sense that there was so much more that could be done with those brands. It was clearly a company that had bold objectives to innovate, to move into new categories, to develop globally. It was a company where the culture seemed to be one that I would appreciate and want to be part of. For all those reasons, I made that shift. That was four months ago. I'm still quite new to the role.

Steimle: How do you take an established company like Hershey and bring it into the digital age with social media and mobile?

Horst: I give the company a ton of credit in that it is being both bold and rigorous as we move into that arena. Over the years, we've seen companies make incredibly aggressive shifts of investments, say, from broadcast to digital, only to dial back and say, "Whoops, that was a little overly aggressive." We're taking a balanced approach whereby we're striding meaningfully into that space with significant investments without losing the rigor and the analytical underpinnings that have made the company so successful to date.

We're being thoughtful in terms of how we manage the portfolio of the tried and true channels, moving assertively and mindfully into digital and social channels, and also being purposeful and devoting some of our time and budget to continuous experimentation and testing of new channels and new tactics so we're always feeding this overall ecosystem with fresh learning.

Steimle: What does the structure of your marketing team look like?

Horst: We have a regional structure, and within that, we have brand groups centered around the clusters of brands, as you'd expect: the confections, the mints, the snacks, and so forth. We have groups that are devoted to digital, to the media, and creative support. We have teams that are focused purely on innovation and feeding the innovation pipeline. We tend to pretty mindfully move people around through those, both to give them international experience and to let them go deep on the craft of marketing in a staff role versus the more general manager/P&L brand manager role. We try and make sure people get a good portfolio of experiences in their careers.

Steimle: What's your philosophy on building and managing a marketing team?

Horst: I couldn't articulate a philosophy of managing a team, but I could tell you some of the things that are important to me that perhaps add up to a philosophy. First, you've got to have the right culture, the right team dynamic, the right environment that enables people to do great work. That starts with who's on the team, what the rules of engagement are, and what the cultural norms and behaviors are that you expect and insist on. For me, those include egoless collaboration, a leaning-in courage-of-your-convictions proclivity to generate and champion bold ideas, a curiosity, a desire to explore, and a team orientation whereby people have each other's backs and seek the best for the whole and are not on a mission to simply do for themselves.

If there's one thing I look for in marketers, it's this restless curiosity to seek, develop, and look for what's new, what's exciting—not chasing squirrels but having a continuous openness to "Is this as great as it could be?"

Another is a collective desire to do great work. Sometimes, effective can be the enemy of great, and sometimes, people set up a false polar dichotomy: it can either be hardworking or it can be great, and award-winning or art for art's sake. I'm a big believer in having to do both. The best stuff does do both, so that as we're thinking about moving the business, driving commerce, and accomplishing our goals, we don't lose sight of the fact that a great way to do that is through powerful, compelling, engaging, talked-about work that gets people excited, that gets them talking about it, that makes your brand part of the popular culture.

As I work with teens and try and establish culture and operating norms, I try and encourage this sense of "Is this great? We challenged ourselves to do something we're excited about instead of just effectively moving a needle somewhere."

Steimle: What are the goals and metrics you've been given to focus on in this new role?

Horst: There are a bunch across the various areas. There are some that are pure P&L-oriented—deliver a bottom line in some of the parts of my role and be a part of delivering the bottom line as a company. There's all the classic ones of share and growth, and there are various brand metrics around awareness, consideration, and so forth.

Innovation-wise, we have goals around what percent of growth is being delivered by innovation and what the help of the pipeline is. Part of what we're working through right now is what the KPIs should be as we move into some of these new channels. We have pretty well-known, time-tested KPIs around, say, broadcast. It's not always as obvious what the success metrics should be around digital engagement, social activities, and so forth. What does good look like? What's the right benchmark to be shooting for? We're in the process of developing some of those because those will certainly become a part of the mix as well.

Steimle: How is globalization affecting marketing for you?

Horst: That's a big one for me. Hershey has had a global agenda for many years now, but over the last several years, it has been more aggressively building that agenda, so it becomes an interesting set of questions around how you both build businesses locally and manage the brands globally. As I look at other companies that have managed that, I see a pretty wide spectrum of how companies approach it. You see some that are quite comfortable allowing significant degrees of freedom region by region to respond to local tastes and preferences and to craft the brand to meet the local realities, and then you see others that are much more strictly managed globally with little to zero deviation in terms of digital identities, positioning, ingredients, presentation, form factor, etc. It is what it is everywhere. At the end of the day, it's a choice. It's a philosophy. I don't perceive one right answer out there. The question becomes, "What's the right answer for the company?"

A set of discussions I'm routinely drawn into and accountable for resolving is as we take Reese's Peanut Butter Cups to China, how far will we go in adjusting the value proposition to address Chinese tastes and sensibilities? How much will we stay the course and try to educate and embrace customers with a more standard global version? That's a big one. There's a built-in tension there. The local teams will always have a bias towards "I need more flexibility." And folks in the home office will always have a bias towards "Let's stay the course." How do you find the right, smart answer in there and stay consistent from a philosophical perspective? That's one whole challenge in the management of the brand.

Another is making sure that as a CMO, you don't presume too much in terms of what you know and what translates and that you're sensitive to the different laws of nature that often apply region by region. The way people think about brands, the channels they use, their tastes both in terms of flavor profiles and how people eat vary so tremendously that you have to keep a nimble and open mind as you engage in conversations from region to region.

Steimle: How do you make sure you're in touch with customers globally and understand what they need and want? How do you balance local needs with staying true to the brand?

Horst: Going back to the notion of philosophies, I have a strong belief that everything starts with good insights and having a high bar for what gets to be called an insight. You have to make sure that in all the markets you're in, you have a well-tuned insights ecosystem whereby you know who your customers are, you know what's on their mind, and you trust what you're getting from that insights ecosystem so that it can be the foundation for absolutely everything you do.

How do you walk that balance? You have to start with where you fall in terms of that spectrum of philosophies I described. Are you Snickers, which is absolutely unchanged pretty much anywhere you go in the world? Are you Oreo, which as it entered China developed a number of forms that were more consistent with the Chinese palate in order to establish that brand and provided many more degrees of flexibility? Decide where you are on that spectrum and what that means in terms of decisions.

Chief Marketing Officers at Work

Then, it's a process of assessing what you are hearing from consumers. What does it mean in terms of implied action steps? There are ways in which you could lead quickly to, "If I hear insight A, that means I must take action B," but there are sometimes more nuanced ways you can navigate through those realities depending on where you've decided your philosophy is. It comes down to having good, open dialog and debate with what's truly necessary to move the business and what's a challenge that can be overcome with great marketing, a little bit of time, perhaps the right level of investment—an education and familiarity challenge versus a fundamental structural barrier. You have to know the difference and have a good lively debate to sort through that. Find that Venn diagram overlap of it that addresses the local realities but doesn't violate your belief system of managing global brands.

Steimle: Do you have any experience breaking down silos? What can the CMO do to facilitate that?

Horst: The breaking down of silos issue is more important than ever in this modern marketing world because with the proliferation of channels, with the growing importance of data and analytics, you cannot afford to operate in silos. It becomes absolutely crippling. Where does PR begin and social end? Who's responsible for data strategy between a CIO organization and a marketing organization? How do you accomplish real-time analytics? I'm a huge believer in egoless collaboration. You need to get to a point where people are able to park their functional identities at the door and come together as multifunctional teams attacking a particular issue.

That may take the form of these agile pods that we were doing so much of at Capital One and that we're starting to do at Hershey. You have someone from PR, someone from social, a digital technologist, a copywriter, and a brand strategist all sitting together in real time co-creating, executing, testing, sharing, learning. That can only happen if people aren't behaving as though they're in competing functions and are concerned about turf, creating borderlines between them.

One form it can take is these established, permanent pod-like things. Another way it comes together is almost like a consulting firm, people coming together around a particular initiative and then reforming around the next initiative. Again, it only works if people are not focused on their turf, if they're not focused on ownership with a capital O, and if it's about jumping in and getting the best out of each other for a common goal. That's a huge cultural tenet that forces dialog around operating principles but also can sometimes force discussions around structure.

Steimle: Are there new forms of marketing or new trends in marketing that you're excited to experiment with in your new role?

Horst: One is this craving for authenticity in brands and craving for aspects of story behind the brand. Everyone points to the craft beer syndrome. The craft beer syndrome is certainly showing up in many categories, including some of the ones I now operate in. It's this desire for realness, for a sense of understanding of what this thing is, why it is, the story behind it, and how it plays into my life in a more meaningful way than satisfying some functional need. That's exciting stuff from the perspective of the marketer because it forces you to go to richer, more nuanced, more interesting places. You can't just do the good, old-fashioned bite and smile TV ad to satisfy that craving for an authentic story.

It also sets up some real challenges. People's natural instinct is to feel that that kind of authenticity doesn't come from a larger, more established company that they're familiar with. There's this joy of discovery of the craft brand. How can you as a larger enterprise address that and play in that space? It's an exciting and challenging trend all at once.

Steimle: How do you get through to a consumer in this day in a world of ad blockers and people skipping ads? Where consumers have so much control, how do you make sure the brand connects and maintains its power and relevance?

Horst: When you do great work and people call each other into the room to see and enjoy experiencing it, then they don't skip it. They don't hit the mute button, but they might even not just watch it all but seek it out because it is giving them something intrinsically rewarding beyond a buy-me message from the manufacturer.

Doing great work is one way. Another way is thinking broadly beyond the "ad unit." How do you leverage some of these channels to become a more integrated part of their experience so it's not about interrupting your programming to bring you this message but seamlessly, authentically, and in an entertaining, rewarding way becoming part of the experience so that you're not forcing that either-or experience on the part of the consumer?

Steimle: What do you see as the biggest challenges facing today's CMOs?

Horst: One is certainly how to drive growth. I have not yet met the company or the executive that isn't consumed with what to do about driving growth. I've never felt a more competitive and challenging business environment, broadly speaking, across industries. How do you grow? And then, challenge number two, how do you do that in a way where you are understanding and demonstrating rigorous ROI in order to get that growth? With this proliferation of channels, getting a handle on how it's all adding up and what you are getting for it is something we all wrestle with. And one of the challenges du jour is the whole notion of ad fraud and what percentage of your digital spend is doing what you think it's doing.

The challenges are driving growth, doing it with ROI, and thirdly, managing a complex ecosystem of channels, of technologies, of data, and of a constantly changing consumer behavior. It's a massive intellectual challenge to stay on top of that, to knit it together, to focus on the things that matter most without getting distracted by the myriad choices, technologies, channels, and tactics that are out there waiting to suck up your time and money.

Steimle: How do you keep up with all the opportunities, tools, and vendors? How do you make sure you're not missing out on something?

Horst: That's a source of constant anxiety. I get about two hundred emails a day, and three quarters of them are people breathlessly telling me about their wonderful solution that will change my life. Some percentage of them are probably right, but I don't begin to have enough time to read all those emails, let alone answer them, let alone engage and explore. It is one of my greatest sources of anxiety: How do I keep up? How do I know what's going on? How do I know what I need to know?

For me, it comes down to a mix of things. One is I try and stay engaged in a small number of peer networks and stay in touch with people, ask smart people I know what they are doing and what they think I need to know. I have a lot of good people that I work with, both at agencies and on the team, who stay busy understanding what's out there and what's going on. From time to time, we'll engage external consultants of various sorts to help us keep our ears to the ground. To me, it's a mosaic of things you do to try and have both a good radar going and a good filtering system for what's worth your time and energy.

Steimle: Are there any common mistakes you see today's CMOs making?

Horst: That's a tough one for me to answer because I'm not sitting looking over other CMOs' shoulders and therefore would hesitate to call things mistakes. Some cautions out there might be getting too caught up in the energy of a trend. I mentioned companies that have made bold declarations of how much money they're going to throw into new channels only to then scratch their heads and say, "Gosh, that wasn't the best move." It's balancing being smart, thoughtful, and prudent while being bold and stepping into new spaces. Getting that balance right is a tough one.

There's another caution, which is delegating too much of your decision making to the data and becoming too paint-by-numbers, too willing to allow the analytics to be the answer to your important questions instead of allowing the data, the analytics, and the numbers to inform, guide, prompt, and stimulate but not relinquish control, decision-making, and judgment in that equation. There are times where if you follow the data out the window, you end up somewhere you don't want to be. That's another aspect of balance. In so many ways, managing the issues of balance is increasingly a challenge for CMOs.

Steimle: What are your thoughts on marketing to millennials?

Horst: It is a hot topic. I recently had some interesting dialog with some folks on the subject of multicultural and how the thought processes around multicultural and millennials are increasingly interrelated dialogs. Addressing a multicultural consumer is as much about addressing a multicultural mindset, perhaps more so than identifying people who would be identifiable as multicultural, and the multicultural mindset is in many ways a millennial mindset.

I wouldn't say it's the happy luxury of killing two birds with one stone, but I thought it was interesting that those two things are more interrelated than not and that a millennial who might be white and suburban could have a multicultural mindset in terms of their consumption, their interests, and their cultural reference points and that to not realize that would be to miss an opportunity. I'm not sure yet where to go with that, but I found it tremendously thought provoking.

Steimle: Over the course of your career in marketing, how have you seen marketing change, and what's stayed the same?

Horst: One thing that's changed is it's gotten so much more complicated—the channels, the technologies, the data, the multifunctional considerations, the complexities of proliferating segments. I look back at the early days of my career and it seems almost childlike in its simplicity. It's a much more multifunctional, multitechnology, multichannel undertaking. Marketing has evolved so much to the point where, in some ways, no two CMO roles are alike.

As you look across companies, it's probably one of the most varied functions in terms of how the job description and the accountabilities play out from one company to the next. The role it plays and what it drives, what it owns, what's expected of it have gone through a lot of change over time.

There are some things that haven't changed. At the end of the day, it's about understanding consumers. It's about finding a catalyzing insight. It's about a big, powerful, enduring idea or the search for a big, powerful, enduring idea that can move hearts and minds. It's about leveraging sights, sounds, language, and ideas to make that happen. There's so much that has simply remained true. I carry the things I learned from early mentors decades ago with me today, even in a world where I'm leveraging those learnings in channels that couldn't remotely have been conceived of twenty-five years ago. Fortunately, there's still plenty that remains constant.

Steimle: What are the skills marketing students should be acquiring that will still be relevant ten or twenty years from now?

Horst: Even years ago when I was doing on-campus recruiting, I would encourage people to go for breadth. One of the wonderful things about the marketing function is that it is so multifunctional. You have to be able to sit with the market researcher and talk about statistics. You have to be able to have a good dialog with someone in the supply chain about manufacturing efficiencies and sourcing. You need to be able to engage in creative dialog with the agencies. That doesn't come from going one hundred miles deep in majoring in advertising.

I would say breadth of capability, agility of learning. In particular, it's a world of data and technology, so being data-savvy, which doesn't mean being a programmer. It doesn't mean being an analyst but knowing enough to be dangerous, knowing enough to have a good conversation with the person who's doing the analytics, and doing the coding of the apps—or whatever it might be—so that you can be a good consumer, a good customer of those activities. It's about breadth with a particular focus on the data and the digital side of things.

Brian Beitler

Executive Vice President & Chief Marketing Officer
Lane Bryant

Brian Beitler is executive vice president and CMO at retailer Lane Bryant. Beitler previously served in senior marketing positions for brands such as David's Bridal, Kohl's Department Stores, Bath & Body Works, Toys"R"Us, and Mattel. Beitler holds a bachelor of science in marketing from the University of Utah and an MBA from Brigham Young University.

Josh Steimle: Give us an overview of your career. How did you get your start?

Brian Beitler: From the time I was young, I had a desire and a knack for persuading others to see my perspectives as well as for selling things. I remember being one of the few kids who actually enjoyed selling the $1 chocolate bars door to door to raise money for Little League Baseball. It was natural for me and I was pretty good at it. As I went through my high school years and worked in various roles, including telemarketing and sales, it became even more clear. I learned that I really loved sales and marketing and my journey through college was soon determined in my mind. When I entered the U of U, marketing was without question my major of choice. I also knew from a young age that I was going to pursue an advanced degree, and it was going to be a business degree and an MBA.

J. Steimle, *Chief Marketing Officers at Work*, DOI 10.1007/978-1-4842-1931-7_20

My focus on business was also shaped by two parents, both of whom worked in the finance industry. They both encouraged business and emphasized that with my natural talents and skills I might have a successful career in marketing.

Up until the start of college my plan was pretty traditional for a middle class kid. Do well in school, get involved, work to pay for college, and hang out with friends. But things changed when I met Amy, my future wife. We fell in love fast and decided to marry even faster; we were married in 1992 at the age of nineteen. We had our first child by twenty-one, our second by twenty-two, and the third by twenty-four—we ended up with six total. So while I was focused on beginning my education, we were starting a family, and figuring out how we were going to provide for this family without amassing huge debt.

I was fortunate to begin my career at Matrixx Marketing, now Convergys, the telemarketing company I started working for in high school. They were flexible at a time when flexibility wasn't common and they allowed me to adjust my schedule to fit my college courses. The company also gave me incredible opportunities as a very young leader. They promoted me quickly and I ended up working as a sales supervisor and then a floor manager on several different accounts selling long-distance. At age twenty-two, they promoted me to account manager and allowed me to run the Clairol account. The account that changed everything for me was Mattel. Mattel had launched one of the first software programs for girls called Barbie Fashion Designer. We provided consumer and technical support for Barbie Fashion Designer, and I was given the opportunity to run the account. During my time on their account, I developed a strong relationship with Mattel. They reached out to me as I was finishing my MBA and offered me a job at their headquarters in El Segundo, California.

I joined Mattel as a manager in their consumer affairs department overseeing call center operations, but only a few months later my boss left, and they gave me the opportunity to run their consumer affairs organization as Director of Worldwide Consumer Affairs. Then, the sales part of their direct marketing arm was added. Mattel had a high-end Barbie collectibles business and a high-end die-cast car business that they sold direct through catalogs. One thing led to another and I ended up in several roles there. I worked on strategy for the Boys' division and then ultimately as marketing director for Hot Wheels.

I had about a five-year journey at Mattel and was enjoying that career path when, as a result of presenting at a conference, I received an invitation from Toys"R"Us to join them on the retail side of the toy business. I wasn't looking for a change, but the thought of living near New York City appealed to me. My father was from NY and my grandmother still resided there and my business travels to NY had always energized me. We decided to make the change to retail for geography reasons and give the East Coast a try.

I spent two years at Toys"R"Us in various marketing roles until that company was taken private by KKR and Bain. At about that time, Limited Brands reached out and talked about the reposition of their Bath & Body Works brand. They were looking for a marketing executive to come in as they were transforming from the country, cracker barrel store into what they termed the "modern apothecary." Having learned to love retail at Toys"R"Us, I was enamored by the speed and pace of retail. You could both learn and affect change so immediately compared to CPG. At Mattel, it took months, even years to bring a product to market. In retail, you could have an idea to improve the business and have it in place within weeks.

I enjoyed the research and diligence in product creation, but could also see the power more immediate data would provide in retail. We just knew so much more about how the product sold, how a promotion worked, who was buying, and what else they were buying. It was truly incredible, compared to what I knew before.

After I had experienced a couple of years in retail, there was no question it was going to be a passion for me. On a less serious note, I love that it is an industry where one day you can be a genius, then the next day you're an idiot, and the day after that you're a genius again. You can affect the business that quickly if you make good decisions.

At Bath & Body Works, I learned that I loved helping to transform a business, particularly one that had stalled a little bit. I also loved learning from incredible leaders—Neil Fiske was the CEO at the time, a remarkable leader—and I learned and gained a lot from him.

After being there a few years, Kohl's Department Stores reached out. They were looking for a newly created senior vice president of marketing strategy position. They had made some changes in their marketing organization and as a company, were getting ready to launch a series of exclusive brands—Simply Vera, Vera Wang, Food Network, ELLE, etc. I would need to come in and develop a truly holistic marketing strategy that leveraged these launches while maintaining their "value" position. And I would have the opportunity to affect the strategy across every channel—traditional media, direct marketing, private label credit card, partnerships, digital.

Although growth had stalled a little bit, they were still a darling of Wall Street at the time and on the track to become the market leader in the discount space. So those facts combined with the opportunity to frame a new role and build a new team made it an easy decision as a next step in my career.

I spent a few years at Kohl's, and had a great run. It was a tough time in retail, as I was there for the recession years—'08, '09, and '10, but I felt like we were perfectly positioned to win in that situation if we did the right things. And we did by focusing on our core position and differentiators at a time when consumers were becoming even more value-oriented. Kohl's was one of the only retail brands to have positive growth through that recessionary period as we positioned the brand as the place to get the best value for your money.

I was at Kohl's for about three years when a Private Equity firm—Leonard Green and Partners—called about helping to turn around David's Bridal, a brand that had gotten stuck during the recession years. They needed a CMO to come in and partner with the CEO as they looked to reshape and change the face of that brand. We introduced a new and important relationship, White by Vera Wang, which was Vera's first diffusion brand in the bridal industry. I had worked with the Vera Wang brand at Kohl's, but now she was leveraging her namesake in the bridal industry. It was an exciting opportunity in an industry that I was absolutely passionate about. I have five daughters, and although none of them was of marrying age, it was fun to go in there and see the journey that a bride goes through. I spent four years at David's. We were successful in getting the business growing which afforded Leonard Green and Partners the opportunity to sell David's to Clayton Deubler & Rice in early 2013.

I left David's in June of 2014 and was spending the time with my family and considering what to do next when Linda Heasley, the CEO of Lane Bryant, called. I knew Linda Heasley from my days at Bath & Body Works. For a period of time, she ran our planning and allocation division while I was head of marketing. I had respect for her leadership style when we worked together, so when she asked if I would come out and have dinner with her and hear the Lane Bryant story, I agreed. After that dinner, it was easy to make the decision to join this brand, at this moment. In many ways, it was a true marketer's dream. A brand with heritage and strong awareness that was stuck and in need of revival, a brand that was focused on a specific and understandable customer segment that had been wildly ignored, and it was led by a CEO that understood purpose and brand building.

Steimle: What special things are you looking forward to doing at Lane Bryant?

Beitler: I look forward to changing the conversation about "plus-size" women, the way we view their bodies, and the way they view fashion. The remarkable thing about our culture in the U.S. is that we have made so much progress on women's equality over the last forty years. There are more women than ever going to college, pursuing advanced degrees, entering the field of science and engineering, and leading some of the Fortune 1000 companies. That said, we still have a long way to go. There are too few women in board or C-suite positions across the Fortune 1000, and I don't even want to get started on pay.

But with all this progress on so many fronts, our view of women and women's beauty remains outdated and, quite honestly, silly. We still judge women first by their looks and not the content of their character or contributions to society. That's not to say that we don't eventually get to women's contributions, because we do. But almost all of our initial impressions start with beauty, and a very narrow standard of beauty at that.

I have five daughters and four of them are in their teenage/early adult years. And while I am excited for all the opportunities ahead, I have seen, first hand, the impact of our rising expectations for women, still coupled with this outdated beauty standard. At times, it's almost as if our culture says, you can be anything you want to be as long as you are a certain size and look a certain way. Because if you don't, that needs to be your first priority and then you can do the rest.

As a brand that has been around for one hundred years, Lane Bryant has always believed that all women are beautiful and deserve to be seen and celebrated as they are. That the content of your character matters more than your body size. That said, we have also always believed that everyone should have the ability to look great and feel great in amazing fashion.

We recognize and understand at a very personal level the pressure women face, and know that all women are beautiful and deserve to feel desirable, sexy, confident, or whatever they want to feel, regardless of body size. We also know fashion can help them to achieve their inner sense of confidence.

So repositioning the brand with this empowering view has become job one. We want the market and consumers to know that all women do truly deserve great fashion and do deserve to be seen and represented in the world. In media, in fashion, in Hollywood. That was Linda's new vision of a 100-year-old purpose. She articulated it very well. In fact, when she joined the company, she put the industry on notice when she said, "We are going to change the conversation around plus size. We're going to change the way she sees the world. We're going to change the way that the world sees her. And in that process, we're not just going to make great fashion, we're going to instill confidence in women." It was a chance to join a company that was going to have a purpose that would drive both growth, as well as an important value and message for women in the country.

Steimle: What does the structure of your marketing team look like? How is it organized?

Beitler: There are five disciplines inside the team. We have a head of creative, who is responsible for working both with our external partners as well as our internal team to develop the work you see projected in the marketplace. We have a head of marketing strategy, who's responsible for building the plan and identifying the opportunities that we have both with our external advertising as well as our internal programs.

We have a team that's focused on insights and what we can learn from both the customer and the marketplace. Then, we have a team that is focused on the operations of the group. They run the finance, production, and planning for the group as a whole. Lastly, we have a team that is responsible for our brand presentation, the way the brand comes to life inside the store, the way the product is merchandised, the way the store experience is laid out and designed. The marketing team in total is about seventy associates.

Steimle: How do you coordinate communication with these individuals? What kinds of meetings do you have? What's the day-to-day?

Beitler: There's a weekly staff meeting that I run with my executive team to set priorities, establish direction, and confirm the projects and ideas that are being developed and worked on. Then, there are a series of cross-functional cadence meetings that are built around each of the key things we're working on, whether it's the promotional plan for brand, the store presentation, our digital marketing strategy, or our advertising approach. In those meetings, we talk about how we're going to execute and go to market from a cross-functional perspective.

We also have a series of broad-based cross-functional meetings with the entire leadership team from the company. In a specialty brand like ours, the brand is not just determined or projected by the marketing organization. We have merchants who are making key decisions on what to buy, what we feel is going to be right. We have a design team that's developing the trends and the fashions for the client as well as the store team that's working on the experience.

Those cross-functional meetings ensure everything about the experience— from product to marketing to web design to the store—is going to happen in the way we all want it to happen and that the product we're creating for the customer is going to be exactly what she wants. It's a very collaborative approach. I don't know that it's that way in all specialty brands, but that's certainly the structure that Linda as a leader and her executive team have worked to lay out here.

Steimle: What's your philosophy on building and managing a marketing team?

Beitler: My view is simply to find the best talent that we can find for a given role and then give them the freedom to use their creativity to move the brand forward, under a clear vision and with agreed to operating principles. My style is not to micromanage decisions, I try and encourage as many ideas to come to the table as possible. I believe great leaders help their team to curate great ideas. That means you need a lot of cross-functional meetings and a lot of places where ideas can be nurtured and developed.

The goal is to teach a team to look, to find associates that they feel could succeed them within a year or two. That's the quality of talent you want to bring into your team. Once you get the quality talent on board, you're going to need to give them the freedom to do what you hired them to do. Get out of their way and focus on providing the structure and framework around which to operate so they understand what the brand stands for and what the guardrails are for, and how we're going to move the brand forward.

Steimle: How do you attract and retain top talent?

Beitler: First, through the results. Our first focus is to put some wins on the board, to do some things that are impactful and meaningful to driving the business and to creating change because I believe great brands have gravity. If you are a great brand, you will attract customers, you will attract partners, you will attract associates, and so the first focus is to show that the marketing team is going to be able to have a real impact on the business and to articulate the purpose and the vision of the business in a compelling way so that people on the outside can see the movement and momentum that's happening with the brand. That's what begins to draw talent away from other great companies, because typically, the only way to find great talent is to convince them to move from great companies. That's where the good talent is.

The focus is quick and early on. I never run in with the desire to change a lot of the talent. Great leaders and great marketers look at the internal team and go, "Is the challenge that I have the wrong players or that this team hasn't been well led and inspired and given the freedom to create?"

As a leader coming onto a team, I've often been told by other internal executives, "This person isn't very good at their job." What you find out as a leader is it's not that they weren't good at their job. It's that they weren't allowed to use the full expression of their creativity. The first step is to see what the team that you have can do; usually, you'll find that they can do pretty amazing things. As you do that and those amazing things start to happen, talent is easily drawn into your brand, into your work, into your teams.

Steimle: What are some of the specific metrics you focus on in order to drive growth?

Beitler: There are several that we start with. We look at whether our advertising is driving an increased awareness across our target audience. Can they see the advertising? Two, does that advertising motivate consideration of the brand? Does it put us in their line of sight for potential shopping? Then, we look deeper: does it increase their purchase intent?

We monitor on an ongoing basis from a national brand tracker of women in our target market to understand how their perception, view, intent, and awareness of the brand are changing. As the leader on an aided basis, our awareness is extremely high, over ninety percent.

The goal is to be top of mind. The goal is for Lane Bryant to be the first brand she thinks of when she thinks she needs new fashion. We measure and monitor those metrics at the start. The digital era has wildly changed your level of understanding if you're being successful in your advertising because you can watch your social and digital engagement. We pay extremely close attention to how our social sentiment is moving, whether it's moving up or down. And we react!

It's not just whether we are attracting people to our Facebook page, increasing the number of likes, the number of Instagram followers. It's whether we are increasing the conversation they're wanting to have with the brand. If we do great advertising, we should see engagement increase.

We can also look at core metrics in their own media space: Is the traffic on the website climbing? Is conversion climbing? Is the time they spend on the site engaged in the brand increasing? As we look externally at those first points of contact, do we see growth? As a bricks-and-mortar retailer, we obviously pay close attention to the store traffic as well. Do we see movement in the traffic as a result of the things we're doing externally? Can we see that translate into conversion? We monitor every metric that we can, and we try and tie back to every activity that we do, even when we're doing what some marketers would call traditional brand advertising or image advertising.

Great image advertising should bring customers to the brand. It should result in action, not just curiosity, interest, or affection for the brand—not "I like that ad" but "I want to go to the store as a result of that." All the way across the marketing funnel, we're trying to measure at every point whether we are seeing movement in the right direction.

Then, at an attribute level, we monitor the attributes. Are we seeing an increase in affection? Is this a brand she loves, is this the brand for me, is this the brand with high-quality products? All of those elements in today's world are important. The beauty of where we are today versus where we were twenty years ago is that it's so much more measurable and so much more finite as you're looking to drive customers into the brand. You can see real time whether or not you're being successful with the messages you're projecting.

Steimle: What do you see as some of the biggest challenges facing today's CMOs?

Beitler: One is the deluge of data that is coming to brands. It's only going to increase. We see sensors coming on the horizon, almost being able to literally let you see a customer navigate the store. These don't exist yet, but between beacons and sensors, just the sheer volume of data is a huge challenge. And so is understanding how to prioritize that data to find insights that you should react to in order to affect the business.

The increasing shift of the consumers' demand for immediacy also creates a challenge for retailers and brands alike to be able to respond immediately, not just to her or him getting the product but also to questions about that product if they want support or service for that product. It's affecting the speed with which all brands have to be able to react and respond to those needs.

The other piece is we have a changing consumer demographic. Technology is entirely reshaping the way young people engage in the business. We don't yet even understand how that effect is going to come. Trying to anticipate where you take your brand when so much new technology, interactions, and ways to communicate are being invented literally on a yearly basis is making it difficult for brands to anticipate where to go next.

Increasingly, CMOs are being tasked with the responsibility of representing the customers' viewpoint, but they don't have immediate answers to the direction they're going. It's a difficult world because there's a lot more data, a lot more tools, and it becomes much more difficult to sift through all of that data to find things that really matter.

Steimle: With those challenges, what are some mistakes you see CMOs making these days?

Beitler: There are a couple of them that I've personally experienced. As you try and embrace social media, sometimes, you fail to anticipate the response in an environment that's not as controlled. Brands and marketers are so used to working in an environment where they control the creative, they control the message, they develop it, they communicate it, they outline it, and then they project it where and how they want. Sometimes you want the social space to behave with those same rules, and it doesn't.

The other day, we did a Twitter chat and it didn't go well. The consumer was much more aggressive than we had anticipated. We have a lot of consumers who have loved this brand, and the brand has grown, but there are people who don't love it yet. Sometimes, when you reach out to engage, those who don't like you become much louder and more aggressive than those who do. Being ready and prepared to respond to that is difficult. It's a personal and recent mistake that we made. The mistake was not in engaging with the customer in social media, it was in not being fully ready for the conversation.

One of the common mistakes is chasing the shiny new toys, investing in technologies or platforms that aren't yet proven to deliver return for the business. Five years ago, there was incredible talk about how social and mobile commerce were going to be the next thing. Many brands ran and chased and spent millions of dollars investing only to arrive there and find very little return from that effort, because even though those technologies emerged and people embraced them quickly, not all parts of their behavior move at the same pace. It's easy to see a technology and desire to try to get ahead of the technology and to go faster than the consumer goes and to overinvest with relatively low return on that investment.

The other mistake that brands and CMOs can make is the view that in this social world, brands need to be ever-changing to keep up with the customer. Some of the best brands on the globe have remained true to their core principles and values even as the world has changed around them. Brands like Apple and Nike have had positions for a long time and have not changed those positions as the consumer has changed but maybe changed their approach on how they convey those core principles and their core values.

We see a lot of brands and a lot of CMOs trying to be very reactionary and fast, not recognizing that great brands have to have deep purpose and intent. It's really about how you engage with the consumer, not necessarily evolving your purpose and your mission. Some brands will become obsolete over time, and that's just the nature of progression.

Steimle: How has marketing stayed the same over the past twenty years? What are those core parts that don't change?

Beitler: Great storytelling—in the sense of the story you tell and the way you respond to the feedback you get from conversation—great creative, and great ideas are still at the core of marketing. When you do that, customers and prospective customers respond to the brand. At the end of the day, marketing is still about creating demand and attention for your brand. That's the focus. It's about getting people to engage and want to have your product be a part of their lives. That hasn't moved.

Traditional media, including television is still the best means of creating impact for your brand, primarily because you affect more senses: sight, sound, and experience.

There's been this huge move to push away from print. Every big department store brand talks about how they wish they didn't have to do Sunday inserts. They want it all to be digital. I often say, "Don't kill off grandpa before he's dead. There's still a lot of value to be extracted from those long-standing channels, and there are a lot of consumers who still engage." A lot of the traditional media tools are still very effective. There are just new tools that have been added to the mix over the last decade and it's about embracing those, not abandoning the traditional ones. It is about reinventing the way you use them.

And you see brands leveraging media the way we did with #ImNoAngel to create a social campaign. We didn't spend a ton of money on #ImNoAngel. We used television advertising as a way to spark the social conversation. The #ImNoAngel campaign had over 15.3 billion media and social impressions over a five-week window with a very small spend on television, but we used a hashtag and an idea to create a social spark. The traditional piece was still important, but you had to change the way you leveraged that traditional piece to recognize the potential and the future and what social media can do.

Steimle: What are some of the skills that students should be acquiring today in order to be future marketing leaders?

Beitler: Some of the most important skills are a true understanding of problem solving and idea generation. At the end of the day, great marketing is still about being able to identify needs, understand insights from those things that you learn, and develop ideas that a customer can respond to. In a world that changes this fast, being adaptable and having great intuitive skills as well as analytical skills to problem-solve are essential to any marketer because the shift is so fast on the ideas you put in place that you have to be in a position to hold to the purpose of your brand but still be able to react.

Steimle: What are some of the skills that CMOs need that don't get enough attention?

Beitler: The notion of collaboration and cooperation internally, building your executive influence, doesn't get the attention it needs. We invest time for CMOs in understanding markets, understanding customers, understanding the data, but we don't invest enough time on whether they understand how to influence an organization and affect the direction of an organization and get it to move in a way that will get other internal executives to align and move together towards the mission and vision that the brand is trying to create.

The other piece is CMOs developing a true understanding of the operating principles and practices of the business. To run a business, a great CMO today has to understand the ins and outs and the levers that are used to operate the business holistically, not just to drive traffic or to create demand.

Steimle: Is there anything we haven't covered today that you're itching to talk about?

Beitler: The only thing I would emphasize is the need for marketers today, and I'll speak specifically about retail marketers, to be focused on the quality and content of their brands and the ideas they generate around them. We see marketing today devolving to price and promotion as a vehicle for driving traffic or driving demand for the brand rather than a focus on the content of the brand, the values of the brand, the purpose for which it exists and the need that it fills in the client's life. Retail marketers in particular need to refocus on what their brand stands for and get diligent about communicating that message and creating differentiation through the content of the brand and not through the price of the brand.

Walter Levitt

Executive Vice President &
Chief Marketing Officer
Comedy Central

Walter Levitt is the executive vice president and CMO of Comedy Central, owned by Viacom. In his role as CMO, Levitt heads brand strategy, advertising and promotion, and ensures Comedy Central's content spreads far and wide. Previous to working at Comedy Central, Levitt served in a variety of marketing positions at Canadian companies such as CTV Television Network, Alliance Atlantis, and Canwest. Levitt holds a bachelor of arts in communication studies from Concordia University. Levitt is a past board chair of the Canadian Marketing Association and is on the board of PromaxBDA and the Banff Media Festival.

Josh Steimle: A lot of people might be surprised to find out that Comedy Central has a CMO. What is your role there? What does it entail?

Walter Levitt: Every great brand needs not just leadership but a strong marketing perspective at the table. Particularly in the entertainment industry, we sometimes think the content will sell itself, that people will find a great new piece of content. While there's historically been some truth to that, the reality is that today there is so much great content that in order for it to be found, smart brands need to have a point of view and need to be aggressively marketing themselves to consumers.

© Josh Steimle 2016
J. Steimle, *Chief Marketing Officers at Work*, DOI 10.1007/978-1-4842-1931-7_21

My job and my team's job is to make sure that all of Comedy Central's businesses are well positioned to the consumer. That starts with having a strong point of view in terms of brand positioning. We think of Comedy Central as a comedy brand that delivers its content in many different places. That's the starting point for our marketing.

On a more practical, tactical basis, week in and week out, the marketing team's job is to make sure that all of our content is being consumed. A big part of the focus is our television content and getting people to watch it. Even then, it's not just on the linear television screen. It's watching our television content wherever consumers choose to watch it. That can be on a TV screen, the Comedy Central app, the Comedy Central website, or even other platforms like Amazon Video or Hulu. That's the starting point—to get people to consume our content on all those platforms.

Then, we are in other businesses. We have an extensive digital business where our content is available in many different ways, formats, and places. For example, Amazon Prime has a Comedy Central Stand-Up Plus channel, where people can subscribe to get our best standup content. My team is responsible for making sure that people consume our content there. We are in the live comedy business, and we are responsible for making sure that we get consumers to be aware of those events and to buy tickets. We're in the radio business, we're in the consumer products business, and so on and so on. That's the long version. The short version, as I explain to my mother, is that my job is to get people to love our brand and to consume our content.

Steimle: What does the structure of your marketing team look like? How many people do you have working with you, and what type of people are they?

Levitt: There are a few different tenets of the marketing team. The biggest part of our team is definitely our creative team. We do all of our creative, all of our advertising, fully in-house at Comedy Central. In our creative team, we have a large team of writer-producers. We have a large team of designers and a large team of copywriters. They are working every day to do the best work from an editorial and design point of view for the brand. They are working to create all the advertising, all the campaigns around our content. That's a large group.

There's a large production and project management team within the marketing group that's responsible for all of the logistics of everything we're doing creatively. There's a brand marketing team that's responsible for our overall marketing strategy, for our media planning and buying, and for our event marketing strategy for our brand. We are big buyers of other people's media, and that brand marketing team is responsible for all that media planning and buying. Tucked in there is our social media marketing, which is handled by some combination of all the groups.

Steimle: What are some of the metrics you focus on and are measured on?

Levitt: There are lots. This is an area where our business has changed a lot. Even ten years ago, there was one primary metric and that was TV ratings. Today, we look at any number of metrics to gauge the success of our work and our brand overall. Certainly, ratings on television still matter. That's a huge part of our business and a huge part of our revenue.

But increasingly, it's not just about live viewing. It's about replay viewing, live plus three or seven days, and commercial ratings on linear TV. That obviously includes people that watch on their DVRs. We look every day at downloads of our app and consumption of content on our app. We look at consumption of content on our website. We look at consumption of our content on Hulu. We look at social media, consumption of our content on our Snapchat Discover channel, but also the volume of conversation about our brand and our content in places like Facebook or Twitter.

As a result, there's not one metric in particular that drives the business. It is looking at any show or franchise genuinely from a 360 perspective, looking at all the inputs, looking at all the ways people can consume it, looking at all the things people say about it. That's how we measure success short term. And long term, that's also how we measure potential.

There was a day when if you made a TV show, the only thing that mattered in getting it renewed would have been its TV ratings. That's no longer the case. We now look at all those other metrics. We have often picked up or renewed shows or franchises that maybe did not have huge success in their season on linear TV but gave other indications that there was a real groundswell of interest, connection, and conversation, which told us there was great potential.

A good example of that would be *Broad City*. For the first season of *Broad City*, the TV ratings were fine, but they certainly were not spectacular. But, we quickly saw the amount of conversation around Abbi and Ilana, the amount of passion for the two of them and for the show, the amount of critical acclaim it got. Every indication was that these were two stars in the making. In fact, what happened was that between seasons of the linear show, we produced a bunch of digital content and the metrics on that content were absolutely phenomenal. The point being that the days of measuring linear TV ratings only are long gone for us and probably for most other media brands.

Steimle: How are millennials changing the marketing landscape? How are they impacting how other groups consume content?

Levitt: Millennials certainly have been at the center of the sharing economy. There's no question that millennials love to share and that they lead the pack in terms of sharing. One of our big strategies in all of our marketing is how we give millennials stuff they can share that allows them to make a statement about their own comedic taste, and from our perspective allows them to spread our brand to their fan base. That's a relatively new idea in the last decade or so.

In the last four or five years, the impact of sharing has been absolutely phenomenal for entertainment brands and all brands in general. That's driven by the millennial sensibility. What's interesting though is that as the millennials start to age up, move out, and have families and perhaps more traditional lives in a sense, we now look at the next generation coming up, called Generation Z. They've grown up in social media. It's always been there for them and sharing has always been part of what they do. They don't think twice about it. It should be interesting to see how they shape the way brands communicate over the next decade.

Steimle: What about globalization and the international market? How does people being able to access your content from anywhere in the world over the Internet affect things in terms of appealing to other markets outside of the traditional North American market?

Levitt: Comedy Central is truly a global brand. At this point, we're in something like seventy-two countries around the world. Our content is seen everywhere. Our brand is widely available. But, we actually look at our business regionally. We're part of Viacom. Viacom has an international group that takes our brand and our content around the world. As a result, much of the content that we make available digitally and socially to our North American fan base is geo-blocked to North America.

As an example, my family's in Toronto. I commute between Toronto and New York. When I'm in Toronto, I can't always see all the content that we post on our website or our app. When I'm back in the U.S., I'm able to. This notion of a global brand is absolutely true and our content is being seen around the world, but the strategies tend to be on a market-by-market basis driven largely by the distribution agreements we have in each of the markets.

Steimle: Are there other trends in the industry or with your customers that are affecting you in your role?

Levitt: The biggest trend is certainly the continued movement of consumers to consume content on the platforms of their choice at the times of their choice. This is not a new trend. It's been going on for a long time, but it's certainly accelerated in the last year or two. Mobile is becoming a preferred place to consume content for millennials. We used to talk about mobile being a second screen. I might argue that for millennials, in many cases, it's a first screen now. The question is now what that means in terms of the consumption of shorter content versus longer content.

I think all the research would suggest that even millennials will defer to the best screen available, all things being equal. If they are in their home or their apartment and they want to watch a long-form piece of content, if they have a giant screen on the wall, which most people do, they are likely to watch that content on that giant screen as opposed to their phone screen. They may be casting that content from their mobile device onto that screen, or they may be watching that screen through a set-top box of some kind, but they're continuing to watch the content on a big screen when the big screen is available.

But, we're seeing that mobile is enabling greater consumption of content at all times. It is an opportunity if you're a brand and particularly an entertainment brand who is trying to connect with fans and be their favorite brand for a category of content. The ability to connect with them anytime, anywhere is amazing.

There was a day at Comedy Central that the only time you could connect with our brand was when you were home in your house or apartment and you had the TV on. Today, we can connect with consumers anytime, anywhere. Increasingly, we're seeing that's what's happening through the use of our app or our mobile website. And through our radio station, Comedy Central Radio, that's available to people anywhere.

It's a relatively new thing in that it is now commonplace for people to consume content in other places. It perhaps used to be more limited to somebody based on data caps, but that era seems to be gone. It's a huge opportunity for brands—and especially brands like ours—to be literally in the palms of people's hands anytime, anywhere. It's a huge opportunity to stay connected, and drive and grow consumption.

Steimle: Certain parts of the entertainment industry have struggled with adjusting to the Internet, social media, and the ease with which copyrighted content can be shared. What do you think is the right mindset for entertainment companies to take with regards to the future?

Levitt: The short answer to that is nobody really knows. We are in an amazing era where the opportunities for an entertainment company are phenomenal, where there are so many places for people to consume your content. There are so many places for people to connect with your brand. There are no easy answers. There's no obvious—if everyone was doing x, then y would happen. The reality is that as an entertainment brand, you need to stay connected to your consumers and you need to be relevant to your consumers. If you're targeting millennials, you need to be relevant to them on digital platforms, where they are spending a lot of their time.

If there is a mistake anybody is making, it's somehow thinking their brand is immune to this evolution of millennials spending more time with digital platforms. That is the reality and we all have to continue to adapt our businesses to that. More broadly speaking, the smartest brands, the best brands, look to the consumer for perspective and say, "What does my consumer want? What is my consumer doing? How do I service their needs?" If you're targeting millennials, that inevitably means placing more resources and focus on places like social media.

Snapchat, as an example, was not a dominant player in the space three years ago. Now, for millennials and for Generation Z, it's a massive platform where they're spending a ton of time. If you're trying to connect with your fans, if you're fan-centric, you will be there because you know that's where your fans are. That's a mistake some media companies are making, which is not necessarily embracing the changing habits of fans.

That all said, of course, monetization in some of those platforms is taking a little longer than everybody would have hoped. The dilemma for media companies is that you can't wait for the monetization to catch up with consumption because it will probably be too late for your brand to have a significant footprint at that point. You need to make some bets, and you need to invest in being where your fans are. Not all platforms are created equal, and not all platforms will ultimately have the same return. You have to pick your spots and make bets where you believe the consumption will continue and the monetization will happen. It is inevitable that consumer habits will continue to change and evolve, and as a brand, you need to change and evolve with them.

Steimle: What are some of the specific tools and technologies that you use in your day-to-day job to get things done?

Levitt: There are all the tools you would expect in the traditional workplace: productivity tools, the suite of Microsoft products that everybody uses. Because social media is a big part of what we do, I spend a lot of time on tools and platforms that are looking at social media, such as the native Twitter or Facebook tools that show the dynamics of how people are using those platforms.

We use Sprinklr to both manage and measure our social media activity and that's a significant tool for us. There's a tool called Nielsen Social, which specifically measures conversations around television content in the social media space. We use that tool actively. We use other tools that measure social conversations and social sharing, tools from companies like Engagement Labs or Shareably. There are any number of tools that we use on any given day.

That suite of tools evolves over time. A tool that may have been what we needed a year ago may no longer be the tool we need now, and we will evolve over time. At the core, they're all about keeping an eye on the consumer and making sure you know what the consumer's talking and thinking about. And that most importantly, as a brand, you're responding to them in real time and servicing their needs. It's less about the tool. It's more about the outcome of how you use that tool and what you learn with it. To me, that's what's really important.

Steimle: How do you keep up with all the different technologies available out there to make sure you are using the best tool to get the job done?

Levitt: There are two parts to that answer. In terms of the actual technologies, to make sure we're doing the job well, we have a team of smart people here who are keeping their ears to the ground on all the new tools that are available and continuously saying, "We should try this. We should try that. Let's give this one a shot." That's certainly not one person's job. It's a shared job of everybody here. The other, broader question is how you keep track of all the technologies, all the platforms that are emerging every day that consumers are using. That's the really interesting part.

If you're a marketer in 2016, you better be on every social platform that exists because that is where your fans are, that's where your consumers are, and that's where the conversation about your brand is happening. It amazes me when I hear about or meet other marketers who are like, "I'm not on Twitter," or "I don't believe in Instagram," or "I'm not sure I understand Snapchat." To me, that's short-sighted thinking. If you're a marketer in 2016 and you are not on all those platforms, you probably shouldn't be a marketer.

Our job as marketers has always been to stay on top of the consumer, to be, in a sense, the voice of the consumer in our organizations. The consumers are on all these platforms, and it is changing, and so as new platforms come in and old platforms get discarded, as a marketer, you have a responsibility to personally be on all those platforms, try them out, experiment, see what they're capable of doing, and in the process, learn along with your consumers. That's something I've always been focused on. I've always been focused on getting on any new platform that emerges that has any scale whatsoever to get to know it, see what it's about, and make sure that if it becomes the next big platform, I'm not late to the party. I think every marketer should be doing the same.

Steimle: Do you have experience breaking down silos? How can a CMO facilitate that?

Levitt: That's always been an issue in organizations. And in some ways, it's a bigger issue today, especially in media companies where there's a bit of a divide between older products and digital products. In many respects, CMOs have the best perspective on the business. They are not beholden necessarily to anyone in the business other than the consumers. CMOs are beholden to the consumers and can play an incredible role in the center of organizations to keep everybody focused on the consumers and conversely to prevent people from getting focused on the stuff in the organization that doesn't really matter to the consumer.

The classic line is, "No consumer cares what department that thing came from. They just know it came from your brand. Consumers don't care what department made it. They just know that your brand made it." As CMOs, our job has always been to play that role. We have an incredible perch from which to see the business holistically.

By definition, CMOs tend to come from some sort of strategic background, have a good view of strategy, have pretty good insight into human beings, and can therefore bring different parts of an organization together. I'm seeing that a lot now as companies like ours make that evolution into the digital space, where people who have only worked in historic parts of the business for many years sometimes have a hard time seeing the evolution happening in front of them. People that come in from the purely digital side of the business sometimes have a very specific view of the world driven entirely by the digital experience.

CMOs can play an important role in bringing those perspectives together and acknowledging that no consumer sits at home and says, "Okay, today I'm going to be digital. Today, I'm going to be analog." That's not how consumers think. Consumers think in a more holistic way. In my experience, CMOs can play that role within organizations—to bring that sort of holistic view to things. It's a tough thing because within large organizations especially, there tend to be historical silos and perspectives, which sometimes inhibit the best ideas from moving forward.

The CMO role is one that has an objective perspective in many senses. Therefore—no surprise—a lot of CMOs tend to rise in the ranks to president and CEO jobs because you need a similar kind of perspective.

Steimle: What's the importance of being data-driven and having data within the CMO role?

Levitt: It's key, and it's an area that has changed a ton in the last number of years. It's both an incredible opportunity and sometimes incredibly overwhelming. The amount of data that's now available is staggering, and every organization, every CMO I've talked to, struggles with how you actually use it all effectively because there's so much time and effort spent in collecting the data.

At its core, the data helps you be a better marketer. It helps you understand your consumer better, it helps you reach your consumer better, it helps you measure more effectively how you're doing as a brand, and it's an incredible amount of information that we never used to have as CMOs. Either you had to go out and do some third-party research of a small sample, wait six months for the results, and hope the results were accurate, if not out of date, or you'd have to use your gut and say, "I think this is probably how consumers are going to react or think," and you would just go for it.

Now, both those techniques are still valuable and useful. But today, the ability to get an instant read on consumers' perspectives or how consumers are reacting to something you're doing, or to be able to focus your entire marketing efforts around the people that matter to you, is phenomenal.

Within this company, we have a massive DMP (data management platform) that is shared across all the brands at Viacom that tracks consumers that are interacting with our digital properties and allows us to be super smart and rich in terms of finding consumers and connecting with consumers for our franchises.

For example, we were able to retarget people who had interacted with MTV and the MTV Movie Awards last spring and introduce them to the new season of *Inside Amy Schumer* because Amy Schumer hosted the MTV Movie Awards. We introduced people who had been exposed to Amy in that context who had not previously been consumers of her Comedy Central show. That's super-effective marketing. That's way more effective than casting a wide net and hoping you find people who might have heard of Amy Schumer. Internally, we use that DMP incredibly effectively. We start everything we do by looking into the DMP and seeing what data we actually have to help us and how we can retarget.

Social media is a huge part of what we do. We are deep in all the rich data we get from social media, and we try to take advantage of it to make our marketing super relevant and effective. That said, it can be overwhelming. There are times where we look over all the data we have and we're like, "That's great. How do we make it actionable?"

Sometimes, the answer is, "We don't know. We don't know that we can make it actionable." That's tough because if you spent time and money collecting data and then realize you can't act on it, it certainly gives you a moment of pause and makes you say, "Wow, why did we spend all that time and money?" Those instances are less frequent than the instances where we go, "Wow, that's incredible. We have a wealth of data at our fingertips that can help us make better decisions and be more effective."

Steimle: What are some of the skills CMOs need that don't get enough attention these days?

Levitt: A facility with data is probably the biggest one because the whole data space has evolved fairly rapidly. When they were practitioners within organizations, most CMOs probably did not have the chance to be working hands-on with the data because it simply didn't exist in those days to the same degree. CMOs increasingly need a facility for understanding and using data that is not as inherent or natural to us.

For many CMOs, when we came up through the ranks, the media choices, for example, were more limited than they are now. Your instinct is to go to what you know. The availability of rich, deep data now allows you to be much smarter about your marketing decision-making. If I were doing a two-week course for CMOs, I would make it entirely about data, entirely about making sure CMOs have a facility with how data is used and can be used.

We all have a facility for things that were important when we were growing up in the marketing ranks. Over time, we all have gotten more comfortable with using data. And perhaps the next generation of CMOs will have come with a different experience as they work through their organizations and inevitably bring a different perspective. By then, there will be some new tools available that they would not have necessarily grown up with. It goes back to the idea that you need to stay on the pulse of your consumers and the pulse of your industry and never let yourself stop learning.

Steimle: What are some of the skills that university students, up-and-coming marketing professionals, can focus on today that are still going to be relevant ten, twenty years from now?

Levitt: Those haven't really changed much. There are three things that make a great marketer. One is focus. Marketing always has been and always will be about focusing. Anybody coming up through university and college and wanting to get into the marketing ranks needs to have the ability to focus because that has always been a core marketing skill. It's one of the reasons CMOs are well positioned in companies to move into CEO roles. They have an incredible ability to find something that's important and focus on it. Other parts of other organizations have less of that ability. Focus has always been number one.

Number two is enthusiasm. Even as the marketing field and practice and techniques have changed, marketers need to be enthusiastic salespeople for their brands, products, and services. If you're coming up into the marketing world, that enthusiasm is a key tenet to make marketers successful. It's extremely difficult to make your consumers or fans enthusiastic about your products, brands, or services if you yourself are not enthusiastic about them. That may seem trite, but enthusiasm for marketers has always been important and will continue to be.

The third skill that has always been important and will continue to be is the ability to have insight into human beings. Marketing, at its core, is about understanding consumers—understanding consumers' head spaces, mindsets, where they've been, where they're going, where you think they might be going in the future. To do that, you need to be the kind of person who has insight into human beings. I don't know if one can learn that. One has that instinct or doesn't.

The best marketers have always understood what makes human beings tick and have been able to evolve their perspective on human beings as people have evolved. Those are the three things: focus, a sense of excitement and enthusiasm, and an insight into human beings. Those have always been and continue to be the magic three.

Steimle: Are there any industry organizations that you're part of that you've found valuable for your role as CMO?

Levitt: I've been involved in a number of organizations, some more vertical in my industry, some more broad-based. I was very involved in the Canadian Marketing Association for many years. I was board chair a couple of years ago. That was always an incredible opportunity, to just be in a room with great marketing minds and to share the good and sometimes the challenging about our industry. I'm a big believer in organizations like the Canadian Marketing Association or the American Marketing Association.

Within my own industry, I'm currently on the board of PromaxBDA, which is an association for entertainment marketers, a global association, and that's valuable because those people are living the same day in, day out experiences as I am. It's very valuable to have that peer group.

More recently, I've gotten involved in organizations like the Banff Media Festival, which is not specifically a marketing organization but puts on an event for media people globally. Having that perspective, being around that board table, is also interesting and fascinating and brings an interesting facet to my role. Being involved in organizations in and around your industry is important, and I've always encouraged everybody I've worked with and everybody on my team to get involved. It's incredibly rewarding.

Steimle: Is there anything we didn't cover that you're itching to say about the CMO role?

Levitt: We've covered a lot of ground, but if you want to know more, you can go to my blog at https://mediamktgguy.wordpress.com. It's fairly wide ranging. It covers things specific to my industry and broader marketing concepts.

Geraldine Calpin

Chief Marketing Officer
Hilton Worldwide

*After over 20 years in the hospitality industry, **Geraldine Calpin** became senior vice president and global head of marketing and digital at Hilton Worldwide in 2015. Previously, Calpin held other roles at Hilton related to digital marketing and e-commerce. In 2015, Calpin was named by CNN as one of 11 People Changing the Way We Travel in Tech and Tourism. Calpin attended the University of Strathclyde and has a degree in economics.*

Josh Steimle: Can you give us an overview of your career? How did you get your start? What were the steps that led you to where you are today, transitioning in as the new CMO of Hilton?

Geraldine Calpin: I have a degree in economics but came out of university and went straight into the hospitality industry. I have been in hospitality pretty much all of my career. When I first joined, I was in functions like operations, sales and IT, and then into marketing—in the time before internet was a commercial reality. I then spent a couple of years in consulting, where I spent a lot of time flying back and forth to New York where my client was based, but I always missed the hospitality industry.

After consulting for two years, I joined Hilton in 2002, when the Internet was just beginning to become a serious commercial channel. I joined Hilton to run an operational function in order to get back into hospitality, and get into Hilton—the "owner" of the hotel brand. After joining the company, about

J. Steimle, *Chief Marketing Officers at Work*, DOI 10.1007/978-1-4842-1931-7_22

three or four months in, I had the operational function ticking along and wanted to do more. It was at the time that Hilton International was launching new language websites, so I raised my hand and asked to get involved in that.

I began to spend a lot of time in the digital space from a commercial point of view, creating the right infrastructure to run commercial sites, running the channel, driving, educating, and motivating the company and all of its stakeholders around the importance of the Internet. I established the commercial online team for Hilton International, including the content team, the search marketing team, and the publishing, retailing, and analytics team.

When Hilton Hotels Corporation and Hilton International joined, I was asked to take on a global e-commerce role. I created an industry-first program to allocate an e-commerce manager to support every one of our hotels in the world in managing their online marketing and digital footprint—everything from which keywords we should buy in search engines to what the banner ads and content should look like. This allowed us to deliver strong consistent content and compelling ads that connected with our customers. The idea was to support them in being excellent—and current—in what is a critically important channel.

My next role was head of digital, which meant running all of our digital advertising programs, product innovation and e-commerce, content, and CRM teams. In the summer of 2015, we combined our marketing and digital teams under one leader—understanding there's not a lot of marketing that's not digital, and everything in digital is marketing. The company decided to bring the two functions together and then created the CMO role. We merged the head of marketing and digital roles from a commercial point of view.

Steimle: What's your philosophy on building and managing a marketing team?

Calpin: One of the first questions the marketing team asked me when I took over was, "What do you expect from us?" My response to that was, "Be happy." The reason I say that is if people are happy in their jobs, they enjoy coming to work, will produce better quality, and stay with us. They will have more fun doing it. They will be better team members. They will be better managers. If you're happy at work, you're generally happy in your life.

I said, "My expectation of you, first and foremost, is to be happy with what you do." My philosophy focuses on creating an environment that is fair, that gives people opportunity both to go up the organization but also to go across and broaden their skills. Hilton is a great company and has many great examples of creating that opportunity for our team members.

We have people who have moved across geographies—across continents. People who have moved across disciplines, who have moved to three or four countries around the world. Big organizations like Hilton can do that for individuals. We owe it to our team members to continually develop and stretch them because that is what makes and keeps successful people happy. The philosophy is clear—leadership and hard work. I expect people to work hard, to give it their all and never accept "okay." Let me explain "okay."

One quote I often use in debates with my teams is "People like to be tested every day on a world-class stage, in world class conditions" because it's all about challenging and asking the question—"are we good enough?" My challenge to the team is always, "Is it good enough?" Good enough has to equal brilliant. Try every day to make things either incrementally or massively better. Do something every day better than it was the day before and better than it's ever been. Constantly push for brilliance and never accept "okay." If it's just okay, then it's not good enough; try again.

Steimle: Tell me more about your experience breaking down silos and making sure silos don't form. How can a CMO facilitate breaking down silos within an organization?

Calpin: We have more than four thousand hotels in over a hundred countries. That size and scale across the globe means that we are a heavily matrixed organization. There have not been a lot of silos in Hilton because if the matrix works, which it does, you can't really have siloed activities. I'm not saying it's perfect, but even outside of marketing and digital, a heavily matrixed global organization isn't very successful if it or some of its functions operate in silos. That said, in terms of bringing marketing and digital together, while they weren't necessarily silos before, they were definitely two different departments and organizations. Our desire, hunger, and reality of a collaborative culture is driven from our CEO, Chris Nassetta, who instilled and enthused the entire enterprise around a few, clear priorities. Silos don't work when everyone is organized around the same goals.

One of the first things I did was bring all the teams together and spend time telling them about my role. Their role. Our collective task. Our collective ambition. What we would be famous for in our first year. Also, what I believe in is to try, first of all, to appeal to the spirit within people and then get them to share their successes and failures and discuss with the leaders of the team: "If that's how we did it in the past, now that we are one, how should we do it going forward?"

Having team members create, write their own story, and develop how they think it should operate going forward is a much more successful way of achieving it than me sitting in a room drawing up a chart and then giving it to them. It's the team members who are at the point of most information to make decisions because they're doing it every day.

How we're bringing the two departments together, how we're organized, and how we share responsibility is not decided by me but by me working with my leadership and their teams to figure out, "How should we organize it in Europe versus the U.S. versus the brand organizations?" It's an effort *with* the team rather than for the team.

Steimle: For those who might not be familiar with a matrixed organization, explain what that is and why it prevents silos from being able to form.

Calpin: The best way to explain Hilton's matrixed organization, where functions and geography support each other, is to give you an example. We have a single *sales* function in the company, and a single *marketing* function in the company. The single sales organization is not only responsible for meeting the goals of the global sales organization, they are also responsible for metrics surrounding the regional organizations.

Additionally, as the CMO, I am responsible not just to my boss but also to every regional president as well as all of the brand heads, because my team supports and markets their brand.

In a non-matrixed organization, for instance, you'd have a European marketing function reporting into Europe or an Asia Pacific marketing function reporting into Asia.

With the global nature of our matrixed organization, clear and constant communication is essential to understanding the business needs of our stakeholders, their goals, and their directions.

Steimle: How is globalization affecting marketing for you? What are some of the hot growth markets for Hilton these days?

Calpin: Globalization is part of our DNA. We are in over 100 countries already. We have to think global. Right now, one of our hot growth markets is China. It's not only a massive market today, but also projected to continue to grow in the next five to ten years. Additionally, as a target audience, outbound travel of the Chinese is predicted to soar alongside of population, so we have a lot of energy and focus going into that market right now.

Steimle: How directly are you involved with the happenings in Asia and China?

Calpin: Our team currently includes a VP of marketing based in Asia Pacific who is responsible for developing and implementing a marketing strategy with the China-based team and the broader Asia Pacific region, that will resonate with our target audience. My role in the process is to ensure that plan aligns with our global strategy and ensures that the channel and distribution networks will deliver the results that we're forecasting long-term.

Steimle: How do you make sure you're in touch with your global customers to understand their needs and wants?

Calpin: To ensure we're in touch with our customers' needs of today, wants of tomorrow, and what no one can yet know they want, we continue to survey guests, listen to feedback through social media, keep a pulse on industry and third-party research, and innovate ourselves.

We have tools on our website that track the changes that we make and how they impact user behavior on the website. How does it impact buying behavior, everything from changing the color of a button to changing the overall page layout? That is not directly asking customers but watching the impact of our changes on user behavior.

Our Hilton app has the ability to ask guests to provide instant feedback about their stay. We hooked up our 24/7 call center so that if a customer says something in the app like "The air conditioning is noisy," or "I'd like extra pillows in my room," we respond within five minutes. We might not get the pillows to you in five minutes, but we reply "we're on it," and get in touch with the hotel to resolve it.

We use the feedback and research findings to build relationships with our guests. We understand customer expectations are changing all the time and differ by region—so it's crucial to keep asking the questions and evolving with our guests.

Steimle: In the hotel industry, online travel agents (OTAs) like Expedia are essentially taking away leads and customers and then charging a fee to give them back to you. How are you addressing that challenge? What are some of the steps that have been taken by Hilton over the years to get those customers back so they're dealing directly with you?

Calpin: It's important to be where our customers want to be. Our hotels are featured on the OTAs because there will always be a type of customer who will want to go to the OTAs to shop or to book and OTAs are great partners. We want to be customer-centric, not Hilton-centric, in our approach.

That said, a direct customer relationship is better for Hilton and is better for the guest, because if we have a direct relationship, we can personalize the stay. We know more about you. We can provide a better experience for you. Some of the ways we do that are through our loyalty program, Hilton HHonors. You don't receive Hilton HHonors benefits if you book through OTAs.

The benefits of the loyalty program traditionally were focused on earning points to redeem for free night stays. We promote the instant benefits that come along with Hilton HHonors, even if you're not a frequent traveler. For example, as a member of Hilton HHonors, at any level, you receive free Wi-Fi at any of our hotels around the world. Additionally, through our Hilton HHonors app, available on both Android and iPhones, you get the ability to check in remotely the day before your stay. Just like you can choose your seats on an airline, when you check in the day before, you can also choose the floor, the room, and the room number you want to stay in. Based on the reviews and ratings, guests absolutely love the choice and control of selecting their room.

Our next step in making travel easier was making it possible to use your phone as your room key. Today, at more than 200 hotels around the world (and soon to be more), you check in the day before, you choose the room, you get to the hotel, and should you prefer not to, you don't need to stop by the front desk. You can go straight to your room and use your phone to open up your door and enjoy free Wi-Fi. You will also receive HHonors points when you are there for future stays.

HHonors points are not just for free stays. Today, you can use your points for unforgettable experiences. Through our partnership with Live Nation, you can redeem points for tickets to concerts or exclusive experiences with some of the top entertainment artists in the world.

Finally, Hilton HHonors members now receive an exclusive discount off our published rate when they book directly with us. We've gone from all of our channels and audiences being equal to rewarding our Hilton HHonors members with a lot of benefits. And anyone can join easily when making a booking.

Steimle: What are some other trends in the hospitality industry that are affecting you in the CMO role?

Calpin: The move to mobile has increased same-day bookings. With mobile continuing to be a priority, we are addressing customers' expectations and desire for personalization. More and more people are traveling greater and greater distances than ever before, which has been enabled, in part, by our growing digital economy.

Steimle: Are millennials a topic that you discuss at Hilton?

Calpin: For sure. We consider millennials important, as well as all other generations. We don't focus specifically on millennials because we believe that people are individuals, not a product of their generation. Our strategy is more customer-driven compared to generation-driven.

Steimle: Do you see the millennials influencing other generations, pushing trends in marketing such that other demographics are adjusting to follow in the millennials' footsteps?

Calpin: Great services, great technology, and great devices are adopted unilaterally if they're simple to use and make people's lives easier. Seventy-five-year-olds are going to adopt solutions to every day obstacles as much as twenty-five-year-olds.

Steimle: What do you see as some of the biggest challenges facing today's CMOs?

Calpin: Prioritizing. There are limitless marketing opportunities for large organizations combined with dozens of great ideas. The opportunities surge, erupt, and disrupt every day. The biggest challenge is making sure we make the right decisions, place the right bets, and test—never let your own assumptions drive. Always test assumptions and make sure to have the courage to take risks, because we need to constantly evolve—disrupt—in order to stay current, to stay relevant, and to give our customers what they want.

Steimle: What are some of the skills that university students or new marketers can be adopting today that are still going to be relevant ten or twenty years from now?

Calpin: Good leadership skills mean you are able to engage and inspire the people who are across from you, above you, or below you. All the technical skills in the world will likely come and go. Program languages will change. Marketing channels will come and go. Understanding how to manage people well, how to be clear on direction, and inspiring those around you, whether they work for you or not, are true life qualities. Leadership also helps you outside of your business life. If you develop strong leadership skills, it means that when the next thing comes along, you're able to harness the opportunity, the resources around you, and go after it quickly.

Steimle: What are some of the skills that CMOs need that don't get enough attention but are important?

Calpin: I don't know whether it's that they don't get enough attention, but successful CMOs need to have a good vision, to be great communicators, to have strong leadership skills, and to be courageously innovative. One of the CMO's roles is to drive the organization forward, to change conventional thinking, to be the voice of the customer in the company. It's having that constant "Is it good enough? Try and get it better than it's ever been before." That's disruptive and courageous innovation. Never accept second best.

Steimle: Where there's a need for courage that means there's a risk. Do you have a story or an experience where you took a risk in your marketing career but it paid off?

Calpin: I have a lot. I'm actually placing a big bet right now, overseeing the biggest marketing campaign in our company's nearly 100-year history. It's very bold for the company.

Another risk I took happened when I was the head of digital and inherited a project. I thought the project was too narrow in its focus, so I went and asked for almost double the money to say, "If we're going to do this, we're going to do it right. We're going to do it everywhere across every platform."

I was talking to the digital floorplans now featured on our Hilton HHonors app. I said, "We have to map six-hundred-fifty-thousand rooms so we can tell our hotel guests, 'You can choose your room anywhere in the world at any one of our brands.'" At that time we didn't know what the adoption rate would be, so we tested and analyzed. But going into a multimillion-dollar project like that, you will never really know the results until you launch. The risk absolutely paid off, resulting in double the adoption rates we saw in the initial tests.

Steimle: How can other marketers learn from your success with that risk? What were you able to do that made that risk turn out successfully?

Calpin: I fundamentally believe in simplicity. If you can make an idea, a product, a campaign, a message simple, customers will understand it. They will appreciate the simplicity of it because people want their lives to be easy. One of the first things I did was look at the proposition I inherited, the product that was in design when I first received it. I looked at it and asked, "Is this simple? If I was to explain this to a consumer, would they understand what it was?" It didn't pass that test. I said, "You'd need a matrix to try and figure this out. When can I get this? Who is it for? What does it do?" I tried to redesign the product so that it would be simple for customers to understand, and it would be at all of our hotels.

Make it simple—simple to understand, easy to use—and do it everywhere. Whether you're designing a new marketing program or a new product to go on the shelf, make it a simple-to-understand proposition, a clear proposition, something that's different from what's already out there. Make it customer-driven, simple, and at-scale, and message it cleanly.

Steimle: Are you a member of any peer groups or industry associations that you've found particularly helpful in your role?

Calpin: In professional life, regardless of level, it's really important to network inside and outside of the industry you work in. I regularly use LinkedIn to connect with people I meet. I also attend a variety of external conferences as speaker and guest, and of course, attend some of our own internal conferences for hotel General Managers and Owners across the world. This all helps me stay close to what our guests, employees, and stakeholders need from a product and marketing perspective.

Matt Price

Senior Vice President of Global Marketing
Zendesk

Matt Price is the current senior vice president of global marketing for Zendesk. Previously, Price served as Zendesk's vice president and general manager for Europe, the Middle East, and Africa, in which role he managed growth, project and customer success, and go-to-market teams. Before coming to Zendesk, Price was CMO at Troux Technologies. Price has held executive roles in marketing, sales, and business development at Wily Technology, Art Technology Group, Multizone International, and Borland International. Price attended the University of Reading, where he earned a bachelor of science with honors in computer science.

Josh Steimle: Tell us a bit about your customers at Zendesk—who they are and what you do for them.

Matt Price: Customers found us. They found us and put up this online customer service software. The first ten thousand customers were purely web-trial buy. They found us on the website, they set up for a trial, they put up their credit card number, and they bought the software. Through that, the customer type was almost self-defining. They were people who were digitally aware. They were people who had the power to purchase themselves. They were very globally dispersed. The demographic of the customer base was very much defined in terms of who could acquire and buy us as opposed to where we had salespeople deployed within the market. So even today, Zendesk has one of the most geographically split customer bases of any of our peer groups because of that.

© Josh Steimle 2016

J. Steimle, *Chief Marketing Officers at Work*, DOI 10.1007/978-1-4842-1931-7_23

It was a beautiful model, heavily analytics-based, transparent, very much a funnel business, understanding the dynamics of that web trial by SaaS business. That remains the core of our business, one of our biggest routes to market. As we've grown, we've found that there are people who want to buy the software who maybe can't put a credit card in or who aren't the sole decision makers and have to justify buying us to another group of people in the company who wanted to buy something else, especially as we've moved more up-market and started to sell to bigger organizations.

Now, we have some distinct go-to-market places. We have a velocity business, which is our web trial buy, and an enterprise business, which is more hands-on, assisted sale with a lot more human interaction. We've also found that the buyer type has changed as we've diversified our product range from being purely somebody responsible for customer service to somebody who's running HR, running IT, or building an app, an e-commerce app. All of them are trying to do some degree of customer experience or relationship, but they're all coming at it from different angles.

That relates back to a lot of the transformation we're trying to do as a business in marketing, which can be summarized in the question of how you evolve from being a single-product, single-channel company to a multi-product, multi-channel company.

Steimle: What's your philosophy on building and managing a marketing team?

Price: It's evolved, and we've learned a lot going through this. We're continually thinking about how to empower people. Especially if you grow as a business, you run a risk as the machine becomes bigger of your people becoming smaller cogs doing less interesting jobs. When you begin a startup business with thirty or forty people, the first marketing person you hire is a total generalist. They are doing everything from strategy all the way to updating the website and going along to a trade show and popping up the stand booth.

Then, you start to specialize a little bit more. You might have your web specialist, your email specialist, your demand specialist. Then, if you go a step further, you end up having teams of those people, and you subdivide labor even more and more.

What we've found is that the smartest people don't want to be doing just one small job. They want to be CMOs themselves one day. How can you create an environment where there can be many CMOs? How can you create a slice of the business for them either in running marketing for a particular territory or offering them a specific part of a sub-business, where they can tangibly own a part of the business and metrics and running multiple different types of campaigns?

Our philosophy here is to continue to reorganize and make sure people feel empowered to do stuff. What that actually translates to, if you can do it, is a lot of agility because it doesn't require fifty people to get a simple campaign out the door. You can distill it down to three or four people who can move quickly and are aligned to business goals. We've seen that. We reached this stage of the business post-IPO. There were people moving on to new roles outside the business. We encouraged that. It's great to see people's careers develop. As we evolved and restructured our business to be more agile, we actually found people come back into the business, those people that left, because we could give them bigger jobs. Also, they realized the grass is not so green on the other side.

Steimle: What kind of skills and abilities do you look for in new hires?

Price: We look for a couple of things—firstly, their ability to do the job. Do they have the relevant technical skills? Have they seen enough different businesses, different worlds where they can actually manage specific tasks? To some degree, it's agility. To some degree, it's experience. Then, we have this other thing we call the "eye of the tiger," which is how well we think that person would operate inside our environment. A lot of people talk about culture and culture fit. Based on the behavior that we see of this person, what they like and don't like, and their personality style, how well would they operate within our business specifically? How quickly could they build relationships, making sure they're not a personality style that would work against the business moving forward? The ability to do the job and eye of the tiger are the two things—and I have no idea how we originated the latter term, but we like it anyway.

I also love to see people have broad backgrounds. I'm a bit biased on that. I like to see people who have stayed with a company for three to four years and been promoted within that business and can show that they can grow and expand their role with it once or twice. I like to see people who have done something entrepreneurial, even if it's like setting up a lemonade stand when they were a kid or doing something to earn money, to show that they can think and operate independently to achieve their own goals. Those things tend to stand out quite a lot.

Steimle: What are some of the timeless skills? For example, for a student coming out of the university today, what are the skills they can acquire that are still going to be relevant in marketing ten, twenty years from now?

Price: Curiosity and a love of data are super useful, no matter what you're doing, for two reasons. Firstly, if you're curious and love data, then you have a mind that allows you to have data or fact-based conversations with people, which helps you move your projects along quickly and bring people with you, especially in a cross-functional world. That's super important. The other thing is that an understanding of data allows you to understand how to scale things and operate to scale.

I remember when I was first introduced to this. It was when I switched from the customer service job to my first marketing role. I was working for a company called Borland that did software development tools. I moved into the marketing department there. Borland, at that point, was just getting into direct mail for PC software. It was the nineties. Everything became so analytical. It was really interesting to see how one small change in copy, or in what you put inside an envelope, or how you addressed an envelope, or what color the envelope was, affected other changes. I now realize that was A/B testing. It's interesting to see that come full circle from a web environment to a digital environment. And guess what? There's going to be something coming along in another fifteen or twenty years in technology. At the same time, we're going to be testing the communications and the adaptation to that as well.

Data and curiosity are really interesting. Something related and particularly important to the class of people coming out of university now is authenticity and transparency within an organization. A marketer's skills have had to change from a world where you totally controlled your output of your message and the perception of the business to a time where your customers control that. You can't fake or spin anything. The *"Mad Men"* days are over.

Actually, authenticity and transparency are important on the basis of that. That depends on who the buyers are as well, because both within a B2B environment and a consumer environment, the consumer base has switched from being baby boomers to Gen X to millennials. I recently saw a study stating there are more millennials in the workplace now than there are Gen Xers, and those guys have a totally different perspective on the way things are.

Steimle: Tell me more about your thoughts on marketing to millennials. How is this group influencing marketing for everyone?

Price: I've learned a lot from how to market to millennials by working with millennials. It's really interesting. In order to understand millennials, most people will have to have them within their workplace, figuring out how to build relationships and what's important in the relationship with a millennial in your workplace. It's similar to how you communicate with millennials from a marketing perspective, so there are some important things to understand.

Firstly, there's this concept of the millennials hungering for meaning, authenticity, and being able to tie things back. What we find within our environment is that the number one source of employee engagement is our community relations programs and the work the business does within the community, and we invest in that. What's interesting is that's also our number-one source of brand publicity within national press and TV. That hunger for meaning, attaching authenticity, and transparency are super important. That's more of a method discussion. That's more content and messaging and understanding that.

The other thing is understanding communications channels. My kids think I'm being weird if I email them. They're seventeen and nineteen. I'll communicate with them on one particular channel and find that they're not communicating with me. They've shifted to another channel. If I'm not communicating with them on Snapchat now, then I can't have a discussion with them. Understanding the communications channels, understanding email within the millennial group—it is a channel, but it is not the most important one. The rise of social media within that environment is important too.

Steimle: Do you feel like millennials are impacting other demographics, other groups, and influencing how we market to those other groups?

Price: Millennials are driving channel change within other groups as well. The millennials are early adopters of new technology that's now being adopted by broader groups. For example, messaging is super important within the millennial group. It's the anchor of what they want—the chat and IM—but we're now seeing, for example, live or online chats as a massive driver in customer engagement within other segment groups. There's a need for businesses to have implemented things like live chat in order to support the millennial group, and those then become available to other segment groups, which are then adopting it.

People of all ages love doing live chat to interface with businesses. That's going to be a significant shift in communications channels over the next few years, this use of things like WhatsApp and Facebook Messenger driving B2C communication. We're already seeing it. At the moment, you look at China with the rise of WeChat. Nobody communicates with a business in China using email unless it's an exporter or an importer. Everybody's communicating through IM and chat messaging.

Steimle: What are some of the key metrics you focus on in your role?

Price: Starting from the inside, we use tools for employee engagement and understanding how well we're performing from an employee perspective. Then, looking at a demand generation perspective, the metrics very much depend on the buyer channel. For example, within our velocity business, it's classic site visits, conversion to trial, conversion from trial to paid customer, ASP, expansion rate within the customer retention. Those are very simple. Within our enterprise channel, it's more of pipeline development, pipeline influence of campaigns, both online and offline campaigns. Within the velocity business, it's a cost per lead or NQL—that's very measurable—and also yield per NQL, whereas within the enterprise business, looking at costs per SQL, yield from an SQL, and conversion is probably more meaningful because there are so many different touch points on it. That's a demand generation perspective. And then there's the highest level: brand awareness.

We're just starting to evolve. We're a B2B customer company with a reasonably tight set of target buyers as well as awareness and understanding within that specific brand and buyer group. It's interesting looking at how we define brand awareness within a B2B buyer group that's reasonably niched but that's also changing. Pretty much every time we buy a new product or company, our buyer group has changed, so getting consistency around that is interesting. It's one thing having metrics, but in a business that's changing so much, getting consistent and comparable metrics can be a bit of a challenge.

Steimle: With everything shifting so quickly, how do you make sure your goals and objectives are aligned with the overall organization at Zendesk?

Price: You need to look for leading indicators of where change is coming down the pipes, how you are going to respond to change, and what a change is going to mean to you. Classically, that change is going to be from external factors, so you have to try to understand what an external market change is going to mean—somebody buying one of your competitors, shifts in demographics, keeping an eye on those types of things and trying to think through what they might mean. That's long term.

The other thing is internal strategic things. When you first engage around a new acquisition, for example, how's that going to impact the business and the team? Finally, it's looking for breakage points. We realized we might need to split up our demand gen into different businesses when we started to see too many people coming to meetings, things taking too long to actually happen, or our information systems not being able to cope with some new type of campaign. It's understanding that those leading indicators are not necessarily because your business is messed up but because it has changed. If something's broken or not working, it's typically time to sit back and think, "We need to respond, and we need to change the way we're doing things."

Steimle: Do you have any experience breaking down silos? How can a CMO facilitate that?

Price: Firstly, taking ownership of certain things is important even if they don't fall within the business itself. An example of that is messaging across the business and understanding brand consistency. For example, that messaging might be communication of your website, but it's just as much what your salespeople are saying, what your analyst relations guys are talking about, and what's being communicated on your earnings call. Take some degree of ownership for that, and when you identify inconsistencies, try to fix them. Step out of your own silo and try to solve problems across the business.

Another thing is proactively making sure you're not building silos yourself. If you see something sitting in your team that would be better sitting in somebody else's team, volunteer that and make sure you get away from a territory agenda in favor of what's best for the business agenda. It's a trust perspective.

Most importantly, have a look at what the customer experience is and always go back for that and remove friction. This is why we reorganized slightly into our velocity and enterprise businesses because we kept building out all of these things that the enterprise guys needed. They needed some prequalification. They needed to speak to a sales rep. Then, if they wanted to have some help in services, they spoke to a services person. If they wanted to get support, they spoke to a services person. All of this stuff was important for the larger businesses. They need specialists in each of those areas, but we realized we'd over-engineered it for the guys that actually had a really simple transaction and all they wanted to do was have a simple question and a single source for the answer.

Take a step back and have a look at the customer experience and the buyer journey. Try to understand what it is that the buyer wants and how they get their information. Try to think less about how we give that information that the customer wants, how we qualify them, or how we convert them and more about how we make their experience with us as frictionless as possible. That helps to break down silos.

We mentioned data as an important driver for having discussions, but framing business or internal discussions around what's best for the customer or the customer experience really helps to remove internal barriers as well.

Steimle: What tools or methods do you have for making sure you're in touch with your customers and understand their wants and needs?

Price: Zendesk is perhaps our best source of information because there's a huge wealth of it. I think Zendesk has had over a million customer interactions since we were born. They're all stored within this fantastic database, which is searchable and allows us to pick up sentiment. We can set up triggers on certain keywords that get routed to certain groups. We can look at analyses of certain areas. That level of rich data is hard to come by, so it's a bottom-up asset, but we're helping our customers use that asset and unlock that for other purposes. It's pretty interesting.

We use standard techniques such as surveys. We look at win-loss analysis. If somebody hasn't converted from a trial, we ask them why, and we gather information from those different sources as well. That's a bottom-up general thing.

We also look for signals. If we see a change in any of our analytics to our business, such as a conversion rate going down, a plan shifting, we take a sample and have conversations with people to try and get behind what that data is. A big mistake I see marketers—or at least inexperienced marketers—make is they feel they have to take the whole data set to interpret a trend or understand what a buyer wants. Whereas actually, it's just as good taking a random sample of one hundred customer feedback records or one hundred deals and sifting through and spending two hours looking at them one by one. You'll probably get more information from there by diving in on a sample set rather than looking at a macro data set.

Steimle: For all the talk about big data, there's something to be said about small data, right?

Price: Totally. It's amazing. We have all these fantastic analytics on Zendesk with insights of how Zendesk helps people convert. This is just the customers, and that's super useful for overall benchmarks, but for getting real insight, there's nothing like sitting down and reading one hundred randomly selected tickets. Talk about the voice of the customer! That's the literal voice of the customer, actually reading what people are saying.

Steimle: How is globalization affecting marketing for you?

Price: We've always been a global customer. In many respects, within a B2B world, because we led with product and web first, Zendesk became an international company on the back of it. In fact, we did some analysis early on when we were looking at our business growth and we wanted to understand what international markets were strong for us. It was really interesting. We took the level of penetration Zendesk had in a particular market, divided it by the GDP, and came up with an index as to what our penetration level was. Then, we tried to match that index to other market factors, what we thought might be big drivers. That number, that index, was directly proportional to the amount of English spoken within that country. In our most mature markets, within the U.S., the UK, and Australia, we had the highest penetration. In countries that had the least English language spoken, it was less. The signal then was easy.

Initially, it was about localization and trying to speak to people within their own language. Actually, the first step on localization was translation: at least let people be able to consume the information and have our product. Then, over time, it was looking at localization. Localization can be a number of things. Most people think it's translation, but actually, localization is how you adjust your messaging in order to suit a particular market. For example, in SaaS, security is super important, and data privacy is more important in some countries than others. Maybe you need to adjust your messaging around that. How do you localize to the way people want to buy and what channels exist within a certain market? In some countries, resellers are quite important. In some markets, the way corporations buy is different. Face to face might be very important as opposed to having an inside sales rep.

Finally, it's understanding how your product fits within a different buyer community. For example, in China, there's no point in trying to sell somebody an email management product if most of their interaction is being done through messaging.

Steimle: What do you see as some of the future growth markets for Zendesk, either in terms of geography or industry?

Price: It's something we think about a lot. We think our penetration in all global markets is reasonably low at this stage based upon the propensity of people to buy. That's a factor of two things. Firstly, the relevance of what we provide to people is changing all the time. Within the SMB (small and medium-sized businesses) community, every day, a new cohort of people wake up and say, "Hang on. I need a better way to manage digital customer relationships.

I need to find something that does that." Every day, more and more people are searching online for that sort of solution, and we're fortunate to be in the right place, and we've got to make sure we serve them well.

Then, there's a whole cohort of people that actually know they've got a problem but don't know how to fix it yet. How do we put marketing plans in place to reach out to those guys? We can expand our own market on that basis. That's very much within SMB. We still see massive growth around that globally, and we will accelerate that growth by localizing within certain markets.

We're also seeing another big dynamic of changes, which is the change happening to enterprises and large businesses. A few things are happening within those businesses that are bringing them to Zendesk. One thing is how people are interacting with those businesses is swinging much more to a blended mix of phone, email, messaging, and digital channels. Because we're a born digital technology, when they're coming up for replacement cycles, they're finding us. At the same time, we've enhanced our offerings significantly, as well as support and product, to make ourselves have the right profile in order to support those businesses.

Through an overall contact center, we've also started to identify other interesting market dynamics where people are using Zendesk for employee service and taking customer service principles: "Hey, why don't I use live chat within IT to serve my people?" or "If I'm in HR, why don't I have a knowledge base other people can have?" That's a very interesting vertical growth market.

Another significant dynamic we're seeing is what we call the embeddable market, whereby businesses are increasingly using applications in order to communicate with their customers. Nearly every enterprise business has an app, which is becoming a major form of customer engagement. We are seeing a lot of companies embed Zendesk technology within those apps. The rate of mobile API usage we have is increasing significantly.

To summarize the overall market changes, the move to digitization is definitely bringing people to us. The way enterprises are buying, fast companies and their need to change technologies, and digital innovations such as web and e-commerce interaction are driving market growth to us.

Steimle: Being a customer support company, what's your opinion on how customer support has become part of marketing? It used to be that marketing was advertising and getting customers, and customer support was a separate part. What are your thoughts on that?

Price: We're seeing a real blurring between the lines of marketing, sales force automation, customer engagement, and customer service. Everybody's coming up with all sorts of different words for that. We're definitely seeing that trend. If we look at the amount of customer data that's available now from customer service interaction and how that can fuel decisions made by marketers, it's incredibly powerful: the way we can use our customer satisfaction data and Net Promoter Score information to segment customers and data. For customer outreach, it's how we can use that to inform marketing buying decisions on media to make sure that stuff isn't wasted. We're at the early stages of that. We see ourselves as playing an important role in that moving forward.

It's kind of interesting because in many respects, the way we think of our brands is evolving significantly as well. When we put out that first website, our strap line was, "Love your help desk." Then, our strap line was, "The new face of customer service." Now, our branding is becoming a lot more about overall customer relationships and customer engagement and marketing to the point where our latest marketing offering, Relate, is a communication device that is a combination of events, content, and education on how you engage with customers, not just focusing on hard marketing techniques but teaching people how to build empathy and transparency into their communication, transform their organization, get the right tone of voice and techniques, and try to join everything up. That's a big project we've been working on recently and it's going pretty well.

Steimle: What are some of the skills that a CMO today needs that don't get enough attention, maybe some of the soft skills or just lesser-appreciated but necessary skills?

Price: People skills. I certainly underestimated those throughout my career, and it's one of the things I've been working on recently, but this notion of empowering people, creating leadership, removing roadblocks for people. Cross-functional leadership, not just being the guys that put the website up or stick adjectives in front of feature names but really looking at the whole and owning bigger solutions. Being analytical, being a data king, and being in touch with new levels of communication. A lot of that is bringing people into the organization who can help you do that. You can be a CMO that's only done marketing and come up through a classic brand route, but more and more, you need to be a full-stack employee, a full-stack CMO who has experience in all of these different areas.

Steimle: What does it mean to be a full-stack CMO?

Price: It's having an understanding and ability to pull together different things. It's being able to understand right across the organization what's happening and pick it up quickly. Understanding the dynamics of what's happening within a sales team. Understanding how your messaging slices through analyst relations. Being able to synthesize lots of information quickly from many different sources of the business, even if they aren't classically within a marketing domain. Being able to understand a sales forecast. Being able to understand customer service data and customer feedback. Being able to understand a financial model or a business plan. Being able to understand the feedback coming in from an employee engagement survey, really taking the overall slice of the business.

It's also being able to operate in an entrepreneurial way: gather that information and propose and look at new things. It's taking huge amounts of information from the organization and understanding it and being able to organize it and put strategies and programs in place in order to change things.

Steimle: Is there anything in your background that's not directly tied to marketing but that has been beneficial to your role as a marketing professional?

Price: Firstly, I would advise anyone in business to spend a period of their early work life with high customer engagement, either working in a retail store, on the telephone, or in customer service. As much as you might think your home life was diverse, nothing prepares you for the level of diversity of attitudes, opinions, and backgrounds of people. Retail and customer service are good for that. Also, putting yourself in the position where you're serving other people is super-important not just for communication skills but for approaching your job with respect and being humble for the people you are serving. That's super important. Approaching any type of marketing or customer engagement with a level of arrogance or disdain for the consumer—we've all see it—it has to be a non-starter, especially when you relate that to millennials.

Carrying a number, running a sales team, running your own business, waking up every morning and thinking, "How the hell am I going to be able to achieve my goal" enables you to think laterally and also gives you empathy, both for the people who are trying to sell the product and those who are going to buy the product. It also creates a certain level of drive, understanding, prioritization, and creativity. Being trained as a computer scientist helps me analytically but also in modeling and building models, whether it's organizing information on a chart, communicating, or understanding how to model the business. Having worked in the U.S. and in Europe has helped to no end, being able to be a bridge within those markets.

Susan Lintonsmith

Global Chief Marketing Officer
Quiznos

Susan Lintonsmith is the global CMO of Quiznos. She came to the role in 2012 after more than 20 years of marketing experience. She has held executive positions at big name brands such as Quiznos, Red Robin Gourmet Burgers, Western Union, Coca-Cola, and Pizza Hut. Lintonsmith has a BA in marketing from the University of Notre Dame and an MBA in finance and marketing from Indiana University.

Josh Steimle: To get us started, give us an overview of your career. How did you get your start? What were the steps that led to where you are today?

Susan Lintonsmith: I started working when I was quite young. My first job was babysitting when I was eleven years old. I took over a brother's paper route at age twelve. I started in the restaurant world at fifteen at a mom-and-pop Italian-Mexican restaurant. I was motivated. I'm the youngest of four, and all of us needed to work to help fund part of our high school and all of our college tuition. I started working early on and learned how to earn and save money. Those early years prepared me for the workforce after I got out of graduate school.

I graduated from the University of Notre Dame with a BA in marketing and a minor in psychology. I went directly through to Indiana University and got

© Josh Steimle 2016
J. Steimle, *Chief Marketing Officers at Work*, DOI 10.1007/978-1-4842-1931-7_24

a marketing and finance MBA. From there, I was recruited to Pizza Hut. It's funny because I had spent many years working in restaurants. When I started graduate school, I did not think getting an MBA would lead me back into restaurants, but at the time, Pizza Hut was owned by PepsiCo, and I was so impressed by the people there and the opportunity to make an impact early on in my career. It was lean and growing very fast, and they said, "We need somebody who can hit the ground running, take ownership of projects, and drive results." I had a wonderful seven and a half years there, spending time at the corporate headquarters, then going out into the field for four years, and then coming back to the headquarters, which at that point had moved to Dallas, Texas.

While in Dallas, I got a call from the Coca-Cola Company to interview for a position. I wanted to get experience outside of restaurants, so I jumped at the opportunity and moved to Atlanta. I spent nearly five years with Coca-Cola leading an innovation team, working in brand marketing, and working with bottlers to drive that business forward. I spent four years in Atlanta, and another year in Denver working directly with several bottlers. After a year, I was asked to move again, but for personal reasons, I needed to stay in Denver so ended up leaving Coca-Cola.

I joined Western Union as global vice president of branding and loyalty marketing. That was a great opportunity for me to learn about the financial services industry and to get some global experience, since Western Union is in all but a few countries. I led the company to one strategic brand platform including one brand logo, global guidelines and a global agency network, as well as the launch of a very successful loyalty program. After more than three years, I was recruited back into packaged goods with WhiteWave Foods, then owned by Dean Foods, as the vice president/general manager of the Horizon Organic dairy line. When I was called for that opportunity, I wasn't looking, but was a loyal consumer and had the product in my refrigerator. I was absolutely the target for that brand, and I loved the organic industry. My proudest achievement was the launch of Horizon Organic milk with omega-3. We were the first to add omega-3 to milk and now it's a major business for the company. I spent a couple of years at WhiteWave Foods before getting a call for the chief marketing officer position for Red Robin Gourmet Burgers where I spent five years. That led me to my current position as global chief marketing officer at Quiznos.

Steimle: Is there anything in your background that's not directly tied to marketing but that has been beneficial in your role as a marketing professional?

Lintonsmith: There're a couple of things that have helped in my background. The first is that I grew up as a competitive figure skater. I bring up my nine years of competitive skating because dedication to a sport like that teaches you self-discipline. I had to get up early and out on the cold ice nearly every morning before school. It really fed my competitive nature. The other thing was having to work, as I mentioned earlier, starting at a young age. That taught me work ethic and the value of money. I got some good experiences working early on. Both of those things prepared me for the business world.

Steimle: What does the structure of your marketing team look like?

Lintonsmith: I have grouped my team into five different areas. The first one is what I call "insights, analysis, and innovation." This team is the front end of marketing responsible for looking at trends and research studies, including a lot of third-party information and our own proprietary research. This area also analyzes our sales results. Innovation and new products are included in this area since many ideas are driven by the insights. Development for a new fast casual concept that we just launched, called Quiznos Grill, was led by this team.

The second area is marketing and advertising, which includes all aspects of the national calendar and every promotional event, whether it's a new product introduction, a new menu launch, or a tie-in with a movie or other partner. This group handles all consumer communications, both inside and outside the stores, from point of purchase materials and menu boards to social, mobile, digital, radio, print, etc.

The third area is a communications and training team that handles internal communication to all company team members and franchisees, and external communications to the media. This team also develops our training materials and job aids for the restaurants.

My fourth area combines quality assurance and research and development. Quality assurance controls our product specifications. Quality ingredients are a key component of our brand. This team works directly with our suppliers to monitor the production of our ingredients to ensure they meet our quality standards. Innovation is also key to the Quiznos brand. We are continually developing new recipes. The R&D team develops the recipes and writes the procedures. It's important in restaurants to make sure the recipes can be easily and consistently executed at all stores. This group will work with our Operations leadership group to ensure the recipes can be implemented as designed.

My fifth leg is international, which includes two direct reports. One person manages marketing and menu development for Canada, and a second person works with our master franchisees in about thirty-seven different countries.

Steimle: What's your philosophy on building and managing a marketing team?

Lintonsmith: I look for passionate leaders—people who truly care about the business and want to make a difference. These are people who will go the extra mile because they love what they do and are motivated by results. These are people who desire to make a difference and have a positive impact on the company.

I try to build a team with people who have intellectual curiosity and look for better ways of doing things. I appreciate those who aren't afraid to ask the tough questions or challenge status quo. I value the person who tells me what I need to know, not what they think I want to hear.

I want people on my team who have great attitudes—people who are positive, upbeat, and have a lot of energy. A positive attitude is a big thing for me. My favorite quote is "attitude is everything." I have a rock on my desk in my office with this quote on it. I love optimists and personally try to keep a positive attitude. We all face a lot in our work and personal life. How we deal with what happens makes all the difference. I frequently say, "You can't control the winds, but you can adjust the sails." Or, from Epictetus: "It's not what happens to you, but how you react to it that matters." You get the idea.

I try to build a team with individuals who work well together. There are a lot of really smart people in the workforce, but I look for people who can work well with others, people who want to personally contribute but also understand that it takes a team to get a lot of these projects accomplished. It's nearly impossible to do anything by yourself in a company. Team players do what is right for the business and don't care who gets the credit.

These are just a few key qualities I look for when I build a team. I believe if you have a great team, then you don't have to manage them. You lead by providing the vision, the resources, ensuring alignment, and then getting out of the way to let them do what they do best.

Steimle: How do you attract and retain top marketing talent?

Lintonsmith: It's currently difficult. It's no secret that Quiznos is in a turn-around situation. This was a brand that had over five thousand stores at one point and experienced rapid growth. We went through a bankruptcy in the first quarter of 2014, and now, we're doing a lot of things to try to grow sales and turn the business around. Unfortunately, I can't attract and retain great marketing talent by throwing a lot of money at them. I have to retain great people by letting them know how much they are appreciated and giving them the opportunity to grow, learn and make a difference.

When recruiting for a position, I let the candidate know that this is a place where you can come in and be part of a turnaround, and help change the lives of franchisees who have bought into this franchise because they want to be financially successful and pass it on to their children. It's an opportunity to work with a great group of people. I can tell you, I love the people I work with. If people enjoy what they're doing, they feel challenged, and if they like the people, that helps to keep them around. I'm trying to make the environment as engaging and fun as possible. I try to let people know when they do a great job and make people feel that they are an essential part of the team. It's important to recognize and reward good work. That's how I'm trying to attract and retain top talent in a competitive industry.

Steimle: Do you have any experience breaking down silos? How can a CMO facilitate that?

Lintonsmith: I have worked for several companies that have had silos. You have silos at almost any company, no matter how big or small. I believe it all starts with the tone set by the executive team. If the executive team of cross-functional leaders works well together, that behavior tends to permeate the organization. Driving teamwork and breaking down silos is something that we work at very hard at Quiznos. The executive team communicates and works well together. Part of the reason is that we spend a lot of time together. We meet every Monday afternoon to discuss the priorities. We do quick check-in calls at the same time every morning. That ensures that we stay connected, even if we're away from the office. We believe that if we work well together, odds are, our teams will as well.

Communication is key too. We're moving fast so ongoing communication is critical. We outline the priorities, define the charter and team roles and responsibilities, and update the rest of the company at a reoccurring monthly meeting. We also have the right meetings in place for cross-functional teams to make sure they are working together to accomplish the key initiatives. We're not perfect, but it's better than situations I've seen at other companies. Again, the executive team plays a huge role in eliminating organizational silos by leading by example, setting the expectations, and communicating frequently.

Steimle: What are some of the key metrics that you focus on?

Lintonsmith: In the restaurant industry, the key focus is on topline sales, and the two components are the number of people coming in—what I call foot traffic—and the guest-check average.

Next, we look at key components of the P&L, including food costs, labor, and gross profit. When we make menu decisions, we'll closely evaluate the impact on both food and labor. In addition, the menu team monitors the product mix. The mix is a key component of the food cost line. I also look at customer input, which we get from a restaurant-level survey, to ask, "How was your experience at the store?" We monitor overall satisfaction, intent to return, and the Net Promoter Score, among others.

I look at a brand-equity tracker to see how the guests are feeling towards the brand nationally and monitor online chatter about the brand and about our competitors, really watching to see what people are saying. I also look at franchise input on promotions, initiatives, and sales results. Those are the key metrics I focus on as CMO.

Steimle: How do you approach the international marketing? How does that factor into your role?

Lintonsmith: I have global responsibilities for both marketing and the menu. Much of our focus is on North America, where we have the majority of our stores. However, we are in over 35 countries that have "master franchisees" that we also support. From a marketing perspective, my team's role is to be brand stewards and to provide resources to the countries as needed. We need to maintain brand standards and consistencies across the countries, so we have guidelines around the restaurant look and feel and all branding elements. We also get involved in the marketing plans for the different countries. We have creative that we can work across borders, with different consumers and address different competitors. We try to keep the partners updated on what we are testing in North America and the results to date. We also share best practices from other countries.

From a menu perspective, we have a set number of recipes that are the same around the world. We then work with our master franchisees to create a few specific recipes that appeal to local preferences.

Steimle: With all these different types of customers or different groups around the world, what tools or methods do you have for making sure you're in touch with those customers and understand their needs and wants?

Lintonsmith: We have a lot of resources for North America and in other countries try to do basic research to understand the market, the competitive environment, and consumer needs and preferences. It really varies from country to country, so I can't say we have one tool that works everywhere, but we are trying to get better at a disciplined approach.

Where we have strong social markets, we're able to monitor online chatter about our brand or watch what people are posting on Facebook. It's important to understand how consumers from different countries are talking about their experiences with our brand. Where possible, we have a tool to gather feedback on specific experiences at a particular store that they visited. We are also working on expanding a loyalty program to more countries. We have a program that is working well for us in a few countries and are working to expand it into more regions.

Steimle: What are some trends in your industry or with your customers that are affecting you? For example, it seems to me there's more of an awareness of healthy eating these days. Are there other trends that are affecting your marketing?

Lintonsmith: What we see in the restaurant world today are people's expectations for higher-quality food and also better environments. In the past, people were perhaps more interested in the quantity of food for the price. The millennials have really changed that. They're expecting better food, wanting food with a story, and want to eat in a nicer environment. That's why we're seeing the huge growth in fast casual concepts, where you order at the counter and the food is typically brought to your table. In addition, we're see-ing successful quick serve restaurants improving their menu and their facilities.

Not a new trend, but a continuing one in restaurants is that consumers are looking for healthier options or minimally, more visibility in terms of nutri-tional information, like calories and sodium, so they can make more informed decisions. In that respect, at my last two companies, we made sure to readily provide the nutritional information, even if it wasn't good, and then promote customization so guests could make informed decisions in order to meet their dietary or personal preferences. We also made sure that allergen infor-mation was available, given the increased focus on food allergies and intoler-ances. There's a growing number of people looking for gluten-free options. While only about one percent of Americans have celiac disease, many more people are choosing not to eat foods with gluten for dietary reasons. So as a bread-based brand, we're trying to make sure there are "gluten-savvy" options and information available. There are many other trends too about where the food comes from, whether antibiotics or hormones were used in raising the animal, sustainability practices, etc. There are several trends impacting the restaurant space. The key is determining what your brand stands for, and for your consumer targets which factors most impact actual purchase behavior.

Steimle: How are millennials affecting marketing for you? Are they affecting how you market to other groups as well?

Lintonsmith: Millennials are definitely having an effect on how we're mar-keting. They not only are expecting a little bit higher quality, but the way they consume their media information has changed the way we have gone to market. We've changed our media mix quite a bit in the last 3 to 5 years. In the past, we could reach a large audience and drive noticeable sales growth with a strong national TV buy. We spent most of our budget on TV spots and media. TV is still very high on the list in terms of driving reach, but it's not as high-usage for millennials. They are using two or three mediums at the same time. They are choosing how they're going to engage with your brand. Instead of marketers talking at the consumer, millennials are choosing when and how they're going to interact with marketers, whether or not they're going to fast-forward and ignore the commercial online or on their television, choose not to engage in print, change the station on the radio, pay to listen to commercial free digital radio, etc. Their media consuming behavior has forced us to be smarter about how we utilize social, digital, and mobile. Most marketers are allocating more money to interactive. Not only is it more cost-effective, but it is a way to engage with this important audience.

Content marketing has become more important in the last several years, and communicating to the millennial consumer in an entertaining way so that they are choosing to spend more time with your brand, and hopefully share the content, instead of choosing to ignore you. Because of the millennials, I've changed how I allocate the marketing budget and put more towards social and digital than in the past five years.

Steimle: What are some specific initiatives you've taken surrounding digital, social media, and mobile?

Lintonsmith: Some of the best ways to connect with our customers has been from a social perspective. We are posting on Facebook and tweeting every day. We try to generate new content that is very timely with what's happening in the world so we can be relevant and resonate with our audience. A specific initiative was the launch of the new platform called Toasty. TV in March of 2014. This is a digital platform that offers engaging content like comedy, music and sports – things we know resonate with millennials. In the first year of the Toasty.TV launch, we created about fifty pieces of original content to engage the consumer and get them to keep coming back to our site. We worked with a great agency to develop, at a very good price, creative mash-up parodies that were a lot of fun and got a lot of views. We also posted these videos on our YouTube channel, which were shared and gained significant number of views.

Our first video parody was called "House of Thrones", which was a mash-up of two very popular cable shows at the time. This was an important launch for us. The site and video launched at the same time as the company announced the Chapter 11 restructuring. Toasty.TV helped change the focus from the restructuring to the launch of our clever and creative marketing tool.

Another of our parody videos was called "Startourage", which we launched the week of the theatrical release of Entourage and the release of the new Star Wars movie teaser. The video got over 1.4 million total views with consumers spending over 2.9 M minutes watching the video. One of our most successful video parody was "The Burn Trials". This was a parody mash-up of Burning Man and the "Scorch Trials" movie, the second in the Maze Runner trilogy. Timing is everything. The video was launched with the movie trailer release and the same week of the annual Burning Man gathering. The video was viewed over 5.1 million minutes, of which 4.6 million were in the first two weeks. The video got over 2.7 million total views and a lot of press coverage given the relevant and timely topics.

All of the parody videos included Quiznos advertising in a very unique and subtle way. The intent was to entertain and not market at the consumer, but engage with them in a fun way that they appreciate. And we got great feedback from our guests and comments on social media. We watched the

Quiznos posts where they say, "Wow, this was fantastic. This was better than advertising and we're going to be coming to Quiznos now because of it." Toasty.TV was a big initiative for us that we continue to support as a way to engage consumers, especially millennials, from a social and digital perspective.

Steimle: Are there any specific tools that are valuable to you in your job, specific software, CRM systems, marketing automation, anything like that? How do you use those tools?

Lintonsmith: We don't use tools like that per se. We are working actively on building a loyalty program. The reason we want to have a loyalty program is more than just giving our guests relevant offers and incentives to return more often. A loyalty program is important to us so we can better understand guest behavior and have more of a one-on-one personalized discussion with them versus marketing at everyone the same way. There is so much we can better understand about our guest through a loyalty database that will give us better insights and help us make better decisions. We are in the process of building a program that's integrated with our new POS system.

Steimle: Talk a bit about data. What kind of data do you have access to? How do you use data in your role?

Lintonsmith: We have a lot of sales data available to us, down to the store level. We can measure sales, traffic, how much the consumer spent, what they purchased, etc. Right now, we can't tie it to a specific consumer, but will be able to once the loyalty program is launched and integrated with the POS. In addition to detailed sales information, we track what guests are saying about the Quiznos brand and about their experience at one of our restaurants. We use a lot of information and data to make decisions on how we market to our guests, to monitor how they feel about our current promotion, how they like the menu, etc. We are constantly trying to innovate. We get a lot of immediate feedback, good and bad, from tests or whenever we make a change. We monitor and can make adjustments as needed.

If we see comments that come through on our surveys or on social monitoring where the guest had a great experience, we'll respond and also recognize the store for great service. If the guest has a bad experience, we'll make sure we connect with that guest to understand what went wrong and try to course-correct to make sure we satisfy or resolve the situation in the best way possible to retain that guest. We will use data in a number of different ways in our business to try to understand behavior and attitudes and to better engage our guests to get them to recommend the brand and come back more often.

Steimle: With all this technology, data, and social media, is there a danger of getting lost in it and forgetting the basics of marketing?

Lintonsmith: There's a lot of data and information out there. Sometimes, you have to step back and say, "What does it all mean" and "What am I going to do with this data to make the right decision for the guest?" As a marketer, you need to look at the information, but quickly boil it down to the "so what?" And of course some decisions may be based on gut feel. We as marketers have a lot of experience as to what works and why, especially when it comes to innovation. Guests or data can't always tell you what the next big idea is. Data may inform or confirm your direction, but may not tell you exactly what you need to do to make a leapfrog change to be stronger and more competitive in the marketplace. There's still a lot of common sense and looking forward at where you want your brand to go and how you stay ahead of the competitors, especially in a very dynamic industry.

Steimle: Do you work with outside agencies? How do you manage those relationships for a successful outcome?

Lintonsmith: We work with a couple of different agencies to help us with some of the media planning, developing the overarching creative, and helping us be relevant in the social digital perspective. On Toasty.tv, for example, we worked with a small but talented and nimble agency called Windowseat. But, we tend to do a lot internally based on trying to make sure we have as much of our budget as possible going against working media versus paying overhead at agencies. Planning, creative development for our restaurant menus and point-of-sale materials, menu development, digital and social execution, etc. are all managed internally. We'll engage help from outside experts as needed, but a lot of our marketing is handled internally.

Steimle: Are you part of any industry organizations? If so, how do those organizations provide value for you?

Lintonsmith: The main one I'm involved in is The CMO Club. I've been a part of that for over six years and I've been the chapter president for Denver for a number of years. There's a lot of value in networking and utilizing the resources that are available. This is a global group of CMOs across industries, across the world, and it is really great when we can all get together to discuss business successes and challenges. There are two summits in the U.S. each year.

We come from different industries and have a lot of differences, but we are facing some common issues. Sometimes I learn how others are addressing things in other industries and I'm like, "Wow, I never thought of that. That is really interesting and could be applied to my business." It's also a safe way for some of us to get together and discuss topics we may not know well and see how others are addressing the issue. That organization is really helpful for me. I participate in a number of other groups as well, but The CMO Club is the one I've spent the most time with in recent years.

Steimle: Is there certain media you turn to or favorite books you've read in the past that have been influential for you in your role?

Lintonsmith: There are a number of books I have read in the past and some that I have gone back to, for example, Jim Collins' *Good to Great*[1] and *Great by Choice*[2]. I read those years ago and I've recently reread them. Those contain great reminders to any kind of company about making sure you have the right people on the bus and that you are focused on the right thing to remain competitive.

Some of my favorites are by Malcolm Gladwell. I read *David and Goliath*[3] and *Outliers*[4] not long ago because we're in a turnaround situation, and sometimes, I feel like we're the little guy from a budget perspective competing against some pretty large budgets and resources.

Another one I've looked at again recently was *Blue Ocean Strategy*.[5] As I'm in a turnaround situation and a cluttered industry, it's a great reminder about the need to carve out a new space and not get stuck in the red ocean thinking. It helps to remind me, as a CMO, to not get caught up on focusing on the competition and fighting over this set or shrinking pool but instead thinking outside the box and creating new opportunities and new directions for this turnaround brand.

Steimle: One of the challenges facing CMOs today is the sheer number of marketing vendors, channels, and opportunities. How do you make sure you stay on top of all these tools and opportunities out there and use those that are going to help you in your role?

Lintonsmith: There are so many new tools and vendors to consider and I have very little time to spend trying to navigate all the options out there. I'm fortunate to have a director of interactive and innovation who spends a majority of his time looking at companies and new tools and exploring these different opportunities. He has a small budget where he can test out different initiatives with these companies. He'll screen the options, test as he deems appropriate, and then come back and say, "Here are the companies or areas where I think we should put a little more money and serious thought." He plays that critical role for my team.

---

[1] HarperCollins, 2001.
[2] HarperCollins, 2011.
[3] Little, Brown and Company, 2013.
[4] Little, Brown and Company, 2008.
[5] W. Chan Kim and Renée Mauborgne (Harvard Business Review Press, 2015).

He is also an important resource because he can connect the dots between marketing and IT. He's a marketer who has IT skills and handles all the coding for our email program, website, etc. Given so many of the opportunities that present themselves are tech-related, you typically need to have both groups in the room at the same time. Given he has marketing and technology knowledge, he is perfect for screening ideas and deciding which ones we should pursue.

You can get lost and spend so much time trying to understand which opportunities to consider and which ones to pass on. Again, I'm fortunate to have a talented person to handle this for the team. My fear is that he's going to know how valuable he is and be stolen away! It's so critical to be able to create the link between marketing and IT and have somebody who really understands both.

Steimle: What do you see as some of the timeless aspects of marketing? What stays the same as we see all this technology changing along with other shifts?

Lintonsmith: There's been so much change over the past twenty years with the traditional mediums, but some of them still transcend time. For example, TV. It's changed so much and marketers aren't spending as much of their budget on TV as they were in the past, but it's still a great medium to reach the largest audience very quickly. Outdoor has transcended time. Outdoor is still used effectively for local brand marketing and for driving traffic to specific locations. There is some printing that has stayed true and remained pretty similar to twenty years ago, whereas social, digital, and mobile change rapidly.

Steimle: For new marketers who are just coming out of universities or getting started in their careers, what are some of the skills they should be acquiring today that will help prepare them to be future marketing leaders?

Lintonsmith: One thing future CMOs need to do is get some general business skills. As a CMO, marketing is only a portion of what I do. I spend so much time involved in so many other aspects of the business. For example, I spend a lot of time working supply chain on getting new or improved ingredients into our system; with operations to make sure we are staying aligned and doing a great job pleasing the guest; with the technology team on our point-of-sales tools, including the loyalty program; with my analytical director reviewing test results, etc.

I have a direct responsibility for the menu and development of new products. I need to have operational skills and understanding so that when we make changes to the menu, we understand how the changes impact purchasing and distribution, the specs and procedures, and how all that plays out within the four walls with every single restaurant across the country. It is so much more than just marketing. It really is about multitasking, having general business skills, and knowing how to work with, influence, and communicate across so many different audiences.

I would tell the future CMOs, "Don't just spend time in one area. Make sure you understand all aspects of the business because you're going to be involved in making decisions that impact the company that are not just in your space."

Steimle: What do you see as some of the mistakes CMOs today are making?

Lintonsmith: CMOs are making mistakes if they're not working closely with their counterparts. As mentioned earlier, the different departments take their cues from the executive team. If the CMO works and communicates well with all the executives, the changes are that the next layers will also work well together. Also, in most industries, CMOs need to make sure they are close with the IT leadership and team, because so much of what we're doing in marketing depends on the technology. It's important to forge those relationships and work as a team.

Also, for a lot of businesses that are more operationally driven, it is a mistake if the CMO is not working well with the head of Operations. I believe a CMO should understand the operations of the company. I also believe this is an important relationship in Ops-focused companies. If marketing and Ops are not working well together, that could limit the CMO's potential to be successful in launching innovative ideas or projects.

Steimle: Is there anything we haven't covered that you're itching to share about what the CMO role is like?

Lintonsmith: What I have found from talking to a lot of CMOs here in Denver and through The CMO Club nationally is that not every CMO has the same responsibilities. We all have slightly different challenges, but the role has become more generalized, and marketing leaders are taking on more and more responsibilities within the CMO role. For myself, that includes quality assurance, product R&D, communications, and training. At one point, I also had U.S. operations reporting to me. CMOs are getting more involved in IT given the growing opportunities that are technology-based.

For someone who is a great general business manager and wants to be a critical part of influencing a company, not just from a marketing perspective but from a business perspective, the CMO role is now broader and more exciting than ever.

Linda Boff

Chief Marketing Officer
General Electric

Linda Boff was recently named CMO at General Electric after serving as executive director of Global Digital Marketing since 2011. Previously, she served as GE's global director of marketing communications. Before coming to GE, Boff was director of marketing and communications at Citi. In 2015, Mashable named Boff the Individual Digital Marketing Innovator of the Year. Boff attended Union College, where she earned a bachelor of arts in political science and psychology.

Josh Steimle: To get us started, give us an overview of your career. How did you get your start in marketing? What were the steps that led to where you are today as the CMO of GE?

Linda Boff: I have been in some form of marketing or communications forever. I started right after college in network radio. I went to the agency side—first PR, then marketing. I worked in marketing on the publishing side. I worked at a big not-for-profit. I worked at a bank, and eventually, I worked at GE. I looked at different forms of marketing and marketing communications through the lens of everything from consumer goods to sports marketing, a major cultural institution, financial services, and ultimately, GE, as diversified an industrial and tech company as you can find.

Steimle: Is there anything in your background or upbringing that's not directly related to marketing that you think has benefited you as a CMO?

Boff: I studied psychology and political science in college. These days, understanding user behavior and how people consume and react to things is more important in marketing than I ever could have imagined way back when. I also

© Josh Steimle 2016
J. Steimle, *Chief Marketing Officers at Work*, DOI 10.1007/978-1-4842-1931-7_25

have a lot of cultural interests, be it theater or modern art. Different perspectives help a great deal in marketing. Being curious helps enormously.

Steimle: The CMO role can differ from one company to another. What's the full scope of your responsibilities as CMO for GE?

Boff: I'll break it into a couple components. It's how we tell our story and bring it to life. Think of that as the creative component. How do we bring GE's brand to life in the right way to the right audiences to drive impact? That's one part. A second part is connecting what we do on the creative and content side to our commercial efforts, connecting the air war and the ground war and how we drive demand among customers.

The third part is experimenting with purpose, how we use social platforms and technologies to bring our brand to life and to do it in a way that is original. The fourth is the functional side. How does marketing as a function behave at GE? The last, but definitely not the least, is increasingly customer experience and how we think about what the experience is that our customers are having with us and what experience we'd like them to have with us.

Steimle: What are some of the challenges for the CMO of a brand as large as GE?

Boff: There are a few. At the top, it's staying relevant and contemporary. Where GE has an advantage and a challenge is that we've been around for nearly one hundred thirty years. We are well known. People are familiar with GE. It's rare, particularly in the developed markets, that you find somebody who has never heard of GE or who can't give you some sense of what they think of when they think of GE. That's an advantage going in, and it's a challenge, because when you've been around for a while, you are known for certain things that may or may not fit into the landscape of where the company currently is and where it's headed. Being contemporary is harder when the buzz and talk value often goes to younger brands in the digital and social space.

Steimle: Give us some insight into how marketing is structured for GE. Are there different product teams for every division, product, and such? How do you fit in and align what you're doing as CMO with different teams and different parts of the company?

Boff: Our portfolio has focused or been refocused around energy, transportation, and healthcare as well as a very small part of our business in finances. Over the last five years or so, we've also transitioned to being more of a digital industrial company. We're a company that still manufactures jet engines, MRI machines, and locomotives, but we have invested and will continue to invest in software and tools, platforms that enable our machines to be more intelligent and to provide predictive solutions to our customers.

I tell you that as background because as we think about the world of marketing and how it works at GE, we have product marketing teams in all of our businesses, people who are looking at our products and how we market them to our customers. That's a key part of what we do. What's the value prop? What's the go-to-market strategy? How do we launch, grow products, and drive margin for the businesses? That's done really well inside our businesses.

Steimle: You have your own team that you work with and there are other separate teams. Is that correct?

Boff: It is. There are marketers across GE. There are probably four thousand marketers in different parts of the company, many of them in our business units, some of them geographically based, so think of them as marketers that sit vertically in our businesses and horizontally across our company in regions around the world. In corporate marketing, where I am, there's quite a small group of folks who are focused on driving the big company themes. Ten years ago, we launched Ecomagination. Today, it's very much about being a digital industrial company. We're focused on the bigger narrative of the company and how the individual efforts at our businesses both drive product success but also map to the bigger initiatives, bigger programs across the company.

Steimle: You've replaced Beth Comstock at GE. What are some of the unique opportunities or challenges in filling the shoes of somebody like Beth, who's very well known as a CMO and has played a big role?

Boff: Beth is one of the great CMOs, period. Beth gave both GE and the industry a real lens on what it is to be a modern marketer and to drive innovation. I don't think you fill those shoes. What I am trying to do is think about how you market in 2016, in 2017. How do we market for today and build on the fantastic blocks, strategies, and innovations that Beth has put in place? That's the only way you can do this. Otherwise, you'd be looking behind you all the time.

I'm so fortunate in that I still work for Beth. She's now our vice chairman for the company and really looking at whether this is innovation. Marketing is a piece of that, but there are so many other parts of it. Luckily, she hasn't gone anywhere. She's continued to grow, but I'm so fortunate to continue to have her as a leader, mentor, and ally.

Steimle: It seems like there are a lot of new CMOs. What are some specific steps that a new CMO can or should take during the first ninety to one hundred twenty days on the job?

Boff: I'll tell you some of the ones I've taken. Be really curious. Everybody has to give themselves that ninety-day period where they are listening hard and talking to everybody. In my case, it was our business leaders and marketing talent across the organization to hear what was on people's minds and to hear about what we could do both as a function and as a company. What we're trying to do is not marketing for marketing's sake. It's marketing to achieve business outcomes and goals and see where we can be stronger by partnering.

In the first ninety days or so, I wrote a charter, but I didn't sit someplace and do it alone. I pulled together a group of senior marketers across GE. We met a number of times to talk about where the opportunities and the challenges are. Then, the question was, "What do we do about it? What's the blueprint we want to follow? How do we bring that to life?" It was "So what? Now what?"

For us, the "Now what?" is a combination of things. It's communicating in a transparent way across the company, across marketing in a way that includes all voices—not just the top leaders in marketing, but people across the functions. It's a sense of shared pride. For instance, I started a podcast about a month ago. I have loved radio going all the way back to many years ago. It's how I started off. I've been interviewing people using a modern, current way to communicate—a podcast—but also identifying how we can marry the art and the science of marketing. The podcast has contained a lot about inspiration, talking to leaders outside and inside the company.

We're launching a series of video TED talks in January that are more practitioner-based, more about the science of marketing. As I've listened, I've realized one part of what we need to do is share and show off some of the great practices we're doing. You can't do everything. I picked customer experience as an area that is going to be a big focus of mine and of the team.

We've created a whole customer experience CX effort across the company. We've done surveys. We're mapping our customer journey and pain points. That is an area where we can make a difference. Digital is another one, mapping what it means to be a digital industrial company. Part of what we've decided to do going forward is to make sure we market as a digital industrial company would and market in the year 2016. Those are some things I've been doing.

Steimle: What is your philosophy on building and managing a marketing team?

Boff: Hire people who are fantastic at what they do and have deep domain expertise. Give them as much runway as possible. Clear the road for them because part of being a leader is giving people the opportunity to do great work and then getting out of their way and letting them do it.

I'm a collaborative leader. I've tried really hard even in the first couple months of this role to create connections where there haven't been connections before, whether that's across business units or new alliances between corporate and some of our business units, finding ways to connect the dots.

Our marketing is both centralized and decentralized. What I mean by that is a lot of our corporate marketing, the external marketing that you see—be it advertising or content development, etc—comes from corporate. Our business units do more in terms of direct customer outreach, demand gen, trade shows, and that sort of thing. It's figuring out how we can create efforts where everybody can find themselves, and by highlighting various efforts, it helps our individual businesses work with their customers.

Steimle: With all these different units, it seems like it could be easy for silos to form. How do you break down silos? How does the CMO facilitate the breaking down of silos?

Boff: It helps to be transparent about what my objectives are, how we're going to get there, and what the priorities are. Silos happen when people don't have the information they want and feel as though something is happening that they're not privy to. That's a way to silo-bust. Creating trust and accountability helps with that. Creating horizontal efforts, horizontal teams, whether they're workforces, councils, or different growth initiatives—which is some of what we're looking at—all help with silo-busting.

Our businesses have more in common across GE than may meet the eye. We talk about this concept of the GE store and what we do as a company that puts things into the store. That can be leadership, technology, brand, and innovation that benefits the greater whole. Brand is a great example. GE is one of the top ten brands in the world. We're valued at about $42 billion. That's something everybody can derive benefit from. We're all GE. We don't go to market as separate brands. We go to market as a brand in-house. That drives a lot of commonality.

Similarly, from a leadership point of view, GE is one of those brands that has been known for creating great leaders. There's some common practices there similar with technology. We have technology in aviation that applies to oil and gas and technology in lighting that benefits health care. All of those things, what we refer to as the GE store, help break down silos.

Steimle: You work with several outside agencies. How do you manage those relationships for successful outcomes?

Boff: There are some similar principles. What I mean by that is we have several agencies—more than several, actually. We try hard to find ways to come together. Once a month, we do an all-agency all-hands meeting, so there's a sense as to what everybody's working on. We put agencies in groups. On any given project, there's a lead agency that is likely to be working with two or three other partners to support those efforts. We believe in not just single marketing efforts but the overall amp that you might get. It's never about an individual television ad. It's rather about the social media that surrounds that, the PR amplification that comes from it. We will frequently have several agencies working together.

Steimle: What are some of the specific metrics that you track and focus on?

Boff: There's a bunch of them. We look at upper funnel metrics. We pay a lot of attention to the value of the GE brand. We look at all kinds of different engagement metrics, from shares and viewership to what kind of commenting we're getting, so both qualitative and quantitative. We look at sentiment. I look at sentiment every day, not because it's noisy every day, but because if you look at it enough, at a quick glance, you get a sense of how good is good and how bad is bad. We do regular polling—reputational polling—globally and domestically, amongst the general public as well as thought leadership and business decision-makers. We look at marketing-qualified leads and sales-qualified leads as part of our marketing automation process. We measure almost everything. It's what you pay the most attention to that matters.

Steimle: With so much data coming in and so much information available, is there an opportunity for you as the CMO to get lost in that and in a way lose touch by being so in touch?

Boff: There's definitely that possibility. I rely on my team, who are great at this, to help me surface what's important and what's less important. In an age where everything can be measured, it gets harder and harder mostly because of the uncertainty of what it is you should pay the most attention to. We've created any number of dashboards, but I find that people who are the closest to any particular project have a better sense than any dashboard can give you. It's not really the data. It's the insights from the data.

Steimle: With GE being a global company, what are some of the specific challenges for you to adapt to all the different markets, countries, languages, and cultures? How does that affect you in your role? How do you deal with that?

Boff: One of the hardest challenges today for a CMO in marketing is how to be globally consistent and locally relevant. It's hard. If you're GE and you go to market as a single brand, you need both. You need that ability to drive a big brand, to drive a set of core messages, to drive certain attributes, to show up a certain way that is nuanced as it is.

At the same time, you want to be locally relevant wherever you are because in India, it's different from how it is in China. It's different from how it is in Indonesia or Nigeria. That challenge of global consistency and local relevancy is one of the biggest challenges, and often, when I talk to other marketers, that's one of the questions that always comes up: How do you marry those two things? It's super hard. I don't think there's a great shortcut, to be honest. I haven't found one. You have to find the partners locally, be they media partners or tech platforms, to be able to figure out how your message resonates locally. There aren't a lot of shortcuts to that.

Steimle: What trends in your industry or with your customers are affecting you?

Boff: Digital and customer experience is the big one. In a world that is increasingly on-demand and real time, our customers are just people. They're human beings. The good experience they're having on Uber, Amazon, or Airbnb is on-demand, customized, and fast. Increasingly, customers are expecting that from whoever they do business with. For all of us, speed is the new intellectual property. We need to be fast. We need to be transparent. As people are able to see that, they expect that from everybody they do business with.

For sure, we see it in customer experience, and that's laced in digital. Digital has enabled all the things we're talking about. It's enabled speed. It's enabled transparency. We as marketers have to be really facile when it comes to digital tools. We have to be pushing what's new and what's next, including the use of platforms, and that could be Fleck or Instagram. It's understanding how tools can make life easier for us and for our customers.

Steimle: With all the different tools coming out every day, how do you keep up with all the different marketing tools, vendors, marketing channels, and opportunities?

Boff: You can't. You can't keep up with everything. What you have to do is pick some and place some bets. But as a team, we can keep up with quite a few of them. I can't be beyond everything or feel like I know everything, but as a team, we can sort of follow the 80/20 rule. We bring in practitioners all the time. We've created forums. The team did something called GE AppFronts, where we brought in a dozen companies that were at the forefront of new applications—Slack was one of them, Wattpad, Poncho. This was a bit of a showcase for us. We invited our customers to come along and see what was new.

Once a quarter at least, we do an emerging media roundtable, where we bring in companies that are debuting new technologies. We meet with startups all the time. We try to keep our finger on what's going on, pick and choose what it is, where we want to activate, and what we want to use. There's no excuse for not trying to learn what's out there.

Steimle: With all the progress and talk about digital and big data and such, what are some of the ways that marketing has stayed the same over the last twenty or thirty years? What's timeless in marketing?

Boff: A great story, well told, is timeless. In this age when there's so much content, everybody hangs their head and says, "What's going to stand out? How do you get heard?" Great stories that are creatively brought to life get heard. There's more. Therefore, you need to be that much better, but that's timeless. Fighting for the user is timeless. With all of the technology we can use and all of the platforms that are out there, I try hard to always come back to the experience for the user. You still have to fight for the user all the time and have a great value proposition. The best marketing in the world doesn't disguise a product or suggest a value that isn't there. That still has to be fundamentally what's there—great experience. The experience the customer has with your company, your product, your service: that's timeless.

Steimle: What are some of the skills that marketing students should be acquiring today that will still be relevant twenty years from now?

Boff: Whether these are skills you can acquire in school or whether they're things you have to learn along the way, I'm not sure, but being able to observe and translate is incredibly important. Great marketers are great translators. You see things happening, but you have to be able to translate them to the products you're working on and what it is you're trying to market. Being a student—and I don't mean this in the pure academic sense—of trends, of what's happening, understanding the value of culture, news, and where all those things intersect are really important. None of us can know enough about data. Being able to draw insights from data is really important.

Steimle: How do you continue to educate yourself? Are there books that have really helped you, or are there media that you turn to, magazines, websites? Which things do you go to to help you in your role as CMO?

Boff: I look at a little bit of everything. I've curated my Twitter feed in such a way that it is my newsfeed. I follow a fraction of the people who follow me so that when I go to my Twitter feed, it's just a super-quick glance at what I need. When I'm coming to work, I always read three different sources on a regular basis: *The Wall Street Journal*, *The New York Times*, and these days, I'm quite attached to something called theSkimm. It's a lot of fun. It tells you the news, but it's got a real voice to it, which I love. Other blogs that I really like are *Business Insider* and BuzzFeed News, which is a different perspective. I read a lot.

I often read fiction as well as nonfiction, but there are three books in the nonfiction world that interest me now. One is *A Curious Mind*,[1] which is Brian Grazer's. I just got it, but I haven't opened it yet. The other two are *Creativity Inc.*,[2] by Ed Catmull, and Peter Thiel's *Zero to One*.[3] I'm one of those people that learns in multisensory ways, so I also learn a lot just by sitting with other people, whether it's other marketers, some of our agency friends, my team, or people in the startup world. That's probably my favorite way to learn.

---

[1] Simon & Schuster, 2015.
[2] Random House, 2014.
[3] Crown Business, 2014.

Steimle: What do you see as some of the biggest challenges facing today's CMOs?

Boff: It's a lot of things. In a world where there's only so much you can pay attention to, what do you pay attention to? Talent is always a challenge, and today, it's more of a challenge because there are more opportunities and places for marketers to work.

Once upon a time, marketers had the choice to work at a brand or at an agency. It wasn't so long ago that we thought in those terms, right? Now, that's expanded dramatically because to be a marketer at a brand, an agency, a tech platform, a content creator—those worlds are merging, and they're merging more every day. The desire for all of those different groups to have top-notch marketers is increasing, so there's a fight for great talent. Marketing is one of those things that is well defined yet at times can be ill defined. As the industry continues to change, marketers must iterate with it. That's always a challenge.

Steimle: What are some of the mistakes you see CMOs today making? What are some of the temptations CMOs are subject to that can lead them in the wrong direction or distract them?

Boff: There are some age-old distractions, which is the reason CMOs have somewhat short tenures. There's pressure to come in, make a mark fast, and show short-term growth over long-term strategy and results. You need to do both. You need to have a strategy and put points on the board. That can be a bit of a vicious cycle. That's a challenge and a pothole. Showing that you can add value and not be the shiny tactician but rather be the strategy partner is a challenge. In some ways, marketers have never been better suited to do that, but it can be a challenge.

It's a challenge to be a fortune-teller. For marketers, the opportunity to define what's new, what's around corners, what's next, and where we're headed is a great challenge, but you need to do it in a way that's thoughtful and lasting. At the same time, there's this idea in *The Lean Startup*[4], the Eric Reis book. There's an opportunity to iterate, and in iterating, sometimes that means you fail. How do you talk about failure in a way that is instructive to the organization, that is about learning, iterating, and moving fast? That's a challenge. Marketers can lead the way in that, but it takes being brave and intrepid to do it. Nobody likes to talk about failure.

Steimle: Are there any organizations that you're a member of—industry groups or other peer groups—that you receive value from? What is the value you receive from those organizations?

---

[4]Crown Business, 2011.

Boff: I'm a member of Marketing 50, one of the World 50 organizations. I joined recently, so I've only been to one meeting. It was incredibly valuable partly because of the agenda, largely because of the colleagues who were there. That one's excellent.

There's a new one that I'm already starting to see value in, and I haven't even been to their annual conference. That's PTTOW!, which is a really good one from everything I can see. It's good because of the level of membership. I'm a proud member of the Ad Council. They do great work. Then, we created some of our own. We have a digital advisory board here at GE that we change out every year with new startup thinkers, people from the edge of the Internet that I find very valuable.

Steimle: What are some of the skills that CMOs need that don't get enough attention, that aren't what magazines or interviewers focus on but that you think are still critical to the role?

Boff: Curiosity, integration. Being a great integrator is valuable because you connect the dots. Sometimes, others are not necessarily paying attention to horizontal thinking. Innovation gets a lot of airtime. It doesn't mean it's unimportant, but it gets a lot of airtime. Creativity is super important. A group that needs to be able to drive creativity and inspire others around them to look for ways to be relentlessly impactful. Those are some that come to mind.

Steimle: There's a lot of chatter these days about millennials. Do you have any thoughts on marketing to millennials or how millennials are changing marketing for the rest of us?

Boff: To me "millennials" is code for talking about marketing today, marketing in the year you live in. Right now, millennials are so talked about because they're such a big part of our population. As a marketer, you have to pay attention to where people are spending their time, who's driving big behavioral trends, and who's driving consumption. Millennials are doing that right now. To only focus on millennials is a mistake, but to ignore them is also a mistake because they're driving too much behavior and sentiment. When I think about that, I think about what millennials are consuming, be that product or media.

We try hard to pay attention to who's consuming what. We are still advertising on television because people are still watching television. If people stop watching television, we won't advertise there. Sometimes, it's that simple. You market where the people you want to reach are. For GE, that's about being in the right place with our audience—not necessarily the biggest audience, but our audience.

We have put a premium at GE in being first on a lot of platforms. On a lot of digital platforms, we are the brand that was there early, and sometimes, we're so early that we're actually the first ones there. We've done that not necessarily to reach millennials—although a byproduct of it has been that we've reached millennials—but because it's a part of our business DNA. We're a company about innovation, about invention. We have been since the days of Thomas Edison. To be on platforms early is a way to show that off, a way to underscore that in our marketing. It's also a way to make our fairly limited budget and dollars go further.

Steimle: Is there anything we haven't covered about the CMO that you think is important to get out—that you're itching to say?

Boff: I work closely with my partner in crime in sales at GE. A big part of that is marrying our product innovation with what we can commercialize. Marketing is uniquely suited to do that, to be able to say, "Here's the value proposition for a product, and here's what the market needs, and how do we bring those two things together?"

In some ways that's obvious, and in other ways, sometimes it isn't. In a world where there can be a food fight between sales and marketing, the roles are so clearly different and need each other so much. You have products that are being developed and a marketplace you want to serve, and I think marketing is uniquely situated in that place to be able to meet, marry, and bridge those two things.

Lauren Crampsie

Senior Partner and Global Chief Marketing Officer
Ogilvy & Mather Worldwide

Lauren Crampsie is senior partner and global CMO at Ogilvy & Mather Worldwide. She first came to Ogilvy & Mather in 2004 and held various executive marketing positions before entering the CMO role in 2012. Previously, Crampsie worked at NBC on The Today Show as the assistant to the style editor. Crampsie attended Lehigh University.

Josh Steimle: What's the full scope of your responsibilities as CMO of Ogilvy? What do you do for North America? How do you address global concerns?

Lauren Crampsie: There are two sides of the coin. One side is growth and new business, and that can mean everything from the macro setting—yearly growth strategies and targets, types of businesses that we want to grow into, and types of verticals that we want to attack for that year, whether it be retail, travel, or what-have-you. Then, it can be as micro as actually running a new business pitch and being hands-on as far as what the talent looks like on the client's team, on the pitch team, what our pitch strategy is, how we will operationalize for the client if we win the business, helping with the whole process and helping the client get the best out of Ogilvy.

© Josh Steimle 2016
J. Steimle, *Chief Marketing Officers at Work*, DOI 10.1007/978-1-4842-1931-7_26

The other side of my job is the marketing PR side. The macro is setting the global marketing agenda for the brand, and the micro side is helping local offices and regions, like New York or London, with their local marketing plans. What are the different ways they want to go to market that year? How much do they want to spend? What do the budgets look like?

As agencies, we don't have anywhere near the kind of marketing budgets that a traditional Fortune 500 client would have, so the question is how we make some impact and how we look at owned and earned media as real sources of value for driving the Ogilvy agenda and brand name through all its different touch points. It's interesting because they go hand in hand. How we want to grow and who we want to grow with is very much about how we go to market and how we think of ourselves and our products. At the same time, they're distinct enough that I need specialized teams in both that I can oversee and direct. There are very few people on my team, maybe two max, that straddle the hybrid of both sales and new business and marketing.

Steimle: What are some of the challenges and opportunities for the CMO of a brand as established as Ogilvy?

Crampsie: I'll start with the opportunities. The rich amount of content that we have to work with is—it's rare for a company to have that much culture rooted in its founder and in its founder's books, stories, memos, and behaviors. Sam Walton is an example that comes close with the culture he created for Walmart. Ogilvy is similar. So much of the foundation that David (Ogilvy) laid down for us—his teachings, the way he felt about talent, the way he felt about the work, the way he felt about the business—is still so relevant today despite all the change and turmoil, three recessions, technology, digital, and everything. So much has been disrupted, yet foundationally, so much of David's beliefs hold true.

The opportunity is having all of that content and an internal brand that's so strong. Some of the hardest components of executing a new enterprise platform are, will my employees rally? Can I get my employees on board? What does the internal branding campaign look like? How do I make sure all my key stakeholders and constituents believe in this platform? I deal with these questions with my clients all the time. For a brand like Ogilvy, that's already so baked into the organization that there's very little I have to do from an employment branding standpoint to get people to buy into David's philosophies.

The challenge, of course, is that David Ogilvy is no longer with us. He hasn't been with us for quite some time, so how do you take everything that he taught us and modernize it and make it relevant? The one thing I'm experiencing lately and with one of the many buzzwords these days is this millennial audience isn't as inspired by a founder-led culture as some of the other generations, particularly a founder that is no longer living and breathing on this planet. It's getting our young people excited about Ogilvy not just through

David. That's a real challenge and something that in a world where the agency landscape has become so saturated, it takes more for a company like Ogilvy to stand out than it ever did before. While David's legacy lives on, and it's strong and it's great, it's not going to get us through the finish line. I'm constantly thinking about how we layer onto the things he taught us and how we continue to innovate and separate ourselves from the competition.

Steimle: What's your philosophy on building and managing a marketing team? What do you look for in hires?

Crampsie: You need believers. One of the amazing things about marketing and advertising is you're tasked with getting someone to believe in the intangible. If you're marketing and you're spending money on advertising budgets and campaigns, it's because it's not enough for someone to have the tangible aspect of your product. You need them to buy into the intangible as well. It's only going to happen with a deep, fundamental belief in your brand.

That's what I look for more than anything with my team of people. Particularly on the marketing side, I need people that really believe in the Ogilvy brand, in our company and the way that we're structured, and who believe that structure, the way we think about our clients, and the value we provide our clients is something they want to be a part of. If I can't feel and see that belief in the first five or ten minutes of meeting someone, I know they're not right.

After that, I think a lot about diversity in terms of the team I have and how I get the most diverse group of people working together. That's always something I look at. I'm a firm believer in diversity being one of the best drivers of business results, so I never hire teams that look, act, and talk the same. I make sure the team is very diverse, both demographically and psychographically, and that people are complementing each other. I believe in tension. Healthy tension is good. When you have that healthy tension, people make each other better. I look for that as well.

I also empower my direct reports to be a key part of the hiring process because in many cases, they might be working with the person more than I would. I want to make sure they're comfortable and happy and that they think they can work with the person as well. The beauty of working in a less structured growth and marketing environment is you can be more risky in terms of talent decisions and can take a bit more time making those decisions. It should be the most fun team to be on. I definitely want people that exude passion and energy and come into work excited and leave every day feeling like they were challenged and that they learned something.

Steimle: What does the structure of your marketing team look like?

Crampsie: Right now, there's the centralized global structure, which has a managing director of content, Nikolaj Birjukow. That's a new position I built particularly for him about two years ago. Nikolaj is my number two on the marketing side and he oversees all of the specialized functions within marketing. He oversees all of our social media and community management, all of our web developers and UX designers for all of our web properties experiences. He oversees our editorial staff. Nikolaj also oversees our internal communication staff—the staff that oversees our internal Internet—and how we communicate with our employees.

My MD oversees that staff as well. It's a real content marketing-driven team. I have a worldwide editorial director, Jeremy Katz. I think Ogilvy was the first agency ever to do a content partnership with a publication. We did one with *Fast Company* about two years ago. I'm a big believer in content marketing and brands as publishers. I completely buy into all of that, and I created the marketing team around that philosophy. The editorial staff is a part of it as well.

On the local level, it depends on the office. The one thing that is not centralized is PR. PR is decentralized at the local level. The only central PR function is me, so I personally take on any big global announcements, crisis management, or anything of that nature because I think it's the most effective way. In many cases—especially with social media and the Internet where it's so hard to control anything—having somebody of my seniority and my tenure take that on personally is the quickest way to get results at the global level.

Steimle: Speaking of that lack of control these days, how do you get through to consumers? How do you work with the customers you're going after in this world of ad blockers where the consumer has so much control over the channel, over the medium?

Crampsie: It's elevating the conversation. It's trying to make the conversation as personalized as possible. We have a CRM program that we use through ogilvydo.com, which is something that our Asia office developed. I launched it globally about two years ago, about the same time I launched the partnership with *Fast Company*.

ogilvydo is our editorial engine, and as part of the opt-in process for that, we clearly tailor content to our consumers based on how they've opted in, who they are, and the type of content they like to digest, whether it's because they've told us directly or because we know enough about them and their habits online that we can hypothesize and target them specifically.

Again, because we don't have massive marketing budgets, we have to be targeted, we have to be personalized, and we have to make the conversation as mutually beneficial as possible. What something like ad blocking has done for the industry is forced us to be even more creative and empathetic to the customer than ever before.

Steimle: Talk more about that empathy. How do you put yourself in the role of the consumer? Do you have any tools to help you do that with all the people you're going after?

Crampsie: One thing Ogilvy does not lack is tools and process, and it's the output of being a company that has been around for as long as we have and has scaled as much as we have. The ability to understand a customer at any point in the buying journey, whether it's pre-, during, or post-sale is not an issue for us. We have enough tools, process, and data that we can completely understand any customer's journey to purchase, what the barriers and drivers are at any given stage in the purchase process, and how to act accordingly depending on those barriers and drivers.

The challenge is less about understanding the consumer and putting ourselves in the consumer's shoes. The challenge for us is more about figuring out which types of messaging are going to resonate. What type of messaging is not just going to resonate but feel true and authentic to the brand because the job now is not only to give the consumer something interesting that they can really engage with. It's also building brand and business value over time. The only way to do that is to be clear about what your brand stands for in the world and continuing to build upon that brand proposition. It's having to do both of those simultaneously that gets tricky, because if you have to do one without the other, you might see a short-term sales spike, but you're not going to see the long-term growth that we want to represent for our clients.

We try to take a long-term as well as short-term approach, and the best way to do that is to look at the brand over time and make sure you're continuing to be true and authentic to the brand.

Steimle: What are some of the specific metrics that you focus on?

Crampsie: It really depends on the client because in a perfect world, we'd focus on the entire funnel, from brand awareness all the way through to sales, conversion, and, depending on the business model, retention of that customer. The more we can be grounded in everything, in both the soft metrics of brand awareness as well as the hard metrics of sales and business results—that is the optimal metric universe that we like to play in.

Sometimes, you have clients that are a bit more private with their information, particularly sales and business information. In many cases, you can see that happening if they're not a publicly traded company. In those cases, we tend to work more with softer metrics, which is fine, but that's not an ideal state for us. The ideal state is having access and accountability over business results.

Steimle: In terms of media, are there are any favorite publications or books that have been especially helpful to you in your role as CMO?

Crampsie: I loved Sam Walton's autobiography. My friend Tristan Walker founded a packaged goods company called Walker & Company, and he does Bevel, which is a subscription razor service. He and I always talk about the Sam Walton autobiography as being a gold standard for everything business—starting a business, keeping a business, taking a business public, continuing to make a business successful. It's a great end-to-end story.

I tend to gravitate more towards real, personal stories. I think that comes from my marketing background. I've read Malcolm Gladwell books. I've read *The Lean Startup*[1] and your typical business books. They're all great for me. They just don't resonate as well as actual, personal stories that I can relate to. I tend to gravitate towards those types of books.

Steimle: How is digital affecting marketing at Ogilvy?

Crampsie: It has greatly affected it. For me in my role, it has done so much positive—the amount that we're able to do with social media and our web properties, being able to have our work live on YouTube, our fans being able to reach us directly in real time on Facebook and others, being able to talk to potential talent on LinkedIn. There's so much we've been able to do at scale that we never could before. It's helped us tremendously. I would even venture to say that from an Ogilvy brand marketing standpoint, it hasn't hurt us at all.

From an organizational standpoint, it's about how you modernize the skill set and the talent in the company for a highly digital adaptive company and a not-so-digitally-based company. The thing about an agency like Ogilvy is we're working with digital at the core companies and clients just as much as we're working with digital clients and companies that are still trying to "figure digital out." We have to be structured to be able to capitalize on both, so we have to have the types of people that are highly innovative, constantly building intellectual property and doing product development, looking at different technologies, thinking about different platforms, and partnering with creative teams on those platforms.

We also need to be able to have teams that are thinking much more in the traditional space and aren't as innovative in the digital space simply because the client is just not there yet in the curve of how they need to go to market in order to be most effective from a sales standpoint.

Digital has made it trickier for us to build the perfect organization from a talent standpoint. That's going to be harder and harder as we go through it and as things change more and more. The optimal talent model for a company as large and diverse as ours is going to become a tougher and tougher nut to crack. A lot of it is about experimenting and trying things out and seeing what works and what doesn't.

At the end of the day, this is a relationship business, and it will always be a relationship business. There will be some bumps in the road, but as long as we put those relationships between agency and our clients at the core of what we

---

[1] Eric Ries (Crown Business, 2011).

do, eventually, I think we'll get to that optimal talent state for any given client in the Ogilvy ecosystem.

Steimle: Do you think there's a danger or temptation for CMOs to focus too much on digital and ignore some of the traditional marketing that still works well?

Crampsie: Absolutely. The best marketers understand what types of data they need to look at and be obsessed with in order to drive the most optimal business results at the highest margin. It's probably an easier question for some of the more traditional companies to answer than for some of the newer companies, but without that answer, it's very hard to figure out the right mixed modeling.

You need to look at your customer not just as a persona but also as a data set, which is why we talk a lot about customer segmentation, understanding who your core target is and the subtargets after that.

As long as you have an understanding of your core and you really understand what's going to make that core your loyalists, what's going to make them buy and what's not, then you can kind of play around with different types of messaging, mediums, digital tactics, and media and whatnot. But you always have to keep your eye on that core customer and how they like to be treated and engaged.

Steimle: What kind of data do you have access to? How do you use data in your role?

Crampsie: Most of our data comes from our online channels. It's the easiest thing to measure because we know exactly who's coming where and when, where they're stopping, what they're engaging with, what other types of content they're looking at. It's all of our owned web properties and all of our social platforms. That's the data I use to optimize the types of content we should be pushing out more, the types of work people are really engaging with. It's helped me look at all of our key audiences and determine the right platform to speak to which type of audience.

We may find that our B2B audience is looking at our LinkedIn page or our SlideShare page, and the way we think about and organize those pages needs to be for an end user that's very much a business user, whereas the majority of people who are going to Ogilvy.com are going there because they want a career at Ogilvy.

The tone of voice and the way we organize information on Ogilvy.com can be a little bit more fun. It can speak more to talent and people that already have an interest in our industry and are looking at Ogilvy as an agency they potentially want to end up at. The way I use it is to define which owned media channels—because I do very little paid—speak to which types of targets and then optimize the messaging based on those targets and how they engage on those platforms.

Steimle: What do you see as some of the biggest challenges facing today's CMOs?

Crampsie: In some ways, it's the age-old challenge, because it's never really gone away, which is that marketing budgets tend to be some of the first budgets to get cut. How do you fight to keep your budgets intact when every single industry is being disrupted at the speed of light? How do you then quantify that those marketing dollars are garnering you ROI on the bottom line?

As more and more industries become disrupted, as more and more legacy companies become entrenched from competitors that started three weeks ago out of their garages, how do you deal with that, and how do you continue to make the customer buy your product and be interested in your brand? How do you do it with less money than you've had before? That's a challenge that has always been there for marketers: The marketing budgets get slashed, and what do I do? How do I prove to my CEO that marketing is actually making a difference on his bottom line?

The challenges haven't changed. They're probably a bit more scary than they used to be mainly because of this disruption that we're seeing and these new types of companies that market through product. If you look at what Uber does, all of their marketing is through Uber the product, the app. If you're a traditional packaged goods company, you can't do that. You have to rely on distributors, and the supply chain is so much more complicated than companies like Uber or Airbnb that operate in more of a shared-economy lifestyle. With the changing business and marketing dynamics being what they are, that's the difference.

Before, we had the changing marketing dynamics but not as much of the business dynamics. Now is a bit of an inflection point where we have these insane changing business dynamics, where every day there's something new—a new technology, a new service, a new competitor. It's being able to stay abreast of that and give it some attention but not so much attention that you lose sight of who you are and why you exist to begin with.

Steimle: As you look at marketing and the history of marketing, what has stayed the same? What hasn't changed in the field?

Crampsie: What's stayed the same is that brands are as important today as they've ever been. Brands still matter to people. People still believe in brands. Consumers still are rooting for brands. What's changed is how they matter to people. The things brands have to do and the ways they have to engage are different. We talk a lot about brands' behavior. It's not enough to be a brand that says. You have to be a brand that does. You have to do what you're saying. That is what has changed. You can't just throw messaging at people.

You have to actually behave in a certain way and what we try to do for all of our clients, whether it be a Watson Food Truck at South by Southwest for IBM or a drinkable billboard for Coke Zero, we try to put our brands in places in the world where they're actually doing something, where they're actually helping a consumer in some way and become utility as much as product. That is the main thing that's changed. The power of brands and the fundamental truth that a consumer will still pick a brand they believe in over anything else hasn't changed at all.

Steimle: What are some of the skills that young marketers or university students can be acquiring today that are still going to be relevant in marketing ten or twenty years from now as they rise through the ranks?

Crampsie: Understand how to use research in the best way. It's not sexy to talk about research anymore, so people don't talk about it. Your customer service channel is now like your Twitter feed. People or brands think that they are getting all this customer feedback and research done in real time, but there's still very much something to be said for pure, old-fashioned customer research. That skill set is never going to go away. It's going to continue to be relevant. Understanding your customer, understanding how your customer buys, understanding why your customer buys, the seasonality of it—you need to have a bit of a research background to really understand that. That's going to be incredibly important.

Understanding media is going to be important—how the media ecosystem fits together, how a piece of content can travel from your television screen to your mobile device, understanding that ecosystem and how to optimize it. Performance marketing is going to continue to be of more and more importance to brands. PR skills will continue to be important. We're going to see more and more crisis management arise as things like data leaks become more common.

We see even the secretary of state's and heads' of movie studios emails getting out there. It's going to be more and more important for people to understand how to react in those types of situations, and good crisis management and PR are going to be important.

Steimle: What are some of the skills CMOs need that perhaps don't get enough attention?

Crampsie: Focus and discipline. There's such perpetual beta at any given moment that it's hard to stay disciplined and focused. It's very easy to just follow the shiny new object. As a marketer, the more focused you can stay on your one priority or objective—and it could be that for the year, your one objective is to move *x* amount of your marketing budget into digital because you know that's where your customer is.

That's fine, but having that one key objective and focus and being fanatical about getting to the end goal is tough right now for most marketers because it's easy to take your eye off the prize to go chase a unicorn that you'll probably never catch, and someone else that has just started their company two months ago might catch it for you.

If you're a marketer at a heritage company, you need to be able to learn. The biggest tool you have is the data, knowledge, and information that company has been collecting over time, and learning from successes, repeating successes, learning from failures, not repeating failures, and optimizing are really overlooked. It's so important, because otherwise, you're running in the hamster wheel.

It sounds obvious and simple, but it gets overlooked. I've seen so many marketing plans that are just sixty-page multiple objectives and marketers who think that if they throw in everything and the kitchen sink, they've touched everything, and now they're good and can go action everything. You end up doing too much of everything, and then you end up doing nothing. This idea of being focused on your objectives and not losing sight of that focus is key.

Steimle: What are your thoughts on millennials and how millennials are changing the marketing landscape?

Crampsie: We're just starting to see the real effects of the purchasing power for that group of people. The jury's still out. Marketers talk a lot about wanting to reach millennials, but I don't think they really know what that means, and I don't think they know why they want to reach them. They just know that they should.

No one can argue that they're an important, growing part of the economy and how brands should go to market, but at the same time, as they mature and gain more purchasing power and experience in life and in business, we might not have such a panicked reaction to them as being these enigmas who don't follow traditional, linear life paths and who drop out of college, don't care about their job, and just want to do good in the world.

I've seen all the studies. Until they have a salary they can actually do something with, until we see the effects they have on our economy and society in a real, monetary way, it's going to be hard to see where the generation is going to net out.

The most important thing about them is that they grew up online, whereas we didn't, and what does that mean? What it means is the online brand experience has to be at the center of every brand strategy in the next five to ten years. Many brands right now are still putting the retail experience at the center. That is going to drastically change because of millennials. It's more based on the fundamental truth of how they've grown up and less about the panicked screaming boomers and Gen-Xers who just can't for the life of them decipher what is going on with these millennials.

Snapchat's a great example of this. Everyone has to figure out their Snapchat strategy because that's where the millennials are. It's kind of like, "Really? Why?" What millennials are doing on Snapchat is optimizing their own selves and acting out on their narcissism with their friends and their like-minded communities. Are millennials engaging with brands on Snapchat? Sure. Are they engaging in a way that leads to a point of purchase? I don't think so. It goes back to my point around focus. The minute you lose focus of what your objectives are and what your core is in terms of your customer and get caught up in Snapchat campaigns or whatever the case may be, that's where we give audiences like millennials too much power.

We've already screwed up because we've basically told them that they're the "Second Coming" and that they should be CEOs and get paid five times the—experience and paycheck are no longer correlated. It's terrifying, but like everything else, this too shall pass. I now hear audiences talking about centennials. I'm like, "Oh, now we're over millennials. Now we're on to centennials."

Steimle: Is there anything we didn't cover that you're just itching to get out about the CMO role?

Crampsie: The only thing I will say is that CMOs now have more power than ever before, and I think they have real power to effect change in an organization. I'm very much of a believer in the CMO being the best consigliere between what your people want inside your organization and what your customers want. The more CMOs start to understand the level of power they have and how much they can use their marketing and targeting strategies to pay back the bottom line, the better the industry will be. We're going to start to see more and more marketers end up in CEO roles over time. Brands matter now more than they ever have, and the person that is responsible for how your brand is seen in the world and within your organization is in a very powerful spot.

Jeff Jones

Executive Vice President and Chief Marketing Officer
Target

Jeff Jones is the executive vice president and CMO at Target. Before coming to Target in 2012, Jones was partner and president at McKinney advertising agency for six years. Previously, Jones held various executive marketing roles such as EVP of global marketing at Gap and global account director at Coca-Cola. Jones holds a bachelor of arts in communications from the University of Dayton.

Josh Steimle: Give us an overview of your career. How did you get your start in marketing? What were the steps that led to where you are today as the CMO of Target?

Jeff Jones: I'm one of those people that knew at a really early age what I wanted to do. Starting in college, I knew I wanted a career in advertising and marketing. Every year of college and every summer between years in college, I interned in the industry. I had a lot of internships all through college, everything from a little internship at *Advertising Age*, to internships at agencies, to studying international advertising for a summer semester in college. My passion for advertising began initially because of an insane curiosity and love of photography. Those are the two things that really got me fascinated by a career in advertising.

There I was, this kid from West Virginia, studying what I always wanted to study in college, the first person in my family to ever go to college. I was terrified to move to New York, so I set my sights on working at Leo Burnett in

Chicago. For most of my senior year, I pursued opportunities at Leo Burnett and got rejected every single time. I moved to Chicago without a job, started working in a restaurant, and ultimately got an informational interview with Leo Burnett. I remember like it was yesterday. In fact, I recently reconnected with the person who interviewed me to thank him for giving me a chance. During the interview, he said, "Tell me about a product that does not exist but should exist." On the spot, I said, "Fingernail clippers that catch the fingernails." I got hired. That began my career.

After accepting the job at Leo Burnett in Chicago, I immediately got offered a chance to move to Detroit to work in the automotive business. I spent about five years right out of school at Leo Burnett, having gotten my dream job, and then I made a difficult choice to leave Leo Burnett. That choice was prompted by a meeting I had at Procter & Gamble, who was my client at the time. A woman who was my most senior client at P&G pulled me aside and asked if I wanted to be a marketer or an ad guy. She went on to hold global leadership roles at P&G, and had an extremely successful career. And she's the one that first taught me the difference between advertising and marketing and really instilled in me what is still a huge hot button for me today. That conversation with her is what prompted me to leave Leo Burnett and join the Coca-Cola Company. That was the first time that I became a client in a corporate marketing job.

I ended up leaving Coca-Cola because I got the Internet bug like so many people did in '99. I joined a friend from college who had started a technology consulting company, very successfully scaled that business and sold it to a public company in Chicago called Whitman-Hart. I ultimately got recruited to go back to Leo Burnett to become the CEO of a subsidiary agency that they had acquired. It had become a massive failure and I was able to turn it into a very successful agency. I then left to become the chief marketing officer at Gap.

I then went back to the agency business. I had a chance to join a former colleague and we ultimately bought a midsized advertising agency in the U.S. that was owned by Havas and took it private. Six years later, I was recruited, really believing that I would never leave, to come to the role I have at Target. I got here in a very circuitous route.

Steimle: So the question is, where do I buy those fingernail clippers?

Jones: What's so funny is that to this day, everywhere in the world I've gone, I look for them. They do make them and they're terrible, so it's still on the long list. Now that I'm at a company with incredible design capabilities, incredible manufacturing relationships, I always think, "Why aren't we making fingernail clippers that catch the fingernails?"

Steimle: Well, if I ever see those on the shelf, I'll know where they came from.

Jones: Exactly.

Steimle: What's the scope of your responsibilities as CMO of Target?

Jones: I always tell people I have one title and three really different jobs. One of my roles is to lead the communications organization. That's the classic corporate communications, team member communications, PR and crisis communication. The other part of my job is as chief marketing officer, and that has all of the classic dimensions of advertising, loyalty, and media operations for the company as well as the brand and category management function.

One of the things that makes it pretty unique and awesome at Target is my team leads the scouting for all of our designer collaborations. One of the things that has made Target famous is how we partner with fashion designers, which happens in marketing or the brand management function. We also play an important role with our owned brands, our proprietary brands. We have a large stable of those brands, ten of which are billion-dollar-plus businesses, all the way through to packaging, packaging engineers and innovators on everything from bottles and vessels to labeling.

We do all loyalty marketing, so we think about starting with a consumer and building lifetime value with really successful digital products like Cartwheel, which is a billion-dollar mobile savings product for Target. All of those things fall into the second bucket as my marketing job.

The third aspect of my job, which is a new responsibility, is as guest architect. That role is really trying to figure out for Target how we architect the ideal consumer journey in this world where consumers want to shop anytime, anywhere, using their mobile phone and tapping into new and different fulfillment and delivery options. It's my job to ask, "What would our guest want?" and "What is the future of experience at Target?" We come from a place where we defined what the physical retailing experience was going to be, and now we have to redefine it.

Steimle: What are some of the challenges and opportunities for the CMO of a brand as large as Target?

Jones: Without question, the first challenge is growth and simply how you grow year-over-year on a base of seventy-two billion dollars. A second big challenge is how we lead the consumer in the rapid pace of change that we're all facing: constant disruption by technology; constant disruption by new competitors entering the market. Many of those things don't cause us to lose share today, but they are changing consumer behavior, and so there are an infinite number of companies that we don't really lose business to, but we lose attention to, and that's a huge challenge.

Steimle: How do you get through to consumers in this new world of ad blockers, where consumers have control?

Jones: Ad blocking is a current reaction to a broader dynamic of consumer control. We have to think about all the ways consumers are in control beyond the fact that they're blocking ads. That means where and how consumers are choosing to purchase. Where and how are they choosing to get information. Where and how are they advocating or not advocating on behalf of a brand. It's a long list of ways that demonstrate that brands aren't in control like they used to be. Every one of those requires a lot of empathy for the consumer and specific strategies on how we engage them.

Ad blocking is one of the current manifestations. What that really says as far as empathy for the consumer is they don't want to be overtaken and interrupted. How do we think about creating content and creating experiences that improve shopping without taking over or interrupting it? That's very much top of mind for us.

Steimle: How do you make sure you're in touch with your customers and understand their needs and wants?

Jones: At Target, we call our shoppers "guests," and I'm lucky from the perspective that we've always been a guest-focused company. We haven't had to teach our team that the guests matter. We have a purpose that is singularly focused on the guests, so the company's clear on what we're here to do. We talk about fulfilling the needs and fueling the potential of our guests, which is a much bigger purpose than selling them things. In order for us to fulfill needs and fuel potential, we have to be empathetic to what it's like to make fifty thousand dollars a year and have a family of four and have to feed and nourish and grow that family.

One of the things that exists inside marketing as the centerpiece for how we help the company be empathetic is what we call the Guest Center of Excellence. That organization is part of my team. Their singular objective is to help the company continue to improve the level of empathy we have for those we serve.

Steimle: What are some of the tools or technologies they have to help them with that?

Jones: A very specific one is that teams are now in the middle of what we call Guest Immersions. An immersion is where we take the leaders of the business into a market and spend two days in homes with our guests, really trying to understand from their perspective what problems they are trying to solve, how they are trying to solve them, what roles different brands play in solving them, and what role Target plays in solving them. Nothing creates empathy for who you're trying to serve more than being with them in their homes, talking about their lives, their families, and their challenges. Those immersions are a very powerful tool.

Obviously, with tens of thousands of team members, we have to be able to scale that capability. We have a centralized portal where we aggregate all of our guest knowledge on topics that people can access and leverage in their business. It ranges from teams in homes gaining true personal empathy to leveraging technology and tools to enable teams that scale to learn from all those lessons. We have to do both of those.

Steimle: What are some of the key metrics that you focus on as CMO?

Jones: Global to specific, it's comp sales, EPS, and ROIC performance. We are rewarded as a team with performance-based compensation, and those are the big three.

Marketing has three roles. We have to drive traffic to one of our assets; we have to deepen engagement with our guests; and we have to strengthen the love they have for Target. So, we are measuring traffic, transactions, basket conversion. We're measuring net promoter. We also are thinking long-term about equity building, and we have four distinct equity pillars to track and measure our relative performance versus that of our competitors. We can also keep drilling down to a program level, looking at campaign effectiveness and advertising, likeability, intent to shop and brand recognition. That's the range—from comp sales, EPS, and ROIC down to an individual piece of creative and how it tests with consumers.

Steimle: What does the structure of your marketing team look like? How is it organized?

Jones: One area is communications, organized around expertise in competencies like corporate communications, PR, team member communication, and crisis communication. Another area is marketing which includes functional experts in brand management, media, marketing operations, creative, and loyalty, all of whom are organized around the categories of business that we serve; style, baby, kids, and wellness. That essentially shapes how we deploy resources, people, and dollars. That's a basic sense of how the team's organized.

Steimle: What's your philosophy on building and managing a marketing team?

Jones: If I don't have the best marketing team possible, we fail. We have assembled a team the last several years that I would hold up against any marketing organization in America. The leaders within marketing are undeniably experts at their functions. That enables them to have enough experience inside and outside Target to help us go faster because they can draw on a lot of references and a lot of experiences in other places.

It's super important to build a team that you want to be with, that you can trust implicitly because of their intentions and their expertise. They're all obsessed with success. Success to them means the success of their people and the success of the business. You learn it everywhere, and I've definitely learned that at this scale, you cannot compete and win without having a great team.

Steimle: How do you attract and retain that top marketing talent?

Jones: They are attracted to the reputation and history of this brand, the nature and quality of the work we do in marketing, and the fact that this company believes deeply that marketing is at the center of everything we do. I'm not fighting for the proverbial seat at the table like many are. We do phenomenal work at a very large scale that can impact lives immediately, and we're able to see the impact of our work.

We invest in marketing, so teams have resources to compete at a very high level. I retain them, hopefully, by keeping them challenged. I say to the team, "I want to have the most revered and the most recruited team in marketing" because then I know I have the best people, and that raises all of our jobs to make sure we're keeping the best people motivated by their work more than by their title.

Steimle: Can you talk a little bit more about what you look for in hires?

Jones: It depends on the level and the nature of the role, but in general, more than anything else right now, I'm looking for a few things: expertise, people who have demonstrated the ability to do these kinds of jobs at other places, so they're bringing an ability to go faster at Target.

I'm looking for people inside the company who have demonstrated a capacity to take on more through the quality of their work, the way they've built their teams, the way they're evaluated by their peers, their ability as great communicators. We are fundamentally transforming Target, and I believe leaders have to be able to share perspective on where we're going and why we're doing what we're doing. I want people who can think strategically, communicate clearly, and bring that expertise, passion, and commitment to keeping people moving forward. Those are some things that are extremely important.

Steimle: Do you have any experience breaking down silos? How can a CMO facilitate that?

Jones: Every company is battling silos. We've been successful at breaking down some, and there are still some we've got to break down. Great marketing people are very lateral thinkers. They are good at connecting people, ideas, and opportunities in very horizontal ways because they're really good at thinking about the consumer.

One of the things I try to do is to stay obsessed with who we're serving. The more I start with the guests, the less the way we're organized is relevant. If I can help people connect across silos in service of the guests, that's what I'm trying to do. In general, based on my experience, marketers tend to think more horizontally than classic operators, for example.

Steimle: Are you a member of any industry organizations, CMO-focused or marketing-focused? If so, what kind of value do you receive from being involved in these organizations?

Jones: There are hundreds, and I have landed on two. One of them is called M50, and for that one, the value to me is a chance to be in person with other CMOs, to really share and learn from each other. The other one I have joined is the board of the ANA, the Association of National Advertisers. The ANA board is a smaller group that truly tackles industry-wide topics that are of importance to any marketer. To have the opportunity to do that with other CMOs is extremely valuable because we have the ability to impact the industry at large.

Steimle: Are there certain media that you turn to to further your career? Are there books or other publications that you've found especially helpful?

Jones: If you saw my bookshelf, you would know that I am insane about reading. I said to my team recently, "I officially now have way more books than I have time to read." I begin every day and end every night with Twitter. I have everything from Al Jazeera as a source for news to TechCrunch and Mashable as sources of innovation and lots in between. Social media, especially Twitter, is a real go-to for me just to stay as absolutely current as possible. I try to spend as much time as I can with our social team to stay close to what our guests are saying about what's happening in the world.

What we're doing with Facebook, Snapchat, Periscope, Pinterest, and Instagram—those don't necessarily fall into the reading category, but they are platforms to help me stay connected in terms of what our guests are thinking and doing.

On the business side of things, most of my reading is focused on anything to do with transformation, change, and human behavior, so books like *Little Bets* by Peter Sims,[1] *The Lean Startup* by Eric Ries,[2] and Dan Ariely's *Predictably Irrational*[3]. Those tend to be the kinds of books and authors that I read to stay current.

Steimle: Which changes do you see as being driven by millennials when it comes to marketing?

Jones: Like every major generation in history, there are things that are true of them and things that turn out not to be true. We're at an interesting place right now on that topic with millennials. It wasn't that long ago when everyone's conversation was, "Everything is different. They don't value brands. They don't pay attention to marketing. They don't buy homes. They don't buy cars. They don't get married. They don't shop in physical stores." Those overarching statements are turning out to be false.

---

[1] Simon & Schuster, 2013.
[2] Crown Business, 2011.
[3] Harper, 2009.

As a marketer, you're always trying to stay in touch with the front edge of all those waves, pay close attention, study over time, and then see where trends ultimately resolve themselves because now we're thinking about the one that's coming behind them. That's where my teenage daughters reside. I see them first-hand, and boy, everything I see about them seems to be an extreme version of what I heard about millennials five years ago.

The point is, the world is changing constantly. As a marketer, you have to be insanely curious and constantly learning because what's true today isn't true tomorrow. That's what we're all trying to figure out. One thing that I do believe is true—and pick the math model that proves it—is the rate of change is absolutely increasing. That's one thing that every generation has in common. They're all changing faster than the ones before.

Steimle: With all this change happening in the marketing world, what are some of the things that do stay the same? What are some things we can depend on?

Jones: Trust. People do business with brands and people they trust. One thing that has changed and I believe will remain true is that consumers, no matter what label we give them, have the ability to know everything they need to know to make a choice in a way they didn't used to. That is forever true. Choice. It's a constant that the instant you disappoint, there's another choice. It almost doesn't matter what age you are, what profile you're assigned, what cohort you're assigned. Those are a few things that come to mind that are fundamentally true now, and it's hard to imagine a day when they're not true.

Steimle: For the young marketers or the university students who are starting out, what are some of the skills they should be acquiring today that are still going to serve them well ten or twenty years into the future?

Jones: I'm obviously biased, but I believe the profession of marketing is the best profession there is. Great marketers are so deeply connected to all parts of the business and that is the best general management path there is. I want students to understand what a career in marketing really is so they choose it as opposed to ending up in it because they weren't sure what they wanted to do.

One of the things I mention to people all the time is "You cannot run from math anymore." So many marketers in my generation and certainly the ones before got into marketing because it was "creative" and they weren't good at math. I talk a lot about data-informed intuition. Experience, gut, creativity, human potential, and original ideas absolutely still matter. I've often said, "I still have never had an algorithm make the hair on the back of my neck stand up." But, I also know that every single day that passes, our ability to make better decisions, faster decisions, more precise decisions is informed by math. You can't enter this profession anymore if you are fundamentally afraid to embrace that.

Steimle: What are some of the skills CMOs need that perhaps don't get enough attention?

Jones: I'm not sure I can judge how much attention they get, but I'm guilty of this at times, as well, where I want to kind of push away from creativity because there's such a current in the world today of, "That's the soft stuff. We can't measure it." Everything is about what I just said: math and quantifiable results. As a result of that, there are fewer and fewer people in the C-suite with the ability to have original thought and are able to connect emotionally and empathetically with consumers. It's part of my job to make sure that skill set is represented with my colleagues.

What I've tried to do in my career is not just be the words and pictures guy but to be able to demonstrate to my boss, my CFO partner, whoever it is, that I can connect that thinking to what matters in the business.

Marketers and CMOs have to own a certain competency in the C-suite, but they also have to move to the middle more to demonstrate to their peers that there is business value for this way of thinking. There's business value for creativity. There's business value by improving the satisfaction, health, and relationship that consumers have with our company. Companies with high Net Promoter Scores are high P/E ratio-companies. They're correlated. Too many CMOs have not had the skill set or the interest in trying to make the business connection, so as a result, they've stayed in this place just being the creative people.

Steimle: What do you see as some of the biggest challenges facing today's CMOs?

Jones: Growth, no question. There are so many industries today that are fundamentally low-growth industries. That requires a different skill set than high-growth industries, not necessarily an easier or harder one, but a different one, because the focus has to be on creating differentiation to steal share. Competing to steal share in a low-growth environment is an enormous challenge that lots of industries and CMOs are facing.

Steimle: What are some of the mistakes that CMOs are making today that you see?

Jones: The mistake CMOs make is probably the mistake that businesses make, which is being too internally focused as opposed to being externally focused on who you're serving and what the competitive landscape holds. It's easy to just do your job and keep your head down and forget what's happening around you. That's a mistake people make. Another one is not spending enough time on testing and experimentation and funding that effort because, as I say regularly, "We have to do what works as long as it works while at the same time figuring out what's next." If you're not doing both of those things, you're probably making a mistake.

CMOs that put their arms around their function and keep people out and draw silos and boundaries as opposed to helping people understand marketing's role in driving growth, in creating value that attracts people to you, are also making mistakes.

Steimle: When it comes to experimentation and seeing what's next, what systems or processes do you have in place to facilitate that?

Jones: It starts with a core belief of the company that design and innovation drive growth. That translates into strategies about testing and experimentation. It continues by funding experimentation and innovation and ensuring we've got a way to close the loop on the learning. Trying to shift the conversation away from simply ROI to a conversation about learning is really the best way to ensure that people aren't just making the math work to prove that everything had a positive business return. They're demonstrating a competency of getting better by what they've learned through experimentation. Those are all things we try to do.

Steimle: Is there anything in your background not directly tied to marketing that you think has been beneficial to your role as a marketing professional?

Jones: A couple of things come to mind. I have had sales jobs. One time at the Coca-Cola Company, I moved from marketing into sales. Nothing gives you empathy like being on the frontline in a sales job. Being president or CEO of smaller companies and the obligation you have to the people you serve in your companies for the livelihood you create with them—that obligation is probably what made me the leader of people that I'm trying to become.

Being involved in starting companies from scratch—I've been part of one from pretty much scratch and I've turned around a failing one. In those environments, it's very much the entrepreneur's mindset of you start with what you have as opposed to what you need. When you're in environments of scarce resources and there is nothing else, it teaches you to be more innovative with how you get results when you don't have the resources you could possibly need.

Steimle: Is there anything we haven't covered about the CMO role that you think is important to communicate?

Jones: The things I would try to emphasize are our obligation as CMOs to help people understand why they should choose a profession in marketing instead of ending up in the profession of marketing because of its access, its impact on business, its diversity. That's one big message. The related one would be that it requires embracing what's possible with data and math.

Then, I want to make a callout to other CMOs. We have an obligation to demonstrate the business and innovation value of marketing and to help our colleagues understand why they should consider marketing an important partner. We shouldn't just get frustrated that they don't. It's incumbent upon marketers to learn the language of finance, learn the language of operations, and connect what we know naturally to what others know naturally in the spirit of breaking down silos. As much as we are students of the consumer, we must also be teachers of the profession to create world-class marketers for the future.

David Doctorow

Chief Marketing and Strategy Officer and Senior Vice President of Global Marketing

Expedia

*In 2011, **David Doctorow** became the chief marketing and strategy officer as well as the senior vice president of global marketing at Expedia. In addition to marketing, Doctorow has held executive business development and management roles. Doctorow was director of marketing strategy and operations for Hewlett-Packard. Prior to joining Expedia, Doctorow led the marketing ROI service line as associate principal of the marketing and sales practice at McKinsey & Company. Doctorow has a bachelor of arts degree in international relations from the University of Pennsylvania and an MBA from the Stanford Graduate School of Business.*

Josh Steimle: Give us an overview of your career. How did you get your start in marketing? What were the steps that led to where you are today?

David Doctorow: I've had a fairly circuitous path to marketing. I started out as an investment banker and then went into corporate development. I worked at an Internet startup along the way during the dot-com boom. I worked at McKinsey two different times and I worked at HP in marketing. All of that background equipped me to be a businessperson, but it was really the experience at HP, which was in between my two tours of duty at McKinsey, where I picked up marketing in depth.

© Josh Steimle 2016
J. Steimle, *Chief Marketing Officers at Work*, DOI 10.1007/978-1-4842-1931-7_28

I ran marketing strategy and operations at HP. I call that job the "blood and guts" of marketing. It's where I learned all the unsexy things that are important to making the marketing function work, such as the quality and granularity of the data you get and the systems that marketers use to do their jobs from planning to evaluating performance, etc, and understanding what kinds of governance processes and approaches make the function work. All these unsexy things turn out to be extremely important when you're actually running the function.

What I learned at HP became important to me at McKinsey my second time around, when I helped McKinsey start their marketing practice serving CMOs. Years down the road that translated into an opportunity for me to switch sides and become a CMO myself. It was a circuitous path, but the skills I picked up along the way were each in their own way helpful to me doing a good job now.

Steimle: Who are your customers at Expedia and what's the scope of your responsibilities there?

Doctorow: In some ways, our customers are everyone. We all travel at one time or another. It's important to talk about customers in the moments they're in, because if you're going on a business trip to Columbus, Ohio, you may want to stay close to where the meeting is, and you may be on a budget and want to have a low-cost hotel option. But if you're going with your family on a beach vacation to a glorious, glamorous place in Mexico, you're going to be looking for something very different. If you're like me, you want a kid-friendly hotel with beach access, a great pool, wonderful room service, etc. Those are very different needs from a business trip. Our customers are everyone, but you have to get down to understanding what it is that they're trying to do at that moment.

Our bread and butter is serving leisure travelers, but we also serve what we call unmanaged business travelers, people who don't have a corporate travel relationship. That's important to our business too. We even have a brand focused on corporate travel. Ultimately, our customers are anybody who's traveling.

Steimle: What are some of the challenges and opportunities for the CMO of a brand that's fairly well established like Expedia?

Doctorow: Number one is keeping the brand fresh. It's critical that the story and the brand proposition continue to evolve. That's because we're in a very competitive marketplace, and we always have to be able to convey a clear reason or reasons why customers should come to us. At Expedia, our story is really about listening to customers.

That leads to the second point: we need to put in place as CMOs—and we do here at Expedia—a listening system at very large scale. We do that through test and learn. Test and learn is an approach whereby we can put different customer experiences, different offers, different messages in front of customers and get feedback from them in real time on or off the site about what is relevant and working for them. That customer feedback is critical to the CMO job today, listening to that and making sure our whole team listens to that is integral to our success.

The third thing is, we try hard to only acquire customers once. When they come to us, we want to make sure we are developing as rich an insight about who they are, what they want, how they want to travel, and what people like them care about so we can serve them extremely well. We believe that if we show them that kind of loyalty, they will in turn show that loyalty to us. Economically, that's important for our business because the cost of retaining customers and serving them well through delightful experiences is way more profitable for us than acquiring customers over and over again.

Four and a half years ago, the brand was in decline by many measures. The turnaround was putting in place some of those elements, focusing on test and learn, and innovating as rapidly as we could. It was repositioning the brand story to stand out from others in the marketplace. For us, that was about personalization. The tagline, "Find Yours," was the theme of our brand campaign. That helped us stand out from others in the marketplace who were emphasizing different attributes.

The other theme was getting in place technology and data that would allow us to continuously learn and improve. It was through these listening systems in all that we do, whether it be our product, our marketing, even the customer experience while people travel.

Those were the core elements of the turn, and now that we have indeed turned the company around, the stock has moved from about twenty bucks to one hundred twenty-five bucks. Today, the question is how we expand on the capabilities that we've built, leverage our global platform, and enable other brands that we've acquired over the last year and a half to come and leverage those insights and still compete effectively on their own.

For example, in the last year and a half alone, we've acquired Travelocity, Orbitz, and Wotif, which is an Australian online travel agency. All of these brands are in one form or another leveraging some of the great traveler insights that have become embedded in the different platforms we've developed, as well as in our product and in our marketing.

Steimle: What are the challenges and opportunities around these acquisitions for you as a CMO? How do you integrate that with the Expedia brand? How do you not integrate it but still utilize it while building the Expedia business?

Doctorow: There's a lot of opportunity here, and we certainly have learned about the challenges and how to overcome them. On the opportunity side, we have some great traveler insights built into our technology platforms and our marketing operations that we've learned over the years with our Expedia brand, and we seek to share what we've learned as aggressively as we can with other Expedia, Inc. brands. However, we believe that competition is good amongst these brands, so we let each brand decide how they're going to leverage all the things we've learned in Expedia.

Likewise, when we do acquire brands, we have learned that each of them has their own unique insights and approaches, and we don't want to destroy those when we acquire companies, so we work hard to listen and find those golden nuggets, and where we can, we transport them back to the other brands as well. All of that sounds clinical and easy, but this is a human process, and it's ultimately about people becoming part of a team when they join a company. That involves creating the right type of dynamic where people feel that not only is there a business opportunity but there's a career expansion opportunity for them personally.

The more that I as a CMO can help people connect to that personal story, the more these mergers tend to go well. I won't claim that we've cracked the code, but we're working hard all the time to get better and better at it. When we do, good things seem to happen.

Steimle: What systems and processes do you have to make sure that you are in touch with customers and that you understand their needs and wants?

Doctorow: We listen to customers in every way we possibly can. Testing and learning through our live sites and the marketing that we execute every single day is a core part of what we do. This year alone, we will complete something like thirteen hundred tests in our core products. We've got about another one thousand on the marketing side. If you break that down, on a daily basis, we're doing roughly five or six tests a day, and all of those tests are about learning. We believe that only about a third of these tests should actually be winners— meaning they get something right with the customer—because if we get too many winners, it means we're not thinking creatively enough and pushing hard enough to put new experiences in front of customers so that we can really learn what works and what doesn't.

To get that all right is pretty unique in that having losers in testing is not just an option. It's a requirement. The insight that comes out of those losses, and quickly learning what works and what doesn't, is part of the secret sauce that makes us one of the most customer-focused companies in the world.

Steimle: Is there a danger in focusing on data too much and losing out on some of the common-sense intelligence that you could gain from customers?

Doctorow: Tests are based on human observations. We make sure we have real, live interactions with customers. In labs, we listen to customer feedback, one by one. We read all the comments that come in. These kinds of sources of data—as well as other surveys that we do which have qualitative elements to them—are all important sources of hypotheses that we then convert into future tests. While we try to bring data to make decisions as much as we possibly can, in the end, we are all travelers, and it's about trying to understand how to make that experience better. We'll look at any data, any anecdote that will help us do that better and better over time.

Steimle: Tell me about the structure of your marketing team. What does it look like?

Doctorow: It is a functional organization that's global for the most part, but there are a couple divisional teams, which are each of our regional brands. For example, I have a leader of paid search, a leader of natural search, a leader of email marketing, etc—which are the functional leaders—but there's also a leader of all online marketing focused on the Travelocity brand and our other regional brands. We do this because we think that to be really world-class, you need to have centers of excellence that attract world-class people, and there aren't so many in any given function.

Plus, we build technology and automation that support execution in each of these channels, and we want to build that once in each of these functions. We set up our regional brands separately because we want them to compete and have control over their own destiny while being able to leverage these world-class assets and shared service teams that exist in the core functions. Ultimately, it's a hybrid model between functional and divisional. So far, that has really worked for us. We're seeing great growth that emanates not only in our mothership brand, Expedia, but also in these regional brands.

Steimle: What are some of your philosophies on building, managing, and leading a marketing team?

Doctorow: Philosophically, the first thing is who is on the team. It's important to me to have people on the team who are hungry and agile learners because the world we live in changes incredibly quickly. If you're a functional expert in paid search or email, while we do value that experience, we have found time and time again that the worlds of paid search, email, or any of these functions change every six to twelve months. We've found that in the medium and long run, people who are agile learners and are hungry to learn and drive results will do the best. It starts out with building the right team.

The second thing is it's important to have a performance and results-oriented culture. We look religiously at results and with high frequency—daily, weekly. It's putting in place the processes, the tools, and the culture of that type of disciplined review of results and paying attention to the data and the facts that are out there. Doing that at a rapid clip allows us to learn faster than anybody else out there. That learning is critical to our success.

The third thing is the use of technology. We believe that to be world-class and operate at large scale like we do on a global basis in many different languages, countries, and channels, we have to put in place automation that both accelerates our ability to learn through these channels, share what we learn across the different teams where we operate, and sense how the outside world is changing.

A simple example of this is we will use techniques—machines, ultimately—to understand and try to optimize our pricing in certain lines of business in which we operate. We're always putting those different prices in front of customers so that we can get that real feedback as to what price makes the most sense. It's a simple example, but the techniques of using technology to help serve customers better are critical to the future of marketing, especially as the outside world has been so dynamic and we expect it to keep being so.

Steimle: Do you have any favorite third-party technology tools that you use in your job?

Doctorow: Because technology is core to our success, we by and large build technology in-house. While we're open to testing all kinds of things, including third-party technologies, the in-house solution is the ultimate winner if we do it right because we have to differentiate ourselves in those assets and those approaches that we take. If we're reliant on a third party, then we have only so many degrees of freedom.

Steimle: Let's talk about international. In a way, Expedia is the ultimate global company, being in travel. But, you have competition from other travel websites, like Ctrip in China. What do you see as some of the future growth markets for Expedia in terms of geography?

Doctorow: We are very global. We operate across Expedia, Inc. in about eighty countries. That's originating countries, and we sell hotels in over two hundred twenty countries around the world, so we are a very global business. Growth in Asia has been a core strategic priority for us. We have a number of brands operating in Asia. Although China definitely represents an important growth market today, it's not only China. There are a number of markets in Asia that are important. Many of them are super attractive.

We have a $1.4 trillion travel industry, which is a big market. That means there's going to be a lot of players that go after it. We try to focus and build capabilities that can scale globally. We work hard to understand where we need to make adjustments on a local basis so that we can compete well. There are examples that come up from time to time around this as we learn more what customers value.

A simple example of this is in Mexico. In order to compete, it is essential to have a certain kind of payment option available to customers called installment payments. It's an important capability that is not something we need worldwide. We may someday decide we want to do so worldwide, but it's critical in some markets. Being global is operating at scale and leveraging what works in some of our core markets, but we do need those listening systems in place so that we can adjust when it makes sense.

Steimle: What are some of the core metrics that you focus on in your day-to-day?

Doctorow: Customer experience is really important to us. We look carefully at Net Promoter Score, which is basically a measure of the number of brand advocates, the number of detractors, and the delta between the two. We're constantly trying to understand the drivers of detractors and advocates and expand upon the advocacy areas and remove the pain points in the detractor areas. That's important to us because providing a great experience to customers means more customers will come back of their own accord.

First, we want to delight customers, but second, it's economically important for our business. We also look at core health metrics to make sure we're getting enough traffic to our site, that it's converting well, and that we are getting the right type of repeat purchasing behavior to happen. Over time, as strategic priorities evolve, we always have a KPI, or two, or three at most that focus on bringing those strategic priorities to life in a simple way.

A few years ago, we were really focused on mobile, and as demand was coming in much more from mobile devices, we wanted to make sure we had appropriate focus on our mobile business. At this point, we have a belief that mobile is everybody's job, so we've evolved to where that actually is not a KPI per se. We want to make sure we're serving customers excellently no matter the device they're on, but as our strategic priorities evolve, we continue to make sure we have the right metric and focus on them at any given time.

We try to have very few top-level KPIs in our business, probably no more than seven or eight. The rationale is you can only be great at so many things, and we don't want to overextend ourselves. That choice of where we'll focus and keeping that pristine is what strategy is all about for us. It's making those conscious tradeoffs upfront about where we want to focus and, as a result, where we won't as much.

Steimle: How do you make sure your goals are aligned with the overall organization, and how do you push that down through marketing to make sure all the different marketing divisions have their goals aligned?

Doctorow: As a senior leadership team member, I'm very involved in helping set the metrics for the overall company. It starts with having an active voice in that conversation. The second thing is we try to have as much one-to-one alignment of the core marketing KPIs to the top seven or eight metrics that are important to the business overall.

Marketing is such a broad function and has so many dimensions to it that we tend to have a very natural alignment to those top-level company measures on a one-to-one basis. Occasionally, we'll end up focusing in a particular functional area where there isn't as natural a marketing focus, and that's fine. We don't need to have one-to-one for every single measure. The point of the exercise is that every marketer can see when they are gold. There's a clear cascade from the top-level company measures to the top measures for the marketing function down to the managers and the individuals. That cascade is critical to making sure that people know where they're to focus, and to focus where we spend our conversation time and our customer listening.

Steimle: With these different divisions in the company, there might be a tendency for silos to develop. Do you have experience breaking down silos? How can a CMO facilitate that?

Doctorow: CMOs are perfectly positioned to break down silos. That's because our job is to listen to the customer first. If we can use what we hear from customers to simply raise the right questions inside our own organization , it is really helpful in driving the right focus and producing the right business results. I'll give you an example. Some years ago in our paid search business, we had a focus on driving hotel traffic. We've since broadened out to focus on all the lines of business that we market and sell, but at the time, getting hotel traffic to convert better was of critical importance to the company.

It was of critical importance to making sure we could figure out the right traffic to acquire. As marketers, we could have been satisfied with simply getting paid search visitors to our site, but the right way to approach it was to understand whether those visitors were converting through. Were we fulfilling customer needs to the point where people actually ended up buying something at the site? When we dug into understanding that data, we found reasons why certain search terms on our site that we were making available were not equipping us to meet customer needs and answer their questions well enough.

As a marketer, I try to foster an environment where we work as one team with those other groups, our product group, and our supply group to simply answer customer questions. It's not about marketing being right. It can't be. It's about serving customers better. As a CMO, fostering that culture is not a right; it's an obligation. Having done that at Expedia, we've seen good success. Now, our whole company tries to take that mindset, and I think we do a pretty good job.

Steimle: Are there any industry organizations or peer groups that you're a member of? If so, what kind of value do you receive from them?

Doctorow: I'm pretty selective about joining industry organizations. Over time, I've joined some here and there, and I sit on panels and participate in some conferences.

Ultimately, these memberships are most important when they help foster bringing new ideas back to the company. That's really what that membership and participation are all about.

Steimle: Are there any favorite books or media that have helped you in your role as CMO?

Doctorow: One of the books I've read and keep rereading is Jim Collins' *Great by Choice*.[1] In that book, Jim talks about the idea of firing bullets and then cannonballs. Great companies fire bullets systematically to reduce the risk for when they fire the cannonballs. But, they do indeed fire cannonballs. It's not only bullets. That philosophy is something that I've personally embraced, and it's something I've tried to espouse here at Expedia. It has served us well.

In the twenty-five hundred–some-odd tests we're doing, that's a lot of bullets. A number of those do become cannonballs over time. We're not bashful. We've recently made one of the biggest bets in travel industry history by rolling up a number of players in the marketplace. That's a cannonball based on a lot of fired bullets that suggests we can help serve customers better if we do that. That's one of the things I really like in the book.

The other thing I enjoy out of that book that keeps me focused is what Jim calls "productive paranoia." The basic idea is you can never rest on your laurels. You must always be asking, "Where can we be blindsided? How can our legs be taken out from under us?" and looking aggressively to try to find where those attackers may come from.

I joke about it: it's got to be *productive* paranoia. It can't be irrational or extreme paranoia, but we do try hard in all of our functions in marketing to always be looking left and right. I ask those teams quite often to comment on where they're seeing the risk and what mitigation approaches we can take. It's a great book.

Steimle: Is there anything in your background that's not directly tied to marketing that you feel has been beneficial to your role as a marketing professional?

Doctorow: First, there's the general business acumen and financial skills that I built up over the years doing both management consulting as well as a couple different finance jobs in investment banking and corporate development. That kind of approach allowed me to be a trusted partner to the CEO because I can think from that background—in fact, it's my job to think like the CEO even though I wear the functional hat of the CMO.

---

[1] HarperBusiness, 2011.

The second thing is my interest in technology. So much of what we do in marketing today and what we will do moving forward is going to be technology-enabled and technology-led. Understanding technology enough that I can partner well with our head of engineering and our head of product to build world-class capabilities that span functions is critical to me being effective.

The final thing is having studied some science over the years. Ultimately, test and learn is about applying a scientific method, and developing that starts with developing hypotheses, but it continues by putting in place the right measurement approaches and learning as quickly as we can. That scientific training along the way has proven helpful.

Steimle: What are some of the skills that marketing students or new marketers should be acquiring today to prepare them to be future marketing leaders ten, twenty years down the road?

Doctorow: I would tell them to learn the basics of business across all the functions so that as a marketer, you not only know about the four Ps but can also partner with the full matrix. That's important for marketers. I would also encourage exposure to science and engineering along the way. Understanding how these things work is no longer an option. It's going to become essential for the future marketer to be really effective. The earlier you start, the easier it will be to be effective as you move up in the ranks.

Steimle: What are your thoughts on the sharing economy and Airbnb and such? Do you view these companies as competitors? Have they influenced how you're marketing to consumers in any way?

Doctorow: This is a big industry. People want to travel. Today, travel is a $1.4 trillion industry, so it isn't surprising that there are constantly people trying to innovate and disrupt in an industry of that size and growth profile. Certainly, Airbnb is a great example of an innovator in the marketplace.

We have seen that one in four people in the last year has participated in a sharing economy travel offering of one kind or another, vacation rentals being an example. This is a real trend in the marketplace. It's one that has recently led us to acquire HomeAway, which is an important innovator in the space. HomeAway is much larger than Airbnb, especially from a revenue and profitability standpoint. We're definitely believers in the sharing economy, and we're putting our money where our mouth is.

Steimle: What are your thoughts on marketing to millennials? How do you see millennials impacting the marketing ecosystem?

Doctorow: It's definitely an important question with the size, growth, and influence of that segment. As a marketer, the basics are the same. Ultimately, we have to execute well in all of these marketing channels that customers will consume. When they go to travel, we have to have a listening system in place to know what it is they want in their travel experiences.

There are differences that we see in the ways we need to tell stories to customers, the channels they tend to use to consume information, and ultimately even the travel experiences they have and how they want to talk about them before, during, and after those trips. We ultimately want to be able to deliver experiences that are relevant to a segment of that scale and importance, so we're testing all the time to see how to optimize all of those things for millennials.

Steimle: What are some of the biggest mistakes you see CMOs today making?

Doctorow: In today's world, with the massive amount of change that's happening outside, CMOs could get caught simply following others, whether that be competitors or channel partners of one kind or another, who have new placements and advertising opportunities. If you're really pursuing and listening to all those things, in some cases, you're chasing noise.

The distinctive CMO will sift through and build teams who will sift through the noise but focus energy on less and have a good instinct and systems in place to quickly determine what is going to work and stand out. Ultimately, the elements that are going to work need to be organized by having a clear perspective on how we win as a company and as marketers in this company. That is a true north in figuring out what is signal and what is noise. CMOs must have that clarity of thinking.

Steimle: Are there any topics we haven't discussed with regards to the CMO role that you feel it's important to cover?

Doctorow: Being a CMO is about as much fun as you can legally have. It is a remarkably exciting role—one that allows you to be in touch with customers. I try to remember every day that we are all about creating moments for people. Some of my favorite memories were formed during some kind of travel or another.

As a CMO, I have a unique opportunity to help customers and travelers create those moments and make the most of them. That is remarkably rewarding. To do it while building an incredible team and having that crew row in tandem is great fun along the way.

Rishi Dave

Chief Marketing Officer
Dun & Bradstreet

Rishi Dave is CMO at Dun & Bradstreet, where he leads brand, digital, and alliance marketing as well as analytics, product marketing, social media, internal and external communications, and demand generation. Prior to working at Dun & Bradstreet, Dave held a number of positions at Dell, including executive director of Digital Marketing and senior manager of Global Online Analytics. Dave holds an MBA in marketing from The Wharton School at the University of Pennsylvania as well as degrees in chemical engineering and economics with honors from Stanford University. In both 2012 and 2013, he was voted BtoB Magazine's Top Digital Marketer. In 2015, Dave was nFusion's Cojones Award winner.

Josh Steimle: Give us an overview of your career. How did you get your start? What were the steps that led to where you are today as the CMO of Dun & Bradstreet?

Rishi Dave: In 2014, I joined Dun & Bradstreet as its first true Chief Marketing Officer. The company's Chief People Officer and I were the first two external hires brought on by Bob Carrigan, who had just been appointed CEO of Dun & Bradstreet. Bob viewed transforming marketing and people/culture as fundamental to the growth of this company, and he saw them as being very closely tied together.

My goal at Dun & Bradstreet has always been to drive marketing-led topline growth for the company. This comes down to three core areas of focus: One was modernizing the brand and culture of an iconic, 175 year-old company.

J. Steimle, *Chief Marketing Officers at Work*, DOI 10.1007/978-1-4842-1931-7_29

We need to build a narrative that shows how Dun & Bradstreet has expanded its business to offer a variety of solutions that help companies of all sizes grow. The second area of focus has been to revamp our go-to-market strategy, putting a customer-first emphasis by developing a persona-based go-to-market strategy. The third area we've focused on is growing pipeline—building relationships with new customers and expanding what we do with our existing customers. To achieve our goals across all three areas, we've leveraged technology, data and analytics, thought leadership, and organizational transformation.

Prior to joining Dun & Bradstreet, I spent ten years at Dell. I started at Dell in corporate strategy, then moved into digital marketing and analytics. Then, I ran digital marketing globally for one of Dell's B2B business units. Over time, my role grew, and by the time I left Dell, I was running digital marketing globally for Dell's B2B business. Before Dell, I was in business school, where I studied marketing. After college, I worked at a number of startups, both in Austin and the Bay Area and at Bain & Company.

Steimle: Tell us a bit about Dun & Bradstreet's customers. Who are they?

Dave: We work with companies of every size, across every key industry, all around the world. Thousands of small businesses work with us, as do most Fortune 500 companies. Customers come to us because they want to grow. Companies know that data and analytics are critical to achieving growth, and with the world's largest commercial database—we manage more than 250 million company records—we're well positioned to help them achieve their goals. We believe that the quality and volume of a company's relationships are the key to growth, and that data and analytics let them build those relationships at a scale never before possible in the digital age we're in.

And that cuts across many of a company's core functions. CMOs, CFOs, CIOs, supply chain leaders, compliance leaders and their teams all work with us.

For instance, working with credit and finance teams, when we marry our data with our customer's own data, we create insights that will help a finance professional balance risk and opportunity as they evaluate customers.

In sales and marketing—one of our fastest-growing segments—our data and analytics help our customers in a very end-to-end way. We can work with them to target new prospects, nurture them effectively, and close them more efficiently. The data drives their digital marketing and website optimization strategies and marketing automation and CRM platforms.

And in supply chain and compliance, customers use our data to make sure they're doing business with ethical, responsible, reliable partners and minimize the risk in their supply chains.

Customers also want to make sure they're getting our data in ways customized to how they operate, so we deliver the data in many different forms. It can be streamed directly via API to our customers' own systems, embedded in our customers' cloud-based applications like Salesforce.com, or used through cloud-based apps that we develop.

Steimle: How do you define customer loyalty, and what does it mean to you to build it?

Dave: You only achieve customer loyalty by truly understanding the unique needs of that customer and then delivering results. We use our own data and analytics—the same solutions we provide our customers—to prioritize the right offering for the right customer at the right time. That's much more customer-centric than pushing what we want to sell. And we also want to create great integrated experiences for our customers. This involves aligning online and offline tactics—content, events, etc.—to show the customer that we understand the challenges they have and know how they can activate data to meet those challenges. Integrating our own data and analytics efforts helps us do this.

Steimle: What steps do you take beyond bringing in the customer to keep them engaged and coming back? How do you build that long-term relationship?

Dave: Our marketing organization works closely with our customer service team. Using data and analytics that show how our customers are using our products let us know how we might be able to provide better experiences in a given moment. We also just talk to our customers a lot. We spend a lot of time in direct dialogue and through surveys to understand what they're facing every day, and we translate what we learn from those conversations into content and experiences that we believe can help.

Steimle: What does the structure of your marketing department look like?

Dave: We've structured our global team to map back to our priorities of driving growth by modernizing our brand, evolving our go-to-market, and growing pipeline. I have leaders heading up the persona-based go-to-market strategy and messaging, our digital/demand generation and technology approach, our customer data and sales and marketing analytics, and our communications, content and branding. These different teams all work very closely together in an agile way in service of our targeted personas.

Steimle: What's your philosophy on building a marketing team?

Dave: Today, if I were to pinpoint the most critical core competency in a word, it would be "agility." We look to hire T-shaped marketers—talented people who have deep expertise in one particular important area, such as content development or analytics, but who also understand enough about the other aspects of marketing that they can contribute to strategic dialogues in service of the customer persona. We combine this with a "tiger team" approach that puts these T-shaped marketers together in an agile unit that works very closely together in pursuit of a shared goal—a persona-focused campaign, a product launch, or another important initiative. My team knows that to be successful they cannot work in silos, and they must collaborate to build something great.

Steimle: What was that process like for you to build your team?

Dave: Create the right culture and brand to attract the best candidates from the outside while leveraging and developing internal talent to succeed in the new strategy. Lastly, we create "just enough" process to allow people to scale their work, but not get them mired in bureaucracy.

In designing my marketing organization, I kept in mind what I thought was needed to drive the strategy into the future.

Steimle: How do you attract and retain the top marketing talent? How do you get the people you want?

Dave: A lot of what attracts people to a company is the culture and the brand. They want to know what a company stands for and that they're going to be doing work they really believe in. We're fortunate that Bob Carrigan, our CEO, really understands this. He talks all the time about being forward-leaning in our culture, and he functions this way himself. He's a big believer in servant leadership, where a leader's success is based on making sure his or her team and customers and partners are successful. Within marketing, we try to have the right balance of process and autonomy; we want to bring in good people and turn them loose to do what they were hired to do with the right tools and structure to succeed.

As a leadership team, we also demonstrate what we say to show that we authentically believe in the purpose and values we espouse. Sometimes that involves divesting businesses, investing in new opportunities, and/or changing policies.

Steimle: What are the practical steps you've taken to ensure the alignment of metrics and good communication with other C-level executives?

Dave: I work closely with my peers to ensure that we are all aligning under the company strategy together.

As we build marketing programs, we do a lot of testing and learning. We start small on tactics and then scale what's working based on the metrics we're seeing. To understand what to scale, when, and how, we must measure every aspect of our operation—and not be afraid to act on what the analysis tells us.

And then communication becomes critical. We must actively communicate with our key internal colleagues on what's working in the smaller-scale experiments, gaining their advocacy as we roll-out the successful tactics more broadly.

CMOs have a great opportunity now because our job is more metric-driven than ever and our contributions are more measurable than ever.

Steimle: What are specific metrics you focus on?

Dave: I look at our overall brand metrics and our pipeline and sales. Are we building the right relationships with customers and prospects and then closing them?

Steimle: How do you work with sales, and what are the challenges and successes you've seen there?

Dave: I've talked a lot about pipeline, and clearly that's as important for us as it is for many marketers. But pipeline doesn't pay the bills. Sales pays the bills. That's why we have as much responsibility for closing pipeline as we do for generating it. We have to work across the entire buyer's journey as a partner to sales, right down to the close.

Personally, I'm in the field all the time working with our sales team to meet with customers. I like speaking directly with our customers and our front line sales teams to get their feedback. Being part of the sales cycle gives me a visceral understanding of both customers and what the field sales team is going through.

Steimle: What other activities do you engage in to make sure you know the customer and understand his or her point of view? How do you know you're creating marketing experiences that align with the customer's interests?

Dave: Number one is actually going to customers and talking to them directly. Number two is constantly talking to our frontline salespeople. Number three is having a strong understanding of what people are doing digitally, what they're reading, where they're going, etc. Number four is constantly doing customer research. Lastly, at any given time, we have a large number of small experiments of marketing programs running live and we scale those that succeed.

Steimle: How are globalization and internationalization affecting your marketing efforts?

Dave: The constant challenge is knowing how much to scale globally and how much to do locally. I don't want to create individual fiefdoms in every region. I want to scale my marketing, but I don't want to be irrelevant to the local market.

One of the things that's unique about Dun & Bradstreet is that we have a multichannel go-to-market. In a lot of countries we're in, we work through channel partners. That helps scale marketing efforts more effectively.

Steimle: Are there any other trends in your industry or with your customers that are affecting you?

Dave: A big one for CMOs is data and analytics. Not just building great models, but also basic things like integrating data, cleaning it, making sure it's all connected across the silos—so that it is usable at scale. One of the biggest trends we're going to see is that the CMOs who are going to succeed in the next four or five years are going to understand data within their corporation and will know how to leverage analytics to make decisions.

Steimle: What changes have you seen in the marketing world since you began your career?

Dave: There are probably three big areas. One is data and analytics. Two is the rise of marketing technology. Three is the increasing importance of great thought leadership and content.

Steimle: How do you manage relationships with outside teams like agencies?

Dave: First, you have to decide when you partner versus execute in house. You have to experiment with the right mix based on what you're good at, where your talent is, what talent you can hire, how fast various aspects of marketing are changing, etc. Then, you need to view partners as extended members of your team.

Steimle: Can you walk us through the process of any specific campaigns or initiatives you've taken and what success you've had with them?

Dave: The biggest one was the modernization of our brand. It's a pretty daunting task to modernize the brand of a 175 year-old iconic company. Along with that, we also wanted to modernize the culture, so we tied the two together. From day one, the Chief People Officer and I were connected at the hip on this work.

We're in an industry that's very complex for customers, and companies in the industry don't often make it any easier to understand. They actually benefit by keeping it complex, making it seem like the only way you can figure it out is to work with them. So we saw a great opportunity to create a simpler, more human message.

We did the work in a relatively short timeframe. The short timeframe forced us to be innovative and prevented us from overthinking things or watering them down. We first started with our purpose because everybody in the organization had a different idea of what it was. We then created the right set of values that supported that purpose in order to create the right supporting culture. We then looked at the creative that would support this change.

We talked to a lot of customers, partners, employees, and people in the industry. We also looked back at our own history. Our history is archived in the Baker Library at Harvard Business School. We dug deep to understand the DNA of why we've succeeded for 175 years and how customers perceived us over time. We brought all that together to develop our purpose and values, and it's truly been a huge success.

Not enough time has passed to fully understand and complete the measurement of the external view, but the employee transformation has been tremendous. That fundamental cultural shift was precisely what we needed to help drive what we needed.

From an agency partner perspective, we picked an agency that worked primarily in the consumer space. The beauty of consumer agencies is that they have an incredible ability to distill things to their simplest form in service of the end customer.

The work defined not only the expanded breadth of work we do today, but also where we are going.

Steimle: Are there things in your background not necessarily tied to marketing that you feel have been beneficial to your role as a marketing professional?

Dave: I studied chemical engineering as an undergrad. I think that the engineering mindset has helped quite a bit. I didn't anticipate being a CMO when I graduated from college. Marketing back then was a very different discipline. As marketing evolved into leveraging data, analytics, and technology, I fell into it because my passion started aligning with the way marketing was evolving. It initially might seem odd that I studied chemical engineering, but now it makes complete sense—that whole engineering mindset, that way of thinking, that analytical orientation, and the creativity are all strong qualities that help you succeed in marketing.

Steimle: Interestingly, not a single CMO I have interviewed has said, "I set out to have a career in marketing. I wanted to rise to the top of the marketing organization."

Dave: When I graduated from college, marketing was a completely different discipline compared to today. There were people who came out of undergrad at that time who said, "I want to be a marketer. I want to rise to the top." Then the marketing profession completely changed on them and became something very different from what they expected. It became something different for those of us who didn't initially set out to pursue a career in marketing too.

Steimle: Do you think that's going to continue happening, or can somebody today leave university and say, "I want to be a CMO someday," and chart a course to that position?

Dave: Marketing is shifting so much that it's hard to say. People who graduate now realize that marketing is constantly changing. Perhaps they are more wired to change with it today.

I tell college kids today that they can be a marketer immediately without a job in marketing by building their own brand through their personal blog, personal website, and social platforms. This will give them a visceral understanding of marketing today and help them stay abreast of changes.

They will quickly learn how fast everything evolves, and they can demonstrate this to a future employer.

Steimle: Are there any other specific skills that young kids today need to know if they want to have a great career in marketing going forward?

Dave: Marketing is becoming a set of specialized disciplines—technology, data, content, messaging, sales enablement—and they require deep, functional expertise. Kids have to invest in a deep expertise in one of these highly specialized areas within marketing. They have to be able to leverage that expertise across all the different disciplines to work in service of their customer. They can pick their deep, functional expertise based on their interests, but they also must understand the overall strategy and how to integrate to get things done. They need to be that T-shaped marketer I spoke about earlier.

Steimle: What other changes do you see coming down the road? Where do you think marketing will be in ten or twenty years?

Dave: Marketing will become increasingly mathematical and algorithmic, but no matter how good your algorithms and mathematics are, unless you have something unique to say and a creative way in which to say it, it doesn't matter. Fundamentally, the best marketers will still be great messengers, great storytellers, and very creative. They also have to be able to drive growth with data, analytics, and technology to make that message come alive effectively.

Steimle: How have you used thought leadership for yourself or for Dun & Bradstreet? What do you think the potential is?

Dave: Thinking about Dun & Bradstreet first, I recognized from the time I got here that we had a great opportunity for thought leadership. We have a ton of intellectual capital around our company by being at the intersection of data, analytics, and business growth. To unlock all that and have it break through all the clutter of the web requires us to do more than just good writing and content development, though. We have to create a forum for it that lets us connect content to commerce. That's why content and thought leadership are so prominent on the completely modernized Dun & Bradstreet website we launched in April 2016. Content is the front door to the entire site. The strategy is to use content from our subject matter experts to engage customers and prospects with great answers to their most pressing questions, and from there, optimize the site experience to move those customers and prospects to the solutions most appropriate for their needs.

I also invest a lot in my digital brand, and it overlaps with what I do for a living and what Dun & Bradstreet does. My personal and professional brand online blend together. As the CMO, I'm one of the faces of the company, so I think a lot about that in my own personal thought leadership.

Steimle: What other channels are you using to connect with customers?

Dave: It depends on the customer and what the best experience is for him or her. Digital is a big component. Social is a useful channel in terms of amplifying our thought leadership. We definitely leverage events as well. As much as we are in the modern world, events still play a big role. We invest a lot in events, both events that we host as well as events that we go to. We try to integrate that with our digital efforts as well. Email is still big, leveraging marketing automation. For our biggest customers, we try to do a lot of in-person workshops throughout their buying process. We use all the channels, but we try to integrate what we do for the customers around those channels. Obviously, our salespeople are one of our biggest channels to connect with our customers.

Steimle: How do you keep up with everything out there in terms of marketing technology?

Dave: I think CMOs have to be voracious consumers of content on the web. I am consuming content digitally like crazy because I'm paranoid that I'm going to lose touch. I talk to our partners, vendors, and agencies all the time. I call up the VCs in the Valley who invest in marketing technology and ask them, "What should I be buying next? What am I not thinking about?" I do all those things because CMOs have to be a bit paranoid and constantly on top of what's happening.

Steimle: What do you think is the biggest challenge facing CMOs today?

Dave: The biggest one is being relevant because many CMOs are not able to embrace what's happening and what's changing. The second challenge is that many CMOs invest in what they think is cool, like marketing technology or data, but they don't always think about the overall strategy around these, so they don't get the ROI they're expecting from those investments. Lastly, balancing the creativity and storytelling with the analytics and technology continues to be a challenge.

Steimle: What are some of the big mistakes you see CMOs making?

Dave: Not building the processes and culture around the changes that are happening in marketing. Another big one is that CMOs don't do as much marketing as they did when they were senior marketing executives, so their role transitions to be more focused on leadership and managing the company overall with a marketing mindset, which can sometimes be a difficult transition. The third piece is collaborating with their peers. The CMO is responsible for the strategy of the company, not just marketing, so collaboration is key but this doesn't always happen to the extent that it should.

Steimle: How do you make sure you're taking time to focus on leadership the way you need to? How do you measure that? When the results take time to come in, how do you judge whether you're being effective in a leadership capacity?

Dave: It can't be something that just happens. It has to be a programmatic set of activities that you do consciously to ensure that you are hiring the right people, motivating them, and challenging them. You have to check in with them often and at all levels.

I

Index

J. Steimle, *Chief Marketing Officers at Work*, DOI 10.1007/978-1-4842-1931-7

60532747R00193

Made in the USA
Lexington, KY
10 February 2017